DATE DUE

DEMCO, INC. 38-2931

CINEMA CLASSICS

A facsimile reprint series of significant books
on film history, and film criticism, including
a number of important screenplays

Selected by
The American Film Institute
Louis B. Mayer Library

A Garland Series

Movies and Society

I. C. Jarvie

Garland Publishing, Inc.
New York & London   1986

For a complete list of the titles in this series
see the final pages of this volume.

This facsimile has been made from a copy in
the library of Southern Connecticut State College.

Reprinted by permission of Basic Books, Inc.
© 1970 by I. C. Jarvie

Library of Congress Cataloging-in-Publication Data

Jarvie, I. C. (Ian Charles), 1937–
   Movies and society.
   (Cinema classics)
   Reprint. Originally published: New York :
Basic Books, 1970.
   Bibliography: p.
   Includes index.
   1. Moving-pictures—Social aspects. I. Title.
II. Series.
PN1995.9.S6J3 1986   302.2'343   82-49213
ISBN 0-8240-5765-1 (alk. paper)

Design by Donna Montalbano

The volumes in this series are printed on
acid-free, 250-year-life paper.

Printed in the United States of America

MOVIES and SOCIETY

MOVIES
and
SOCIETY

I. C. Jarvie

BASIC BOOKS, Inc., Publishers
New York

Library of Congress Catalog Card Number: 77-135620
SBN 465-04737-8

Published in Great Britain under the title
Towards a Sociology of the Cinema

Printed in the United States of America

For
May and Suzanne

Contents

PART TWO
THE SOCIOLOGY OF AN AUDIENCE: WHO SEES FILMS
AND WHY?

PART THREE
THE SOCIOLOGY OF AN EXPERIENCE: WHO SEES FILMS
AND WHY?

CONTENTS

CONTENTS

Note to the Reader

The reader coming 'cold' to the subject may find it helpful to read the Appendix, 'Film and the Communication of Values', first. This Appendix is a talk delivered at the Centre for Culture and Technology, University of Toronto, while the book was being written. It introduces and applies some of the ideas in the book in a general manner, and so may help the general reader to get used to some of the idiosyncrasies of the literature to which this volume is a modest contribution. But, that Appendix revolves around a special topic, namely, the communication of values, and I therefore felt that it would be inappropriate to place it at the beginning of the book as an Introduction proper.

Preface

First, a limit to aims: this is an essay towards, no more, a sociology of the cinema. Merely compiling a near-complete bibliography is far beyond my present resources. As for planning and directing empirical research into the subject, that is a dream which may one day come true. What I attempt here, in lieu of such new empirical research, is to sift and put together some of the innumerable snippets of information that are to be found scattered throughout the very large literature on the cinema. No satisfactory overall framework has yet been proposed which will incorporate all this information. My task shall be to construct a tentative sociological framework within which these snippets can be arranged. The primary purpose of such a framework is to explain or make sense of the facts (see my (1964)). But it can do other jobs as well. It will pose questions and indicate answers which will serve to organize the confused discussion of the topics; the discussion may thereby be enabled to progress, i.e., to go beyond my questions and answers. Another job the framework will do is to reveal where there are gaps in the scattered information. Of course, I shall be exposing far more gaps than I can possibly close. My reason for doing this is that there is so much unsurveyed ground that closing the gaps is not urgent. If my framework manages to support even that much – a survey – however inadequately, I shall be satisfied.

Second, a limit to scope. This work tries to be about the sociology of the cinema. The trouble with most previous works which pretended to be about the sociology of the cinema, was that they were *not* about the sociology of the cinema; the authors have hardly seemed aware of the more obvious sociological questions which the cinema gives rise to. Judging by the published literature, 'the sociology of the cinema' has come to mean (not the sociology, but) the psychology (not of the cinema, but) of the audiences in the cinema, their responses, etc. Thus, a sample of the topics discussed most frequently in the literature: the frequency of cinemagoing and its relation to intelligence; the degree of identification of the audience with screen stars and characters; the degree of influence of films on children's *mores*; and so on. Mayer's two books *British Cinemas and their Audiences* and *Sociology of Film* are paradigms of this kind of literature.

If one is interested in such economic and sociological topics as the

xiii

financial, industrial and social structure of the film industry, its basis of recruitment, the role the institution of cinemagoing plays in the social structure of modern Western societies, the typicai kinds of society and social situation that are portrayed on the screen, the problem of why certain films have appeal and others do not, one will find very little of interest in the works of Mayer. Indeed one will find precious little even in the otherwise fascinating anthologies of Rosenberg and White (1957), McCann (1964), Robinson (1967), Deer and Deer (1967) and White and Averson (1968). There is virtually no institutional analysis in these works. Such content analyses as exist, as those in Jones (1942), Wolfenstein and Leites (1950, 1955), and Mead (1959), are fragmentary and tantalizing. When psychologists and social psychologists like Kracauer (1947) and Huaco (1965) are turned loose they either make unacceptable sociological assumptions,[1] or treat films as though they existed in a sociological vacuum.[2]

The present work views the cinema as a social phenomenon – one social institution among many. In trying to fit it into a framework I have divided the problems into four main areas, covering the making, viewing, experiencing and evaluating of films.

In the course of this study I have drawn on published information, good, or bad, or, as usual, fragmentary, as well as on my own experience. The film industries in America, Britain and France are best documented, with those of Germany, India, Italy, Japan, Russia and Poland somewhere behind. In addition I have found out a little about the industries of Hong Kong, Singapore, Taipeh and Bangkok. But my aim is not to generalize – the data has been used merely to draw contrasts with Britain and America, my central concerns.

While I claim that there is research – even empirical research – in this book, there may be those purists who are surprised at the amount of *a priori* sociology there too. As this is a topic I have entered upon elsewhere (1964, 1967b), I shall put up only two explanatory arguments. The first is that sorting out and clarifying problems is an *a priori* activity. The second is that surveying possible solutions, and deciding which are obviously false or inadequate, begins on the

---

[1] Kracauer simply assumes that because certain themes are clear to him in German films of the twenties and thirties these themes reflect the hidden underside of the German national psyche in those years. He evades the question of whether the films he analyses were popular or not; or whether their creators had any special claims to be regarded as reflecting the 'national syndrome'.

[2] Hauco's book relies to a very large extent on plot summaries. This guarantees that the book is concerned neither with the sociology of the production of film art, nor with the sociology of experienced screen art. It is solely about what sociological conclusions can be drawn from plot summaries of film art. See J. R. Taylor's review (1965).

a priori level, regardless of whether or not any of the solutions are actually held to be true by anyone.[3]

I can imagine a disappointed reaction from those friends of mine – film critics, aestheticians, and others – whose concern is less with the cinema as a social institution than with good *films*. Since what writing there is on the sociology of the cinema often concerns itself with films that are trash, those concerned with good cinema would naturally want to urge me not to waste time by discussing bad films and their audiences. In the name of *good* films they may also complain that, since discussion in current literature on the sociology of the cinema very often proceeds on the basis of plot summaries, neither authors nor readers are able to discern if the films are trash or not – which is worse than frankly indulging in trash. Were authors (including myself) to forswear discussing films they have not seen, this situation would not arise. It is not plots, but those special and important qualities possessed by film as a unique medium which should be of aesthetic concern and, perhaps, aesthetic concern in the cinema should be primary. If this be so, much of the study in the present volume should have been omitted, not so much because it concerns itself with trash, as because it is sociological rather than aesthetic.

Sociology must involve the study of trash. The cinema is – sociologically, at least – a mass art; and it would be silly to pretend that mass taste is very high, or that the average product reaches above mass taste to any high standard of excellence. Thus, my defence in discussing trash is complete: chiefly, I am doing sociology. Yet I wish to defend my study aesthetically too: although I confess to highbrow biases, I am critical of the view that the average good entertainment movie ('trash', in the broadest sense) is of no aesthetic interest; it is one of the most pleasurable entertainments I know and, loath though I am to say this, occasionally it even satisfies highbrow criteria: it can be informative, well done, sophisticated. It is snobbish, then, to ignore mass cinema either as a sociological or as an aesthetic phenomenon. Going further, one can argue that the best *and* the worst films come from the same social structure of production, enter into the same mass market, present their particular views of the world, and have certain images in the public mind. Further: even a poor film may raise or explore an interesting social, moral, or personal problem.[4] Later on I shall try to intrigue the reader with some.

[3] The philosopher P. K. Feyerabend has argued that the more solutions to problems that are entertained the better the chances for knowledge to grow.

[4] For instance, the aesthetically and intellectually leaden 'problem-pictures' of Stanley Kramer: *On the Beach* (The Bomb: how will people behave after the

My concern, then, in writing about the sociology of the cinema, is with the whole galaxy of production, marketing, portraying and being-reflected-in-the-audience, and to a certain extent with appraisal and the sociological factors which may help explain why a film is good or bad. In the end, of course, the artist's technical mastery, imagination, creative discipline and control over his material, must make at least some of the difference between good and bad films. Yet these qualities are not totally individual: possibly certain social structures and organizations are more conducive than others to giving the artist the opportunity and incentive to do well. This is the way the problem of good and bad films will be introduced here. In the body of this book, the problems are set so that sometimes quality is relevant, sometimes not.

The complaint that a sociology of the cinema should not be manifestly such that it could have been written without having ever entered a cinema and seen films, is a serious one to which I have paid considerable attention. For example, when I discuss the western or the musical, I am studying them primarily in terms of their effects as cinema: I do not confine myself to searching their plots for social significance. Of course, plots are an integral part of most films and cannot be entirely ignored; but the special visual and aural cinematic qualities of, say, western and gangster films, contribute considerably to their effect. I have tried not to forget this – as most of my predecessors have done, to their loss and ours.

As to the contents of films and other background material, I shall summarize all that I do not expect the reader to be familiar with, but nothing else. I must ask the indulgence both of the reader who thinks a film I regurgitate painstakingly is part of the standard film repertoire and can be described briefly, and also of the reader who thinks he knows the standard film repertoire but finds me giving a cursory description of a film I consider part of the standard repertoire but which he has not seen. There is as yet no agreement on what constitutes the standard film repertoire.

A further comment on the other complaint. Very often we are perturbed less by the feeling that a writer on the sociology of the film has not seen the films he discusses, than by his apparent lack of sympathy with film as a medium. Such writers don't go to the cinema mainly because they don't really like films. Thus they have little understanding of the people they are studying. Now this seems to me

holocaust and before the bitter end?); *Inherit the Wind* (The Tennessee Monkey Trial: Biblical literalism *versus* liberalism over the introduction of Darwin to the Bible Belt); *Judgement at Nuremberg* (Nazi war crimes: how does Germany view its guilt, and how is the guilt to be shared?).

a serious complaint, because sociology without human sympathy is
not only appalling, it is also methodologically dubious. This observation of mine should not be construed as a demand for fieldwork,
although in general I favour some measure of critical fieldwork.[5]
Rather, what I am urging is a Collingwoodian exercise in 'putting
oneself in the other chap's shoes'. A thought-experiment will do; but
if one is totally out of sympathy, one had better quit the whole
venture. Comic books are unlikely to be illuminated much by writers
who detest comic books: detestation will not develop understanding,
only abet condemnation. My argument here must not be misunderstood. It is not in general essential that one approve of, like, or
sympathize with, the subjects of one's intellectual inquiries. But
where such attitudes are lacking in the human sciences the scope of
inquiry is severely limited. It will scarcely be possible to explain what
the adherents of comic books and pop music get out of these things
if one is utterly out of sympathy with them. Some great imaginative
writers appear to get inside antithetical characters, so perhaps one
should just say: unless you are a great writer, stick to subjects you
have some sympathy for if your purpose is to illuminate.

Few writers appear to detest films in the way comic books are
detested; more commonly, films are a matter of indifference or
detachment. Neither attitude is a good heuristic device for the study
of films. The medium is a sophisticated and refined one which cannot
be appreciated without a degree of involvement and learning. A
corollary of this is that highbrowism itself may be a form of lack of
sympathy, and in some senses it quite definitely is. As a professed
highbrow, I will go to see and sometimes enjoy the most *avant-garde*
cinema that is available. But I can also thoroughly enjoy a good Joan
Crawford or Lana Turner vehicle, a weepie courtesy of Douglas Sirk
or Jean Negulesco, a rousing action film like *The Vikings* or *Vera
Cruz*, or a mere glossy adventure like *Charade* or *Arabesque*. I do not
feel that this involves abrogating my critical standards. It involves,
rather, appreciative tolerance of diversity, which is part of a well-
controlled critical apparatus. One does not apply the standards of
English literature classes to dime-store novels, or else, if one does,
one becomes hypercritical and risks making a fool of oneself.[6] If one
happens to develop an interest in dime-store novels, one must first
have learned to tolerate them, to discriminate among them to an
extent and even to like the better ones – using criteria which may

---

[5] Not, let it be said, for the usual reasons. See my (1964) and (1967*b*).

[6] An example of this may be the discussion of Raymond Chandler and Hank
Janson in Hall and Whannel (1964). Chandler is a writer to take seriously but,
Janson does not pretend to be. To score the one for not attempting the successes
of the other seems a foolish piece of critical argument.

be quite new to one's experience. The fault of such volumes by Hall and Whannel (1964) and Thompson (1964), and they are very big faults, is that their authors are more concerned with uplift than with understanding; they are out to grind certain socio-political axes, arguing from the need to raise public taste, to the need to reform the media, to the need to reform society itself. In their ideal world there would be no room for television's *Peyton Place* and *Batman*, for the meretricious novels of Hank Janson and Mickey Spillane, for the splendour of the Hollywood musical, for the gushy romanticism of the 'woman's' picture. Their austere reformer's world is too dull for me. On the whole, while I agree that there could be more good films, there are surprisingly few that are as unspeakably bad as some critics like to think; and though public taste could be better, I do not want to see it lose the capacity to enjoy the ordinary, slick, superbly professional film: public taste should be expanded, not narrowed.[7]

My sympathies, then, are deeply with the films as they are, along with all their engaging virtues and admitted faults. This puts me in the classic anthropological posture of being a participant observer. Thus, on occasion, the argument of the book is autobiographical, like any other field report. Moreover, I have done fieldwork because I love the community of the cinema to which I belong; I write about it the better to understand it.

[7] This, incidentally, would be my defence if my anti-purism was attacked as slumming. Intellectuals may draw out of ordinary films what plain folk do not, but there is no reason to think they are unable to experience what the plain folk do as well.

Acknowledgements

This book is in part the fruit of five happy years at the University of Hong Kong, a unique opportunity for contact with a non-European society and a non-European film industry. It was a revelation to find that close on three hundred pictures a year were produced there, making Hong Kong for a time the third-ranking world producer. The first jottings for the book were made in 1962 in Hong Kong, when I was much encouraged by my friend Joseph Agassi. We were to renew our discussions in 1966 in Boston where much of the volume was drafted. The systematic research was spread out before and after that meeting, not being completed until this year.

I am indebted to the University of Hong Kong for study leave at the end of 1964, which I utilized to make a preliminary survey of the collections of the British Library of Political and Economic Science and the Library of the British Film Institute, and for a research grant the following year. The Canada Council gave me generous travel funds to finish my research in 1968. A grant from York University helped that research along. It is a pleasure to thank Professor W. J. H. Sprott for helpful discussion when the book was still in the planning stages. For permission to search the stacks at the University of Southern California and the Royal Danish Film Museum, I am grateful to the authorities. Help and hospitality were generously given by the Belgian Cinémathèque and by Mr and Mrs William Kugel of Beverly Hills.

I. C. J.

MOVIES and SOCIETY

Introduction

The Relevance of Cinema and of Sociology in General to the Sociology of the Medium-at-Large

1 *The cinema as an art form comes of age*

The cinema was the first among the new communications media developed in this century to mature into an art form. An art form might be characterized as a medium an artist would consciously choose for purposes of putting forward his vision.[1] Radio did not become a medium of choice until the Second World War and after, and as I write, television is still in process of becoming a medium of choice. Certainly the television series, operating with a basic situation and set of characters, which allies television with radio as opposed to films where by and large each film stands by itself, would – if this is not sacrilege – provide a very interesting realization of the great omnibus novels of Richardson, Proust, Galsworthy and Powell.[2] Or, putting it another way: one day, someone familiar with television may want to execute his omnibus vision in a television series.

It would be safe to say that by 1914, when D. W. Griffith made his Civil War masterpiece *Birth of a Nation*, the feature-length silent film had matured as a medium of choice. By this I mean that the expressive resources of the medium were sufficiently developed to enable it to satisfy serious creators. By the early 1930s the sound documentary film and the sound cartoon were maturing in this sense. It is difficult to say when the sound feature film matured, although the brilliant dance sequences directed by Busby Berkeley in films like *Whoopee* (1930), *42nd Street* (1933), and *Gold Diggers of 1933* were already paving the way. Certainly by the time of Orson Welles' *Citizen Kane* (1941) the medium of the sound feature film was rich enough to be considered mature.

If we date the beginning of the cinema's maturity from 1914 in the

---

[1] Thus science and business can be art forms too.
[2] In 1967 a: d 1968 Britain's BBC television did some very successful adaptions of Victorian novels spread over many episodes.

1

way I have indicated, then it has a history as a medium of choice of more than fifty years. Over those years it has proliferated into such a complex medium, that a creator wishing to work in film has quite a few different possibilities: two-dimensional, silent movies, in a rectangle proportioned 3:4 height to length; two-dimensional sound movies in 3:4 ratio; silent and sound films in other ratios; silent and sound films in other ratios and three-dimensions; and each of the foregoing can be either coloured or black and white. All these variations of technique involve using a camera, and some, a microphone as well: yet film images *can* be produced by photographing drawings, or even drawing directly on film; sound tracks can be electronically produced, or again, even painted on to film.[3] Nowadays, these means of making films are all available, and the creator selects that which he finds most appropriate to his needs. Not so long ago their availability was limited because sound film was an expensive, almost exclusively professional medium. Since then, the advent of cheaper and cheaper equipment has put film making within the reach of almost anyone determined enough. The Underground cinema movement in the USA[4] could not have existed were it not for the new ease with which films can be made, despite limited budgets; once the movement surfaced, however, it could easily support itself.

In these fifty years film has come to fill our world, from the amateur baby movies thrust by their proud creators upon reluctant guests, through the ubiquitous television screen and movie projectors in classrooms and libraries, to the cinema screens, no longer housed on every other street corner, but still surprisingly plentiful. My generation is authentically a product of education by film. At a very tender age I was hiding under the seat when the witch appeared in *Snow White and the Seven Dwarfs*. By the end of the war I was making weekly trips to the Saturday morning cinema club to see programmes consisting of cartoon, 'interest' film, serial and feature, all for ninepence – with the Odeon Cinema Club song of 'happy girls and boys' thrown in. At school we had lots of fun as our schoolmasters wrestled with the intricacies of sound film projection in the darkness of furtive classrooms. Finding adults to take one into 'A' pictures was also a major preoccupation.

It was not our fate to face the cinema as a strange and rather vulgar new invention into whose darkness one might escape from the troubles of the world outside – as the philosopher Wittgenstein, for

---

[3] Because optical sound is simply a changing strip of white on the edge of a film and can thus be painted on.
[4] Described in Battock (1967) and Renan (1967).

example, used to.[5] The inside of a cinema became a home from home for my generation, the central focus for many of our interests, values, images, fantasies – even intellectual efforts. Unlike our elders, we are familiar with the cinema world and its language: we can with ease follow patterns of flashback which verge on being indescribable;[6] we can spot at once the use of a 'stock shot' in a new film;[7] we can 'see' when filmed excerpts are inserted into a live television show, such is our sensitivity to the surface of the medium we have been gazing at all our lives.

2 Critique of intellectual hauteur towards the cinema

This does not mean that the cinema is taken seriously enough by the intellectuals of this society, or that its products are prized – as I think they should be – as among the greatest achievements of our culture and civilization. Only the French official cultural mandarins acknowledge the cinema (they seem to regard films as a good cultural export) and, maybe as a result, French intellectual attitudes to the film mix heavy over-intellectualization with a sort of slumming among the B-picture dross for undiscovered masterpieces. True enough, what one considers great art has elements of personal predilection in it, but I think I can enter a short list of cinema giants

[5] Norman Malcolm in *Ludwig Wittgenstein: A Memoir* (London 1958) tells it thus: 'Wittgenstein was always disgusted with what he had said and with himself. Often he would rush off to a cinema immediately after the class ended. As the members of the class began to move their chairs out of the room he might look imploringly at a friend and say in a low tone, "Could you go to a flick?" On the way to the cinema Wittgenstein would buy a bun or cold pork pie and munch it while he watched the film. He insisted on sitting in the very first row of seats, so that the screen would occupy his entire field of vision, and his mind would be turned away from the thoughts of the lecture and his feelings of revulsion. Once he whispered to me, "This is like a shower bath". His observation of the film was not relaxed or detached. He leaned tensely forward in his seat and rarely took his eyes off the screen. He hardly ever uttered comments on the episodes of the film and did not like his companion to do so. He wished to become totally absorbed into the film no matter how trivial or artificial it was, in order to free his mind temporarily from the philosophical thoughts that tortured and exhausted him. He liked American films and detested English ones. He was inclined to think that there *could not* be a decent English film. This was connected with a great distaste he had for English culture and mental habits in general. He was fond of the film stars Carmen Miranda and Betty Hutton. Before he came to visit me in America he demanded in jest that I should introduce him to Miss Hutton.' (pp. 27–8.) If philosophy was torture, what was a front row seat for a bad Betty Hutton movie (and they nearly all were bad)? Should one view the case as philosophy as suffering becoming cinema-going as counter-phobic defensive suffering?

[6] Could *Dear John, Mirage, Two For the Road, La Guerre est Finie* have been successful with the general audience any earlier?

[7] See Everson (1953).

3

who, by any reasonable criterion, must rank with the top artists of our century in painting, fiction, poetry, music, etc.: Michelangelo Antonioni, Ingmar Bergman, Robert Bresson, John Ford, Jean-Luc Godard, Buster Keaton, Akira Kurosawa, Fritz Lang, Orson Welles. While it is less true now than it was, I think it would be easy to find 'cultivated' people who have never heard of these names, still less could accurately locate their films and the countries they work in, and, worst of all, would have trouble in seeing why these film makers are better than others.

I do not know how to explain this continued lack of cultural respectability for the cinema in the Anglo-Saxon world: it may be because of its newness and vulgar associations, past and present. Dime-store novels do not besmirch books of poetry, yet the same cinema plays *Le Journal d'un Curé de Campagne* and *Drag Strip Riot*. The intellectual (allegedly) doesn't root in the paperback store: pornography and poetry have similar covers these days and confusion is easy: needing to know where he is, the intellectual shops in stores which help him in that. Perhaps the solution is film societies and specialized 'art-houses' where only 'quality' films are shown. For the time being, however, these seem to attract little cliques of devotees; you have to be devoted to the cause to know of their existence. And so on. If we have to wait as long for the cinema to become respectable as the Elizabethan popular theatre waited, we shall wait some time. The process may be being speeded up by the increasing number of educators who want to teach children to be 'critical' of films in school.

On top of the lack of respectability, which is slowly improving simply because of the mass of film in the environment of all but the most determinedly insulated, there is also a monumental ignorance about the nature of the cinema as a social institution — among the most significant in the world. And *this* ignorance is not getting any better, despite the heroic efforts of writers like Marshall McLuhan who are battling to increase awareness. To explain this phenomenon I would cite not the dearth of studies, but their poverty: the more or less complete failure of their authors to grasp what a medium does to a society and why.

This medium that is apparently so hard to understand was at one point the third largest of America's industries. Since the First World War it has been one of her principal exports. It is a major vehicle for the dissemination of her national culture. Apart from anthropological fieldwork, I know of nothing comparable from the point of view of getting inside the skin of another society as viewing films made for the home market.[8] One is not in a good position to judge

---

[8] Cf. Benedict (1946) and Weakland (1971).

4

their truth, but it is safe to say that they are made for and seen by a mass audience; this is both a secure and highly significant as well as informative starting point.[*] Ozu's films about Japanese middle-class life, Satyajit Ray's of Bengal, the majority of American films, are a mine of information and insights into the societies they portray or misportray. Moreover, the film medium has penetrated almost every society in the world, and imposed its standard pattern of exhibition, distribution, and even production. There can be little doubt of its considerable influence and importance. Most people, though, still do not know the first thing about how films are made, or ever reflect on the nature of the experience and the institution.

This study is a preliminary exploration of the questions that need to be asked.

The cinema is both a social and an aesthetic occasion, and these two aspects are intertwined, since its social character may affect art; and its artistic effects may affect society. Like any institution, the cinema has a pre-history, a history, and a structure. Unlike some institutions it was not designed or created by any one individual or group with plans or visions. Still less did its pioneers imagine that their pursuit of the profit motive would have profound effects on society, communication, and world culture. How portentous that would have seemed! But then, like all social institutions, the cinema has its unintended as well as its intended consequences. The profits were sought and intended, the star-system was quite unintended, but grew despite the stiff resistance of the producers. Some of the unintended consequences were welcome, others were not. The profits lead to cut-throat competition which the producers attempted to stem by forming cartels. The fantastic development whereby a weekly trip to the cinema became a world-wide pastime was fostered by the same producers, who soon so took it for granted, that they were quite dismayed when it began to decay around 1949–50.

The cinema as an institution, then, came into being as suddenly as it was invented, and in no time it swept the world. It is one of the key social institutions of our society, and one of the liveliest art forms of our age. Yet while books abound on its history and its art, its social dimensions have only been lightly explored. It is difficult to explain this omission, but let me try. A number of things perhaps contribute:

[*] One among the many faults of Kracauer's (1947) is that he ignores altogether the question of how widely the films he discussed were seen, or appreciated. It is enough for him that the psyches of film makers were making films apparently pregnant with authoritarian symbolism. With this technique it would be easy to jump to the most extraordinary conclusions from Eisenstein's *Ivan the Terrible Part II* – such as, that religion and decadent madness weighed heavily in Stalin's Russia, even 'hough the film was seen by no-one as it was suppressed for twelve years.

5

(1) misconceptions about what sociology is and what sociological studies should consist of; (2) a general lack of descriptive sociology of the main institutions of our society; (3) the vulgar associations attached to the cinema, partly because of its very newness and popularity; (4) the feeling that what little there is to be said on the subject of the sociology of the cinema is trite and/or well-known. This last point, if true, is especially unfortunate: questions are laboured over and over again in the literature, when they could easily be disposed of once and for all by sociological analysis. I am thinking of questions like: is there a relation between popularity and profit? - do audiences get what they want or what they deserve? - and so on. This I will take up later; for now, I want to elaborate on (1), (2), (3), and (4).

3 Sociology is not psychology of social consciousness

(1) The most influential misconceptions about sociology are those on the part of writers about films. However, they are participants in general misconceptions about sociology which were quite widespread even fifteen years ago. It was constantly confused with social science and social work. This perhaps explains why the study of sociological aspects of the cinema has hitherto meant topics like film and crime, film and children, censorship, 'social' (i.e., factual documentary) film, etc., i.e., socially significant aspects of the cinema. Further, film writers have tended to confound sociology with social psychology. The questions which are concentrated on in putative sociological studies of the cinema are: how effective is the cinema as a propaganda medium? - what of its ability to influence people for good or evil (also the censorship problem)? - what of its psychological effects in creating a glamourous world of escape? None of these questions will concern us much in this volume, partly because they have been fruitlessly bandied about quite enough for the time being, partly because they have little to do with a study of social structure, and partly because they are so primitive as to warrant dismissal out of hand. The obvious answers to them are: all media can be effectively adapted to propaganda use and, under certain specifiable conditions, these will be highly effective (see below); media and their products have only marginal effects on the amount of good or evil in democratic society but under certain kinds of totalitarian conditions they can have significant effects; practically any medium is an outlet for escapist fantasy and under specifiable social conditions the role of the media as escape may be marginal (in training) or central (in war). Thus the questions are badly put; they are not sociological enough. In order to render them deeper and of

more interest, as well as to make them more malleable, they have to be reformulated so as to take into account: the interplay between the cinema and the society – the social conditions – it serves/portrays/ attacks; the structural impact of films as an institution among existing institutions, not as content among possible contents; the uses to which the audience can put the cinema situation they are in.[10]

It appears that ever since the cinema became a subject of (minor) intellectual interest, a tradition of film criticism which might be said to be 'sociologically oriented' has existed. That is to say, attempts have been made to relate films to what is known of the sociology and social psychology of the societies which produced them. It may seem a trifle odd to speak of societies 'producing' things; all that is meant is that to some extent the attitudes, values and interests of their makers are conditioned by the social context in which they were raised and in which they work.

Serious film writing began in the twenties but was mostly aesthetic. Let me briefly recapitulate the development of 'sociologically oriented' criticism and its journals. The British school of documentary film makers in the 1930s doubled as vigorous critics, and the journal *Close Up* reflected their deep interest in the social questions raised by the film medium.[11] Since the war the group of British critics thrown up by the highbrow aesthetic journals *Sequence* and *Sight and Sound* have become preoccupied by the social value implicit in films – and this preoccupation triggered off the violent and tedious debate about 'commitment' in 1956–7. The younger generation has gone even further, viz. the neo-Marxist analyses of the political journal *The Universities and Left Review*. In the penultimate case the urge to talk sociology – or what sociology was thought to be – used up the store of actual sociological knowledge very quickly, leaving only a sort of journalistic impressionism. The neo-Marxists had the strength of a tradition of sorts, and the power of the analytical tool of economism. But their unconcealed loathing of our society heavily coloured everything. In the United States, Lewis Jacobs' classic history book *The Rise of the American Film* (1939) was primarily an attempt to set the cinema – one of the most important social institutions in American society – in its social context. The 'social' approach was carried to absurd lengths in the turgid social Freudianism of Kracauer's book *From Caligari to Hitler* (1947); here an ingenious but misplaced hindsight was utilized to blend the facts to the theory

[10] The next nine paragraphs were published separately as an article 'Sociology and the Film Critics' in *Film Journal* (Melbourne) #17, April 1961, pp. 101-2.
[11] The ideclogy of this group is the subject of interesting discussion in an article by Neil Beggs in *Film Journal*, #15.

that incipient Nazism was evident in many German films made between the years 1919 and 1933. Later, in the fifties and sixties the critics of the far out *Film Culture* and the sober *Film Quarterly* at times indulged a socio-political whim; at least in the case of *Film Quarterly* they have been able or equipped to carry it off.

The attitude held in common in these works is that of treating films as though they were statements about, or reflections of, the society they portray; statements, that is, of an attitude or a point of view towards, criticism or evaluation of, what they portray.

To one used to the ways of the other arts this seems, at first glance, an odd approach. Films deal with people in society, certainly; but so do novels, plays and, often enough, poems. And, to be sure, a reviewer of novels will occasionally discuss, for instance, an author's psychological or sociological insight in the course of a more technical discussion of whether the book is a good one or not. Much the same applies to drama. But to concentrate exclusively upon these aspects and, furthermore, to evaluate the work purely on such a basis would be unthinkable.

Without going into the point in too much detail, the following passage from Gombrich's *Art and Illusion* seems relevant:

Logicians tell us – and they are not people to be easily gainsaid – that the terms 'true' and 'false' can only be applied to statements, propositions. And whatever may be the usage of critical parlance, a picture [film] is *never* a statement in that sense of the term. It can no more be true or false than a statement can be blue or green. Much confusion has been caused in aesthetics by disregarding this simple fact. It is an understandable confusion because in our culture pictures are usually labelled, and labels, or captions, can be understood as abbreviated statements. Propaganda in wartime often made use of photographs falsely labelled to accuse or exculpate one of the warring parties.   (pp. 67–8)[12]

Sometimes film critics will condescend to be 'technical' when discussing the merits of a film; they more often, especially if they are highbrows, judge the film on social or moral grounds.[13] We are all familiar with the kinds of words they use.[14] Some of these same

---

[12] It is instructive to see the despair of the addicts of silent cinema, confronted with sound, in these terms; an art form as 'pure' as painting suddenly had words added to it. Previously there had been titles – but the purest cinema (e.g., *The Last Laugh*) went without.

[13] There is an intriguing passage in Brecht (1964) where he reverses the procedure and declares that despite its social and political shortcomings, he enjoyed and praised the film *Gunga Din* (see p. 151).

[14] In the hope that no-one will use them again, here is a selection. *Words of*

critics will labour the theory that in its total effect film resembles nothing so much as poetry. The absurdity of mixing these two ideas is apparent if we imagine a discussion of Shakespeare's merits as a poet solely in terms of the social and moral content of his work.

The retention of this clearly inconsistent position by critics requires some explanation, and a number of possible explanations suggest themselves. There is the coincidence (at least, I assume it is a coincidence) that many people who write about films are politically leftish[15] and, faced with the undoubted commercialism of the cinema's 'bread-and-butter' output, they are continually on the defensive. Unlike the novel, and not unlike the theatre, the cinema is a high cost industry tending to produce a large proportion of trash. Anyone unprepared must find it heartbreaking that *The Ten Commandments* cleans up, while *The Sweet Smell of Success* loses money. Just as drama critics flay the drawing-room comedy, so the 'pink' film critic shows no mercy to the average Hollywood or Pinewood product. Many of these films, remember, seem technically impeccable; yet it is quite plausible to argue that what they principally lack *is* a sense of reality, a point of view, and so on. Therefore, critics concentrate on these deficiencies.

The trouble is that such analyses of their faults are superficial; in fact the real faults of the poor commercial film are much more often technical. They suffer from slack, stilted script-writing, implausible story lines, cursory or inappropriate direction, incompetent playing, excessive music, and (the fault of 90% of films since *The Robe*) a failure to prune at both script and editing stages. Bored, perhaps, at having to complain about excessive length in every other article they write, critics attack instead escapism, distortion of life, vicarious indulgence in what is ostensibly being condemned, and so on. Such criticism looks both deeper and the result of hard thinking. True, when well done this criticism can be incisive, as was the case with Derek Prouse's joint review of *Picnic* and *The Rose Tattoo* in *Sight and Sound* (Spring 1956); perhaps he did overlook the entertainment value of *Picnic*, but he certainly saw through the 'profound'

---

approval: 'aware of the real issues', 'committed', 'concerned', '*engagé*', 'honest', 'real', 'serious', 'sincere', 'socially conscious', 'true', 'valid', 'vital'. *Words of disapproval:* 'cynical', 'deceptive', 'empty', 'equivocal', 'escapist', 'evasive', 'false', 'frivolous', 'glossy', 'hollow', 'invalid', 'irresponsible', 'professional' 'shallow', 'slick', 'smooth', 'superficial'.
[15] My conjecture is that unconsciously they revere it as a propaganda medium and rationalize this into an artistic appreciation. At heart their views are Lenin's. For how the socially conscious attitude paradoxically comes round to opposing the individualist film, see Neil Beggs article referred to in note 11.

philosophy-of-life pretensions of Inge, Miller, Williams, and Co. Poorly done such criticism can lead to ingenuousness, as in the undiscussed assumption behind John Gillett's 'Westfront 1957' (*Sight and Sound*, Winter 1957–8) that all good war films are pacifist. But the truth is that such criticism is the easy way out: it is child's play for an intellectual to pour out that sort of thing. You don't have to know anything about the cinema to write it – or about art for that matter. You can (and sometimes do) write it after merely reading the plot summary. Analysing and discussing the filmic qualities of films like, for example, *Bonnie and Clyde* and *Point Blank* and explaining their merits and demerits is an altogether more difficult task.

A second explanation for the prevalence of 'sociologically oriented' criticism was offered during the first 'commitment' debate, and this is that *cinéastes* proselytizing for the cinema, were wont to meet the indifference and superiority of 'old-fashioned' intellectuals by stressing not its value as entertainment but its seriousness. The problem was a tough one. Assuming you must proselytize, the question is, how are you to convince people simply bored by what they consider frivolous popular entertainment? Answer: you try to prove the opposite: you try to show how realistic, how concerned with serious issues, the cinema is (at least potentially). You argue that the cinema is involved with life, that life should be taken seriously and that therefore the cinema should be taken seriously. The fallacy here is that so much should ever have been conceded. What should have been attacked is the disingenuousness of an aloofness from 'frivolous', 'popular', and 'entertaining' things. The cinema is an art; the function of art is to enrich our experience through entertainment; it no more needs an apologia in sociological terms, than poetry does. In the face of the attitude that poetry is a trivial woman's pastime, the critic would not argue its social significance! Certainly, the cinema medium has as great a capacity for 'seriousness' as any other: but when concerned with its artistic not its propaganda aspect it is impermissible for a critic to mobilize the latter to support the former. The very assumption that the cinema needs such an intellectual justification is to insult the medium and reflects a basic lack of confidence in its intrinsic value and importance. Films are there as films – some committed, some not, some artistic, some not; and in a variety of manners. It so happens that movies often can be 'read' in any number of ways. But of necessity they must be entertainment; as the fine critic Gavin Lambert put it: '*all* art is entertainment, but not all entertainment is art'.

The conclusion my argument reaches is that the critics' retreat into sociology is sheer moralizing; ultimately, it reflects a betrayal or denial of the artistic possibilities of the film medium. The very same people who take it seriously enough to hotly proclaim its artistic possibilities betray it by moralizing about them instead of showing them.

4 More descriptive sociology needed

(2) Neglect of the basic sociological spadework by mass media specialists is one thing; neglect by sociologists is another. In general, there has been surprisingly little descriptive study of the major institutions of our society from the sociological point of view. Much of what does exist in the sociology of institutions is postwar, and even more recent. Sociologists tended for a long time to concentrate on social class, religion, etc., leaving the field of industrial sociology sorely neglected. For example, neither Parliament, nor Congress, nor the theatre, nor the motor industry has yet had its sociological maps even superficially drawn. Mapping an institution is not to be thought of as a simple empirical task. Map-making is primarily interpretative – what kind of information do you want to show, what kind of questions is the map supposed to answer? The four parts of this book could be looked upon as providing four superficial maps of the same territory. Part I on the industry is an historical map of the main 'physical' features. Part II on the audience is a map of the whole concept using a peculiar projection. Part III on the experience is a discussion of the relation between the maps I (industry) and II (audience) and the map of society projected on the screen. Part IV is a discussion of various attempts to map the relative standing of films one to another. Within this overall neglect by sociologists, there is the further oddity that among the mass media, cinema is neglected as against television. Although the cinema antedates television, there is more literature on the sociology of television than of cinema. Indeed almost anything under the heading 'mass media' by a sociologist or a social psychologist will be about television, with glancing references to radio, newspapers, and films, in that order. Riesman (1952) explains this by saying the effects of radio and television needed to be demonstrated to the advertisers. On behalf of the sociologists it needs to be said that they perhaps face special difficulties in mapping the cinema as compared with, e.g., radio and television. There is a notorious difficulty of access to facts about the film industry, which is secretive and insular, and the intermittent 'flow' of films (both in the sense of output and of exhibition), and their lack of dispersion compared with the other three media, makes basic mapping research more difficult. In the course of what follows we shall be exploring how far these difficulties and this neglect make theories of the mass media inapplicable to cinema.

11

5 *Turning aside from the vulgar*

(3) The vulgar associations of popular art seem genuinely to deter academic study, and to leave the field open to the preachers and the do-gooders. A classic example of this is the currently total neglect of the phenomenal cultural ferment going on in the pop music scene since the advent of the Beatles. It is one of the most active areas of popular culture, it is a window into an otherwise closed-off teenage world, reaches heights of sophistication in music and verse which only a very few trendy and strenuously *au courant* intellectuals are noticing. Although *The Times* music critic saw that something was going on when he called Beatles Lennon and McCartney perhaps the most interesting British composers of 1964. Elsewhere it has been noted that *The Beach Boys* and the West Coast groups (*Jefferson Airplane, The Doors*) are making new music. But there is little commentary on the lyrics, e.g., the remarkable surrealism of Simon and Garfunkel's 'Dangling Conversation', and the sociology of the whole scene: how groups form, are discovered, promoted, and how material is gained; the question of why certain discs and not others make the top and so on – all these are totally unexplored. One exception is the comic strips: indeed several tomes have been devoted to this subject.[16] The playfulness of comic strips, the fact that they can be read at leisure, and the lack of complication in their industrial and structural analysis perhaps explains why they especially have been studied.

A close reading of many of the critics of the twenties and thirties, especially Rotha, Arnheim, Grierson, reveals one recurring theme: we must persuade people to take the film seriously. One has the impression the average intellectual paid no more attention to films than he paid to the stack of polite detective thrillers he would demolish from time to time. The earnest attempts being made to show what the medium can do, how important it is, and how aesthetic, explain much of the content of criticism right up to the fifties (Roger Manvell's seminal *Film* and Hall and Whannel's *The Popular Arts* are still of that tradition), as well as some of the judgments. The high rating given to Eisenstein's silent efforts, despite their nowadays crude-looking air of propaganda, was because he treated the medium seriously and was trying to extend it. Disney was loved for a while (until he was thought to have 'sold out'

---

[16] Namely, Wertham (1954); in addition there are White and Abel (1963), Jules Feiffer *The Great Comic Book Heroes*, New York, 1966, and George Perry and Alan Aldridge *The Penguin Book of Comics*, Harmondsworth, 1967.

to commercial success) because he did wonders with the sound cartoon, and was easily mistaken for a folk artist like Chaplin.[17] One cannot perhaps overestimate the amount of this moralizing, which was directly attributable to a reaction against Hollywood and all it stood for. Certainly in the United States in the twenties and thirties there was an intellectual snobbery that focused interest exclusively on European, Russian, Japanese, etc., movies: Hollywood was regarded as just a trash factory. One came across these views even after the war. Hollywood's open brashness and vulgarity, its scandals and notoriety, probably did grave damage-by-association to the image of the cinema: why should, and how could, one take that place and its works seriously? To the snobs the best thing to do with nasty ephemera was to turn away and hope that it moves. Contemplating all those well-scrubbed Russian peasants driving tractors to the rhythms of *montage* was much more edifying.

Judgment was seriously clouded by such attitudes. Hollywood, which was forging the true language of film, and was later to instruct the rest of the world (e.g., Japan, France, etc.), was beyond the pale. Instead, anything Russian was 'OK'; a lot of wispy French romanticism was 'OK' (who now views Carné-Prevert films?); nice little documentaries were built into cults, with a theology and high priests – but few followers. A sober, non-prejudiced, non-extreme perspective appears to have been very hard to achieve among both advocates and detractors of the cinema.

6 *Against the allegation that sociology is trite*

(4) The feeling that sociology generally has little to say is easy to counter. Many of the sociological superstitions aroused by the cinema will be bared and blown away in this volume. Blowing away sociological superstitions is a major task of sociology. People, for example, believe that cinema (and television) influence their children, and, if the programme content is 'bad', so will their children be. Studies, like Himmelweit (1958) and Schramm (1961) unmask this as nonsense. We may be influenced by the cinema for good or ill, but if we are, how we are is much more complicated than it looks at first sight, and possibly even counter-intuitive. Further to confound those who expect no surprises from sociology, we have McLuhan who argues that all this literal-minded searching for influences completely misses the point. Whether he is right or wrong, it is very illuminating to discuss his idea that the media are extensions of our sensorium and as such play a large part in, if they do not govern, the way we sense and understand the world. They carry a cosmos,

[17] Schickel (1968) and Jungersen (1968) are excellent sources for all this.

13

in a Kantian sense, with them. Such a sociological idea is not obvious, not easy to get a hold of, and is full of fascinating implications for future thought. Q.E.D.

7 The major sociological questions about cinema

If these factors (1), (2), (3) and (4) together do not explain why the present study has so little by way of predecessors, at least they should convince readers that effort in this direction may be of interest. The mass media is a fascinating area about which there are many complex and unsolved problems, problems which by extension are in some significant sense major problems of our society. I do not mean such portentous problems as, 'does the cinema corrupt?', or, how can we get more, better, pictures made?' These problems exercise others, but not me. I already find the cinema too rich and exciting and the number of worthwhile films outstripping my ability to see them. Instead I have tried to answer four questions which have long bothered me, and have then tried to study the implication of the answers I've given. The first question is, '*who makes films, and why?*' This is of course the anti-purist question: 'don't tell me who wrote the poem or how, tell me whether it is good or not', the purists cry. '*Who sees films, how and why?*', is a much easier question and takes less space to answer. '*What is seen, how and why?*' is much more involved and fascinating since it takes in the content of the films and the character of the medium as such. And '*How do films get evaluated, by whom and why?*' is again a minor topic but vital if there is to be any semblance of completeness. These questions progress chronologically through the manufacture of a film from conception and production, to sales, to distribution, to viewing and experience, to evaluation. I hope that in addition to being chronological, their order is also logical.

8 An outline of critical sociological method

My intention being to write on or towards a sociology of the cinema, it behoves me to say something about sociology. The four questions just listed, which form the basis for the four parts of the book, are the *problems* from which I start. To some of them I think I know the answers, but it is my intention to discuss different candidate answers in a critical manner, so that no opportunity is lost for eliminating error. This, roughly, is a microcosm of my view of the nature of intellectual inquiry, a view taught to me by a great contemporary philosopher, Sir Karl Popper. *Eo ipse* I believe this to be the way of conducting sociological enquiry. The starting point is best seen as a

14

problem in a concrete society – in my case several closely connected problems manifest in the three societies I know tolerably well: England, Hong Kong, and North America. To this problem or problems various solutions exist or can be discovered, and these can be subjected to criticism. It is crucial that the problems be genuine ones, and that the criticism of them be as severe as possible.

Aside from this general methodological approach, there is the question of what constitutes a sociological explanation of the problems set. Two views on this matter I reject. One, functionalism, says that social regularities ought to be explained exclusively with reference to other social regularities in that same society. Of course, interconnections between social regularities can be very illuminating, as when we show that the social class position of people interlocks in interesting ways with the kind of church they attend. But unless one thinks that people conveniently adopt religions (as barristers adopt pin-striped trousers) as protective colouring when they have entered a certain class, then the interlocking serves chiefly to stimulate the sociologists: the interlocking of regularities is another regularity to be explained, it does not in itself explain anything.

The second view of sociological explanation I reject is that which says an action can be explained by reference to basic psychological drives and/or basic biological needs. Both these factors seem to me to be 'given' when a sociological problem is formulated. They cannot therefore be used to explain it. We know perfectly well that people have something like a psycho-biological need to be gregarious. But that gregariousness does not explain their class system. That they fulfil this need by class and not by colour of eyes, or height, indicates the presence of social institutions and beliefs about what is desirable and acceptable, and these include the marks of class, but not those of eye-colour and height.

So if as sociologists we compare the cinema with the church, describe its church-like buildings and respectful atmosphere, its regular, often weekly, attendance, its place as a community centre for ritual foregathering, all of which make it the competitor to religion we know it is, we do no more than describe some of the decline in religion and the ready acceptance of the cinema.

Sociological explanation is something like this: a man acts, we assume, because he wants to; he wants to because he wants something, he wants to achieve something, to gain some end, and he expects to do so by acting. His want and his expectations form a context, or situation, against which, or in which, he acts. His aim is given to us and striven for by him. The better his appreciation of his own wants and their possibility of attainment in a given situation,

15

the more likely is his aim to be realized by the action intended to realize it.

Let us say that a man wants to make a film for profit. His want may be solely that, or he may also desire to make a good film: unless good films are all profitable this additional urge may yield problems. However, his view of the situation in film making, its past successes and its present trends, and his 'feel' for the possibilities in a film subject, may provide good grounds for going ahead. Let us say this same man, despite proven ability to make profitable and good films, produces a lemon which is a box-office disaster. Dismiss, for the moment, the possibility that he had a 'bad day' or series of days, and see whether his acting as he sees in his own best interests, will explain the badness of this movie without auxiliary assumptions. The classical case is the foreign film maker who is a novice in Hollywood: lured by salary, promises, and the superb professionalism of Hollywood's technology and players, he may come. There follows a sad, and repeated story. Little by little he is asked to make compromises; to shoot scenes he dislikes; to select angles to show off sets or stars' profiles and not solely what he wants to convey; he is persuaded to put certain kinds of music over scenes; to edit this and that in these and those ways; etc., etc. In the end a film is released which he may very well disown – depending on whether he wants further employment in Hollywood or not.

This explanation is, I think, purely sociological, be it true or false, in the sense that it utilizes only social institutions and conditions. For example, those insinuating the compromises upon the novice are acting in what they see as the defence of their investment, or their bosses' investment. The director is naive of their ways, and yields because each point in its turn is small, and hardly seems worth a battle. The accumulation, however, can spell ruin for film and director. The social structure of Hollywood in this case is (or was) such that only the most fiercely meticulous and dictatorial personalities managed the transition easily. Others swallowed what happened and learned how to manipulate the Hollywood set-up, for example, Robert Siodmak, Max Ophuls, Jean Renoir. Others wrote off their early efforts but relied on success finally to give them the strength to throw off compromises (Billy Wilder, William Wyler, Alfred Hitchcock, etc.). Others disappeared without trace.

No psychological or other quirks are needed to explain what happens: everything follows from the clashing aims of the (sociological) actors, and their different degrees of appreciation of the facts of the situation. Such is the sort of explanation I shall be seeking for the topics explored in this book.

16

9 *Fitting cinema into a sociological frame of reference*

Having looked at the questions to be raised, and at some ideas about how to answer them, one further delay is required before we can move on to treat them directly. This must be a general review of what sociology tells us about the cinema; a sociological framework within which the cinema can be viewed. This will involve us in some jargon, and readers allergic to sociologese are welcome to skip a few pages. In searching indexes for references to the cinema, in addition to 'cinema', 'motion-pictures', 'movies', 'films' and so on, one looks at each of the above words, and their prefix of 'the sociology of'. What discussions I have found on the cinema in the literature of the social sciences revolves around certain basic categories: *leisure— art—entertainment*; *communication—propaganda*; and *mass culture— mass media*.

How to organize and present all this? A recent volume by Stephenson (1967) offers a way of classifying sociological ideas about the mass media that is helpful and illuminating. Stephenson argues that most sociological studies of the media have considered them as forms of *social control*: i.e., the media are seen as providing information and propaganda by means of which the society influences or controls behaviour. Stephenson endeavours to redress the balance by focusing on what he rather clumsily labels *convergent selectivity*. By this neologism he simply means the choosing by an individual of the things which please and entertain him from among the wide selection available. The individual wishes to play or conjure with these and not others, and in selecting them he in a sense 'links' himself with all those other persons whose choices have converged at the same point. Their selections, or selectivities, converge.

It is clear, utilizing Stephenson's distinction, that leisure, art, and entertainment are cases of convergent selectivity. The films *qua* leisure-time activity, *qua* art, *qua* entertainment, are simply one among many offerings our incredibly rich and diverse societies produce. This isolation of leisure as a special kind of human activity no doubt has its roots deeply in puritanism, *via* Marx. For the Puritan work was not only good, it was virtuous – idleness was sin. For Marx the means of production, man's relation to them, and especially his productive work, were the fundamental reality. Such (diminishing) time as he had left over from exploitation was for family and recreation. Nowadays in view of the decreasing need for productive work, and the gradual elimination of routine and unpleasant tasks, there are arising new categories: for example one might toy with the idea of a play theory of work. Many kinds of work with many differing rewards are on offer. Do we not choose increasingly that combination of work and reward which we are best able to play with and tolerate, if not positively enjoy?

Be that as it may, for the moment there is still quite a sharp distinction between work and play, and a huge demand for those activities that man can enjoy when he is not engaged in productive work. As the society grows richer it can generally be expected that more and more leisure activities will be needed and each in greater quantity. With the exception of vaudeville, almost no form of entertainment has been squeezed out by the advent of new ones. Reading and home entertainment may have been affected by radio, films, television, but after a period of adjustment each has settled down to live amicably with the others – providing the customer with pluralities of choice when he has moments to spare. Stephenson's emphasis is a valuable corrective, but the media as mechanisms of social control cannot be neglected.

Communication and propaganda are also social control functions that the mass media can clearly fulfil as well as, if not better than, traditional arts and entertainments like books and music-making. One of the comforting things about research into *overt* propaganda is the discovery that by and large it is ineffective and strongly under the control of the primary groups, rather than, as had been feared, controlled by the manipulators or by the collective behaviour of the unstructured groups, e.g., the crowd and the audience. However, the media are also sometimes thought of as vehicles for *covert* propaganda, e.g., political, escapist, etc., etc. This kind of 'reading in' of messages is very difficult to discuss since there is little agreement on what constitutes the facts. That any creator presents people and society as he sees them, and that his vision will almost certainly be shared by some party or group in the society, cannot be disputed. That high costs of entry into the industry, and preferential and discriminatory restrictions on entry effectively prevent certain minority viewpoints from being represented seems true enough. Communists on the whole are sparsely represented in the American film and TV industry; conservatives and social democrats are on the whole sparsely represented in the ranks of film makers in Eastern Europe. To take this charge any further we have to look at the curious view occasionally dignified with the name 'the theory of mass society'.

The idea behind this 'theory' is that mass-production alienates or endistances man from his product and creates the work/pleasure dichotomy. Moreover, urbanization creates huge anonymous conglomerates of people, with no sense of community or shared experience and tradition – in short a lonely crowd. Lacking culture and tradition, with circumscribed life-chances and experience, this atomized society is increasingly bound together by the media.

The mass media give 'culture' and vicarious 'experience' to the mass, and function as a form of social cement. Housewives plug in to their soap-operas for a 'fix' of experience and emotions to fill the emptiness in their lives. More radical devotees of the theory proclaim that mass 'culture' is inescapably *kitsch* because it must appeal to the lowest common denominator, or, it is dealing with an audience that cannot tell the difference between *kitsch* and the real thing and in this situation *kitsch* will win. It will even, if Dwight Macdonald is to be believed, destroy 'high culture' because it will swamp it and the essential elite that sustains high culture. In Macdonald's view the cinema and television are inherently *kitsch*, they are impoverished as media of artistic choice because of their being forged for a mass audience and not a select and sensitive one.[18]

The mixture of pessimism, snobbery, perversity and plausibility in this 'theory of mass society' has been critically discussed by R. and A. Bauer (1960). Their argument is that all the evidence that exists either undermines this theory and its premises, or can as easily be interpreted to go against it as to count for it. They do not try to offer a fully-fledged alternative view; only Stephenson does that. Riley and Riley's approach (1959) to a sociological view of mass communications is programmatic, but useful. Perhaps this is the place to essay a few remarks of my own.

When one enters a cinema one does not suffer a change of roles akin to the change one suffers when one enters a classroom or a courtroom. The roles pursued in the primary group (the family) and in the secondary groups (e.g., work) can be sustained as a member of an audience. However, these roles are largely irrelevant to the interaction process of viewing a film. Whether with family, friends, workmates, or strangers, an audience has as first approximation its own patterns of coherence in relation to the film. To enter a cinema is both a social act constituting something (an audience, different on each occasion), and a private act in which one experiences the film in one's own way. The impulses for picture-going are extremely diverse. Some people just go to see a good film they've heard about. Others go for a rest. Others go to distract themselves from their pressing problems. Still others go there to neck and pet. Some go there because it is necessary to be *au courant* with the preoccupations of their reference-groups; or to learn; or in pursuit of art; or in pursuit of private fantasies. Some go there as part of a love-affair with a star-icon; others go as part of a dare (can you stand it?), in a state of thrill-terror. And so on. No simplistic account of what cinema-going

---

[18] See his (1954). Macdonald allows silent films to aspire to folk-art; sound films are inherently *kitsch*. Less than ten years later Macdonald was film critic for *Esquire*.

amounts to is possible. Audience moods and reactions, individual moods and reactions, are just as involved as the indiv'dual act of cinema-going. Like any other act of consumption, cinema-going is very rich. Let us simplify and take it as read that, for reasons of their own, people want to go to see films. We can now concentrate on how they achieve this and what happens to them in the course of the undertaking. They don't change roles, although they do forge new temporary group alliances. After the initial audience has dispersed they still belong to the group that, e.g., loves *Bonnie and Clyde*, as opposed to the group or groups which, to varying degrees, detract from *Bonnie and Clyde*. Just as McLuhan distinguishes a 'hot' medium as one that is all-absorbing, high-definition, and tending to impose itself, from a cool medium, low-definition, fuzzy, requiring much audience effort if it is to work, so one might look at groups that way. The audience itself is a temporary, loose, but rather 'hot' group which imposes itself – the theory of crowds and collective behaviour is interesting here. The family or primary group, on the other hand, is rather 'cool', and requires a high degree of involvement to make it work. It is perhaps significant that the cool medium, television, has come into its own in homes, family homes, while the hot medium films, adapts best to audiences in the mass. Home-movie audiences are curiously uneasy and out of place, as is a room of people watching a large-screen projection of normal television programming. Television is a constant flow which does not bother one and which one can plug one's concentration into as one sees fit. This explains the success of the rambling and repetitive (deliberately so) soap operas and of the late-night talk shows; they are microcosms of the medium itself. Of course, both media can be adapted to either scale, but the mainstream of each has settled down in a curiously appropriate social slot.

A few words, finally, about learning-theory. Films are a language which is highly conventional and has to be learned. It is foolish to compare languages in their degrees of nuance and subtlety: they are all open-ended and what it seemed impossible to convey one day is being done the next. Each language has its inimitable aspects, as in film dissolves, overlapping sound, and jump-cuts. Learning is usually thought to be either mechanical and repetitive, where the responses approach motor reactions after a while; or trial and error, where the learner probes his environment and modifies the later probes in accordance with the feedback from the previous ones. For there to be signals or symbols there must be uncertainty in the environment being probed: otherwise there is only confirmatory feedback and therefore no learning. Communication theory is a

20

model of learning-theory. There seems little doubt that we learn about cinema-going, about what it does for us, and learn when to select it for our purposes. We also learn from the direct content of films, although here one has to be circumspect. Information absorption, like value-acceptance, doubtless has much to do with the reference group of the learner. Increasingly, however, the reference group is broadening and becoming identical with the total audience, which is becoming identical with mankind: the global village. The technological and information gap between those in the global village and those outside grows larger all the time, and the differences of perception of the world grow acute. Failure to perceive the world in the same way as those who have learned to use the media can lead to disastrous consequences and, if one is to take McLuhan literally on this, to Vietnam.[19]

[19] See his piece on the war as Westernizing the Orient by using out-of-date technology, p. 49 of Wolf and Bagguley (1967).

Part One

THE SOCIOLOGY OF
AN INDUSTRY:
WHO MAKES FILMS, HOW AND WHY?

I wish to deal with the industry first and with its audience second; films must be made before they can be seen. True, there must be demand before there can be supply; however, it is sufficient to explain supply by saying demand is anticipated; this is known as risk. In brief the answer to 'who makes films, how and why?' is this. First, who: films are made principally by a specialized industry which recruits widely. Second, how: the industry operates like any other, bringing together land, labour and capital. Further detail involves exploring the rather interesting history and present social structure of that industry. Third, why: simple enough; the industry produces films in order to make profit, and/or to make propaganda; the individuals who man the industry do so either to make money, and/or quality films, not to mention some other desires that cinema gratifies, such as fame or sex.

I

The Relevance of the Sociology
of the Industry to the Sociology
of the Medium-at-Large

1 *Individual* versus *collective arts*

A film is a product to be produced, consumed, reacted to and evaluated. Mostly we shall be concerned with those produced by an industry. Films are also the objects of action. People wish to see them, for whatever reason. Mostly we shall be concerned with how they accomplish this desire in the commercial structure the industry provides. What difference does it make to a study of this kind that films are produced by an industry and not by a man with a chisel; that it takes a sub-society of the society to make them? It makes both more and less difference than at first sight.

Unlike some of the longer established arts, e.g., poetry and music, and more like the theatre, films are rarely the product of one man's unaided creative effort. In the last five years it has become *possible* for one man, even one with limited resources, to make a film that is up to professional standards. To do so, to make a film entirely on one's own, requires at least the abilities to operate a film camera, develop the film, splice film together, and record sound on to it. Few professional film makers do or did possess any or all of these abilities. In the period since the pioneer days when almost everybody in films could handle several jobs, a high degree of division of labour has been introduced, and directors, for example, have rarely mastered more than one other function of the film-making process.[1] Part of the amateurishness of amateur films stems from the sheer difficulty of mastering these different processes in all their current complexity. What does all this matter? Is there an inherent difference between arts which can only be produced collectively, and those, like writing or painting, which can be produced by an unaided individual? Does such an alleged difference tell us that a drama differs from a novel in

[1] Directors often came either straight from editing, or from writing, or from the stage or television, etc.

the same way that a building differs from a statue? To answer this question it might be helpful to look at architecture: film, like architecture, is a collective art. To complete the final product an architect must use the services of a good many highly specialized concerns. And although architectural education is very thorough in giving an architect an understanding of all these different specialities, it is not necessary for him actually to be able to mix and pour concrete, weld steel, glaze glass, cut wood or master other processes which he decrees must go into the realization of his conceptions.

That such differences as these between collective and individual arts *cannot* be inherent is shown by the exceptions to this on both sides. Against the architect one can put a man who designs and builds his own log cabin; against a professional in Hollywood, one can put a film maker who does everything himself.[2] Against the writer or artist, one can put cases where novels and poems were co-authored, paintings and sculptures worked on by several persons.

There are, then, no *inherently* collective or individual arts. There are, however, important differences of organizational complexity in the production processes of different arts. Even the organizational complexity of films and architecture differ in that the latter is a profession with legally enforced status; the former has only a trade union closed shop, with no legal and little professional status given its members. The building industry is as complex and subdivided as the film-making industry – not to mention the book publishing industry and the music-publishing and recording industry. But a comparison of degrees of complexity is of no interest in itself. What is interesting is the question of who if anyone is the key creative person in a collective art. There is little doubt about the answer, indeed there are no competing claims, in the fields of making buildings and making books.[3] The situation is by no means as clear in the making of records, much less of films. Since it is *possible* for one man to make a film, I would contend that there is nothing *inherent* in the film medium which complicates the assignment of responsibility. Instead, I maintain – to begin with at least – that the problem arises purely because of the way the complex organization of film-making is structured. Films can be made or marred in such a large number of ways, and decisions made at such a number of levels in the organization, that there is a genuine question as to whether there is sufficient

---

[2] Norman McLaren has made some animated films in which he drew both sound and visuals directly on to film; 'underground' film maker Stan Brakhage gives the impression that he shot, developed, edited and wailed the sound tracks of several of his films unaided.

[3] Although the making of non-books is another matter; as must be the making of non-buildings.

centralization of decision-making to attribute the finished product to any one individual.

An informed film critic is well aware of this. Yet being convinced that films are an art, and that art demands an artist, he seeks to identify a centre or essence of the film and attribute responsibility to that one person. This is not hard to do, since it is the critic who decides what the essence is. In the early fifties the journal *Sight and Sound* printed two articles by film makers which, incredibly, disputed this issue. Howard Koch, a writer, made the case for the script being the essence of the film; Thorold Dickinson, a writer-director, argued that the director, even when he realizes someone else's script, gives the film its essence.[4] A couple of years later in the same journal an unknown young critic, Tony Richardson,[5] went even further. He distinguished directors who were genuine creative artists and the essence of whose films had some personal vision, from brilliant technicians who had no central vision, but were adept at realizing scripts written by others. It is not clear whether Richardson believed that only creative film makers made films with essences, or whether it was simply that their essences were better or truer.[6]

When a question is turned into one of defining an essence,[7] all answers are of necessity either arbitrary or verbal or both. Yet the underlying problem – the attribution of responsibility for the work – is a genuine one. Film makers sometimes find themselves complimented for a touch in a film that was someone else's idea. For example, a critic once complimented John Ford on the perfection of his film *They Were Expendable*. It transpired that the film had been edited after Ford had gone on to other things: the result was over two hours long; Ford insisted he shot it to be 1¾ hours and he ought to know.[8] Acid things were said by many about Marlon Brando's

---

[4] See Dickinson (1950) and Koch (1950).   [5] See Richardson (1961).

[6] Richardson's subsequent career is ironic. He became a successful stage director after directing the play *Look Back in Anger*, and then made a series of films: *Look Back in Anger, The Entertainer, The Loneliness of the Long Distance Runner, Sanctuary, A Taste of Honey, Tom Jones, The Loved One, Mademoiselle, The Sailor from Gibraltar, Charge of the Light Brigade*. One outstanding feature of these films is their complete lack of a consistent style, their technical fluency is unable to conceal that their author has nothing to say, no personal vision of his own. He is also unable to discipline himself and to be content as a *metteur en scène*.

[7] For the critique of essentialism see K. R. Popper, *The Open Society and its Enimies*, London 1946, rev. ed. 1962, vol II, pp. 9–21.

[8] Lindsay Anderson, 'The Quiet Man', *Sequence*, no. 14, New Year, 1952, esp. p. 24: ' "I didn't put a godammed thing into that picture" . . . said [John] Ford [of *They Were Expendable*]. I [Anderson] said: "But *Expendable* runs 2½ hours as it is . . ." Ford said: "I shot the picture to run an hour and forty minutes – it should have been cut down to that". I said that this could not be done without ruining the f lm. "I think I know more about making pictures than you do," said Ford'.

performance in, and general behaviour during the making of, *Mutiny on the Bounty*, yet the result was superbly original. Since film is a collective art it is a truism that all those involved are collectively responsible. But there is a limit to this, as the examples show: what one remembers about *Expendable* is the dignified pace – for which Ford was at most partly responsible;[9] what one remembers about *Bounty* is Brando's sparkling performance – for which no-one else – not the director or the other actors – can take the slightest credit. With the general run of films the question of overall responsibility rarely arises. Nice touches which aid the total effect may or may not have been contributed by photographers, editors, designers, actors. Where the question of responsibility becomes interesting is in the case of good films, and especially those chains of good films which display something we call a 'personal style'.

In general in these cases, we find it convenient to assume what fits most of the evidence, that the director is the key man, i.e., the person ultimately responsible for what appears on our screens. (It needs to be said that the person who 'produces' a play on the stage is the equivalent of a *film director*. A *film producer*, as will be made clear below, is equivalent to a theatrical impresario. Confusion is further aided by a recent tendency of producers of plays to call themselves, aping film terminology, 'directors'.) Our assumption is, though, one of convenience, because we know perfectly well that even a director with a personal style can have a film he has made spoiled by bad photography, bad editing, bad casting, bad performances, bad sound, bad production design, etc. Each of these is usually the province of a different individual, or even department, whose work is sometimes executed after the director has performed his allotted tasks. Therefore, he is not always responsible. It is still advisable to start with the assumption that the director is responsible, and only where the evidence seems to conflict with that assumption shall we offer different theories, such as that the director was aided or abetted by this or that collaborator or specialist despite himself (if he was helped intentionally then he takes the responsibility as chooser). Remember we are discussing here those special individuals in whose work we perceive a style. The assumption of directorial supremacy is not only false but absurd where routine big studio production is concerned, since here the director may have had only a minimal say in the casting and staffing of the production team. We cannot hold those responsible who have had no control. It is nevertheless

[9] A director as experienced as Ford can retain some control over pace by 'cutting in the camera'. This means shooting each scene in such a concise and economical way, with no overlap between shots, and no duplications of scenes from other angles, that it is virtually impossible to edit it in more than one way.

remarkable how personal was much of the work done in the heyday of the Hollywood machine: Val Lewton horror films, MGM musicals, the films of Cukor, Ford, Hawks, Hitchcock, Lang, Lubitsch, Mamoulian, McCarey, Milestone, Siodmak, Stevens, Sturges, Vidor, Von Sternberg, Wyler, to mention only a few of those securely established in Hollywood before the war.

What about eminent directors who have full control? They, we agree, must take full responsibility. By full control we mean selecting the personnel and okaying the final product – usually by leaving their names on it. Alfred Hitchcock might say[10] that Technicolor assured him that a Baltimore street set (in *Marnie*) would look realistic in the final print, and he believed them, but the result was very poor in fact. This does not relieve him of the responsibility for what he called a poor shot (nor did he disclaim it). He appointed Technicolor, he accepted their reassurance, and he decided to pass the final print with the poor shot in it, for whatever reasons. So although it seems responsibility lies squarely on the shoulders of eminent directors, we certainly cannot assume this of all, especially those who are cogs in studio machines.

What does it matter who is responsible? Isn't the main question: 'is film x good or bad?' Indeed, this *is* the main question. But, do we need to know who is responsible for the film as a whole in order to answer the question? The answer to this would *seem* to be 'no'. There is a standard view that the way to evaluate a film or any work of art is to see it a few times, think about it, try out various interpretations, argue about it and endeavour to make up one's mind. Nowhere here does the question of personal artistic responsibility arise. Whether the film was made by a robot or by Alfred Hitchcock is quite irrelevant. I shall try to explain why this standard view is utterly mistaken.[11]

2 *Internal interpretation* versus *external interpretation*

There are other questions, not so central, but certainly not peripheral even at a first glance, such as why is film x so similar to film y in so many respects and yet so superior to it? The two films may have been produced by the same company, on the same sets, with roughly the same actors playing roughly the same roles, in almost the same story. Such a comparison may look like a typical philosopher's thought-experiment: beautiful to contemplate but nothing to do with reality. Then, consider the following pairs of films:

---

[10] He said this at a question-and-answer session organized by the Harvard Dramatic Club on 14 July 1966.
[11] Cf. Gombrich on 'ape' art in *Art and Illusion* (*1960*).

SUPERIOR	INFERIOR
Frankenstein	*House of Frankenstein*
Dr No	*Goldfinger*
A Night at the Opera	*Go West*
Adventures of Robin Hood	*Captain Blood*
(Errol Flynn)	*Sirocco*
Casablanca	*Return to Peyton Place*
Peyton Place	

And in case you are theorizing that the second film is worse *because* it is a follow up:

Sylvia	*The Carpetbaggers*
any good Randolph Scott western	any bad Randolph Scott western

Explaining evaluations like these is not only an academic exercise in comparative evaluation, but also a means of improving the general level of film – for instance, by trying to learn from those films that do it better. This must involve the question of who is responsible for the good things in a good film, how was it done, and is it something we can learn? Is it simply that a good film comes from a good man, or does a good film come from placing responsibility in good hands?

There are purists who contend that evaluations in art should only be allowed on the basis of evidence internal to the work itself. We can now ask whether the problem of responsibility for the good or bad in a film can be settled with reference to external evidence. It might be clear to the sensitive viewer that the ending of Orson Welles' *The Magnificent Ambersons* is slightly out of key with the rest of the film. Several viewings later, one has only progressed to knowing that *something* went wrong. Did Welles foul up, or was his work tampered with? It is important to decide a question like this both for the critical assessment of Welles' judgment, and for the question of how films can be improved. Only external evidence can decide these questions for us, and thus it has a place.

Yet once it is admitted that the question of responsibility is interesting and relevant, it is difficult to defend the 'internal evidence' purists. After all, even if films were produced by robots, we would be interested in getting to know which robot was producing good films, which bad, if only to decide which to see. Then commonsense presses in on us: the film *x* is good to a certain extent *because* it has the signature of Alfred Hitchcock on every sequence. This commonsense remark can only be unpacked by reference to Hitchcock's style and mannerisms, which involves comparison with other films he is known to have made. Pedagogically, of course, this sort of assignment of responsibility is vital. Only then can one show how a

30

director has learned and matured as his career in films has progressed. This object lesson may or may not help others to do the same. Certainly, some of the pleasure art gives us is that of recognition. Simply enjoying Hitchcock's confident exposition can be like marvelling at Bach's way with a fugue.

Later, in chapter XVI, I shall press for the inclusion of external evidence in the evaluation of films on the more abstract aesthetic ground that no work of art can be interpreted, still less understood, without some background information and that once this is agreed the critical critic must admit: 'the more information the better'.[12] The rational pursuit for the writer on films, I shall argue, and this goes for the informed filmgoer too, is to try to find out, from internal and external evidence, what happened during the making of a film, and to distribute praise and blame as best he can in accordance with this knowledge, or to make critical guesses where he has none. Internal evidence *can* be used to help assign responsibilities also, but the precision with which it can be used varies greatly. The time comes when its interpretation becomes overly subtle and to insist on it exclusively is purist; that is, the belief that a work of art is an organic and self-explanatory whole. Yet films are the complex products of elaborate processes; how bold to imagine that what goes on in them can be explained without other evidence!

Is it a corollary to our assumption of directorial supremacy, that increased organizational complexity in the production of an art reduces individual artistic responsibility more or less inexorably? By this I do not mean to ask whether there is more front-office and executive interference with the final product – that can arise even when the organization is very rudimentary. Rather, I want to consider the situation created by the existence of complex hierarchies and intervening stages between the artist and his work. For example, does the tendency to sycophancy in an organization muffle criticism of the work in progress that the artist might otherwise have taken account of? Does the subdivision of functions inevitably bring forward people not totally sympathetic to or even on the same level with, the director, and who perhaps lack the ability to carry out the director's instructions perfectly? Does the size of the director's staff, and the amount of money committed to each enterprise, lead the artist to make compromises which he would not hesitate to reject if he felt he had a free hand, or was interested only in learning about his medium and its possibilities? And so on.

None of this in fact reduces individual artistic responsibility, provided there is an initial centralization of control; and even the

---

[12] The intellectual arguments for this are to be found in my (1961*b*), and (1967*a*); my views converge with those of P. K. Feyerabend, see especially his (1967).

lack of centralized control does not eliminate individual artistic responsibility. Supposing a director finishes a film and then it is altered; this is a case of decentralization. In such a case, you may think he is not responsible. But this need not be so if the situation is such that he can demand to have his name removed from the film. No doubt some directing contracts simply hire a man to direct operations on the studio floor for the length of shooting. Other functions, like casting, approving the script, editing the first cut, supervising the sound, okaying the final cut, may not be under his control. In such a case he might fail to get his name taken off. He was paid to do a job and has no contractual rights to disown it. But he could institute proceedings, which are not very expensive, for a writ of restraint. If he lost, then he could claim to have publicly disowned the work. Of course, wherever the contract gives the director supervisory or other controls over aspects of the finished product he should have no difficulty in removing his name. Thus I would maintain that as a first approximation a director can be held responsible for everything he has his name on, even if responsible only in the minimal sense that he didn't attempt to have his name removed.

There are documented cases to which we can apply this analysis: perhaps one of the best is Tony Richardson's narrative (1961) of his Hollywood experience in making *Sanctuary*. He claims he was promised freedom before he came, was manoeuvred into making one or two minor compromises, not realizing that this was the thin edge of what turned out to be quite a thick wedge. The film was further altered, he continues to complain, after he had returned to Britain. It is not clear, however, whether an artist can, by complaining, excuse himself so easily. He could have asked to have his name removed from the film and have sued if they refused. Then at least he would have covered himself. So far we have treated responsibility as a sociological category: where, in an organization, is the source of what is in a given film? Let us keep this in mind when we turn to the problem of sycophancy. It is not of interest as a moral problem but as a problem of centralization: when one is surrounded by sycophants vital information is likely to be filtered and deflected. Realizing this danger, which is part of being competent, an artist can either construct his staff so as to avoid sycophants, or he can take corrective measures against them. Similarly, it is the responsibility of the artist to search until he finds technical personnel with whom he has the right *rapport* (and also not to confuse *rapport* with sycophancy). Most of all, he needs to have constantly in the forefront of his mind the problem of his own artistic integrity: not his conscience, but his judgment. Self-awareness is part of it; but the hiring of personnel and their organization is also a way of taking care of such things as a tendency to get either too soft or too tough in face of challenges to his central responsibility. Moreover, he can for example shoot a scene in several different ways and appraise the results before making a final choice. His responsibility for his organization and his collaborators and his treatment of both is never really removed, and any criticism of his failures which cuts as deep as to point to these is bound to be of interest to him, provided he recognizes the problems, is trying to cope with them critically, and uses his own mistakes – when they become apparent – to learn.[13]

We started this chapter with the problem, is the film maker at a special disadvantage as an artist because of the complex organization of film making? Our subsidiary question so far was, to what extent is individual (artistic) responsibility destroyed by complex production organization? It is now time to switch from looking at the individual in the organization to looking at the organization itself and asking the further subsidiary question: since individual responsibility remains, despite organization (although complete freedom of expression does not[14]), and the organization is not invidious to art in that sense, is it beneficial to art? The implicit assumption at the beginning of the chapter, which created the problem of locating responsibility, was that high quality art could not be a collective product. We are now treating the reverse assumption: that the highly professional standards of Hollywood have only been achieved from a high degree of organization. Hollywood's professionalism is sometimes criticized as stultifying by film makers who equate art with self-expression, but they are not to be taken seriously. I take it

---

[13] In footnote 6, I echoed several critics who have remarked negatively on how Tony Richardson seems to draw eclectically on the style of other people's films. In principle his behaviour seems admirable in its way. Perhaps he is searching for his style. But how long should he persist before realizing he lacks a cinematic sense and therefore may never have a style of his own? To use his own categories, when will he reconcile himself to being an efficient *metteur en scène?*

[14] The demand by artists for freedom of expression seems to me to be of little interest. I cannot think of any argument which would warrant either business or the state giving single individuals large sums of money, and allowing them make what films they like with it. Artists should count themselves lucky that this happens as often as it does. Meanwhile they are forced to argue for their projects in terms of quality and popularity. This is a useful discipline, since they can learn how to say what they want to say in highly prescribed and controlled forms. When they have proved their mettle in this way they may, if they are lucky, gain complete freedom to make what they wish. After all, scientists are not simply given grants to do as they see fit. Both indiscriminate giving and discriminate giving are utterly impractical – the solution is competition for giving, which, whatever its faults, is at least practical. For those who believe that science is ennobled because the profit motive is removed, we need to recall that feasibility and long and short term benefits are highly important criteria in the financing of scientific research.

that high professional standards, while neither necessary nor sufficient for good films, are not *in themselves* bad. The question then is, could a comparable professionalism be achieved if the organization was less complex? Undoubtedly the main benefit is division of labour, and complexity is the outcome of it (Adam Smith[15]). So we can assume that as long as complexity reflects chiefly division of labour (rather than, say, multiplying subordinates (Parkinson's Factor 1)), and as long as the problems of complexity are manageable (as the examples above show they are), complexity is improvement (but see Parkinson's third law).[16] This can help us solve a very different problem.

3 *Artistic success* versus *industrial success*

The different problem is, why are Hollywood films so popular?

This amounts to asking whether there is any connection between the world-wide success of the Hollywood product, and the way they organize production in Hollywood. My unsurprising answer to this question is 'yes'. The triumph of Hollywood, *is* the triumph of raising the general standard of films by concentrating on improving the quality of the average product. Hollywood, since the 'teens of this century, has produced a wide swathe of middle-ground pictures that are highly professional in script, acting, direction, photography, sound, design and so on. This is the Hollywood secret. It only rarely (in terms of total output) produced masterpieces, but it also produced only a small quantity of atrocious work, whereas the big film industries of so many other countries in the rest of the world produced unrelievedly bad work across the board (India, Egypt, China, etc.). What is true of Hollywood efficiency is true of American efficiency in general: it aims to raise the general standard, the average, mostly by eroding the lower end of the scale, but also perhaps at the price of less encouragement to the higher end. Very much like Detroit, then,

[15] That is, the breaking down of a manufacturing process into a series of distinct operations, in each of which different workmen will specialize. This increases their output owing: 'first, to the increase of dexterity in every particular workman; secondly, to the saving of the time which is commonly lost in passing from one species of work to another; and lastly, to the invention of a greater number of machines which facilitate and abridge labour, and enable one man to do the work of many.' Adam Smith, *An Inquiry Into the Nature and Causes of the Wealth of Nations*, London 1775–6, chapter I.

[16] I am quite serious about taking Parkinson seriously. The satirical manner of his books should not blind us to the importance and truth of their matter. Factor 1 is 'An official wants to multiply subordinates, not rivals'. See C. Northcote Parkinson, *Parkinson's Law*, London 1958. The third law 'Expansion means complexity, and complexity decay', is in C. Northcote Parkinson, *In-laws and Outlaws*, London 1962.

Hollywood, by raising standards, created standards that for a long time few other national film industries could emulate; by inducing higher expectations in their audiences they forced the world to meet their standards of professional competence if it wanted to compete at all; it was then up to the world to match and surpass these. When several industries did in fact do so (Britain, Japan, Sweden, France, Germany, Italy) the heyday of Hollywood was over and ways of organizing production had to be found which would enable the general standard of picture-making to be pushed up still further – even if the price was to be fewer films. One consequence of this was also that the previous effect of flattening off the top quality was eased too. That is my explanation of why American films are better and more various than ever.

Until the advent of television in the late forties Hollywood was peerless. Then television began to eat into film audiences, cinemas began to close in America, and the production figures fell seriously. This was a booster to native industries elsewhere, which now had vacant cinematime to fill in their own and other countries not yet benefiting from television. The result is that in all the countries I have listed there was a cinema renaissance in the late fifties. The resultant lack of competition from Hollywood was of course bad for, e.g., British production. But, television was soon to lead to serious closures of cinemas in other places too.

What this did to Hollywood's standards is difficult to appraise. There appears to be a lot of extremely entertaining, colourful, star-packed films being released every year now. The question is whether they are in fact any better; has the standard been raised? A glance at the product that was appearing in the thirties and the forties suggests that while 'production values' (colour, 'scope, location-shooting, length) had been heaped on, pictures were not noticeably better.[17] One explanation of this may be a failure to adapt the organization of picture-making sufficiently to new circumstances. Production values could have been improved within the existing mass-production machinery; the main requirement was expanded budgets. But, it could be argued, to raise creative standards more creative freedom needed to be introduced into the system; and if that made it difficult for the system to work, so much the worse for the system – change it. Yet this is a fair description of the facts: Hollywood now allows its top men unprecedented freedom to make what they want in the way they want. The great producer-directors: Ford, Wyler, Wilder, Hitchcock, Wise – even some of the new men like

[17] Indeed Manny Farber (1957) and Pauline Kael (1956) might claim they are noticeably worse. My own feeling is that in the mid-sixties they were getting exciting again.

35

Frankenheimer – work outside the studio machine (or what is left of it, see chapter III) and are more able to carry through their original intentions than they would have been in the thirties and forties. In this sense the product has improved, and the organizational changes have worked. Big men are freer than ever, and with some of them this has led to new triumphs and heights, with while others it has led to self-indulgence and slovenliness.[18]

What was the content of the organizational changes and how specifically did it affect the general product? There has been radical shrinkage and rationalization of the existing studios. Production is no longer initiated on the assumption that studio space, technicians, and contracted artists have to be used. Much more, nowadays, the pattern begins with a producer or entrepreneur getting an idea and packaging it, then going to the sources of money directly. Investment advice and distribution are big functions of the studio now; previously they put their money into their own operation and distributed only their own films. The new pattern is not new, but was invented by the founders of United Artists. This was a corporation founded in 1919 by Chaplin, Fairbanks, Griffith and Pickford to distribute the films they produced. It gradually broadened its catchment area as its founders made fewer and fewer films, and the company almost collapsed during the television slump. But it was taken over by good businessmen who reverted to distributing and investment exclusively – no overheads.

Such people might have been expected to be more conservative than before in what sorts of films they supported financially, since self-financing studios could build-in the costs of experimental films as overheads. Nowadays, when so many films are made by a special company set up and financed solely for that purpose, loss cannot be a tolerated aim. Yet, I cannot explain this, the flow of out-of-the-ordinary films has not shrunk. My only suggestion is that this must somehow be explained by the human factor: the creative producers and the surge of new talent thrown up by television, artists still able to work on modest budgets. Of course, 'the human factor' sounds profound and is in fact trivial. Why was the reorganization such as to allow the human factor to come to the forefront? Here I would cite the critique of Gans (1957) who shows convincingly that the major studio system's main fault was its reluctance to narrow the audience for a film. Hollywood seemed afraid of appealing to the minority audience – forgetting perhaps that a plural society is made up of minorities. Gans noted that the rise of independent producers was better suited to, and did indeed result in, films being made for

[18] Stevens (*Giant, The Greatest Story Ever Told*), Ford (most of the films he has made since *The Searchers*).

sub-cultural audiences rather than for all tastes and all levels, or the standard taste of the largest group.

To sum up, we have tried to answer sociologically the question of whether the film maker is at any special disadvantage because he must needs work within a complex production organization. Our answer has been that the advantages outweigh the disadvantages, which anyway tend to be made up of artistic idealizing, and naive juxtapositions of art and commerce. It is not at all clear that responsibility gets lost in organizational complexity; but it is true that organizational advantages have tended to favour the middle ground as far as quality is concerned. However, under the challenge of competition from television, the organization of film making has been loosened the world over, largely in favour of making a higher quality possible, without lowering the general standard, the average, at all.

II

The Development of an Industry

1 *Origins of the industry*

Conveniently for the historian, the cinema has a clear beginning, and an early history that it is still possible to reconstruct.[1] Roughly, the idea of recording and reproducing motion by using a rapid series of drawings or photographs seems to have occurred to several inventors in several countries at around the same time – the 1880s and 1890s. So our first problem is why the device emerged at this particular stage of human history. In my view there is no answer to this question; it simply happened that way. In particular I reject the Marxist view that pressure of economic need or necessity produces inventions at the time they can be used; and I also reject in this case the classical economic theory that entrepreneurial initiative creates supply to meet existing demand. The cinema is a clear case of where there was first an invention, with no apparent commercial possibilities, a toy, a plaything; and was then dimly seen to have possibilities if only an audience, a demand could be *created*. In this case, supply created demand, in accord with another classical economic theory, Say's 'law'. Certainly there is some truth in the other two views. Inventors had been working feverishly during last quarter of the nineteenth century to make a camera which would reproduce motion. The problem of reproduction of motion (and colour and sound) was 'in the air'. This may account for the competing claims to priority of Lumière, Edison, Friese-Grene and others. But it was not economics or history that drove them on; it was the feeling that such an invention was within reach. And indeed it was, even though Edison's original camera was the size of a baby upright piano. Of

---

[1] And has been quite well served by its historians. Quigley (1948), Ceram (1965) and Hendricks (1961) explore the prehistory. For the American industry Terry Ramsaye's monumental *A Million and One Nights*, Lewis Jacobs' *Rise of the American Film*, Gertrude Jobes' *Motion Picture Empire* are basic. Recently, Brownlow (1968b) must be added. For the British industry Manvell and Low's three volumes so far only reach to 1929. Two general works, Arthur Knight's *The Liveliest Art* and Rotha and Griffith's *The Film Till Now* might also be recommended, although the judgments in the latter are not to be trusted. In the bibliography will be found listed works in English on other industries.

course there is a sense in which demand has, logically, to precede supply. There must have been, so to speak, 'economic room' for a film industry; there had to be enough people with enough surplus wealth to sustain a new entertainment industry. But the new industry was eventually to flourish partly at the expense of older industries, e.g., the live theatre, and to be in its turn squeezed by a still newer industry – television. True, the market was open to expansion, but then the greedy newcomer competes also for a share of older industries in the new market. The fact remains that the film industry had to fight to create itself and its demand. Once it was established it was able, with low prices, successfully to siphon off some of the demand for the theatre and the music hall.

The controversy over who invented the cinematograph was essentially *post-hoc*. In the first instance the invention was regarded as no more than a novelty which would have a certain very limited exploitation value, and certainly no potential as a large-scale money-maker. It is often said that Edison's only bothering to patent it for the USA and not for other countries, indicated his feeling that the invention had little long-term future. Certainly at first neither he nor anyone else knew *how* to exploit it. They shot films of trains arriving, or processions, of numerous events of interest merely because they were moving and – wonder of wonders – this movement could be reproduced. These strips were exhibited in music halls and at fairgrounds as just another 'act'. But by the mid-1890s, the attraction and exploitation-value of these novelty snippets was rapidly wearing thin. It was as though Edison's doubts as to the long-term prospects of this machine were amply justified.

However, it was not to turn into a quick fade-out. The solution to falling audiences was to do something interesting with the gimmick; not to be content with the fact that it moved. One obvious possibility was to record current events: a fire, a race, a boxing match. Another was to show people and places – exotic locales. A variant was a home-produced simulation of these, like faked boxing matches, etc. Keep up a flow of this sort and audience interest is sustained. But this was precarious too, dependent on exploiting the right moments. It served, however, to set up the beginnings of a film making industry. Very rapidly, its principal product was films which told stories. All kinds of stories: fantastic ones of visits to the moon (*A Trip to the Moon*, Méliès, France 1902), simple ones of kidnap (*Rescued by Rover*, Hepworth, UK 1905) and above all, perhaps, western adventures like *The Great Train Robbery*, Porter (USA 1903). These early films were made by semi-amateurs, by eccentrics, and often by genuine creative artists, and they were financed hand to mouth. Méliès in France and Hepworth in Britain after initial success

39

were both financially ruined by film making; only Porter in the USA prospered, although he was not to remain long in films after he was superseded as the leading director by D. W. Griffith. Men like these laid the foundation for an industry – for film making rapidly became an industry. Indeed, industry was what it quickly *had* to become, simply because once the demand was created it was well-nigh insatiable.

The building of the industry began with the production of sufficient story films to allow frequent changes of programme, and thus an adequate flow of revenue to justify the building of permanent places of exhibition. Once these 'cinemas' had been invested in, they demanded a steady and predictable supply of sufficiently new material to keep the audiences coming back again and again. For this to happen, the production amateurs had to become, or give way before, the professionals. The odd camera, plus hastily recruited actors and a shoe-string budget, were no longer enough. Studios needed to put players on permanent payroll to keep them on call, capital was needed to finance programmes of film production which would not pay for themselves until months later. Permanent yet flexible buildings needed to be constructed where equipment could be assembled and stored. This of course, meant the business-men and the financiers had to come in. From its earliest days, the cinema has been a high cost industry, heavy both on overhead fixed costs and on variable costs.

Capital was required, then, both for exhibition, the building and equipping of cinemas; and for production, the financing of studios and their personnel. It was here that films broke away entirely from the theatre and vaudeville. These latter were also relatively high-cost, but they were much less industrialized than films. Films were expensive therefore they had to be industrialized: cinemas had to be filled, returns had to flow in to finance next year's production programme. The amount of money needed, the kind of people needed, were quite different from the theatre. The theatre was on a small scale, each production was floated separately, the returns were modest. Films were large scale, dozens of productions were floated simultaneously, the returns could be astronomical.[2] Everything about the cinema was bigger, brasher and slicker than the theatre.

---

[2] The all-time money makers to date are *The Sound of Music* (US $120 million + initial cost $8–10 million); *The Graduate*, $78 million domestic gross (domestic: foreign gross is usually 50:50); and *Gone with the Wind* (US $77·5 million; initial cost $4 million). These figures are from *Esquire*, January 1968, p. 62, and *Weekly Variety*, 20 November 1968, p. 30. Schickel (1964) gives a gross of $125 million for *Gone With the Wind* on p. 168. Associated Press, reporting the shelving of *The Sound of Music* on 22 November 1969, gives a gross of $112 million.

But, perhaps worst of all, they paid more for talent and finally made more profit. The theatre never forgave the cinema.

2 Later developments

In the early days films, cameras, projectors, and film stock were produced by the same manufacturers: the Lumières, the Edisons, etc. But soon there appeared companies devoted solely to making pictures and hiring their equipment from the manufacturers. The costs of hiring studio space and financing production in advance required that they borrow money, and here big finance came in. The New York banks were and are the principal sources of finance for films. Once, they merely loaned; later they became members of the boards of motion picture companies; finally, and inevitably, they began to direct operations, especially when the Old Guard of film magnates proved unable to cope with either new audience trends or the arrival of television. A case study in this development is the company Metro-Goldwyn-Mayer (MGM). MGM originally belonged to Marcus Loew, Sam Goldwyn and Louis B. Mayer. By the late 1940s the real power seems to have been in the hands of Schenck, a friend of Loew's, who had always controlled the New York end of the business. His impact is felt very sharply in Lillian Ross's book of the making of a film at MGM in 1949, *Picture*.[3]

This economic development of the film industry, especially in the United States and the United Kingdom, is well documented. At first the film theatre owners and the film makers were quite distinct. The first forms of integration were purely horizontal – chains of cinemas. But for cinemas it was wasteful to buy copies of films, they might only want to show it a few days. Yet the studios needed to sell to finance their next productions. Hence the emergence of the third force in the industry, the distributors or renters, to perform an agency function: they took films from the studios and made them available to cinemas. For as long as most cinemas were independently owned they were invaluable. They were a channel of communication between the factories and the retailers. They also off-set specialization. A studio (like Sennett) might concentrate on producing slapstick comedies. A cinema wanting to include a western in its programme, or a drama, would have to negotiate separately with each studio, whereas distributors could obtain films from several sources and offer a variety. This had its economic logic, since the studios were able to sell their films outright, thus releasing the money tied up in completed productions for further production without

---

[3] The full story of MGM is told in Bosley Crowther's hagiographical works *The Lion's Share* (1957), and *Hollywood Rajah* (1960).

waiting for the finished film to earn its money at the box office. This distribution system, though, soon gained a lot of say in what was made. The distributors would not buy films they *thought* the cinemas wouldn't show. Just as the cinemas wouldn't show films they *thought* the public wouldn't pay to see. Thus did production decisions become further removed from any actual contact with the audience: the artists were controlled by what the producers *thought*, the producers were controlled by what the distributors *thought* (or what the producers expected the distributors would *think*), the distributors were controlled by what they *thought* the cinema owners *thought* and the cinema owners were controlled by what they *thought* the audience wanted. If all this does affect taste and thus confirms erroneous expectations, it can easily be seen how the trend could narrow the range of marketable products – which it did, at least in the medium run.

This endistancing of the audience has always been a source of creative frustration in the industry, but it is difficult to see how things could be better organized. No society is affluent enough to allow *anyone* with the urge to create in the cinema the resources to do so. And, since resources are scarce, some criterion of what shall be made has to be adopted. In communist countries the criteria are primarily political. The Poles have developed a sort of film makers' co-operative under a general political supervision. This has resulted in some good films. But I do not see that the argument which attributes these faults in the organization to their capitalist mode has much force. The American cinema has produced the largest number of good films of any country, both absolutely, and as a percentage. And artists in other countries – Kurosawa, Ichikawa, Ozu, Mizoguchi and Kobayashi in Japan; Clair, Renoir, and the New Wave in France; Fellini, Antonioni, in Italy; have all worked within the capitalist framework. There are many individual stories, admittedly some of them true, of potential masterpieces being still-born, or mutilated, or of brilliant people unable to get work, because of 'the system'. But there are also a lot of fishermen's tales about 'the one that got away' present too.

Besides, it was not long before the distribution function began to change hands. Whether the result reduced the problem of audience endistancing is another matter. The distributors had trouble from both the production and the exhibition sides of the industry. Horizontal integration on the production and cinema levels cut at the distributor's feet. The bigger the chain of cinemas, the more economical it became to be their own distributor, and to bargain with the studio direct. The fewer studios there were, the more diverse their products became with size; the stronger their cartel – the Motion

Picture Producers Association of America – the more they could hold the distributors and cinemas to ransom. Thus big studios became their own distributors; cinema chains shopped directly with production companies. And when, ultimately, the producers began buying cinema-chains, a howl broke out. It was logical enough, really; as owning cinemas a producer had a guaranteed *market* for his product even if not guaranteed *custom*. He would never be left with a production nobody would touch. Also, as a cinema owner, the producer was perhaps closer to his audience than previously. At least, the endistancing was within one organization. But the economic arguments against monopoly were to win the day (anti-trust suits were successfully prosecuted in the twenties and forties especially).[4] It is not clear that only benefit accrued, since the cinema owner had to find films to fill his cinema; but, in so far as entry to the industry was inhibited by the organizations set up to do this, perhaps the decision was right. The strength of the capitalist mode of production is usually given as that it rewards initiative and thereby ensures the public will be allowed the widest choice. The rise of monopoly structures both restricts entry and narrows choice, thus undermining any merits capitalism may have for the moviegoer.

The American film industry was and is the paradigm for all film industries not state-run. Such vast amounts of money were there involved, that what happened elsewhere looked like very small beer indeed. However, the general pattern was similar in the industries of Britain, Germany, Japan, and so on. Economies of scale, and attempts to minimize market uncertainty, led to simultaneous horizontal and vertical integration. International trade in films, when they were silent, was more or less unlimited. The restriction on trade brought on by the First World War, however, allowed the American industry to dominate markets right up until the sound era. With an enormous home market in which to recoup costs and make a profit, Hollywood could afford to take whatever price it could get for its products abroad.

Sound, of course, bringing back the language barrier silents had transcended, altered the position again. But even before this, industries were growing up in the East – Egypt, China, India, Japan – with traditions and styles all of their own. Sound gave new economic impetus to this separation and, especially in the case of the first three, the low-cost-endless-musical-folk-costume-melodrama-style was perfected. Egyptian films go to the entire Arab world,

---

[4] Among the large literature I would pick out, for the USA: Bertrand (1936, 1941), Huettig (1944), Brady (1947a, 1947b), and Conant (1960). For the UK: Klingender ar d Legg (1937), Palache (1944), Kelly (1966) and Monopolies Commission (1967).

Indian films across India and to Indian communities everywhere from Kenya to Birmingham, and films in the various Chinese languages for overseas Chinese originate in Hong Kong and Taiwan. All these three industries are devoted to the same cheap-endless-musical-folk-costume-melodrama in a manner and to an extent undreamt of by Hollywood.

Naturally, the organization of the production and exhibition industries is different where the state is in charge. However, differences are not that great. Someone still has to come up with an idea – either off the cuff, or in a committee. Directions can come from above – 'make a film to commemorate the nth anniversary of the revolution' – but in the heyday of Hollywood the same was true. The political as well as the financial aspects of a script may be taken into account when it is being considered, but this is not untrue of capitalist industries also.

Russia, for example, has a large film industry which must show economic returns. The degree of monopoly tolerated is much greater than in the USA, but the development of the industry as a response to the patterns of demand has come about nevertheless. Political liberalization has made more difference to films made in Russia, Poland, Hungary, Czechoslovakia, than, for example, the influence of television. Even so the ability of quality East European films to earn prestige and dollars abroad has no doubt strengthened the hands of those creators *in their own country*. Economic facts are nowhere completely ignored.

Television ended the seller's market which had existed for the American cinema during the twenties, thirties and forties. To economists, a seller's market is one where the supply grows more slowly than the demand because of low elasticity, and as a result the seller controls the market. In pure price theory, the price of the goods is fixed at that point where supply equals (in the technical sense) demand. Consider the cinema situation. A product is offered for viewing which cannot be altered – a film booked for a day normally can't be replaced sooner than overnight. A cinema with a fixed number of seats cannot be enlarged or duplicated except over many months. Moreover, *this* film with this star is not a perfect substitute for *that* film with those stars. As a result, the supply situation is hedged around to such an extent, that one might say there is low substitutability of supply in areas of the film market. There may be indifference curves between one product and another (10 hours of television and 2 hours of film, 15 hours of television and 0 hours of film), but with films they may also vary from film to film because of this low substitutability.

Until the last ten years or so it was the seat at a particular cinema that was priced – regardless of what was showing. (First-run houses in large cities, where only new films were shown, charged more than average, but all the time, not depending on the film.) The cinema began as a cheap entertainment, and production costs rose because they could be sustained together with low prices and high profits. It is difficult to explain this adherence to an across-the-board policy of cheap pricing in a seller's market unless we remember the kind of people the suppliers were. Intuitively realizing, perhaps, that habitual cinemagoing was a form of market-building, and that audience resistance was high when prices were high, they followed a low pricing policy and successfully established the habit. This, then, became a large guaranteed market more or less secure from invasion until television arrived.

Pricing policy had then to become more flexible. Some of the products were now clearly not substitutes: certain films were especially expensive and were given a longer run at higher prices than the common-or-garden product. There was an acknowledgement that cinema-seats were no longer being sold, *this* film was now being sold. Cinemas still had to be filled, but by an audience no longer habituated, able now to go elsewhere if it saw fit.

For a time, around 1950, there were fears that television competition would cause the demise of the cinema in the way the cinema had killed vaudeville before it. The industry mounted frantic 'Let's Go to the Pictures', 'Films are better than ever' campaigns; give-aways, prizes, promotional link-ups with products, 3-D, wide-screen – a host of gimmicks was trundled out to try to stave off disaster. Disaster did not come, but not because of what the industry did – the necessary contraction and re-structuring had to take place. With hindsight it is clear that television functionally overlaps the cinema very little – the things each can do well are different. The type of audience each suits is different, etc. As a result the industry, despite itself, re-defined its role and went forward with increased strength.

III

The Present Structure of Capitalist Production

1 *Initiating and financing production*

My interest is not in the economics of film production itself, but in its contribution to the social structure of the cinema through the fact that films are being made to be sold. There are today, as there has been for the last forty-five years, two production structures: the big studio and the independents. The big studio is run on the factory principle; the independent resembles the free-lance. Big studios own land and buildings and keep technical and creative staff on contract. It is therefore in their interests to keep all this production capacity in full-time use. This was only possible when there was a large market, enough to sustain six or seven such organizations and five hundred films a year (Table 1). This was the case in America in the twenties, thirties and forties of this century. Moreover the monopoly of talent and the efficiency of the big studio effectively kept the independents at bay. They produced a lot of films ('other' in Table 1), but mostly B-pictures, cheap westerns and serials. The few who made the big-time: Goldwyn and De Mille at Paramount, Disney at RKO, and Stanley Kramer at Columbia, were more or less forced to become parts of the machine in order to obtain finance and distribution. But when, under the impact of television in the fifties, audiences shrank, the big studios became casualties: Republic, Allied Artists, Monogram, United Artists were the first, RKO later. The last disappeared, while UA was reorganized on its original pattern as an umbrella over independents with almost no overheads (i.e., no studio facilities), becoming merely a distribution organization. MGM and Fox tottered, so did Columbia. Universal nearly fell, but was resuscitated. They survive still, but their factories have either been sold to television or to developers, or are hired out for much of the time to independents and television. Only Warners seems to have come through more or less unscathed.

It was the reorganization of United Artists that marked the resurgence of independents, like Hecht-Hill-Lancaster, Batjak, the

46

TABLE 1

Feature length production in Hollywood's heyday

	All Cos.	Paramount	Leow's	Fox	Warner	RKO	Columbia	Universal	UA	Other
1930–31	510	58	43	48	69	32	27	22	13	198
1931–32	490	56	40	46	56	48	31	32	14	167
1932–33	510	51	37	41	53	45	36	28	16	203
1933–34	480	55	44	46	63	40	44	38	20	130
1934–35	520	44	42	40	51	40	39	39	19	206
1935–36	517	50	43	52	58	43	36	27	17	191
1936–37	535	41	40	52	58	39	38	40	19	208
1937–38	450	40	41	49	52	41	39	45	16	127
1938–39	526	58	51	56	54	49	54	45	18	141

Source: United States v. Paramount Pictures Inc., et al., Civil Action no. 87–273 in the District Court of the United States for the Southern District of New York, amended and supplemental complaint, 14 November 1940.

Mirisch Brothers (now Corp.), etc. These were men from outside Hollywood with a yen or a flair, like Martin Ransonoff or Ross Hunter or Joseph E. Levine, for collecting talent and raising money, or actors turned producers, or ex-big studio men. No doubt this recent increase in recruitment, diversity and thus choice (good old classic capitalist virtues) partly explains why we now see better and more varied films from Hollywood.

The set-up now is this.[1] The key person is a producer. He usually initiates a film. Perhaps he buys a finished script, or a book which someone reads for him. On the basis of the reader's report he may have some tentative costing done and if the result is pleasing offer it to the finance boys – either through channels of the big studio he works in, or his own channels. Producers with the golden touch have little trouble in getting plausible projects approved, those with no recent hits have big trouble in getting the ear of the right people.

Who are the right people? The bank balance used to payroll the film is provided by . . . a bank, what else? But banks, as Howe (1965) in his authoritative and fascinating article points out, only loan against collateral. In estimating collateral the bank has for the last twelve years assumed films only break even, so the full cost has to be covered. The collateral is usually provided by 'selling' the project to a distributor, who agrees to pay a certain sum upon completion of the film. In this case the bank requires also a completion guarantor who undertakes to fork out additional cash if the project runs over budget. This latter business is *extremely* risky – no United

---

[1] Much of the descriptive material in Hortense Powdermaker's book (1950) still stands, although her strictures on the vices of the big studio system are largely out of date.

States firm specializing in it has been successful. Most of the successful completion guarantors operate out of London. Just how risky completion can be is illustrated by *Cleopatra*, originally buageted at $5 million and completed for between $37–42 million (see Wanger 1963 and Brodsky and Weiss 1964). In Britain, the initial distribution guarantee is called the 'front money', and may be borrowed in part from state as well as private sources. The completion guarantee is called 'the end money', sometimes divided into the 'front end' and 'the end' of 'the end money'.

Who is the producer? Sometimes the producer is also a writer or director or star, but more often not. Once a project has finance, the director and stars can be contracted by the producer and studio space booked. Under the old factory system, division of labour was practised. The producer (and his boss) was boss, he hired and fired and had a final say in all, including creative, decisions (like editing and reshooting). There are cases of famous directors like Welles, Huston and Peckinpah disowning films they've made (*Journey into Fear*, *Red Badge of Courage*, *Major Dundee*) because of *post hoc* tampering by producers and/or executives. This strict control may explain a certain homogenized quality in second-rate American 'B' films, and a high technical standard in American 'A' films. But with the decline of the big studios, and their shorts and B-picture departments (good training ground), the situation now has become immensely complicated. Alfred Hitchcock and Billy Wilder supervise and okay every detail of their films, from writing to editing. George Cukor, John Ford, Vincente Minnelli take a script, shoot it and hand the film over to their principals. These big-name directors now have more freedom in the capitalist-structured industry than they have ever had. Antonioni and Fellini (Italy), Preminger and Wilder (USA), Godard and Renoir (France), make and release films as they wish. Naturally they are open to financial considerations and other influences – but so is any film maker, any artist, any person. If they succumb, it is *their* decision. This, however, is not to say that the kind of situation pictured by Tony Richardson is typical (p. 23 above). Directors recruited by Hollywood like Lee Thompson, Leacock, and Richardson are no doubt expected to show that they can take discipline and make money before they achieve complete freedom. Richardson had that in England already.

Whether the producer will get a project approved or financed will depend on a host of factors, some of them as remote as the whim of whoever he is supplicating to. In general, however, within a big studio with many contract technicians and artists, the key factor will be the script. If the story and action are thought to be capable of becoming a film that people will want to see, then it is made. Just how many people will want to see it, affects the amount of money the project can get – although in the big studio system budgets were relatively on a par, the differences being mainly between A and B pictures. With the independent producer the script is not a sufficient basis for a decision on finance. He may raise interest in a project on that count, but clearly the factors of which stars will play the parts and who will direct it are decisive. It is my guess that Richard Brooks would never have raised the finance for his *Lord Jim* (which, predictably, flopped), despite having worked on the script for years, had he not the stars Peter O'Toole, James Mason, Jack Hawkins and Eli Wallach lined up as his cast.

This system, where a project is not just a script and a budget, but also stars and a director, is known as 'packaging'. Frequently a company is set up solely for the film in question, and producer, writer, director and stars take part-ownership as well as salary. One of the factors that previously militated against independent production in the heyday of the big-studio system, was that the box-office stars were contracted to studios, who would not release them to do pictures for others, except on a *quid pro quo* basis. Thus, however good a film idea a potential independent had, he would rarely be financed unless he more or less joined forces with a major studio and drew upon its contracted artists and financial resources, so sacrificing to a degree his independence. Shrewd independents put potential stars under personal contracts to themselves, in order to have bargaining counters in the game of *quid pro quo*.

Given then, that he has the money, the producer hires a complete production team, which books studio space, and begins to cast the film. Hollywood is strongly unionized and the producer has to cost against what he knows to be union rules on the minimum number of technicians for particular jobs. Attempts to evade these merely lead to boycotts or other sabotage against the production. Moreover, the majority of the most highly professional personnel are in unions. A recent exception in America has been to make the film in Europe or simply New York, where union rules are different.

The key appointment of the whole production is the director. He may be the producer himself (e.g., Brooks, Hitchcock, Wilder) or the writer and thus in on the film from its inception, or he may be brought in at the last moment when the film has been written, cast and staffed. A producer, depending on his personality and style, may then let the personnel take over and keep only a budget check on the proceedings; or he may keep closely in touch with every detail, visit the set often, view the rushes and make free with his advice to all and sundry. It is not hard to imagine how the latter behaviour is received in a community of professionals and specialists. Although in a famous comment about Wyler's *The Best Years of Our Lives*, producer Sam Goldwyn snapped: 'I made that picture. Wyler only directed it.'

There is little further to be said about finance without going to inordinate detail. It proceeds much as financing proceeds in industry and commerce generally. In the days of the big studios, overall profit on the year's operations was the determining factor as to whether finance would be forthcoming for current operations, and the company decided internally how to parcel out its resources in a year's productions. With the fragmentation of production, financing came more to resemble the floating of new companies, or of Broadway plays, or even of the financing of trade unseen. The companies set up to produce films are private companies not given to share issues, etc. Howe stresses very strongly that bankers do not control the industry and never intervene in its affairs unless a company becomes insolvent. However, it is clear that there are banks who specialize in film finance, who know which distribution company's guarantees are cast-iron, which independent film makers have proved their mettle. Like the labyrinths of finance in any field, film finance has its peculiar methods of promotion, its customs and proprieties. It is not an impenetrable mystery; but it is also not wide open to inspection by the outside world. Despite being constantly referred to as a risky business, it is interesting that large numbers of films go on being produced. This is *prima facie* evidence that the system works, i.e., makes substantial profits for those who have mastered its intricacies. Although Wood (1952) makes the amusing point in discussing the period when Rank was more than £4 million in the red and yet continued to find finance, that big debts are better than small since, if the backers ever want to get their money back, they must continue giving support until profitability is restored.

2 Control and responsibility during production

On the studio floor itself the director is in charge of what is put on film. He places the camera, controls the actors (so far as he can), and makes the emphases[2] – if the producer wishes to interfere he has to work through (or sack) the director. A prestigious director may demand that he be allowed in on a film from its inception, and will stay with it until the final copy is prepared for release. More commonly, he supervises the assembling, by the editor, of the developed film (which has, of course, been shot disjointedly and out of sequence). At this stage he will be able to indicate where he thinks

[2] Obviously, a script can be shot to emphasize one interpretation or another, one star or another, and so forth.

close-ups should go in, what sequence should be cut fast, what slow, and so on. The so-called 'fine cutting', the final selection of which scenes are to be removed altogether, plus the music and other sound work are yet to be done. It is the producer who normally dominates again at these stages, and who, in the face of samples of audience reaction, tries to decide (perhaps with front office help) what final changes should be made.

From the point of view of directors, the great advantage of independent production is that a producer includes them as part of the 'package' he has sold to the financiers and distributor, and this allows them to develop an early and intimate relationship with the project, and to make clear how far their authority will extend over the final film. Not being salaried employees of big studios, directors have the chance to team up with producers with whom they see eye to eye and know they can work with or, ultimately, to become their own producers. Some even use a brother, in-law, or other relative, as producer.

The finished film is then shown to the distributors, and hopefully, is approved. It is then reproduced in sufficient copies, and publicity is devised to key-in with its showing.

Thus, the picture we get is of a highly subdivided industry with only one true co-ordinator – the producer. This fact explains why ambitious and successful actors, writers and directors strive to be the producers of their own work if they can. Only in this way can they get as much control over their material as they want.

In sociology, we analyse men's actions in terms of their *aims, knowledge, beliefs* and *objective social and physical situation* (Jarvie 1969c). We should now try to apply this analysis to the making of films. First of all, the *aim*. As noted before, we are not solely concerned in this book with the role of the director, the key creative figure in films, but also with producers, bankers, writers, cameramen, stars, etc. This perhaps is where we must disappoint the highbrow critic in not being only concerned with the director. *Producers' aims may be different from directors' aims, which may be different again from writers' aims, cameramen's aims, and especially stars' aims.* The aim of the *producer* is to make money by making a 'good' film: of course many a producer is exclusively concerned with the first, acknowledging that certain technically professional standards are required to allow a film to be successful. A producer's *knowledge* will consist of his knowledge of the techniques of film making, his beliefs concerning many things, including the economic and social pressures which surround him.

But in acting on the basis of their knowledge and belief to achieve their aims, producers are limited by their circumstances – these include clashes with the aims of others. The notorious cases of producers recutting films or even reshooting scenes indicate how directors' and producers' aims may differ and, of course, it is seldom that the director wins in these clashes. The amusing stories of stars who like to be shot from certain angles, who want parts of a certain length and no less, also indicate clashes of aims between stars, producers, and directors. In general, the star is more concerned with his own overall image than with the particular film; this is less true of all the other participants, though never entirely. And why should it be? People have their careers to think of in film as in anything else. Vanity and status enter into the star's calculations a great deal, rather more than into those of the others. The ideal set-up may be where everyone is pulling to make a good film that will also make money; but circumstances never are ideal, aims never do perfectly coincide.

Besides conflicts of aims, there may be conflicts rooted in differences of knowledge and belief, especially about the audience. Lillian Ross's book *Picture* (1951) is illustrative of this. There is little doubt of the good intentions of producers Gottfried Reinhart and Dore Schary: yet they genuinely came to believe that the film *The Red Badge of Courage*, as director John Huston had finished it, lacked dramatic shape, was too long, and would bore the audience. They interfered with it only as much as they thought absolutely necessary for its success. Now this is the point where the artist gets engaged. But a film is a costly enterprise, and I do not see where one can blame these men for displaying their sense of responsibility in that manner. We cannot tell now whether *The Red Badge of Courage* was good or bad as Huston finished it. Certainly the poor preview response was real enough, and although the suggestion was made that the film be sold on a road-show basis, the industry was still too complacent to try. The mutilation of the film was an unintended consequence of the situation and clashes of aims. Writers may want things done that cannot be done; producers may believe they cannot get away with the certain things which directors want. And then, of course, their objective situations are certainly different: the producer is under different pressures from the director, who is under different pressures than the star. What can be said is, that by not even putting in the archive a copy of the Huston original, the studio displayed contempt for the artist; for not staying to minister to his film, for not having a say in the final cut, and for not procuring a personal print of his own (as other directors do), Huston displayed casualness.

In the heyday of the big studio, writers and directors were reduced in effect to the status of mere technicians, and were pushed around like the rest. This situation was a product of the sellers' market. The studios had no difficulty getting people to work for them, their personnel were well rewarded, and they felt justified in demanding control of artistic temperaments and egos. Further it must be said, that there was also a muted battle going on for the kudos: the producers believing they were decisive, the directors thinking the same. It is notable that in the Academy Awards there is an award for best film, which goes to the producer, and one for best director as well. Whereas in France the normal phrasing for directors' credits is 'un film de . . .'.

This clash between two claimants for the credit, and the fact that executives had usually been producers, at times fostered an anti-intellectualism. Rosten (1941) senses this is especially directed towards writers, and Powdermaker (1950) concurs. A writer-director like Orson Welles, who was in Hollywood eyes a prodigy, was perhaps a victim of this. Given the red carpet treatment in Hollywood at first, he made brilliant and imaginative films which lost money. So much did the moguls come to distrust him, that there are signs they cut his later films almost for the sake of doing so – having no real idea that their tampering would in any way make the film fare better.

Hortense Powdermaker, in her *Hollywood, The Dream Factory* (1950), gets understandably enraged at the stupidity and obtuseness of the people in the system who have power, and who use it to force sincere, decent, serious, and genuinely artistic people to 'compromise'. Now, obviously, these decent artistic people are also in positions of power – otherwise they would not be being pressured to compromise. What is their power? Their contracts, and their talents for doing essential jobs. If they are essential, what is it that producers force them to compromise over? Is what they consider a good film one which cannot be commercially successful? Is the clash of aims so acute? Indeed Dr Powdermaker does toy with the conflicting demands of art and commerce. But this way out is not available to her, since she stresses how well (what she considers) well-made films have been received. So she falls back on this curious view that somehow the industry has come to be bossed by idiots, vulgarians, boors, and anti-intellectuals. No doubt it is, but this does not explain why they act as they do. They are idiots who believe they are infallible gods. This too requires to be explained: how do Hollywood executives get swollen heads? The answer has to be The System. What is wrong with the system, I would argue, stems from the fundamental tension between the economic pressure to improve supply by breaking down production into distinct operations as in a factory, and the creative pressure to let the artists interfere at all stages of the making. Writers, directors, and editors came to find their functions ruthlessly circumscribed. They became ciphers, because that way industrial production was simplified and increased. What the industry has learned only very slowly is that when the sellers' market is gone and they have to work hard at making good films, the system can be modified. The advent of the writer-producer, the producer-director, the star-producer has shown that these key artists can make intelligent and profitable use of more control and responsibility. And, of course, the banks were convinced by the results. Thus the upsurge of independent production was a wise adaptation to the challenge of television, the challenge that both shrank the film market and made it more competitive.

The god-like delusions of producers undoubtedly were bred by the sycophancy and huge profits of the system in its heyday. Executives could in a sense do little wrong: on the whole films and studios made money, a great deal of money. Underlings wanted to stay on the gravy train, so the tradition of sycophancy grew up. This has its pleasures, but also its drawbacks – such as poor-quality feedback and contempt on the part of those outside looking in.

However, putting the quirks of the system to one side, let us glance at what constitutes a job well-done. Let us try to compare the objective situations of the following key figures: producer, director, writer, leading actor and senior technicians (director of photography, editor, sound man, composer). A producer must satisfy his backers – that, above all. This means, the film must be produced on (1 P) schedule, (2 P) within budget, and then (3 P) show a significant profit. Producers have their specialities and their own predilections, but once the film is underway, these three are the elements in the situation by which their performance will be judged. The director is somewhat different – of course, he must (1 D) finish on schedule, (2 D) keep the personnel happy, and, he hopes, (3 D) make a profitable film. Often he will also be primarily aware of (4 D) making a first-rate film which will display his mastery of action, rhythm, the handling of actors, and so on because his future employment will have almost as much to do with these as with a straight profit and loss accounting.

A writer is usually paid a flat rate for his work. True, if his pictures constantly satisfy producer's factor (3 P), i.e., make money, his prestige will go up (1 W). If his cogent and nicely-written script helps the director with factor (2 D) as well as (3 D), a further increment will be added to his prestige. But the intangible matter of (3 W), professional Hollywood public opinion about his calibre is just as important, as is (4 W) the approval of his peers, other writers.

The leading actor or actress is the most obvious case of the person who refers his work to criteria beyond the situation of any particular films. An established star is not usually blamed if a film flops – as some with very big stars do. Naturally, being a (1 S) big box-office attraction is invaluable (3 P), (3 D); as is (2 S) a reputation for professionalism (2 P). But a star is known to a wide public outside the industry, a public not necessarily aware of the profit and loss account picture by picture. The star's 'image', (3 S) popularity in a broad sense, and personal qualities, affect their decisions just as much as anything else. Personal idiosyncrasies come in too – Larry Parks refused ever again to hold a gun in a film; Doris Day is steadfast in avoiding the seamy side of life in her films; Audrey Hepburn is always dressed by Givenchy.

Senior technicians get credit for their work more or less regardless of the profitability of the film – the appreciation their peers (1 T), and (2 T) of the producer, director, and actors, is what counts. Their skills are so esoterically professional that their direct impact on the box-office is disregarded.

To 'map' these differences of situation we might use the following table:

TABLE 2

Vital factors in the situation of different film workers

	On schedule	Under budget	Profit	Personnel happy	Art/ Peers	Hollywood opinion	Public opinion
Producers	(1 P)	(2 P)	(3 P)				
Directors	(1 D)		(3 D)	(2 D)	(4 D)		
Writers			(1 W)	(2 W)	(4 W)	(3 W)	
Stars			(1 S)		(2 S)		(3 S)
Technicians					(1 T)	(2 T)	

These are rough and ready weightings, and doubtless others will want to correct them; they nevertheless sharply bring out the possible sources of conflict. For example, during production a producer is above all concerned with getting the film in on time and budget. A star may be far more interested in ultimate profitability. Only the star looks to public opinion as a separate category from profit. Director and producer can easily clash over the one's concern with budget, the need of the other to keep the team working happily; one's terminal aim is profit, the other's is art. And so on.

Let us take an example – a single scene in a longish film is being debated, let's say a scene where an actress appears nude. The advantage is that such scenes are greatly talked and written about; the disadvantage is that delicate handling needs time. The producer is primarily concerned with the publicity shooting the scene will get, the extra audience who will remember hearing about the scene and on balance decide to see the film. The director and the writer are primarily concerned with whether the scene 'works' in the film, whether the film will come over more or less without it. Recall a few such scenes:

Star	Film	Left in	Must be left in
Elizabeth Taylor	*Cleopatra*	yes	no
Carroll Baker	*The Carpetbaggers*	no	no
Carroll Baker	*Sylvia*	yes	?
Brigitte Bardot	any film	yes	no
Sarah Miles	*The Ceremony*	yes	no
Paula Prentiss	*What's New, Pussycat?*	no	no
Julie Christie	*Darling*	yes	yes
Monica Vitti	*Modesty Blaise*	yes	?
Vanessa Redgrave	*Blow-Up*	yes	yes
Hayley Mills	*The Family Way*	yes	yes
Audrey Hepburn	*Two For the Road*	no	no
Faye Dunaway	*Bonnie and Clyde*	yes	yes
Angie Dickinson	*Point Blank*	yes	yes
Carol White	*Poor Cow*	yes	yes
Ingrid Thulin	*La Guerre est Finie*	yes	?

The balance where elimination would make little difference and where it would is fairly even. The fascinating cases are those three where nude scenes were shot, but then removed in the final editing. What of the star's view? Some obviously take it in their stride (Swedish and French actresses, for example), others seemingly need to be persuaded that their integrity to the role demands it. No doubt vanity, publicity and even jumping on the band-wagon (everybody's doing it) play their parts too.

In other words, the situations of producer, director, writer, and star can impinge in quite different ways on their decisions regarding what to make, what scene to do, how to do it, and so on. In these circumstances it is to be expected that there will be clashes from time to time, not at all due to stupidity, arrogance, vanity, bullying, anti-intellectualism or anything else. To see this point, we need only attend to what we know of the structure of production behind the Iron Curtain.

3 Comparison with communist countries

Large-scale film making began in Russia soon after the Bolshevik triumph, following Lenin's dictum that films were the supreme mass art and thus the supreme instrument of propaganda.[3] Serving political rather than financial interests, the Russian film industry was notable for the degree to which political control and interference were built in. Instead of Hollywood's 'Front Office' there was the Party and its officers; instead of conformity to the criterion of profitability, there was conformity to the Party line. But the parallel is not perfect: while the American system has permitted films which include bitter attacks on capitalist high finance in general and on the Hollywood 'Front Office' in particular, there is no Russian film which attacks the Party and the Party line; not even accepted anti-Stalinist texts like *A Day in the Life of Ivan Denisovich* by Solzhenitsyn, have been made into a film.

Apart from Russia, Poland, Czechoslovakia, Hungary, Bulgaria, etc., have state-controlled film industries. When Russia gained most of central Europe as a prize at the end of the Second World War, they too copied the Russian mode of film production, although with individual variations, as we shall see. The *theory* on which they are organized is artistic autonomy: syndicalism. The artists themselves constitute the production organization and they collectively decide how to spend their budget. In fact, of course, this theory of autonomy is not fully carried out in practice. Good Communist practice demands that every 'secular' organization must be paralleled or infiltrated by Party officials.

It is not hard to construct an *a priori* sociological model of the set-up which resulted. There will be two feed-ins to the system: ideas for films from the film makers; and Party directives, lines, policies, encouragement. More than likely, the film makers will be broken down into small units of manageable committee size. These will then be under a committee of superiors in the organization and either at this point, or higher still in the hierarchy, film ideas will be authoritatively checked against Party policy. Direct Party interference is dispensable for two reasons. One is that the Party's tentacles control the distribution and exhibition sides of film making and when, as with Eisenstein's *Ivan the Terrible Part II*, an objectionable film has come so far as to be finished, its showing can be very easily prevented. The stronger reason, however, is a generalization of this one: the Party has many sanctions against organizations and individuals – which it seldom invokes just because they constitute such a big threat as to cause artists to toe the line without much ado.

The two feed-ins posited are quite general, and the details are undetermined. We cannot know what auto-sanctions artists will impose upon themselves because of the Party, and we cannot predict what

[3] See letter from Lunacharsky to Boltyansky, 9 January 1925, Leyda (1961), p. 161.

sort of themes they would choose if they felt themselves to be free. However, about the Party's interest something can be said. It is the interest of the Party to see films made, which instruct and educate the masses in the general philosophy and Party line. The artists, on the other hand, may have some artistic interests. Almost certainly, then, this divergence will lead to clashes between the Party organization and the film makers. The latter may wish, for example, to make a film which explores the problems and conflicts of an individual. Since any individualism, however implicit, is objectionable to collectivists, the film maker's proposal will be trimmed. Since the Party line changes from time to time, prudence will dictate that the film maker avoid contemporary themes. If individuals and the contemporary world are almost ruled out, what is left? History and respectable causes is the short answer. Respectable causes include socialism, nationalism, law abidance, respectability, also hard-work, self-sacrifice, adjustment to new conditions (agriculturalization, industrialization, collectivization), as well as selfless courage, devotion, honesty, optimism, understanding, wisdom. In Russia and elsewhere the result was a flush of films about the Second World War and film versions of their great classical writers. Anti-nazism, anti-anti-semitism, heroics, etc., are also uncontroversial and offer some small scope for creative ideas; even for personal doubts, conflicts, and a tiny bit of sex. This pattern has continued for some time now, even after the death of Stalin. Serious appraisal of contemporary Russian life has yet to be the subject of a film. This is less true of the satellites Poland, Hungary, Czechoslovakia, where elements of de-Stalinization have hit the screen in the form of individualism, sex, bourgeois problems, and so on.

There would seem to have been three periods of film making in Russia since the Revolution. First, there was the lively and thoughtful cinema of the pre-Stalin era – which lasts until Stalin completely consolidated his power around 1928-9. Even then, however, ideological unorthodoxy was almost unknown. Then there were the dreary Stalinist years themselves, lasting until around 1956, during which time about the only interesting Russian films were made by directors who had established their pre-eminence in the twenties. The main way in which post-1956 de-Stalinization showed itself in Russia was in the surge of more individualisitic films about the war, and in the sudden appearance of a crop of new directors, some of whom displayed a moderate degree of talent.

The process went much further in the satellite countries. In Poland, especially, there arose an avant-garde making impressive experimental films (*Two Men with a Wardrobe*, *Dom*), and a group of young directors with exceptional talent: Wajda (*Ashes and Diamonds*,

Lotna, Innocent Sorcerers, Siberian Lady Macbeth), Munk (*Eroica, Passenger*), Polanski (*Knife in the Water*), Kawalerowicz (*Night Train, The Pharaoh*). Hungary too had a minor renaissance. . . .

Before discussing other satellites let us ask: what is the socio-political explanation for this sort of upsurge? Is it because freedom, after so much repression, produces good art, the way women are supposed to be extrafertile when they stop taking the pill after being on it for some time? This topic is one I shall not enter. But I will take up the point that our understanding of these state-controlled industries is still very poor. An illustration to this point is an article in *Newsweek* (18 July 1966) which tries to explain the renaissance in the Czech cinema, and which succeeds in revealing just how little we understand.

The article indicates that once upon a time the Czech industry produced strings of drab propaganda films. Then, it is argued, the state was forced by public opinion ('bored audiences and sagging revenues') to allow its film makers creative freedom. They were raring to go and set out consciously 'to make the kind of films that would make the Poles envious'. Although their system of control over the making of films is bureaucratic, according to the article, at least it is otherwise free and controlled by the intellectuals. Result, masterpieces which are *popular*. This assertion of the article is difficult to reconcile with the later comment that 'Czech studios spend much of their energy turning out tasteless comedies, stereo-typed copies of American westerns and bad musicals'. In fact 'the masses all want to see Hollywood productions. The Czech renais-sance is happening *in spite of* the audiences'. So much for *Newsweek*.

The presence of so many non-sequiturs and inconsistencies cannot but make us suspicious of the whole article. If the masses want Hollywood, why should the state be forced to free its intellectual film makers? If public opinion forced the state into action about the poor propaganda films, why didn't it also force the state to supply more Hollywood and *ersatz*-Hollywood films? Whoever heard of a Communist *apparat* being forced to bow to public opinion in matters of taste? And if it did so, why is it not now terribly unhappy that the intellectuals are producing unpopular films (although perhaps less unpopular than the previous propaganda pap)? What the article mentions, but hardly plays up, is that competition has developed among the satellites as to which group of intellectuals and artists can squeeze the most freedom out of their state in order to make the films they wish. The Poles they're endeavouring to make envious, are not the Polish people, but the Polish film makers. In other words, the Poles set professional standards for the Eastern bloc: standards which can hardly, like Hollywood's, be politically gainsaid as long

59

as Poland is Communist. So competition has something to do with it. So what the article secretly admires is that Czech film makers can grind out the films they want to make and to hell with the public. There speaks the frustrated film maker!

De-Stalinization has in general led to an overestimation of how much freedom is allowed in Communist film-making structures – perhaps because we underestimate how difficult the system is to understand. My own analysis is more cautious. The film maker in countries like the USSR and Poland has two main obstacles to surmount: one is to get his ideas accepted for filming; the other is to get the finished film released. It seems that final decisions on showing go higher in the political hierarchy than decisions to shoot. The Russian *Ivan the Terrible Part II* was withheld for ten years[4] and films have been seen in China and then their existence denied.[5] Not being controlled by profit, these industries can afford to make films for export only. In Poland, and some of the other East European countries, there is a degree of creative and artistic freedom, but it is often quite easy to interpret what results as ideologically orthodox. *Innocent Sorcerers*, and *Knife in the Water*, which are often cited as examples of ideological thaw, are certainly ideologically neutral, or, not overtly propagandist. But while the Poles allow the individual artist tremendous stylistic control over his films – he either can't or isn't inclined to treat subjects as freely as capitalist countries. Especially missing, are sophisticated and biting films and savage social criticism.[6]

Because the first film by Andrej Wajda to be seen in the West came immediately after the 1956 'thaw' brought on by Krushchev's dethronement of Stalin, it was too easily assumed that the director is an ideological renegade. This mistake has been compounded by *Ashes and Diamonds*, a difficult film to interpret. However, I think it is easy to interpret all of Wajda's films as orthodox – as might be expected of a successful artist working in the Communist bloc.

The message of *A Generation* is that only in the Communist Party is an objective resistance to Fascism to be found. All other forms of resistance are bourgeois futilities. Only the organized revolution of the masses will do.

Kanal seems to be the corollary of this: those who did not appreciate this fact about the historical nature of the resistance to Fascism

[4] It was first publicly shown at the Brussels World's Fair.
[5] Film buffs in Peking have tried to see *New Year Sacrifice* and have had knowledge of it denied. 'You are misinformed . . .' is the standard phrase.
[6] America with its crusading journalists, etc., has a tradition of films indicting society which go to amazing lengths. Most of the anti-American views of the European left wing are based on information from critical American sources like the press and films.

died bravely, but uselessly. Misdirected bravery, it seems, has no objective value in the class struggle.

Ashes and Diamonds shows the futility and destructiveness of the nationalist element in the resistance. Even though it was temporarily on top, it was historically doomed to be replaced by Communism. Again, the idea seems to be that sincerity and bravery and a cause are not enough, it must be the right cause. The picture Wajda draws of the dingy nostalgia for the old days, in the drunken and joyless party sequence towards the end of the film, is clearly intended as a direct comment on all lost causes: what seems best in them is only apparent, not real.

And finally *Lotna*, which seems to have baffled every commentator. What was Wajda trying to do with a film about a beautiful, white, cavalry horse? The answer is really quite simple and the most explicit statement yet, applying Marxism-Leninism to a concrete historical situation and developing the symbolism already present in *Kanal* and *Ashes and Diamonds*. *Lotna*, the beautiful, elegant, white horse, fleet, strong and brave, symbolizes the proud nationalism of pre-war Poland. Magnificent in its way but, in the progress of history, ultimately doomed. *Lotna* represents at once all that was best in that old Poland, and also the inadequacy of old Poland when faced with militant Fascism. *This* is the meaning of the cavalry charge against German tanks. Splendid though the best of the old was, it was out-of-date, not viable in the new conditions created by the progress of objective history.

Elsewhere (1967) Joseph Agassi and I have argued that symbolic interpretations like those just applied to the films of Wajda are a kind of game – one which it is easy to win since one makes one's own rules. Thus my interpretation of Wajda is not to be taken too seriously – no hidden 'truth' is revealed by it. But in a Communist state films must, I claim, be susceptible to some such interpretations if they are to be acceptable. A few films from Poland, and several Czechoslovak films have managed to be ideologically neutral. This is most exciting, whether or not the danger remains of a reversion to a Russian-style clamp-down. If my argument towards the end of this chapter has any thrust on this question, I suppose it is that all known production structures have their weaknesses. For my part, the fact that no year goes by without dozens of entertaining films emerging from capitalist structures, while decades have gone by with only a handful of entertaining films coming from Communist structures, at the least argues for pluralism: let us never allow one structure to have exclusive domain. Personal predilection inclines me to a stronger endorsement of capitalist production, but I shall make the argument for it at a later stage.

IV

Roles and Recruitment to them

1 Roles: defined and ill-defined

For purposes of structural analysis, the categories produced by the division of labour in film making could be regarded as social roles. A role (Banton 1965) is the part a person plays in an institutional structure. Roles can be *achieved* or *ascribed*. We are *sons, daughters*, by ascription; we are *executives, leaders, cameramen* by achievement. We can play our roles more or less well, and they can be more or less well defined by the institutions within which we play them. People who are good at their well-defined role of *college administrator*, might not be so good at their poorly-defined role of *college teacher*. The role of *leader* is not so clearly defined in our society as that of, say, *banker*.

Producers and directors have fairly clearly defined roles in film production. Executives should have similarly well-defined roles but in fact do not. Some executives confine their role-definition, others expand it until they are overlapping with the creative functions of producer, director, writer, etc. (cf. Fitzgerald 1949). Whether or not this role-expansion happens depends not on the structure or the organization but on the individual filling the role, but it would be an over-simplification to say that self-selection for high rank ensures that the expansionist individual will win. There is obviously a flaw in the institutions which permit this latitude in role-definition, and then find their workings disrupted by its consequences. Dictatorial executives are both an embarrassment and, all other things being equal, a liability. Some creators find dictatorship at the top intolerable and quit. One could paraphrase Dr Powdermaker's entire volume (1950), by saying that she clearly shows Hollywood to be plagued by personalism – people who are performing roles are constantly allowing personal factors, rather than institutional factors, to govern their behaviour. Harry Cohn was the 'Czar' of Columbia and held everyone in his grip (Thomas 1967). Louis B. Mayer seems to have thought of his job more as a matter of choosing people and letting them get on with it (this is his attitude as revealed to Doré Schary in Lillian Ross' 1951). The role of the executive not being well-defined, there was wide scope for personal predilection to enter into its definition. Moreover, the extraordinary personal language used in Hollywood, that is, the extensive use of terms of endearment – men and women call each other 'sweetie', 'honey', 'lover', 'baby', 'darling', etc.,[1] indicates how far the personalism has gone. Everyone in a big studio knew that a script or a project would not be judged purely on whether it was promising or not. A lot depended on the personal inclinations of whoever was involved, including how much he liked certain individuals and whether they had been sufficiently nice, servile, flattering to him, or whatever. One can imagine that role-playing in other industries could be carried to this extreme, but one cannot quite see how a successful industry can function in this way.[2] My suggestion, as previously, is that the success was an accident of market conditions – a sellers' gift-horse. However, the continuance of this personalism must partly be explained by the fact that the executive role cannot easily be better defined. This is because shrewd judgment, taste, and insight are all involved in the sieving of projects. Since calculating what will do well involves a large element of crystal-gazing, it is as though any random system of choosing projects would work equally well. Thus, relying on executive idiosyncrasies may be as good a way of operating as any. Yet I think that crystal-gazing literally would be better for the industry. Not because it is objectively random (it is not), but rather because with that system everyone would know where they were and the wretched fawning, flattery and self-degradation which abounds everywhere would be reduced. Currying favour in Hollywood was so vital that it resulted in trimming, compromise, and the destruction, in some cases, of character and self-respect. This cannot be good for any industry, and it must stand to Hollywood's discredit that the system flourished for so long.

To advocate substituting a crystal ball, even half seriously, is to hint that the colossal salaries Hollywood affords its executives (Louis B. Mayer was for a time the highest-paid executive in the United States) are without reason. But on the contrary, however 'irrational' people think the capitalist system is, it is presumptuous to indict its estimates of worth in this sweeping way. Hollywood in its formative years was a highly competitive place, and those who emerged at the

---

[1] See Richard Brooks' novel *The Producer* (1952). Brooks was then a script writer who later became a writer-director and then a producer-writer-director. His novel seems to be factually quite authentic, inside stuff. See also the selections in *Sight and Sound*, 1950, 19, 323f: 'The World Inside'.
[2] In a paper on Hong Kong business Dr M. Topley shows how, despite a similar lack of impersonalism, Chinese business flourishes. *Vide* 'The Role of Savings and Wealth Among Hong Kong Chinese', in Jarvie, ed., (1969a), esp. pp. 198ff.

top did so because they had ability, if only the ability of coming out on top. Even so, the long period of profitability enjoyed by Hollywood could be explained by the sellers' market situation, not entrepreneurial ability. Evidence from the industries of Egypt, India, and Hong Kong tends to confirm this – these industries can, and do, make a profit on almost any film, whoever is in charge. This argument has a weakness. Profligate and spendthrift executives could succeed in ruining any firm, no matter how favourable market conditions. There must therefore be an essential element of prudence without which no executive can succeed. What I am trying to avoid is arguing from a hypothetical standpoint: if only Hollywood had had different executives, maybe better films, perhaps greater profits, could have been made. These assertions strike me as profitless and vague. In public companies executives are paid by performance. The film industry was ruthless in disposing of executives once they had lost the golden touch. It is a pity that there was little or no experimentation with more tightly defined executive roles, backed by not quite such awe-inspiring salaries. It is said that the secret of good administration is picking subordinates and delegating to them. The film industry coasted along flouting this rule, and rewarding exorbitantly those who did so. The new production structures have, in a way, enforced such delegation and practically eliminated the finger-in-every-pie executive.

Let it be noted that under these dictators the roles of other members of the production team were strictly defined, by contract, and by the executive's writ.

2 Recruitment to roles not systematic

In addition to the way roles connect to form a structure, the manner in which people play them, and the degree of definition and circumscription that surrounds them, sociologists pay attention to how they are recruited. Ascribed roles are recruited in well-understood ways, of course; but what of achieved roles? Some, like the Civil Service, are recruited by a fairly straightforward method: competitive public examination, followed by promotion closely governed by selection boards charged to look for certain qualities. Other roles, like that of *poet*, are almost indescribably obscure in the way they are recruited. People simply begin writing poems and, if they are lucky, have them published, and, hopefully, acquire thereby the social role of a poet.

But why, one asks, is this question of recruitment of any intellectual interest? The only answer is that there are theories in which recruitment to roles plays a vital part. The main theory which stresses recruitment is of course Marxism – which could be formulated as:

64

class interest is the principal determinant of outlook and values; the way people act, the sorts of films they make, will be closely related to their outlook, which is connected with their class origin and with their class achievement. Hollywood, together with all film industries, has its working class (labourers, grips, etc.), its skilled craftsmen (carpenters, painters, etc.), its lower middle class (clerks, etc.), its middle class and professionals (moderately successful actors, executives, cameramen, etc.), its upper middle class (top professional photographers, designers) and its upper class. In moving *from* the outside society *to* Hollywood, the question is to what extent recruitment to these classes is by movement at the same class level within their class of origin, or how much downward and upward mobility there is between levels.

The levels are part of the social structure, and yet a structure itself can have a class orientation. There is a theory, widely diffused in sociology, to the effect that the formal rules of any organization may not constitute a true account of its functioning in, e.g., personnel recruitment patterns. That the British Foreign Office, although part of the British Civil Service which has a long tradition of open competition in entry, has for generations managed to recruit almost exclusively public school and Oxbridge-educated people suggests the recruitment procedures are not quite what they seem. What, one asks in such cases, is the *real* basis of recruitment; how are the formal rules circumvented; why, and what difference does this make?

How, then, does Hollywood's social structure introduce, add-to, and replace its personnel: the (sociological) actors who play its institutionalized roles? I shall divide the question into producers, directors, writers, technical personnel, and finally actors. Material on these questions is easily accessible and there are several published sources. Principal among these are Powdermaker (1950), where many individual (anonymous) case histories are given; Rosten (1941); and Morin (1960).

Production executives and producers, the most powerful men in the industry, are certainly the hardest to generalize about. The early pioneers, like Laemmle, Loew, Zukor, Mayer, Fox, Schenck, Warner, and Goldwyn, all were successful in other trades before moving over into films. They seem to have foreseen some of the opportunities to make money and got in early while it was relatively cheap to do so. By and large, they moved in at the theatre end of the business, and only gradually expanded into distribution and then production. Most of these entrepreneurs were products of that extraordinary immigrant ghetto that was New York at the turn of the century. They were mostly Jews and of lower – or lower-middle – class origin. They rose rapidly to command a thriving, vigorous industry. But a certain show-biz brashness, vulgarity (in the literal sense) and folksiness was never rubbed off. These tycoons came up the hard way and as a result possessed the utmost self-confidence. They ran their empires personally, idiosyncratically and – allegedly – ruthlessly. To a large extent they shared and believed in the same values as their audience who, if they were not themselves making good, accepted the American dream that making good was a noble part of a noble society.

Equally interesting cases, and so far unscrutinized,[3] are those of the creative producers: Jack Warner, Louis de Rochement, John Houseman, Arthur Freed, David O. Selznick, Mark Hellinger, Val Lewton, Hal Wallis, etc. In many cases these men came from the theatre or journalism and perhaps for that reason displayed special sensitivity to their medium and an ability to work well with, and even to impose a certain overall character on the products of, creative people.

However, it is safe to make a few generalizations about producers of both kinds. The vast majority of them are men; I have yet to learn of a woman producer. None that I can trace has come from the higher socio-economic strata, indeed, the numbers who have come from quite humble lower-middle–class origins is remarkable. This may account for the two characteristics one most associates with Hollywood in its heyday, namely: vulgarity and showmanship. I am not, of course, suggesting that vulgarity has any direct connection with social class, although I would suggest that cultivated taste and intellectual refinement are more likely to be found among those whose education and environment has trained them for it. The gorgeous and flamboyant vulgarity of Cecil B. DeMille's biblical epics, contrasts sharply with the portentousness and sentimentality of D. W. Griffith (who was his own producer in his major productions). While DeMille went from strength to strength at the box office and enjoyed a long career, Griffith never repeated his enormous success of *Birth of a Nation* and ceased working soon after the arrival of sound. But vulgarity is perhaps less interesting than showmanship – which need not be vulgar at all. One has only to compare the rather limp attempts British films have made to utilize current pop singers, with American efforts. Elvis Presley, Ricky Nelson, Fabian and Bobby Darin were put into carefully tailored films, encouraged gradually to extend their acting range, and thus did well at the box office. In Britain the attempts to film Tommy Steele, Billy Fury, Helen Shapiro, etc., had such a painful awkwardness, a total unawareness of cinematic values, a failure to sell the films as well as the singers, that one despairs. (Steele finally made it ten years later

[3] See the papers by Marlowe (1947) and Reisz (1951).

when Hollywood filmed him in *Half a Sixpence*.) Where success has at last come to England in this way, it has been in part a by-product of the superb showmanship of the Beatles. They drew on their own tastes and values, chose their film debut carefully, vetted the personnel, and as a result succeeded in a big way both at the box office and in producing hugely entertaining cinema (*A Hard Day's Night, Help*).

Indeed the sixties has seen a new flair in the British cinema, traceable to a variety of factors. Together they add up to a bridging of the gap which existed for decades between British film makers and their audiences. Gans (1959) expatiates on all this, showing, convincingly to my mind, that American films only make successful inroads into the British market because they represent values and a point of view missing from the domestic industry and its product. These values and point of view are primarily the aspirations and situation of the working and lower-middle classes, which are heavily catered to in the American product. But American personnel have crossed the Atlantic too. A top American writer-producer (Carl Foreman) and a top director (Joseph Losey) did wonders for the morale of the British industry. *The Guns of Navarone* (Foreman) and Losey's *The Servant* and *Modesty Blaise* have been international smash hits. Even more, Sam Spiegel spotted an unused talent in David Lean and teamed up with him to produce *Bridge on the River Kwai, Lawrence of Arabia* and *Dr Zhivago* – all superbly mounted, superlative entertainments. Of course the most phenomenal of all British successes in the sixties, the James Bond films, are a mixture of American know-how and British creative talent. The producers Albert Broccolli and Harry Saltzman welded Fleming's books, Ken Adam's production design, Sean Connery's good looks, and a welter of other talents into the fabulously successful series: *Dr No, From Russia with Love, Goldfinger, Thunderball,* and *You Only Live Twice.* In my article (1969*b*) I have tried to chart the struggle to re-orient the class bias of British films.

The independent producer constitutes a separate phenomenon. These men are more like impresarios than regular producers. Unlike other creative producers, they make a point of not being employees of a big studio. They find scripts and artists and sell this package deal to the distributor directly. Naturally, men with this talent are rare: generally they seem either to be priorly successful businessmen (Martin Ransohoff) or television producers (David Susskind), or exceptionally successful men within the industry who broke away (Selznick, Zanuck), or writers, directors, even actors turned producers. The first independent producers were Chaplin, Pickford, Fairbanks and Griffith, the top money makers of the American

67

cinema, who formed themselves into United Artists in 1919 to produce and distribute their own films.[4] Chaplin was born in South-East London, and came to America in a vaudeville troupe; Pickford and Griffith were petty-bourgeoisie. Mary Pickford recalls (1956) how she too entered films *via* the theatre. An aspiring young actress without work, she was tempted by the cinema where the work was anonymous and the money real: a good stand-by for those in the theatre who hadn't quite made it yet. Meeting Griffith in the Biograph offices, and being confronted with his vision of what the cinema could become, his comparison with the humble origins of the theatre, swayed her. She was speaking to, and was to work with, the greatest director of the time. Griffith himself had started as an actor, while Fairbanks conforms to much the same pattern.

In brief, while producers and executives have by and large been recruited from humble backgrounds, many of the early stars and directors were lower middle class. The clashes between them might have been predicted on this basis. The social pretensions of D. W. Griffith, Douglas Fairbanks, Erich von Stroheim, etc., would not fare well with the tough businessmen from the garment district. Independent producers are almost by definition recruited after they have had some industry experience, or experience in a related industry, or have accumulated enough money to back their own early projects while they prove themselves. The cinema is now well into its third generation and the rags to riches cases are very few indeed. The general pattern now is that film people come from solidly middle-class backgrounds, with a good deal more education than found by Rosten (the cost-accountants and the sons of first-generation moguls who are now so plentiful, are well-educated and well-heeled before they enter the industry) and they make more diverse pictures. Some of those from humblest origins are now in the ranks of the stars – who have occasionally come from rock bottom (Marilyn Monroe was an orphan) and who may have been through countless humiliations on the way up.

To turn to the key creative personnel: directors and writers. Here the situation of recruitment is rather more complicated. Perhaps the broadest range of class and educational backgrounds is to be found in these parts of the industry. Writers, for example, range from pulp fiction authors through to Hugh Walpole, Christopher Isherwood, and Anthony Powell, each highly educated and literate. The vast majority of writers, however, come from radio, television, and journalism. The ability to work on a part of the script, to revise and improve someone else's work, is not something most authors' pride

[4] Provoking the immortal comment, 'So, the lunatics have taken charge of the asylum', see Ramsaye (1926a), p. 795.

will allow them to do. Of late, British playwrights like John Osborne, Robert Bolt, John Mortimer and Harold Pinter have all done film adaptations of their own work or that of others. They have also usually demanded and obtained control of the final script. Be that as it may, writing is a profession with many avenues in it and films have a huge ready-made storehouse in which to seek recruits. Making the transition from newspaper and magazine writing, or from fiction, to screen-writing is not too daunting a step. It is interesting the way a number of actors, simply by being in contact with films have been able to discover within themselves a talent for writing: Bryan Forbes, Michael Craig, and Jerry Lewis, for example.

The recruitment of directors is more difficult to pin down, naturally, because until the advent of television there was no comparable job where recruits could be sought. Cameramen and theatre directors were utilized, but the one didn't necessarily know anything about actors and the other definitely had problems adjusting to a totally different, much more fluid, medium. Indeed, to talk about recruitment of directors is to speak of innovation and the adaptation of innovation. Just as early films were made by film and camera manufacturers, so early direction was done by camera operators. The function of directing emerged slowly as longer films, with more involved plots and bigger casts came to require more organization. Griffith's greatness lies largely in his invention of much of the expressive and dramatic language of the film, a language which became the special province of the director to master. This invention by Griffith of so much of the language of the cinema: close-ups, intercutting, ellipsis, dissolves, seems unlikely to have been able to come from anyone whose imagination was imprisoned by theatrical conventions. Indeed, in the development of Griffith's many films, one can see how he explores and learns about each device until in the astonishing two years 1914–1916, in the masterpieces *Birth of a Nation* and its successor *Intolerance*, he has forged a rich and sophisticated language which enables him to convey almost any nuance he desires.[5] In the twenties others made further extensions to the language of the cinema: the expressionists of the German theatre influenced heavily the epics of Fritz Lang, and the cranial theories of Eisenstein and Pudovkin became the vanguard of the Soviet cinema. So once again the theatre was an important influence, as it had not been since the early days. These innovations, often accompanied by their innovators, crossed into France (Clair, Vigo), Britain (Hitchcock)

---

[5] This argument needs modification in the light of Vardac (1949), which I came across only when the book was in proof. He situates Griffith firmly within the aspirations of the theatre, even if his camera technique was less 'stagy' than that of his contemporaries.

and over to Hollywood. The first impact of sound was to impose such severe limitation on shooting that films became static and wooden.

The next great revolutionizer was to be Orson Welles, again in America, and he had a mixed background in the theatre, but, perhaps more importantly, in radio. The demands of radio technique, yet its great imaginative freedom, may have been responsible for the daring way Welles did things in his films which no-one had believed possible before. Working with a cameraman of genius, Gregg Toland, he perfected depth-of-field shooting, continuous camera takes, and editing and script devices which, ironically, were contained in commercially unsuccessful films, but which enriched the resources of the rest of the commercial cinema immeasurably. Hollywood is in his debt in more ways than one. The shooting style of, to take four disparate examples, Japan's Akira Kurosawa, Sweden's Ingmar Bergman, America's Robert Aldrich and Joseph Losey are immensely indebted to Welles. Some directors, like David Lean, worked their way up the ladder of apprenticeship from tea boy; while other directors got there rather more easily.

Alfred Hitchcock began as a designer of titles and somehow or other became a director. Of recent years many directors have been recruited from television. There are differences between the media, of course, but television is undoubtedly the best possible training ground. When the industry was big, both Hollywood and the UK used to make a great number of 'B' pictures and shorts. It was here that new and likely directorial talent was tried out. Thus, television has flourished at a convenient time when the B-picture training ground has dried up. Of late, a new method of coming into the cinema has been invented in France: this is to be an enthusiastic film critic and amateur or experimental film maker. In the phenomenon of the *Nouvelle Vague*, we had the astonishing spectacle of the entire editorial staffs of 'little' film magazines getting a chance to direct feature-length films. Amazingly many were successful, and several geniuses were discovered: Hanoun, Truffaut, Godard – and several others who are extremely gifted. Much has been made of the fact that these directors are young enough to have been raised and educated almost entirely in the era of the sound cinema, and that it is in terms of this medium they instinctively think. There can be little doubt that they have a peculiar and interesting sensibility – as witness their reverence for commercial directors like Howard Hawks, and Alfred Hitchcock. Nothing quite like this has ever happened before.

(To take another case which is reasonably well documented:

Poland. It appears that there is an organized film school, with admission arrangements much like any other art school (although perhaps a little stiffer) and its students graduate into the industry. Of course, the fundamental aim of the industry is not above making a good return on investment. What is interesting is how this easing of pressure doesn't necessarily do much for the product. On the other hand, it does ensure a high degree of technical competence even in inexperienced recent recruits to the industry, and it also appears to encourage more experiment and exploration than any other industry.)

Only in the technical areas of film production is there anything like an apprenticeship and training system organized by the unions. The directors and writers have their unions too, but they don't seem to prevent anyone with an appointment as a director from directing, however new he may be.

About the class backgrounds of independent producers, writers, and directors, I have said very little. This is because they have usually entered the industry not directly, but by way of another business or profession. To go into the class origins of these multiple and diverse backgrounds would take us too far afield. With the exception of those countries with film schools, like Poland, or France, film making has not been organized like a business or profession with an open and understandable recruitment policy and requirements which aspirants can set out to meet. On the contrary, in the capitalist world, the cinema has for long cashed in on the enormous numbers of people from multivarious backgrounds and educational levels who have been clamouring to enter. All honour to the French critics for being the first group of intellectuals to make a breakthrough into an industry. A similar breakthrough was made in Britain by using the more rational recruitment policies of the legitimate theatre and of television as stepping stones (see Jarvie 1969b). The enormous prestige of Hollywood has always enabled it to draw into its orbit almost any film maker from any country it desired. Of late, Kurosawa, Bergman, Antonioni and Godard have all spurned offers to work in Hollywood. These men have achieved complete creative freedom on their own terms at home. In years past, only Hollywood commanded the technical and financial resources to satisfy everybody. It no longer has that monopoly. Yet it still lures talents from Canada, Britain, France, Poland, etc. There is still a magic and a quality about Hollywood that has not been dispelled. Hollywood is the only industry with a worldwide mass distribution and remains the only industry where both massive financial returns and high quality can be combined. To conquer it is still a challenge to far and away the majority of those who aspire to make a career in films.

With the dispersal of the big studios the class background of

71

Hollywood denizens has ceased to signify much. The Hollywood social system of old, with its strict marks of status by salary and perks, has fallen apart. It is a world which continues to centre around films, but now on a film to film basis, and on less of a corporate basis. Finally, it might be worth looking at those most prominent citizens of the film world, the actors and actresses who decorate it. The public's idea that films are the modern road from rags to riches is certainly not false. Nor is it false that anyone, from any background, and often with the minimum intellectual capacity, can travel that road. But that the road is at all easy or comfortable is a myth. Los Angeles, for example, is full of the most beautiful waitresses, lifeguards, usherettes, and so on, who flock there and who continue to flock there. These are what filmland calls the 'hopefuls'; the ones who, when hard up like Marilyn Monroe once was, will turn their hand to almost anything just to stay on the scene in the hope of making it, of being discovered. It is indicative of how strong their desires are that some even pose nude for photographers, make 'blue' films, try to get that 'big break' with their bodies. Men, as well as. women. Many who are big stars now have had no previous acting experience. Lana Turner was discovered in a drug store, Rock Hudson was a truck driver, Jean Seberg was found in a talent contest. Yet it remains true to say that theatre, television or modelling are still the main ways to that first foot on the ladder. *Some* have arrived *via* the bedroom, of course. There is an eminent lady star of whom it is said that however wholesome she looks, she got there by sleeping with more people more often than anyone had believed possible even in jaundiced Hollywood. One must hope the rewards of fame and fortune compensate her for those years. Kenneth Anger's astonishing and scatological *Hollywood Babylon* (1965) is a compendium of such tales. But I would say it is apparent that no-one stays at the top nowadays unless they have something, and that something is usually not just looking good. Look at any group of extras in the background of a film shot. Many of the younger men are handsome, many of the girls extremely pretty. These commodities are ten-a-penny in Hollywood, both inside the industry, as well as outside, trying to get in. What makes the difference between the extra and the star? This question is for Part Three, but I will not listen to the idea that the answer is 'nothing', or 'luck'.

After all, merely to learn to relax in front of a camera and a microphone is quite a difficult thing to achieve. To learn also to act and react at will, to modulate one's voice, to hold a mood from scene to scene as shooting stretches over days (while the action of the film may be all taking place in a short space of time), this too is not easy.

In the bad old days of studio factory output many hopefuls were given 'exposure' and one could clearly see the difference between those who had screen presence and those who had not. Yet, the loss of the studio training schools and the B-pictures has made the process more selective and severe. Now stars are really big, the way they were in the very early days. They are also classless and regionless. One fact is surprising; almost none of the top actors and actresses have university degrees. Those that have can practically be enumerated on the fingers of one hand. This applies to a great many in Hollywood; and with lack of a degree (alas!) is associated lack of education; and with lack of education plus great affluence is associated a manifest lack of taste. This may account for the much remarked on gaudy vulgarity of Hollywood and its denizens.

3 Social consequences of recruitment

What does all this matter? That the cinema is a classless industry, recruited broadly if somewhat haphazardly, across most of the socioeconomic strata of America. The lower middle classes are strongly represented everywhere, but films hardly carry the ethos of that class. That films have a broad class base does not refute the theory that they are politically or otherwise influenced. But explanation of such alleged bias as a consequence of class structures is not possible since the facts belie it. Moreover, the broad base of recruitment to the industry may well have some effect upon its product; the unerring Hollywood instinct for the world market is clearly no accident.

A question, not touched upon so far, is what sort of social class system these diversely recruited role-fillers constitute when they have been recruited. Roughly, the answer to this is that they make up a continuum from middle-class to the very rich. However, the stresses, the unbridled power-struggles, the nepotism, and the general personalism, lead to the adoption of behaviour patterns that are far from those that this generalization would suggest. Gaudy and flamboyant display, in particular, is found at every level. Loud voices, uncouth manners and opinions, ostentatious homes and clothing, claques of lackeys, lavish spending, are all to be found there. But then this is an extraordinary society. It is conventional in sociology to attribute prostitution to economic causes. Hollywood may be a counter-example. It is a town with many beautiful and successful people in it. Some of them have used their bodies to get there. People who could easily have found good jobs, marriage, and security, came to Hollywood and used sex as a means to get their talent tested. Sex is cheap; but it generally doesn't get one anywhere by itself; no-one is obliged to behave this way; yet they do.

Another generalization might be that Hollywood's atypicality consists mainly in its extremism. Successful people are very well-off there, and those who are flamboyant by nature are consequently very flamboyant.

Rosten, in his careful book (1941), managed to obtain statistics on the numbers of people in different salary ranks in Hollywood. He found, what is perhaps predictable, but previously unnoticed, that from a sample of 253 actors more than 60% earned less than $8,000 a year in 1939; that more than 50% of the actors at 20th Century Fox, Warner Brothers and Columbia earned less than $7,200. These salary levels were comfortable enough in 1939, but hardly sufficient to sustain the high living of the 'night life of the gods'. In other areas: writing, directing, producing, there is not, as there is in acting, a whole class of people who barely have work from one year's end to the next. Professionals and technicians are not hired by the day or the part as actors are – but at least by the film, possibly by the year. Whereas those in acting feel the necessity to be on call if the studio contacts them, they can't take a chance on losing that 'big break'. Consequently, Rosten was able to disclose the pathetic spectacle of a large group of intermittent actors, living on very little, always in hope. . . . That the situation is not much better now, can be gleaned from Pauline Kael's piece on casting *The Group* (1968). The dreadful fears, insecurities, and humiliations are there graphically described. To play confident and perhaps lose a needed part; to alienate by a naked appeal; what to do? Partly, the state of the theatre and the lack of jobs in New York explains it. Otherwise, who knows what keeps them hoping? As Miss Kael remarks, 'Many don't, of course, and I met some of them later. They were the "crew": from the director on down, they were almost all actors who had given up.'

This raises a final question, since I am trying to make it clear that the reason most people want to be recruited is because of the high salaries. The wish to express oneself in film is a more fashionable motif in the autobiographies of writers and directors now than before. This is partly because when the personnel who manned films up to the fifties were seeking their identities as teenagers, films were not a medium of choice at all, or not one in which a gifted person could see the possibilities. In the old days people just drifted in and stayed because of the money. Front-of-camera people seem to be attracted more by the 'glamour' (which includes the money) than the money *tout court*. The adulation, the vanity-satisfaction, the ego-boost, plus the salary, seem to warrant hideously long hours, often poor working conditions and endless time spent fiddling over minutiae.

4 *Money the magnet*

Money, above all, is the magnet. Thus arises the problem of why and with what justification film people command high salaries. First it should be said that film *technicians* – electricians, carpenters, painters, grips – are well paid by the standards of their craft but not enormously so. The high monies were once the province of the executives, then of stars, producers, directors, writers, tip-top designers. Once, Louis B. Mayer was the highest paid executive in the USA. Now there are quite a few stars who take a half a million per picture, plus a percentage of the profits (Elizabeth Taylor, and one or two others, take one million). Frequently, producer-directors and stars set up a company solely to make one film, wholly owned by them and their associates. This ensures the net take goes where it should (!) and it has interesting income-tax uses.

Are these high salaries justifiable? What would count as justification? Is Picasso justified in collecting whatever the market for his paintings will bear? If the answer is 'yes', then Elizabeth Taylor can say 'me too' (cp. Walker 1966). Her, or rather my, temerity in making the comparison with Picasso is irrelevant, since I did not say 'is Picasso justified if he is a good painter . . . ?' If the answer is, 'Picasso is *only* justified *if* he is a great artist', my question is, 'who is to judge?' And, especially, who is to judge the public that judges Elizabeth Taylor worthy of enough of its money that she can command the salaries she does?

If the answer about Picasso's market price is, 'no, no art is worth that much', then this applies *a fortiori* to the salary of Henry Ford II (not Henry Ford – he invented auto mass production) since his services to humanity are deemed by no-one to be greater than those of Picasso. Is then the president of the US underpaid? The objection to Picasso's high prices becomes a matter of distribution of wealth rather than of the economic value of art, and we have no criteria for judging the just distribution of wealth. A lot of social philosophers have spilt a lot of ink in trying to give us criteria of this kind. Economists agree that none of these theories are workable (implementable), or satisfactory (because of unintended effects, some of which are self-vitiating).

The reader may be dissatisfied with this treatment of the problem of high salaries in the film industry. So is the author. The purpose of the discussion was not to settle an issue, but rather to set it against a background. It transpires that the background does not sustain an adequate treatment of the problem. This may become more amenable to solution, if we pursue the question of what exactly is a Picasso worth? Someone denies that it is worth $25,000, because no daubed canvas is worth that much blood and sweat. Rather than take him up on the 'because', I want to show the feebleness of the statement by asking him how much blood and sweat a Picasso is worth? $1,000? Surely $10? (a man has to make a living). It is told of the late social philosopher Lord Beaverbrook that he approached a *belle* at a party and said to her, 'would you sleep with me for a million dollars?' After an instant's thought the lady said, 'Yes'. 'And how about for five dollars?' 'What do you think I am?', she replied indignantly. 'We know what you are, my dear; it is the price we are discussing.'

V

Case Studies and Recapitulation

In this chapter, I shall survey a few of the detailed published case studies on the production of particular films. There are only a few of these and they deserve careful study. For a picture of the grinding of the Hollywood machine in its heyday, we have Lillian Ross's account of how Gottfried Reinhart produced, and John Huston directed, *The Red Badge of Courage* for MGM. This is by far the best of the studies as a book; it is so revealingly funny that Miss Ross was told never to darken the doors of MGM again. An official account of the making of an MGM picture, (*The Next Voice you Hear*), is Doré Schary's *Case History of a Movie*. Although incomplete, Wanger's *My Life with Cleopatra* is fascinating. No comparable full-length studies of the British machine at work exist, but Lindsay Anderson chronicled the making of Thorold Dickinson's *The Secret People*. The life and work of Akira Kurosawa have been exhaustively studied by Donald Richie in *The Films of Akira Kurosawa* where, naturally, much material on the Japanese industry is to be found. Then, also, the story of the making of the James Bond films has become well known. Finally, there are two wonderful stories of how the individualists make out: Jean Cocteau's own *Diary of a Film*, the story of his making *La Belle et la Bête*; and Michael Macliammoir's *Put Money in Thy Purse* – about the making of Orson Welles' *Othello*.

In the biographies (auto and ghosted) of Pickford, Crawford, Astaire, Chaplin, Von Sternberg, Von Stroheim, King Vidor Keaton, Davis, The Marx Brothers, there is scattered a great deal of inside information on the picture business. In fiction, the most terrifying portraits of the industry are in Scott Fitzgerald's *The Last Tycoon* and Richard Brooks' *The Producer*.

1 The Red Badge of Courage *and* The Secret People

To begin, then, with *Picture*. The MGM hierarchy consisted of Nick Schenck in New York, Louis B. Mayer in Hollywood, Doré Schary under Mayer, and then the individual producers. Reinhart and Schary, both somewhat idealistic, wanted to film Stephen Crane's novel of the American Civil War *The Red Badge of Courage*. Louis B.

Mayer, suspicious of 'art', blue-ribbon films and pretensions (during discussion of an explanatory commentary he comments, 'jabber, jabber, jabber, who wants to listen?') is against the film, but gives Schary his head and $1·5 million to help him gain 'experience'. The film is made and previewed. Mayer hates it and the previews are none-too-successful. Realizing it cannot be turned commercial, it is ordered to be re-edited, dressed up with commentary to tell everyone that the book is a classic, and released in the hope of it at least covering its costs.

This is a story which reveals where the power was in Hollywood, and just how little freedom successful creators had. Although never liking the project, Mayer was prepared to let Schary make it; he was not, however, prepared to expose it to the public as Schary or Huston wanted it. Schary wavered and suggested changes. Reinhart and Huston resisted. Huston got fed up and went off to his next project, *The African Queen*, over which he had a great deal of control. The ultimate power at MGM lay in New York and in the hands of the remorselessly folksy Mayer, and that power was used to fix the final form of the film.

Picture shows us, perhaps, the Big Studio at its worst. At least as Miss Ross saw it, whether a good project got made or not depended largely on the personal caprice of an opinionated and eccentric boss, who was surrounded by yes men and sycophants. Moreover, once the creators had the approval, a budget, and even the film's shooting over, they could see their work at the mercy of further caprice, the god-like opinions of New York financiers, and the inane, instant reactions of excited teenagers at previews. Overall, it was a depressing prospect, and only left one wondering how it was that all those beautiful musicals were ever made at MGM.

Despite this, in the end *The Red Badge of Courage* was an eminently watchable picture. This is not so small a point, as perhaps a comparison will bear out. *The Secret People,* a tale of anarchists in London, did not please the London critics. Thorold Dickinson's previous films like *Next of Kin* and *Queen of Spades* were widely admired. Unlike Lillian Ross, Lindsay Anderson did not delay his book long enough to see the final release version of the film, which was shortened legally, but without the knowledge or consent of the director. The film was on a controversial subject and the cuts seem to have been an attempt to tone it down. It is thus very difficult to draw any lessons from this case. After a feature made in Israel, Dickinson was appointed Chief of film production at the United Nations, in 1956. He has conducted Film Studies in the University of London where he is now Professor of Film. While *The Red Badge of Courage* shows that despite heroic efforts, the MGM machine could not erase

78

all traces of the Huston touch from his film, *Secret People* shows how even when everything is going for a director, if he does not have control right up to the release print, the possibility remains of his work being spoiled. A recent, glaring example of a similar case is Richard Brooks' earnest adaptation of Joseph Conrad's *Lord Jim*. Two years spent on the script, a dazzling cast, a large budget, etc., didn't stop this film being dreary and unsuccessful. This is no fault of Conrad: Carol Reed's *The Outcast of the Islands* was powerful and successful.

2 Cocteau, Welles, and Kurosawa

Case one: intervention yet mild success; case two: some intervention, some disappointment. Cases three and four: acute difficulties yet ultimate success. Jean Cocteau's *Diary of a Film* and Macliammoir's story (1952) of Orson Welles' *Othello*, illustrates how the persistent and dedicated artist can press on against almost inconceivable difficulties (recurring skin ailments in Cocteau's case; running completely out of money in Welles'), without benefit or hindrance from big studios, and yet emerge with a film not unlike their intention and conception, a work which in all integrity they are responsible for. Cocteau, shooting a fairytale in the appalling conditions of France in 1946, lacking electric power and money, constantly ill, unable to tolerate the glare of the lamps, and so on. Yet the completed work is pure Cocteau, and, in some ways, one of his most charming and delicate films. Cocteau always managed to operate inside the commercial structure of French films, but without interference. Perhaps French respect for Cocteau's cultural prestige allowed them to finance the odd Cocteau venture. Welles, on the other hand, was the *bête noir* of Hollywood. He went there in 1940, aged twenty-six, and made two masterpieces: *Citizen Kane* and *The Magnificent Ambersons*; both failed to make money, at least on their first release. The studio interfered slightly with *Ambersons*. After two more of his films were drastically re-edited (*Journey Into Fear, The Lady From Shanghai*) Welles quit Hollywood, returning only occasionally to act, to direct an experiment (*Macbeth*), and to make his superb *Touch of Evil*. Otherwise, he has lived and worked in Europe. Beginning with *Othello*, he seems to have financed his films with the money earned by acting. This method produced also *Mr Arkadin* and *Chimes at Midnight*. *The Trial* was made with French backing. A dynamic and overwhelming personality, Welles has been able to triumph over incredible vicissitudes. His *Othello* may not be Shakespeare, but it is splendid Welles. There is hardly a shot that lacks his distinctive imprint. Yet it was shot in fragments, here there and everywhere, in constant danger of running out of money, between September 1948 and March 1950.

Case five, the career of Akira Kurosawa, illustrates another way an artist may beat the system. Beginning very humbly and working his way up to director, Kurosawa learnt his trade slowly. His early films are all extant and vary in quality. Sometimes the plots and scripts are not too good, sometimes Kurosawa's control is insufficient for him to do what he wants. Gradually, however, he gained the degree of competence required for his first masterpiece, *Rashomon*, made in 1950. Since that time, he has been regarded as one of the world's greatest, boldest and most powerful film makers. However, his *Seven Samurai* was shortened by his studio, and this began to happen on a number of his films, despite his prestige and money-making capacity. He was given complete creative freedom to film what he wanted, as he wanted, with expense hardly spared. But at times his end product was tampered with. This resulted in him becoming his own producer, making his old studio only his distribution agent; he thus gained full control.

3 *James Bond's inner man*

The final case I want to consider is what appears to be a new trend in the industry, the joint production purely *ad hoc*, neither freedom nor interference being relevant. I am thinking of the way the phenomenally successful series of James Bond films has been made. *Dr No, From Russia with Love, Goldfinger, Thunderball* have made a mint of money for their producers, Harry Salzman and Albert Broccoli. The Bond books had been appearing since 1953, but for one reason or another no-one had got around to filming them. Then they became a hit in the US market during the late fifties, and Salzman and Broccoli procured the film rights to them all except for the first. Based in London, but with the backing of the US United Artists Corporation, they decided to mix fidelity to Fleming's level, with new stars, and elaborate locations, sets, and adventures. A relatively unknown British actor was employed in Sean Connery, and he was teamed with up-and-coming young women for each film. Design and scripting were very carefully designed to fit a half-serious, fantasy life. Quips ('The Things I do for England') and gags, quite alien to Fleming, were inserted (as on the occasion when Bond, having seduced a Chinese girl then overheard her plotting against his life, calmly glances at his watch before succumbing to her embraces again, knowing he has time before precautions from ambush are needed). The West Indies, Turkey, Switzerland, Florida, Bermuda and Japan have been their locations. Lots of money was lavished on these films, not on inflated payments to actors and actresses, but on sets and on sending the crew on location for weeks on end. Salzman and Broccoli displayed a shrewd insight when making their decisions on these films. Some of the other films they have made have been bombs. It would have been easy with the Bond films to have squandered what were basically wonderful properties. They succeeded only because they pulled out all the stops: they decided the films had to be made tongue in cheek, that elements of self-mockery already present in Fleming had to be utilized if his plots were to come off in such a graphic medium as the cinema. Money appears to have been no object, but it was also spent wisely. This showmanship has paid off, and these men are now thought to have the golden touch. It is interesting to compare what their rivals did with *Casino Royale*, which tried to outdo and out spoof them, with incomprehensibility the result. Yet the Bond films are all of a piece. Although writer, directors and cameramen changed from time to time, and although only Connery was the common star, they are homogeneous. These are films without a personal touch, with the possible exception of Ken Adam's sets. But they are somehow fully realized conceptions.

To sum up. The system was bad, but it was possible to beat it. John Ford, Alfred Hitchcock, worked comfortably within it; others, like Jean Cocteau, Akira Kurosawa, Ingmar Bergman, Federico Fellini found a *niche* where they could work undisturbed. Orson Welles had to leave the system altogether. The fundamental problems are created by the fact that there are two roles in the film world which are poorly defined: the executive and the actor. Producers, directors, writers, directors of photography know what they are and what they want. What they are up against is the executive with great financial, but no creative, responsibility and no structural controls on his caprices. With independent production this problem has eased greatly. On the other hand, the film maker really has to show his mettle quickly now. No longer can he afford to learn slowly through B and low-budget pictures – he may go straight from television to a multi-million dollar film. One slip and the jig is up. The film maker also clashes with the poor role-definition of the actor. The actor is the most highly paid and the most insecure. Many a time a 'package' will or will not be made depending on who has agreed to appear in it. Yet the most visible participant has a comparatively humble creative role to play.

These role clashes are not extraneous to the system: there is little old-boy network in such a highly competitive industry as the cinema. Apart from competition, any class distinctions there are in film production, are only those of salary and status. The structural comparison of the two will at once explain the clashes: within the industry, actors have high salaries and low status; directors vice versa; executives are high on both counts. Finally, techn:cians and professionals are graded by their salaries, which tend to reflect their association with success. This, obviously, means conflict. The status system is not in accord with the income distribution; and income distribution is unsystematically related to success.

This series of conflicts in Hollywood is a paradigm for similar conflicts wherever films are made under capitalism. In countries like India, Egypt, and Hong Kong, additional complications are introduced by the low status attached to the profession of acting itself. In face of this, it is to be expected that films everywhere will be made within rather loose and involved forms of organisation – which enable the clashes between these status and role conflicts to be minimized.

Having in this part of the book analysed how films come to be, logically we next focus on the consumer, before we look at the content of what is consumed. However it should be borne in mind, for we will return to it, that in addition to these role clashes within film making, there is the question of the role the industry plays, the interests it serves, in society at large. Recruited and structured in a certain way, a consumer industry is going to reflect itself and its relation to the wider society in a certain kind of product, best suited to a certain kind of audience.

Part Two

THE SOCIOLOGY OF
AN AUDIENCE:
WHO SEES FILMS AND WHY?

My plan is to confine this part of the essay to answering the question 'who sees films and why?' In thus trying to sketch the structure of the audience, so to speak, I cannot avoid the 'why' question of how is it that these people and not some others constitute the audience. However, the next logical question: 'what effect has what is seen on those who see it?', will not be taken up until we get to Part Three. We must first say something about what is seen, before we discuss its effects. Insofar as what is seen is relevant to the 'why' of audience composition, we may have to touch on it in this part as well.

Chapter VI: 'The Role of the Audience in the Medium-at-Large', criticizes the notion that cinema-going is a passive activity. Chapter VII: 'Cinemagoing as a Social Institution', will view the cinema as part of the institutions of mass entertainment and show how these socialize and teach. In Chapter VIII: 'The Screen Audience', I shall try to describe what we know about the structure of the cinema audience, and seriously take up the question of why it is this audience and not some other.

VI

The Role of the Audience in the Medium-at-Large

1 'Passive' audiences a myth

What constitutes an audience, and what is special about cinema audiences? The standard view is that there are active pleasures and passive pleasures and that being an audience is one of the latter, whereas music-making and needlework belong to the former. Often, this kind of division is utilized in order to hold up for our admiration a by-gone age when, it is alleged, people sang, played, sewed and read aloud, and generally made their own amusements. Certainly, before amusements were an industry, it was necessary to make one's own, or, rather, to take them within one's own environment. Yet even then people silently read books, and there are few more passive-*looking* activities than that. Reading a book is being a one-man audience. Going to a film is being an audience on a different scale, and also of a different quality. My thesis would be that passivity in mass audiences should earn no more disapprobation than passivity in reading a book; and that it is quite misleading to interpret 'passive' as 'mentally and physically lazy' – the book example should make that clear.

There are, after all, various ways of being an audience, in the mass media as in everything else. The audience of radio and television can continue with a great many normal home activities while it is watching. A film audience can barrack, sleep, pet and neck, eat, drink, and do a number of other things. A reader of a book, however, can hardly do anything but sit or lie, drink, smoke, and concentrate.

What does all this matter? Even if the activity is totally passive, as with a book, or involves concentration as well, as does a book or the films in certain cases, why should that state be regarded as less acceptable, less deserving of our approval than, say, a do-it-yourself madrigal or folk-song session? The usual answer is a kind of puritanism; a feeling that work is good for one, even work in pursuit of pleasure. You have to focus on a book and work at it; a film serves it up on a p'ate. This whole argument is foolish to an incredible degree. It is snobbish and inaccurate. Is listening to the St Matthew Passion

85

more passive or more active than needlework or dishwashing? The English and American working classes, in the country and the towns, did not sit around in salons of an evening. They worked and they played. Some danced, but others watched. Watching has always been a widespread, and quite legitimate activity. Being lazy at dances and sing-songs is not an occasion for suffering censure: let each of us take his pleasure as he will, provided he does not positively harm others. The whole puritan do-it-yourself thing is a bore. It would give me no pleasure to have to write books before reading them, or to make films before I could see them. Therefore I conclude that some pleasures you make, others you buy: *chacun à son goût.* Buying a cinema ticket is exactly like buying a book, and the film has the great additional quality of being pleasurable to people who cannot read.

All this is obvious, but the puritan theory is too widespread to be dismissed without an explanation. In my view there is a sinister and snobbish paternalism here, which sometimes shows its anti-democratic face, as in the theories of censorship and brainwash. An amazing range of intellectuals (shall we call them 'P and P' – the professor and the priest?) fear and denounce mass media, including films because, they argue, they are awash in violence and sex; serious problems are fatuously simplified; they allow escape from reality into a dream-world, instead of facing up to the problems of life. Hollywood is 'the dream factory', films 'the vampire art', etc. The snobbishness lies in the view that audiences are dumb and simply soak up what they see. My own experience is that far from being sponges, ordinary people who regularly see films are down-to-earth and sceptical about them, and take much of what they see with a pinch of salt. The paternalism comes in the cry for censorship and for 'higher standards'. Censorship needs censors, i.e., setting certain people apart as incorruptible and allowing them to protect us from corruption. But this is a case where most men, if asked, would demand to be judge in their own cause. The anti-democratic tendency is already inherent in not allowing people to be their own censors. It is more striking in the demand for higher standards – Shakespeare, not circuses, is the underlying notion, and to prefer the latter is to be a lesser person. I have indicated how strongly I oppose this in other parts of the book. Here, my concern is to explore the view further.

All too often, crude negative evaluations of the mass media, including cinema and television, are peddled by professors and priests alike. Most of them amount to little more than this: media watching is passive brainwash. One comes across this view again and again. Films, radio, television, pop music are described (Meyersohn

1961) as having an undifferentiated output: the differences between programmes is so trivial, it doesn't count. Quite frankly, this sort of remark can only come from someone who in a strict sense does not watch or listen to these media *at all*. Should they accidentally expose themselves to it from time to time, their mental set is so overloaded with preconceptions that nothing gets through. In the preface, I indicate that this aloof disdain of the media is deplorable, especially in those who pose as experts on it. In my earlier argument that the cinema is becoming the media of choice for some artists, I have the core of a rebuttal. So far from being just an undifferentiated stream washing out over ennervated audiences, films, radio, television, and the pop song, are among the most vital and contemporary media of choice for what in pretentious circles would be known as creative artists. The products of their work are very clearly differentiated for anyone who cares to learn the language these artists are working in. As yet television still goes in waves, or cycles, or series, like 'Star Trek', early 'Man from UNCLE', and Rowan and Martin's 'Laugh-In'. But it, too, is highly differentiated to the cognoscenti, i.e., those, like myself, who begin by taking it seriously.

Happily, the fact remains that despite the exhortations, we go on enjoying the media. The brainwash must be succeeding in short-circuiting P and P counter-brainwash – which is also explained by the P and P counter-brainwash: people like myself, it is argued, are so brainwashed they are immune to being shown they are brainwashed. So the theory underlying the P and P counter-brainwash becomes further confirmed by the empirical evidence that media-watching is getting out of control [*sic*]. Even the victims acknowledge their passivity and credulity by defending the indefensible, the media. Sociological investigation reveals that greater exposure to mass-media goes together with an overall passivity and credulity, and media-watching also increases with a decrease in social standing.

Logical analysis, however, shows that any evidence collected will support the P and P theory (and this is especially so, when the evidence consists of people who deny the theory and are obviously therefore thoroughly brainwashed), and the resulting confirmation is thus rendered vacuous because no evidence whatsoever can possibly tell against the theory. But it would seem that a theory with such good credentials is not to be shrugged off with mere irony, such as I have directed at priests and professors.

Summary so far: a plausible theory of the media has been ironic-ally dismissed by a logical trick; the dismissal has been declared inadequate; in the name of logical analysis the dismissal of the dismissal has been dismissed. Hence, it is about time to look seriously at what the priests and professors say. And it is not very difficult to defend it – after all, watching the media *is* easier than reading a novel. This is because reading a novel involves imaginative participation by the reader, in re-constructing in the mind the scenes and people sketchily described. This is so much so that seeing the film of the book before reading the book, short-circuits this act of imaginative reading, and interferes with any conceivable intention the author had of activating the reader's imagination in certain ways. This applies to seeing the film of the book *after* reading the book: the film's realization of scenes and people is always disappointing because it never conforms to the reader's own act of imagination, which he naturally prefers. Hence, having read the book, he prefers it to the film; yet, empirically, we can say, more people have seen the film of any book than ever read that book. Why? Clearly, watching is easier than reading. One might argue that it is less a question of ease and more a question of the expenditure of time: two hours per film, *x* hours plus, per book: it takes a few sentences at least to describe a setting or a face, but no time at all to flash these on to the screen. This means that we are either impatient or lazy. If we are impatient, the correct move would be to look at the last page of the book. *Ergo*, we are lazy.

What exactly is wrong with our being lazy? Puritanism rears its head again. As to short-circuiting the imaginative process, we can learn to know better and refrain from spoiling our own pleasure. Literary snobs to the contrary, people are not going to benefit from reading books just because films are unavailable. Book *vs.* film is as false a contrast as trash book *vs.* good book. The lack of one does not channel people to the other: they are only substitutes to a negligible degree. Failing to obtain a Mickey Spillane novel does not lead to spontaneous acceptance of Jane Austen. Evidence from the USSR notwithstanding, deprived of films, deprived of Spillane, a person might equally well read a tabloid, play a juke-box, take a drink, buy a pack of cigarettes. Only education and the cultivation of tastes within a tolerant and pluralist aesthetic is reconcilable with democracy. Gans, in a very important series of papers (1959*b*, 1960, 1961, 1966), has attacked the monolithic model of aesthetics which places high culture at the top, with everything else individiously ranked beneath. Some broad rankings of whole *genres* may be possible, e.g., chamber music *vs.* folk-music, but it is not very illuminating and easily becomes snobbish.

Within pluralism we can argue that viewing a film can be as rich a way of using two hours as any other. If people bring up Jane Austen or Charles Dickens, we must counter with Michelangelo Antonioni and Akira Kurosawa. If the passivity of film-going is suggested, then comics must be mentioned. Films use a language which is rich and complex, and it can be used to illustrate things the language of prose cannot. Or, perhaps more interestingly, fiction and poetic technique has been enriched by contact with the cinema. *A fortiori* the reverse also. Being a film audience is as complex and rewarding an experience as being the audience at a live drama. True, it is different, because the medium is different. But misplaced attacks comparing it with do-it-yourself and reading miss the point entirely.

2 The audience as unstructured group

Our society, in a way, is a society of audiences. We are all members of audiences many times a day, to different media, at different places, in different contexts. We are radio and newspaper audiences in the morning. Hoardings audiences while we travel to work. Radio, television, gramophone, film, theatre, and book audiences in the evening. At times we are audiences for pleasure, other times from necessity – as when we read signs and letterheads for information, often despite ourselves[1] (e.g., television commercials). Many things we know and enjoy are gained when we are participating as audiences. Most communications of any kind, even face to face, involve transmitter and receiver; source, medium and audience.

What is an audience? Sociologists call it an unstructured group. Group it certainly is, despite the fact that it exists as a group only intermittently and for a short while; that it shifts and reforms itself constantly with different membership. Blumer (1946) suggests that an unstructured group has 'no social organization, no body of custom and tradition, no established set of rules or rituals, no organized group of sentiments, no structure of status roles, and no established leadership'. (p. 186). With the exception of the lack of rules and rituals, these negative differences mark off an unstructured group like an audience from a structured group, like a political party, or a high school class. 'The' audience for 'the' cinema is presumably the unstructured group par excellence, as pictured in such a definition. Any particular neighbourhood audience, which in suburb or drive-in is likely to reflect some of the characteristics of the surrounding society it is recruited from, is less unstructured. But, 'the' audience in that sense doesn't exist. Or, at least, it exists only in the minds of some sociologists of mass society.

When a writer writes a book, or a film maker makes a film, we usually assume he wants to say or do something in the medium and that he wants to say it to or do it for a certain audience more or less

[1] I once crashed my car because my attention was seized by a gigantic Coca-cola hoarding (billboard in the USA).

clearly envisaged. Thus, his work is to a certain extent tailored to and by his hypothetical audience (Gans 1957). One of the main problems of sponsored television, is this tailoring of the programmes to the expected audience to such an extent that experiment is hard to get underway. A business must pay attention to its sales charts, but there are questions of public responsibility where the air waves are concerned. The enormous overheads severely interfere with free competition, and corrective measures of some kind are essential. Britain has its BBC and ITA; the USA its FCC. The film business is perhaps free from government regulation since it is less a medium for purveying news and information, than traditionally a vehicle for works of creative imagination. But, above all, it is not subject to the shortage of channels.

Films are freer in the sense that they do not need correcting. They are not freer in the sense that they have ignored their audience. The question is, just what is the extent of audience participation in the medium-at-large?

I want to start by saying, bluntly, that the audience presents a serious problem which it is irresponsible for the film makers to ignore. Now we have come full circle. We first argued the position that it is slavish for the film maker to pander to his audience; now we say that it is irresponsible for him to ignore it. What should he do? What is the correct relationship of the film maker to his audience?

In fact, what Hollywood does is to sample its audience, to pre-test the product, as described in Chapter XV. The question here resolves itself into what regard is taken of the information. On record are a number of cases of films being re-cut after sneak previews, and the comments on reaction cards. These have gained publicity because famous directors were involved; it seems obvious that there are many cases of this re-cutting, indeed it is virtually standard practice. Far more frequently, alterations are instigated by executives – the notorious Front Office of memory, which now more often means the executive producer. These men order changes on the basis of their guesses as to public reaction. Their aim: to please the audience, to avoid offending significant minorities within it. Such interference drove Orson Welles, John Huston and Stanley Kubrick from Hollywood. Time and again young directors complain bitterly of changes – *Sanctuary* (Tony Richardson), *Major Dundee* (Sam Peckinpah) – which distort their films, render them meaningless, etc. The complaint is less that the films have been changed, than that they have been changed at someone's speculation or whim, and without consultation with those whose names are upon it as creators. For years the Screen Directors Guild tried to gain directors the contractual right to do the first cut. This is reasonable enough – at least a man should have the opportunity to work out a problem his way before interference starts. However, the final decision can reasonably be demanded by those who are accountable for the enormous investment involved. It is surprising how many creators get a free hand in this high-cost industry.

Yet, were there ready information about audience reaction to films, would anyone be justified in tailoring films on that basis? I do not see how the answer can be categorical. If a film is a little slow, and the audience gets bored, then tightening it up will prevent the word spreading that it is slow and dull. Any critical director would go along with this if it was pointed out to him, and any responsible executive would clear proposed changes with the director.[2] What is intolerable is allowing a director to make a film that is out of the ordinary, and then to try to force it into the ordinary mould after completion – as a sort of box office insurance. This happened over Huston's *The Red Badge of Courage* which we discussed earlier. Huston and his producer Gottfried Reinhardt, it will be recalled, wanted to film Stephen Crane's classic in an heroic and deliberate style. Executive producer Doré Schary agreed with them. After letting Schary have his head, executives Louis B. Mayer and Nick Schenck pressured Schary to reconsider and re-cut the picture. It was obvious to everyone from the start that the film wasn't going to make huge profits. But it could easily have recouped if it had had special treatment as an 'art' film and been distributed not only in cinemas but on the art-house and lecture-hall circuit. Mayer didn't want to bother with this. In the interests of the fast buck it was mauled around, did poorly commercially, and even was looked at askance by the art houses as a ruined masterpiece.

With the majority of films of the factory system period, the degree of personal creative involvement was so low that re-cutting, etc., was of little concern. This made it especially reprehensible when producers refused to take risks in the odd cases where there was a genuine creative involvement. Especially when it could be quite easily shown that changing shots about does not make *that* much difference to receipts. (In the later discussion of what makes a film successful (Chapter XV), I suggest that niceties of style and pace play no role at all.) Publishers, at least, edit manuscripts *with* their authors and rarely consider overriding the judgment of someone they take seriously. Of course, their investment in advances is small against the film investment. Therefore, film executives must be more critical of

---

[2] On p. D 19 of *The New York Times*, 28 April 1968, Stanley Kubrick is reported to have 'clipped nineteen minutes from some of the scenes of *2001: A Space Odyssey*'. He said, 'These were simply short cuts here and there – it's a common practice – to tighten and make the film move more rapidly.'

whom they regard as serious artists. The borderline is hard to draw, as all borderlines are. Nevertheless, the treatment of Orson Welles, Eric von Stroheim and Joseph von Sternberg stands as an accusation against Hollywood.

Similar cases occur in Britain. Alexander Mackendrick almost stopped working at one time because of it. He became known as a 'difficult' director, and was not allowed to create in freedom. On the other hand, there is the case of Gabriel Pascal, who, in a megalomaniac display, had astronomers calculate how the night sky would have looked in a certain year for backdrops in *Caesar and Cleopatra*; for desert scenes, sand was exported to Egypt because the sand there didn't 'look' right, etc. Robert Flaherty apparently disappeared to India to shoot *Elephant Boy*, and for a long while sent back nothing but takes and retakes of one shot: an elephant lifting Sabu on to his back. One could multiply examples. A watch certainly has to be kept for this sort of thing. But contrast the situation in Sweden with Bergman, or Japan with Kurosawa, or France with Godard. These artists have a towering stature in their own countries, and large international reputations. They have, also, virtually complete creative freedom. Finance is glad to back them (Godard has some trouble, but he is nevertheless as prolific as Simenon). This comes about because they are serious and responsible, and because their films make a modest amount of money. Their backers do not expect huge returns, but know they can be relied upon. They make more or less what they want. Even American directors of great eminence, who may command freedom once a project is started, cherish many pet projects which they have never been able to get backing for.

If Hollywood's renegades had shown talent at producing commercial flops, one could understand their being treated harshly. But this is not the case. They stopped work because they fought for creative freedom against ruthless production executives, whose strength lay in the knowledge that in a factory no-one is indispensable.

My own position on the issue is by no means a 'liberal' one. I cannot see that those who invest millions in a business venture, whether film, building, airline, or new product, can be gainsaid the right to watch over their investment. On occasion, I think that creative film makers have come by money too easily and have grown uncritical because of this. A certain indulgence in some of the later films of George Stevens and William Wyler is quite apparent. And there was a time in Paris, when the New Wave was all the rage, when it seemed that anyone with enough push could get backing for a film. This led to Claude Chabrol, for instance, churning out a series of more or less dud films. I am not saying that these cases argue for a tougher policy. Freedom to waste is probably something a society like ours can afford and should afford.

Even if investors and their agents have some right to watch over their money, there can be no apology for the stupidity of the way they do so. For one thing, deception: they promise a film maker creative control and freedom and then interfere with his work at every possible stage. For another thing, they may interfere solely on capricious grounds, including their hunches about the public, and so on. This conduct seems to me as bad as it is claimed to be. Degrees of control should be specified from the beginning and adhered to. Such interference as is agreed upon should be based less on vague hunches and prejudices, and on induction from past successes, and have more of an eye to the image-quality of the product and the market for that kind of image-quality. Because of cost, *Cleopatra* obviously had to aim at the broadest possible audience. Modest, one or two million dollar films on the other hand, can make a handsome profit in a specialist audience. Against self-indulgence and against front office ruination, I find myself saying that the audience should be much more critically a factor than it is in each separate case.

A glaring fault of the factory system was that practically all films aimed for the biggest possible audience, and thus the maximum in profits. Those customers queueing insatiably twice a week, were undifferentiated in the film producers' minds. Or were they? Perhaps not entirely. The B-picture was definitely intended as a filler to distract but not enthuse; to recoup modestly. One factor in the European film ethos that has always been different from Hollywood, is this awareness of audience differential. Doubtless, this has a lot to do with their being smaller industries with lower costs, and rather smaller markets to attack. Forced to produce a certain number of films to fill the cinemas and satiate the demand, Hollywood, as we have seen, had to set up a factory system of production with considerable division of labour. However, these moves had the effect of increasing both the fixed overhead and the variable costs of production far beyond those of any other film industry, anywhere in the world. This large investment, and huge attractive market, geared Hollywood into making every film as though for the entire, undifferentiated, world audience. As witness the contortions suffered in trying to have films passed as innocuous to audiences throughout the world (Hansen 1945). Meanwhile, in Europe, Ingmar Bergman makes modestly successful, inexpensive films for people who can understand him. Jean-Luc Godard, similarly limits his aims. When Laurence Olivier films Shakespeare, he doesn't expect a roaring profit, but ? modest one over a number of years. The British film industry fell flat on its face in the late forties when it tried to make big-budget, widely popular films – with pathetic ineptitude (Wood 1952). There weren't many film makers in the old Hollywood who had an audience they wanted to reach specifically and profitably, other than the mass audience. The climate of opinion there seemed to be such that that kind of approach to film making would be rejected at the executive level. Here a serious criticism is to be made of the unbridled, capitalist mode of production. Not because any capitalist will necessarily go for the highest profits. That is actually quite false. But because of the difficulty of new entrepreneurs entering the industry. The initial cost of entering the industry was by then so great, that those who would have been satisfied to conduct business on a more modest scale were effectively kept out. This is very difficult to remedy, since any source of entry money, including an enlightened state – would want to have a say in what is made.

We may perhaps explain the Hollywood lack of interest in the structure of their audience as partly a consequence of the sellers' market. The cinema was such a booming business that there was little incentive to explore and cultivate the audience. There is also little doubt that the vulgarity and stupidity of some of the early executives is reflected in their films. Men of the people, proud of the fortunes they have made, felt they *knew* the audience – it would like and want what they liked and wanted. So long as there was a sellers' market, nothing could prove them wrong. The role of the audience in the industry was for a long time a small one. This resulted in a lack of diversity and a rather haphazard production policy, not to mention creative dissatisfaction.

The role of the audience was taken for granted – a passive, anonymous, easily-pleased mass. They could be expected, it seems, to sit through tiresome second features, trailers, newsreels, advertisements, and cartoons, before the big picture arrived. Presumably, this was on the assumption that picturegoing was more of a social occasion, a 'night out', than a purposive rendezvous to see such and such a film or star. The cinema was merely the climax of a well-established social routine, and could do little wrong. Whereas legitimate theatre was not at all like this, being expensive and intermittent, it simplified the rituals and preliminaries. This institution of the night out at the pictures was in competition with other social activities, like bowling, drinking, entertaining guests at home, or listening to radio. A principal effect of television was drastically to restructure the audience and force film exhibitors to concentrate more on the film and less on the occasion. As a result the feature has come to be stressed and sold as a product, rather than the studio, or the star, or the local cinema.

The film moguls did not impose this social occasion pattern on their audience; it was something that developed over the years as the cinema became a focus of social activity. In the early days, when films were a fairground side show, the audience was casual, stayed a very short time, and needed to be drawn in by frequent programme changes. The introduction of the feature film and the gradual crystallization of the pattern of changing programmes weekly or every three days, tallied well with the weekend mentality of the emerging 5½ then 5-day week. Thus, throughout England and America a weekly visit to the cinema became a widespread social habit. (See Table 3.)

TABLE 3

The growth of weekly motion picture attendance in the United States (1922–55)

Year	Average weekly cinema attendance	Total number of households	Weekly attendance per household
1922	40,000,000	25,687,000	1·56
1927	57,000,000	28,632,000	1·99
1932	60,000,000	30,439,000	1·97
1937	88,000,000	33,088,000	2·66[1]
1942	85,000,000	36,445,000	2·33
1947	90,000,000	39,107,000	2·30
1952	51,000,000	45,504,000	1·12
1955	46,000,000	47,788,000	0·96

Source: Adapted from De Fleur (1966), p. 40; his sources: US Bureau of Census, *Historical Studies of the United States, Colonial Times to 1957,* Washington 1960, Series H 522, p. 225, Series A 242-244, p. 15.

One remembers exactly the attitude: not so much 'shall we go to the pictures on Saturday?', but 'which film shall we go to on Saturday?' Big studio production was geared to this pattern: there had to be enough films made to give cinemas at least fifty-two changes a year. When the choice element came in, when Saturday night also offered television for nothing, or discothèques, or what not, radical reshaping of the industry was forced upon it. Cinemas closed, the number of films produced shrank, more concentrated attention was

[1] The all-time-high average was in 1930, when audiences were at 90 million and average weekly attendance per household reached 3·00. This fantastic peak (how frequently were some people going that the average was 3?) immediately preceded the Depression – cinema attendance was down 15 million the following year and did not rise to 90 million again until the peak years of 1946, '47, and '48. The other peak years for average weekly attendance were 1929 (2·70), 1936 (2·71) and 1937 (2·66).

given to the production of individual films. Films, rather than slogans like 'Let's go to the pictures', was the way to keep the audiences coming. What really happened was that the audience for the first time was able to speak. What it demanded was a *reason* for going to the pictures, i.e., *pictures* should be differentiated for it. Walt Disney, be it noted, who always tailored his product to well-identified audiences, never failed to grow and show an increase in profits year to year. The big studios writhed and threshed with gimmicks like 3-D and 'Scope' to avoid having to make films for specific audiences. In the end they gave in, but at a cost – dismantling the factory-system, the contract talent, the industry. From then on people came together to do a film, not to serve a business corporation. The film received more care, more individual attention and was more closely designed for a special public: teenagers, families, the middle-aged, etc. The audience has its ultimate weapon – to stay away. But, because television is by no means a perfect substitute for films, there is no question of films disappearing. In many ways they are more prosperous than ever – thanks to their audiences.

The role of audiences in the medium-at-large, then, is somewhat obscure. They are huge, unknown, and inarticulate – they can only vote by staying away; walkouts do not count unless they have a chain-reaction on attendance by means of word-of-mouth reports. Once, film makers were only interested in reaching as many people as possible and thus in the LCD; they saw the alternative as being hyper-selective and directing their films to those who want to see and listen. Rare were those film makers who combined creative freedom and modest aims with considerable popular success. Ingmar Bergman and Akira Kurosawa were culture heroes in their own countries long ago and showed the way. Nothing quite comparable exists in the UK or the USA, but it is coming. Hitchcock is a legend, and he is unpretentious about 'art'. It is smart to be a film maker in trendy London, e.g., Richard Lester, or New York – Arthur Penn (*Bonnie and Clyde*). The audience of this generation will go much further with its film makers than ever before.

VII

Cinemagoing as a Social Institution

1 *The sociology of entertainment*

The question, 'what does an audience get out of going to the cinema?',
is being worked over several times in the course of this volume. At
this stage of the argument the question is not quite that, but rather,
'what does society get out of its members going to the cinema?' Put
in sociological jargon this might read, 'what is the social function of
cinema entertainment?' This question is clearly a subdivision of the
general problem, 'what is the social function of mass entertainment?'
There is literature enough on this, which I do not propose to review in
detail. It will be sufficient to suggest some lines of analysis before we
turn to the subquestion. Doubtless, I am ignoring the possibility of
there being psychological functions of cinema entertainment. This
choice was not forced on me, but arose simply because of the veri-
table barrage of literature there exists on psychological aspects of the
media generally, and the cinema in particular. Indeed, as has been
indicated elsewhere, even studies ostensibly about sociology slide
over into psychology if not social psychology.[1]

But it is primarily as a social institution in a social context that the
cinema interests me. Until we have asked, and tried to answer, some
questions about this aspect of it, I believe we have no framework for
the greater detail of psychological studies.

The entertainment industry *can* be studied as a means of fulfilling
psychological needs. What strikes me as an error is the idea that this
can comprise more than an aspect of it. My concern with it is as a
social institution, only one function of which may be the fulfilling of
these psychological needs. The psychology of the matter need not
concern us here any more than the questions of why people need
religion, or why people need love, bear on the sociological study of
the social institutions of church and marriage. We can take the
psychological aspects as 'the given', and interest ourselves purely in
the social realm. Thus, if and when we ask, 'why do people go to the
cinema?', we shall not construe this as a request for a psychological

---

[1] Examples are the Payne Fund Studies, Thorp (1947), Mayer (1945) and
(1948), Wolfenstein and Leites (1950b), and Wilner (1951).

97

explanation of the desire for entertainment, but, rather, as, 'why do people go to the cinema rather than to any other socia[1] institution of entertainment?' 'What are the social attractions, advantages, and functions of the cinema?' A general sociology of film entertainment barely exists. Such studies as there are[2] concentrate on one or other particular aspect of the subject – audience responses, film workers, economic structure – and sociological study of the social *context* of films and their audience, has often been an incidental to critical or historical studies of the cinema. Film specialists might be unsure of their sociology. This explanation does not account for there being no coverage of cinemagoing in general works of sociology, save as an incidental to passages on the mass media in general – as though they were un-differentiated. In the overall maps of our current social institutions, there is either a blank or a blur here. Only in Dr Powdermaker's book (1950), which, besides being by a cultural anthropologist, is about the film makers, do we find a useful if uneven[3] discussion of some of the issues – in the first chapter and elsewhere.

This poverty of material is my excuse for beginning at the beginning; hoping, thereby, to cover more ground than would be possible by drawing together the fragmentary attempts of others.

Approaching cinemagoing as entertainment, and assuming entertainment to be a non-productive, leisure-time activity, seems to involve one in making some sort of distinction between productive, serious activities, i.e., work, and non-productive, leisure, non-serious, non-important activities, i.e., play. A little reflection on some counter-examples should dispel the illusion that there is a tenable distinction here. A man who loves his job, gets immense and intense pleasure from doing it, and who gives it first call on his time, is working. But then he never plays outside of his work, which he often takes less than seriously, and to which he gives much of what would ordinarily be classed as his leisure time. Similarly, there are activities which are serious without seeming to be, and productive without being pro-ductive of goods or services. Such ritualized activities as spectator sports, debates, amateur theatricals, visits to places of mass enter-tainment like cinemas, theatres, and pubs, are very important to society. Is there not in these an element of need, a desire to participate

[2] Especially the monographs of Mayer (1945, 1948) and Manvell (1946, 1955) in Great Britain, and Jacobs (1939), Rosten (1941) and Powdermaker (1950) in the USA, and the anthologies of Rosenberg and White (1957), Mccann (1964), and White and Averson (1968).

[3] For example, her scary discussion at pp. 327ff. of the incipient totalitarianism of Hollywood is a clear case of over-intellectualized analysis. In no sense do Hollywood films promote or predispose one towards totalitarianism.

and communicate which is as serious a business as the actual actions involved in making a livelihood? We can work frivolously and play seriously; some people's work is also their play, some people's play is almost worked at.

Yet there might seem to be an element of the unnecessary in all these play activities. Society could, perhaps, function without them. As an illustration of this, we may be tempted to instance the 'primitive' societies studied by social anthropologists. Of course, in none of these is the struggle for existence so hard that people must work all of the time. Where life is pretty hard, though, we still find elaborate rituals connected with directly productive activities like planting or fishing or hunting, and with decisive events of the life-cycle like birth, marriage, and death. Children's games and parents playing with children are by no means unknown in these societies too. There is even evidence that where the life is easy, as in places like Tahiti, a greater proportion of time is spent on these play activities. Yet we must not make the mistake of thinking that such playing of games is less important to the peoples concerned than their means of getting a livelihood. In many cases, for example, dances – which we might consider a form of play – are considered quite essential for the general well-being of the people. Moreover, Durkheim has taught us that collective activities have a vital part to play in society, since they are to a certain extent a means of social organization. Participation in them cuts across role patterning and allows people to experience a sense of participation in the wider grouping of the society at large. The primary difference, perhaps, between such mass arts as have been instanced, and 'primitive' dances, rituals, and ceremonies, is that wealth and division of labour have enabled the advanced Western societies to support entire industries and classes of people who provide the ceremonies (entertainment).

This point applies to events like church-going and dances, and even, on a restricted scale, to visits to theatre, concerts, and opera. To be seen going to these activities is in some ways as important socially as is the end product: the performance. Curiously, with the cinema this cannot be so. Cinema is in a real sense a mass art, not only in that it appeals to the mass audience, but also in that the individual is lost in the darkness of the continuous performance. He is unaware of who surrounds him, has no social intercourse during the film, and can slip out of the side exit to isolation very easily. However, some element of socializing is present in cinemagoing. It is not necessarily a solitary activity. Families will go, or schools, or groups of friends, or lovers; the cinema is an activity all these groups of people like to do together. Then there is, precisely because of the universal popularity of the cinema, the social activity of discussing and commenting on the film, its stars, etc. Unless one has seen it this can be quite difficult, and this is another way in which cinema-going is involved with an element of socializing.

The degree of collective participation of an audience during a cinema show is virtually zero (although collective moods, like a rollicking one, will often make all the difference to one's enjoyment of comedies, for example, as will a send-up mood to one's enjoyment of something serious – I will cite my own rather lonely and solitary pleasure at Jerry Lewis films in Hong Kong among a stony and uncomprehending audience; and two viewings of *Psycho*, one in a packed, eager, and terrified cinema, a second in a determinedly unimpressed, loudly commenting and rude-noise-making house). This contrasts with primitive society where almost all collective ceremonial activities involve active participation, and this does a lot to create the right mood. In this respect, magazines and books, radio and television have parallels and differences with the cinema. They are even more isolated social activities, but they too create an invisible community grouping: those who have experienced and share exposure to the same content. Aside from these examples, most other leisure activities are more or less social. But how social? It is a common complaint heard from older people that leisure activities in their days were more creative and participatory than they are now in a world of canned entertainment. Not so long ago, most entertainment was a family activity taking place in the family home and involving only the family circle. Moreover, it consisted of games, or songs, or walking, or reading aloud or other pastimes in which there was much participation by everyone concerned.

2 The cinema as entertainment

Now it seems we have come to an age of passive, solitary entertainment. Or have we?

The cinema is not the first institution of entertainment which involved a large number of seemingly passive spectators. Cinema and television are outgrowths of the theatre arts, the history of which, and the roots of which, in religious ritual both in Greece and in Medieval Christendom, are well known. Also, cinema is not the first mass or popular art. We know that both the Greek and Elizabethan theatres were popular theatres, not the province of the privileged few. What the cinema is is the first mass-communications medium to yield an entertainment industry of its own. In that respect it antedates the other two mass-media, radio and television, which came later, and which, curiously enough, pull in a different direction from the cinema – if sociologically regarded. For, whereas the cinema took people out of their houses and into huge theatres or, in other words, it accentuated the effect of theatre and music hall, radio and television are, like books, disseminated media which penetrate the home. Since, in modern society, the home is the family centre, and since families are rarely together except at meal times and times of leisure, the effect of radio and television is to keep the family together in the house where they can interact.

When the cinema was invented, at the end of the nineteenth century, theatre and opera were socially specialized or socially exclusive media. Price and a certain esotericism denied them to some classes. The popular art of the time was the music hall (or 'vaudeville') and close on its heels, melodrama. Soon after the cinema developed to its full strength in the First World War, its competition killed vaudeville in the United States as it was later, after the Second World War, to decimate the music hall in the United Kingdom. The same pattern was not repeated with television. True, the cinema was forced to contract severely in the United States and the United Kingdom but, as might have been foreseen, television is not a perfect substitute for the cinema, and so at a new and lower level, stability returned to the cinema. Indeed, as I write (1968), films are fewer but as profitable as ever.

I believe that we can only properly understand these effects from a sociological point of view. In so far as the cinema is a better substitute for the theatre arts, it has replaced them. Instead of knockabout comedians touring music halls they have preferred to stay in one place and film themselves. In this way more people saw their work, paid less money to do so, and the artists themselves received higher incomes. When sound came and *all* vaudeville acts could be put on film, the music hall was doomed, only to revive a little under the stimulus of television and the night club where programme formats involving discontinuous 'acts' have become very popular. But why did the theatre and opera not suffer a similar fate to vaudeville? The blunt answer is that they are minority and specialized arts: they do not provide the sort of things the cinema provides and, especially, they have a different audience to that which goes to the cinema.[4]

To the extent that radio and television are substitutes for the cinema, they replaced it (screen size and picture quality are the principal differences). We know now, in fact, that the cinema has reached a new plateau – cinema attendances have stabilized, television set sales have also stabilized. The old rivals, which once saw themselves competing bitterly for the same audience, have come in

[4] Herbert Gans' ideas (1959) on the plurality of audiences (or subcultures) in our pluralist society are important here.

101

the end to live together in amicable symbiosis. The film companies have yielded their libraries of past film treasures for television showing, and have ceased to decline to show a film previously pioneered on television. Television has come to rely on film talent, technique, and personnel simply to aid it to prefilm enough material to keep the screens from going blank. This has a lot to do with the realization that the entertainment audience is bigger and more diverse than at first sight, and that a single product can be marketed several ways without losing any of its money-making potential from one exposure to the other. But there is one respect in which these two are not substitutes for each other, and that is socially. *They are totally different social activities.* This reinforces the symbiosis, because these different social activities are complementary. Whereas the cinema performance is a set occasion, it has a tension-building ritual associated with it that television, stuck in the informality of the home, available at the touch of a switch, cannot reproduce. For connected reasons, television can rarely reproduce the grandeur of the screen: the size of its image and the lack of audience tension is responsible for this. Moreover, the stars, a crucial factor in the sociological significance of the cinema, are still much bigger and better defined on the film screen. Film stars, unlike television stars, are not confined to one role in a series, plus guest appearances, or to the modest means of hasty television production. In fact, those television stars who begin to become really well-known usually make the effort to graduate to films.

These distinctions between the great mass media, run counter to much of the literature by sociologists analysing them. Taking a generally critical standpoint, sociologists are inclined to lump the media together and declare that they perform similar social functions. Herbert Gans has labelled the two most popular theories 'The Hypodermic Theory' and 'The Selective Perception Theory'. The Hypodermic Theory views mass culture as injections of propaganda or socialization into a totally passive, anaesthetized audience. Indeed, it is sometimes claimed that the *function* of the media is to anaesthetize the audience; the present-day equivalent to Marx's 'opiate of the masses'. Man in mass society is alienated from his work, which has become mechanical drudgery, his society is atomized by the breakdown of social and kin ties because of urbanization, and the media have been a god-send to keep the social cement intact. They allow man to experience vicariously, and encourage the growth of 'substitute living'.

The Selective Perception Theory argues that, roughly speaking, people select out from what they see in a way controlled by their own preconceptions, prejudices, pre-formed opinions, etc. What we see, as philosophers and psychologists have long agreed, is a strong function of the mental set which we impose on the phenomena. Consequently, the mass media perform the social function of reinforcing people's prejudices and blind spots, rather than enlightening and correcting them.

Both theories are highly critical of the mass media: one for providing vicarious escape from real living – although Leavis, oddly as always, sees salvation in literary criticism – the other for making a bad situation worse. Otherwise the theories have nothing in common, indeed they are contradictory. The Hypodermic Theory is optimistic: inject the right ideas, immunize people to propaganda and anaesthetization, and things will look up. The Selective Perception Theory is deeply pessimistic, leaving us no hope for the triumph of truth. The Hypodermic Theory sees the media as manipulative propaganda; the Selective Perception Theory sees the media as propagandistically ineffective. The Hypodermic Theory allows that the media are omnipotent, the audience passive; the Selective Perception Theory allows that the media are impotent, the audience all-powerful. The one theory demands manipulators, or a manipulative 'system' (the bogey-word of the age); the other imagines film makers as supine before the audience: to be successful they must provide the audience with what it wants – otherwise they might move from selective perception to selective attendance.

However, in recent years a number of authors have put forward theories which give us an equally coherent vision of the media, but which deny omnipotence or impotence to the cinema. These theories are to be found in the work of Haley (1952), Brodbeck (1955), Fearing (1962), Gans (1959, etc.) and Roberts (1959, 1962, 1963). Roughly, one might say the connection is between games, learning theory, and socialization. Haley, in an early piece, attacked the idea of films as escape and suggested they were rather a way of making the world bearable, or, more forcefully, of helping people cope with their world. In an increasingly complicated environment, films help social organization by reducing that complexity to order, as once did religion. This is not a theory to apply to individual films, be it noted, although I shall argue later that single films can be regarded as resembling a meditation on some problem or situation; rather is it a theory of a general character. Generally speaking, what the shaping of experience into orderly dramatic form does for its audience is to pattern and control experience, and to teach ways of patterning and controlling. This is similar to the way a newspaper reporter, to make his research digestible, shapes it into a 'story'.

The anthropologist, Roberts, has developed a general theory of children's game-playing as learning techniques of power-play, and shows how game-playing skill correlates with many other socially advantageous characteristics. Game-playing, for Roberts, and especially competitive games of skill, perform important functions in children's socializing. This can be extended to adults watching competitive sport or even driving automobiles (which is a form of self-testing for some people). However, Roberts maintains that competitive games are to be distinguished from 'amusements' – these do not involve organized play, competition, two or more sides, criteria for determining the winner, and agreed upon rules. Games model competitive behaviour occurring in other settings. But the notion of media of expression modelling the so-called real world, is a suggestive one which we will take up in Part Three. For the moment we consider that cinemagoing is part of play – but not a game. Riesman (1955), confessing how little we know of play, suggests:

> Play, far from having to be the residue sphere left over from work-time and work-feeling, can increasingly become the sphere for the development of skill and competence in the art of living. Play may prove to be the sphere in which there is still some room left for the would-be autonomous man to reclaim his individual character from the pervasive demands of his social character. (p. 315.)

Riesman's thesis is directly applicable to such a phenomenon as the upsurge of teenage pop-music groups and indeed teenage play-culture generally. It is more difficult to apply to cinemagoing, which is so subtle it seems passive. Film-watching play is an important way of enriching experience and sharing experience. Talking together about what has been seen at the pictures is a significant social and socializing transaction in our society.

With the help of the exciting work of Gans all this can be brought together. He argues that audience self-selection is not indiscriminate, but tends to form along lines he labels 'subcultures' of our society. These are distinct groups with a certain 'brow level', and associated educational, social, and economic attributes. He points out that there is a high culture dominating much of the literary and academic worlds which effortlessly assumes its own exclusive possession of universally applicable standards of taste and discrimination, and the lowliness of all deviations from these exacting standards. The media are sometimes taken as inherently uncultivated, and, certainly, discriminations are not allowed to be made within the soap opera, the pop song, the musical comedy *genres*. Beneath this high culture, Gans detects various subcultures, or taste agglomerations, which, allowing for some cultural items being appreciated at several different levels, can be labelled upper-middlebrow, lower-middlebrow, and lowbrow. Each 'brow' is a potential audience, with its own notions of what is good and bad in the *genres* it favours, with its own ways of using entertainment.

Once upon a time, good westerns, good detective films, good women's pictures, were trimmed to reach the widest possible audience – a complete misconception because the audience was plural and should have been selectively sold to. Nowadays, there is some experiment – teenage films, camp-spy films are clearly selectively directed. Walt Disney has been Hollywood's most consistently successful showman – perhaps because he knew what audience and subculture he was aiming at.[5] I would add to Gans, and say that the Disney case allows one to argue that fine achievements in a *genre* with an association with a specific subculture, on account of that excellence, may cross over and be acceptable to other subcultures. This applies to cultures as well as subcultures: it is often said that the best works of art in a tradition are those most universal, most easily appreciated by another culture. What is true of cultures can be true of subcultures. One day we shall perhaps have a universally acclaimed masterpiece of skin-flick,[6] as we have masterpieces of the western, the cartoon, the musical, the who-dun-it, the soap opera.

Gans' theory has the sensible consequence of postulating an interaction and feedback between the audience and the film maker which hardly arises with hypodermics or selective perception. Gans shows (1957) that the film maker is a member of the wider society, a newspaper and book reader, a consumer, a person with values, education, and peers. In trying to communicate, he consciously or unconsciously has an idea of who he is trying to get through to. Apart from box-office, however, he has little useable information on whether he *is* getting across. Gans echoes Fenin's plea (1955) that even if films are a product, there should be conscious market research and product development. Even though the acute sellers' market of the thirties and forties has gone, that market research has not materialized. Must one perhaps salute the skill of Hollywood's entrepreneurs, or is their continued prosperity just luck?

[5] In Houlton (1966), there is a table comparing the percentage change in gross income 1955–65 of the Hollywood big eight (Disney, United Artists, Universal, Columbia, Fox, Warners, Paramount and MGM). Disney showed a 345% growth, only UA came anywhere near with a 257% growth.

[6] Cp. Chappell's 'Twenty-six Propositions About Skin Flicks' in Robinson (1967).

VIII

The Screen Audiences

1 The emergence of audience subcultures

Who does go to the cinema and why? The question is not now difficult to answer although the answers are hard to document. Before the advent of television everyone went except the very old, the very young, or the nonconformists. They went because they enjoyed films; because they wanted to see the stars; because they liked to get out of their homes, and perhaps eat out too. They did this rather than read books or listen to the radio because they liked variety, because films were a social activity providing a quite different kind of stimulus and enjoyment to radio and reading. As with bowling alleys, there was an element of meeting people in the foyer before, in the interval, and afterwards (especially in small towns), an element therefore of showing off, and there was something to talk about subsequently at home, office, school and on dates. In an age of literacy and relative wealth, there is little in the claim that people went to the cinema because there was nothing else to do. Yet it could be said that since films provided – in a double feature programme – up to three hours plus of entertainment for 75c in the USA, or one or two shillings in the UK they were value for money.

This then was the picture once upon a time. Up to the television boom beginning around 1949–50. Since then it is clear that audiences have changed drastically both in size and in composition. For one thing, there are less films being made to see, for another there are less places to see them, and for a third more has to be paid to get in. However, films now appear to last longer, and to be in all senses bigger. Have the reasons for going changed?

It is generally agreed that youngsters now constitute a much bigger percentage of the audience than previously. Perhaps more significant, they are the basic *regular* cinemagoers. Adults and families do go to the cinema, but no longer once or twice a week; they are attracted out for the special film. By 'the special film' I mean the film which they have been sold on. I discuss the mechanics of this process in Part Four. It suffices here to say that my recollection is that in the forties we used on Saturday nights to say: 'shall we go to the Odeon, the Granada, or the Plaza?' Nowadays, we will only stir from our books or our tellies if we have made a mental note: e.g., 'I want to see *Lawrence of Arabia* before it comes off'. Films need not be big for people to want to see them; and hard-selling will not do either. The first James Bond film was by no means particularly costly; on the other hand, all the hard-sell in the world didn't make *Cleopatra* a bonanza. Exactly what makes people go to films, I will take up in Part Four, but I want to mention the phenomenal success of Alfred Hitchcock and Walt Disney at this point. One might say that these two are film makers with a definite image, who can be relied on to produce a certain kind of product. Hitchcock will produce the offbeat suspense film or thriller; Disney will produce films suitable for the family. People know and trust these names. When a Disney product is in town, people who have been saying they must take the kids out for a treat at the pictures will head that way. When a Hitchcock turns up people who saw a previous film of his will note that they want to see it before it comes off.

My reading of the changes in the audience under the impact of television can be put in Gansian terms: there is increasingly greater articulation of the subcultures in the audience competition situation. In converting from being producers of a sample product in a sellers' market, to producers of something more marginal in a competitive market, film makers have groped towards those things that make television an imperfect substitute for films. At first they tried all sorts of gimmickry, but that was to be expected in such a frenetic industry. Slowly, however, a formula for success involving the selling of each film as a package, rather than a whole studio output as a package, has emerged. What this signifies is that each package is looked at separately. Has it an audience? The cycle of teenage films and of horror films certainly was directed specifically at sections of the youth subculture. The spy-cycle began because the Bond films discovered there was an audience for this new *genre*: an audience a good deal more sophisticated and self-congratulating than had ever been thought of before. And the follow-throughs on these cycles have developed, as teenage films became self-parodies, ever more bizarre; spy-camp, smart violence, led to a climate in which masterpieces like *Bonnie and Clyde* and *Point Blank* could be made and be very successful. The old idea when a film was successful, was simply to re-make it with slight variations until diminishing returns set in.

Many changes can be explained in this Gansian way. The new importance of foreign films in the English-speaking market has to do with it now being economically worthwhile to articulate the audience for cultural or naughty (different audiences, with overlap) foreign films. The Italian director Antonioni, with *Blow-Up*, showed that there was a world-wide audience fascinated by swinging Britain and there has resulted a string of films about English sex mores (real and imaginary). Remembering the days when Britis'. film makers squirmed as American audiences called for the subtitling of British films, it was a cheering experience to sit recently among an American audience lapping up the thick prole accents and slang of *Here we go Round the Mulberry Bush* – on Wilshire Boulevard in Hollywood, yet!

In that filmgoing has become selective, so has film making, and the result is that a film is capable of doing just as well or better at the box-office with its select audience as it ever did with its routinized audience.

2 *Facts and figures*

If one expects the cinema audience to be a well researched one, disappointment is in the offing. Hollywood and Wardour Street seem extraordinarily shy about probing their market. Again, I attribute this to the complacency engendered by a long period of the sellers' market. Moreover, those studies which do exist are fairly rudimentary. For example, only two of them touch the question as to whether cinemagoers are solitary, and in what percentage.[1] (Less than 20% of cinemagoers go alone – see Table 4.) This is hard to understand. Another thing, most of the surveys have been done by interviewing people outside the cinema before or after a performance. Thus, when figures are compiled about the frequency of cinemagoing, they apply to that audience, not to the population as a whole. We have few, it any, figures on the population as a whole.

What we do have tells us a few interesting things. First of all on the audience's decision to take in a film. The three tables 5, 6, and 7, suggest that the film audience is well-informed since some 71% of them declare they had either a very good idea or a fairly good idea of the type of film they were going to see before they went; 75% of them indicate that it was the stars, the type of story, or word-of-mouth recommendation that interested them. And, most interesting of all, 83% thought they had obtained value for money, 80% found the film as good as, or better than, expected. Moreover, there is not that much fluctuation in the percentages of those claiming they knew what to expect, either over the age ranges or the frequency of visits ranges, with an odd exception or so, except for the crucial 13% of

---

[1] Handel (1950) who cites a study showing that some 22% of the audience is solitary. This is by calculation from his figures showing 86% of women and 70% of men were accompanied by another person the last time they went to the cinema (pp. 113–15). See also Federation of British Film Makers (1963) table 1.6.

TABLE 4

All cinemagoers: party in which respondent went on last occasion analysed by frequency of going to the cinema within age:

| | 16–24 | | | 25–34 | | 35–44 | |
	Once a week %	Once a month %	Less often %	Once a month %	Less often %	All goers %	Total all goers %
Alone	9	8	11	27	14	19	16
With spouse	8	18	39	39	43	36	30
With one of opposite sex	47	35	20	12	7	5	19
With one of same sex	15	19	12	15	7	9	12
With more than one of same sex	10	6	5	1	1	2	4
With mixed party	10	13	18	3	12	6	9
With children (with or without other adults)	1	1	5	2	16	23	10
n(100%)=	91	101	74	114	99	181	660

Source: Federation of British Film Makers (1963) table 1.6.

TABLE 5

All cinemagoers: whether they had a good idea of type of last film before seeing it: analysed by frequency of cinemagoing within age:

| | 16–24 | | | 25–34 | | 35–44 | |
	Once a week %	Once a month %	Less often %	Once a month %	Less often %	All goers %	Total all goers %
A very good idea	32	23	23	34	38	29	30
A fairly good idea	32	48	42	43	32	42	41
Not much idea	19	19	22	13	19	16	17
No idea	13	8	8	7	7	7	8
Don't know	4	2	5	3	4	6	4
n(100%)=	91	101	74	114	99	181	660

Source: Federation of British Film Makers (1963) table 2.9.

TABLE 6
*All cinemagoers: what it was about the last film seen that made them
interested before they went:*

Total %

The stars in it	32
The type of story	30
'Heard it was good'	13
The music	5
The fact that it was suitable for children	4
The photography	2
The acting	1
The title	1
The director, producer or author	1
Because it was British	1
$n(100\%)=$	660

Source: Federation of British Film Makers (1963)
table 2.8a.

TABLE 7
*Cinemagoers: two measures of satisfaction with the last visit, analysed
by whether the type of film seen had been correctly assessed beforehand
or not:*

	The type of film expected %	Not the type of film expected %	Total %
Satisfaction with film:			
1. Very good value for money	25	18	24
Good value for money	59	47	57
Not particularly good value	12	23	14
Poor value	2	8	3
Don't know	2	4	2
$n(100\%)=$	337	71	429[1]
(cinemagoers paying on last visit)			
2. Better than expected	25	28	26
As good as expected	61	23	54
Not as good as expected	13	47	18
Don't know	1	2	2
$n(100\%)=$	526	106	660[1]
(all cinemagoers)			

Source: Federation of British Film Makers (1963) table 5.6.

[1] The totals include those who said 'don't know' to the question of the sort of film.

once-a-week goers, aged sixteen to twenty-four, who had no idea what they were going to see.

Four sets of figures for frequency of cinemagoing have come into my hands. Table 8, published in 1947, and therefore obviously based

TABLE 8
Frequency of cinemagoing 1947 (USA)

1 or more a week	37%
1–3 a month	27%
Few times a year or hardly ever	25%
Never	11%

Source: P. F. Lazarsfeld, 'Audience Research in the Movie Field', *Annals of the American Academy of Political and Social Science*, November 1947.

on a survey long before the television boom of 1949 onwards, indicates that 37% of cinemagoers went once or more a week.

Table 9, researched just as television was getting under way, shows

TABLE 9
Frequency of cinemagoing 1950 (USA)

Times per month

0	22·6%
1–2	19·3%
3–5	30·7%
6–9	17·7%
10 plus	9·7%

Source: Hollywood Looks at its Audience, Leo A. Handel, Urbana 1950.

58·1% going once or more a week. Table 10, which is from the war period, gives much lower values, 17·50% once or more per week (adding the last two figures). This latter table, however, is different from the other two. It was a survey of the radio audience, and questions about film going were introduced for purposes of comparison. In Table 11, we have another very different figure, one for the British cinema audience in 1960, and in that the figures for once or more per week are 63%. How to explain this discrepancy? How is it

TABLE 10

Frequency of cinemagoing 1942 (USA)

Times per month	Men %	Women %	All %
0	49·7	49·2	49·45
1	15·5	16·8	16·15
2–3	16·6	17·2	16·9
3–4	11·1	11·4	11·25
5 plus	7·1	5·4	6·25

Source: The Iowa study reported in Handel, and my own calculations on final column. Iowa Study equals F. L. Whan and H. B. Summers, *The 1942 Iowa Radio Audience Survey*, Des Moines 1942. See Handel, p. 100: 'Whan reported that no significant differences were found between the attendance of people living in cities, in villages and on farms. All attended with the same degree of frequency.' The reverse is reported for the UK in Box (1943).

TABLE 11

Frequency of cinemagoing 1961 (UK)

Frequency per week

2 plus	30%
1	33%
1 fortnight	11%
1 month	11%
1 3 months	7%
less	7%

Source: The Cinema Audience, a National Survey, Screen Advertising Assn., London 1961.

that, when cinemas have been closing and audience numbers dropping, we find in the British figures a large percentage of people still going frequently to the cinema? The obvious answer is, of course, that British and American cinemagoing patterns are different. If they are not different, though, the table suggests a fall in numbers has been offset against a rise in frequency by those who do go to the cinema. This would appear implausible. Why should the intensity of visits increase? An explanation I am shy of, is the sheer inaccuracy of the figures and the respondents. I know from my own work on a survey of cinemagoing I did at school as a sixth-former learning statistics, that audience surveys are both hard to construct and extremely unreliable. It is all too easy to invalidate results simply by doubling up the simple question 'How many times, on average, do you go to the cinema in a week?', say, and, 'When were you last at the cinema and what did you see?' But if nearly all the informants contradict themselves on this, what can one do?

Although the figures are difficult to accept, one indication they do give is that while television has made a big change, there still exists a hard core of cinemagoers who attend regularly and frequently in a definite pattern. Woefully, what these figures do not do is to compare attendances at different films. One would like to know how many one-time people there were in the huge audiences for *The Bridge on the River Kwai, The Sound of Music*, or the James Bond films. These have been enormous, popular successes, and my own guess is that this was because they drew in filmgoers who are very choosy, normally reluctant to leave their television sets, and who probably go to the cinema only a handful of times a year. Now this sort of audience, if it exists, is more like the audience for the theatre in London, it is a special occasion audience. It will almost certainly be a married and settled audience, with money, and prepared to treat the whole business as a real night out. If this new pattern exists, it would suggest many changes might be made in film exhibiting policy. For example, that weekly changes might be jettisoned for such films, that prices might be high, but that cinemas should be lavish, like theatres, perhaps with bars, since so many of these films have intervals, etc.

For the hard core, who I would guess to be mainly the young and unmarried who want to escape home and thus television, the ordinary 'local' cinema, with frequent programme changes is just right, so long as prices are kept down. Although these days the early close-down of cinemas in the United States and the United Kingdom is well out of date. Confirmation that the hard core is young, comes from the British figures in Tables 12 and 13. We will concentrate on 13 because it shows greater detail. The ages 16–24 account for 39% of the audience, the ages 12–24 for 48% of the audience, and the ages 12–29 accounted for 60% of the audience. The age group 30–64 accounted for 34% of the audience. 60% of the audience, then, lay in the 17 years between 12 and 29, only 34% lay in the 34 years between 30 and 64. There is an odd drop in the audience's otherwise steady decline with age between the years 30–34: my own guess would be that these are the ages when people are coping with young children and setting up their home, etc. Anyway, this remarkable youthfulness of the audience must also have implications for the film

TABLE 12

Profiles of cinemagoers (under 45):

		Once a week %	Once a month %	At least once a month %	Less often %	Total all cinema-goers %
AGE						
	16–24	54	47	50	27	40
	25–34	25	33	30	36	33
	35–44	21	20	20	37	27
MALE						
	Married	20	23	21	32	26
	Unmarried	40	27	33	15	25
FEMALE						
	Married	20	30	26	42	33
	Unmarried	20	20	20	11	16
CLASS						
	AB	9	17	14	21	17
	C1	28	33	31	25	28
	C2	43	37	39	38	39
	DE	20	13	16	16	16
Nights out in a fortnight:						
4 nights or less		20	69	33	60	44
5 nights or more		80	31	67	40	56
$n(100\%)=$		169	216	385	275	660

Source: Federation of British Film Makers (1963) table 6.3c.

TABLE 13

Composition of UK audience, 1960

8–11	2%		
12–15	9%		
16–20	24%	} 39%	} 48%
21–24	15%		
25–29	12%		
30–34	9%		
35–44	13%		
45–64	12%		
65 plus	4%		

Source: The Cinema Audience, A National Survey, Screen Advertising Assn., London 1961.

TABLE 14
Sample estimates of frequency of adult cinemagoing, by social class (UK)

Cinema visits per head of adult population per week

| Class[1] | Hulton survey | | | | |
	1950	1952	1953	1954	1955[2]
AB	0·42	0·33	0·28	0·23	0·25
C	0·49	0·39	0·34	0·31	0·37
DE	0·56	0·55	0·50	0·47	0·54

| | IPA survey | | | | | | |
| | 1956–57 | | | 1959–60 | | | |
Class	Regu-larly[3] %	Occasion-ally[3] %	Never[3] %	Regu-larly[3] %	Occasion-ally[3] %	Infre-quently[3] %	Never[3] %
AB	13	54	33	7	12	39	42
C1	20	46	34	10	13	32	45
C2	29	36	35	14	10	26	50
DE	28	31	41	16	7	19	58

Source: Spraos (1962), p. 30; his sources are the Hulton Readership Survey and the IPA National Readership Survey.

makers. In both Britain and America, the fifties and sixties have seen many more films tailored for the kids' market: especially the various high school films, pop singer films, and beach and surfing films. This was to be expected if only because the cinema faces competition on the teenage front too. Perhaps its biggest rival is the whole complex of what I can only describe as the pop song subculture. The intensity and involvement of the young in listening to records, going to

[1] 'In the Hulton classification, AB stands roughly for the upper and upper middle class, C for the lower middle, and DE for the working class and the poor (e.g., pensioners) of whatever background. The IPA classification is broadly analogous except that the skilled manual workers, who are included under DE in Hulton, are classified separately under C2.'

[2] 'Not comparable with earlier years because subjected to adjustment to compensate for systematic underestimate of true cinemagoing frequency, which becomes apparent in all Hulton Surveys when checked by Board of Trade figures.'

[3] ' "Regularly" means once a week or more. "Occasionally" ranges from less than once a week to once a month. "Infrequently" means less than once a month. Where "infrequently" is not given as a separate heading, the definition of "occasionally" is extended to include it.'

discothèques and dance halls to hear the groups, and tinkering at being groups themselves is not to be underrated.

The figures on frequency of cinemagoing by social class (Table 14) are intriguing. From 1950 through 1955, working class cinemagoing hardly declines at all. However, 1955 is a key year in Britain since commercial television arrived then and began to eat at working class habits. At that time, it would have been fair to describe the BBC as determinedly middle class in outlook and appeal. This is only slightly less so now. In 1956–7 and 1959–60, we notice sharp drops in the DE category in all frequencies: only the 'nevers' go up. In the other classes, regular cinemagoing figures are halved between 1956–7 and 1959–60, 'occasionally-infrequently' figures stay the same, and 'never' shows significant gains. This tale is repeated in the figures for admissions in Table15. Attendance had been slipping since the war,

TABLE 15

Cinema admissions and net box-office takings (UK)

	Admissions (millions)	Net takings (millions)
1945	1,585	73
1947	1,462	68
1949	1,430	67
1951	1,365	71
1953	1,285	72
1955	1,182	73
1957	915	65
1959	581	59
1961	449	60
1963	357	55
1965	327	62
1967	273[1]	59[1]

Source: Kelly (1966), p. 11, adapted from Board of Trade Statistics. Last two entries taken from same source.

but between 1955 and 1959, there is the quite startling drop of more than 50%. The explanation for the failure of the industry to collapse is in the net takings column. One way or another, takings have been sustained, partly because of the abolition of entertainment tax; mainly by boosting admission prices. Higher admission prices do

[1] Estimated.

116

not drive people away, as the jam-packed houses for certain films adequately indicates. The shrinkage and increased selectivity of the audience makes it quite understandable that when they are prepared to go to see a film of their choice, the difference of a few shillings in price is of no consequence. The first-run theatres of large cities quite often trail long queues, despite prices several times those of local cinemas and grind-houses.

My own expectations are that the drop in cinema audience figures will slow down and plane off as these two groups, the young, and the occasional, cinemagoers become steady and consolidated (see Table 16). The days when the cinema was among America's top half-dozen

TABLE 16

Proportion of adults who went to the cinema at least once a week, 1945, 1947, 1957, by age:

| | Cinema attendance | | |
| | 1945 | 1947 | 1957 |
Age	%	%	%
21–29	48	39	—
20–29	—	—	50
30–39	28	25	29
40–49	27	21	22
50 and older	13	23	8

Source: Meyersohn (1961), p. 259.

industries are long gone. But that it will fade out, or cease to make money, or anything of that kind, is inconceivable. As the cinema develops and matures, and becomes technically still more refined, and, especially as more and more people become 'literate' in its grammar and syntax, it can be expected to grow a little.

Our society is encouraging filmgoing in the increasing number of schools and universities where film is used and studied (especially in America), as evidenced by the phenomenal increase in the number of books on and about the cinema published. I can well remember the mid-fifties when cinema books were rare and quickly remaindered. Now the outflow is so fast it is hard to keep up, a great many are excellent, and they are bought and read avidly by young people.

In due course, it might be reasonable to expect that technical developments will allow the local cinema to draw on a central bank of films through television links, in colour and of high quality, which cannot be reproduced in the home. This will sustain the regular audience.

Part Three

THE SOCIOLOGY OF
AN EXPERIENCE:
WHO SEES FILMS AND WHY?

The problems in this part are: How much sociological information does one absorb from viewing and experiencing films, and does this affect one? How true is this film sociology and does it matter if it is not? My answers are that one absorbs a great deal of sociological information, but that it affects one far less than alarmist critics of the media like to imagine; similarly, the sociology is far more true and critical of the society it portrays than is allowed by the media's detractors.

IX

The Role of Experience in the Medium-at-Large

1 Films as an influence

In previous chapters, we have touched upon questions concerning whether or not the audience affects the film as product, and whether the film as product affects the audience as consumers. We have followed Gans (1957) in arguing that the audience affects the product only through the mediation of the image of the audience held by those shaping the film. Film makers, in this regard, differ little from 'opinion leaders' in the 'two-step flow' of communications (Katz, Lazarsfeld 1955): communication and feedback are always mediated. This leads us to reject the Hypodermic and Selective Perception theories of film effects. It is time for a further confrontation with the widespread, commonsense theory that films do influence their audience, whether that influence is mediated or not, and do so quite radically (see Motion Pictures Producers and Distributors of America, 1932). Certainly, all over the world, behaviour is observed which would appear to have been learned from the cinema or from television: from children's games to the way people perform their social roles. Particularly noticeable is the influence of American material. This behaviour is imitative, and I think there need be little dispute that on that level there is *some* influence. However, the stronger hypothesis, that children and young people, being highly impressionable, are tempted to act out violent and sexual scenes from films is a different matter. On the whole, the Payne Fund Studies (1933–5) revealed nothing alarming. Himmelweit, Oppenheim and Vince (1958) explored this hypothesis with respect to television and could find no evidence whatsoever to support it; Schramm, Lyle and Parker (1961) also found little. The conclusions of these studies were so counter-intuitive that they were swept aside, and proponents of the hypothesis (like procensorship politicians) don't even do them the courtesy of rebutting their study (see United States, 1956). Personally, I am of the opinion that since it is absurd to blame e.g., Dostoievsky for the crimes of those who were impressed by one of his characters, so it is to blame the cinema for the juvenile delinquent who claims he did it because he saw it in the movies. It is impossible to establish cause-effect relationships in these matters: reading *Karamazov* did not make *me* commit crimes. The reader who is deeply impressed and acts it out may already be predisposed to be impressed, and there is every reason to suppose that if censorship stopped one of his sources, he would find another. Closing off all the sources of shock and stimulation is virtually impossible. Moreover, the whole theory is old fashioned, rather resembling that of traumatic shock. Yet we now know very well that psychological illnesses are not normally attributable to shock, and that they take their own courses of development just as often as they are pushed along by outside events. Old-fashioned, not to say crude, ideas on this subject are by no means unknown. The work of Bandura (1963), Berkowitz (1963b, 1964, 1966), Lovaas (1961), and their co-workers, strikes this particular layman as coming into that category. Their idea has been to expose adults and children to frustrating or aggression-arousing situations, then expose them to 'aggressive' films and note how their aggression ratings went up. The crudities are in the over-simplification of the equation: violence = aggression; the idea that aggression exists in films and has effects independent of the context and the social surroundings of viewing (film as hypodermic again), and so on. Klapper delivers a few broadsides of his own in the panel discussion in Larsen (1968).

Another argument for concern over media effects is that of *sustained* propaganda for violence. Film after film, from cartoons, and feature films, to documentaries and newsreels of war and riot, exposes us to a steady level of violence. Does this brutalize? Does it contain the danger of imitation? There is as yet no 'hard' evidence that it does. Therefore, those inclined to presume it does will go on thinking that; and those of us inclined to think it doesn't will go on thinking that as well. With a slightly shamefaced attitude, I will suggest an *ad hominem* argument for my side. The strength of my case is related to the fact that I am an avid devotee of the media, and have been exposed to them, indeed have exposed myself to them, uninterruptedly since childhood. This connects up with my remarks in the preface: a great many bewailers of the media are talking in the abstract about what they might do to others. I am arguing from a standpoint of what they have not done to me, and from my non-atypicality, to pooh-poohing what they might do to others. This seems to me a rational *ad hominem* argument: the superficiality and confusions of the media pessimists may have a lot to do with their not themselves being much exposed. However, just as I would admit this genetic explanation of their views does not speak to the truth of those views, so they could say: you must also admit that the fact that

122

you seem not to have been brutalized or inclined to imitate screen violence, does not allow a valid interference to the conclusion that no-one else will be. True enough, and so perhaps the balance of the argument is even. Let us leave the whole question of brutalization and imitation, which are low-level mechanisms through which the film experience can make its influence felt. Let us now consider some other forms influence could take. Film experience also provides: information; social, moral and political argument; distraction; and catharsis That films inform is too obvious to discuss. If they distract too, in the sense that I feel refreshed and happy after seeing a good film, and I feel better disposed towards the world, and am in a better frame of mind to do my work, then films have a very definite effect on me and my surroundings which has nothing to do with imitation. Now what about argument? The newspaper tradition of the exposé, has several times been carried over into the films. A series of films made by Warner Brothers in the thirties peddled the idea that delinquency and gangsterism had social (as well as psychological) roots. Lynch law and conditions in prison were exposed and strongly criticized. Continuing this tradition, Stanley Kramer filmed, in 1960, the Scopes monkey trial case and preached tolerance of opposing points of view. The film as a whole (*Inherit the Wind*) was not good, but the performances (Spencer Tracy and Frederick March) and the message were. Corruption, and its opposite, integrity, have been the centre of many gangster films and of the Elliot Ness television series (*The Untouchables*). Many films on lynching, on social and political intimidation, have discussed the moral cowardice of ordinary people, and the necessity of joint action if they are to overcome their enemies. The highly successful western, *High Noon*, argued that a man should have nothing but contempt for people who wouldn't stand by the representatives of law and order. In a much profounder examination of the same issues, the Japanese genius Akira Kurosawa puts over the idea in *Seven Samurai* that, even given leadership and training, simple people still need a remarkable degree of strength and tenacity if they are to defend themselves against determined enemies. As well as exposing the seamier sides of life, films occasionally enter a living debate of the day. In Britain the film *Chance of a Lifetime* took up the problems of worker control in industry; *The Man in the White Suit* explored incidentally the conservatism of both unions and management in face of a marvellous new invention; the richly comic *I'm All Right Jack* and the equally richly melodramatic *The Angry Silence* explored further facets of industrial relations in Britain.

Many more examples of a critical cinema could be cited in the

123

English-speaking cinema, and in the cinemas of Western Europe and Scandinavia. A few examples have come to us from the more western of the Eastern European satellites, and that is all. However, the bulk of films produced has a more affectionate attitude towards the surrounding society. And, on occasion, especially occasions of national crisis, films appear which set out to praise and glorify aspects of the society. This is manifest in the patriotic type of war film, of which there are examples from Hollywood through to Moscow and on to Peking. At other times, the re-seeing of glorification films can induce nausea: as in the Russian films glorifying collectivization of the peasants – sickening in their romanticization of what it transpires was a ruthless and brutal process. Similarly, Hollywood, to its discredit, made in the heyday of McCarthy-ism a number of very dubious anti-Communist films like *My Son John*, *Big Jim McLain* and *I Was a Communist for the FBI*. These were poorly done and not popular. They were ideologically bankrupt and reduced to devices like flag-waving, identifying communists with foreigners, intellectuals, and people with modernistic furniture; counterposing these horrors with honest mother love and apple-pie.[1]

It goes without saying that films, like any dramatic art, can provide catharsis. They have this effect of triggering off or vicariously releasing our emotions.

These many ways in which films influence their audience seem to me much more important, though frequently overlooked, than simple imitation. Overriding the three of them: argument, distraction, and catharsis, is the sheer amount of information one is fed. In this matter the cinema has great power, since it can tell us truth or it can tell us falsehoods and lies. In the chapter on the western, below, I mention some of the information about the West we can learn from films. Here are some different cases. It was from films that I first learned (in 1953, at the age of fifteen), that there was corruption and gangsterism in the American labour movement (*On the Waterfront*). It was from the great quartet of war films by Lewis Milestone (*All Quiet on the Western Front*; *A Walk in the Sun*; *The Halls of Montezuma*; *Pork Chop Hill*), that I learned something of what it must be like to be an infantryman in the front line. Every one of us learns an immense amount of facts about other countries whenever we see a foreign film. We not only learn what the place looks like; we learn things about the sensibility of that nation, how they approach common human topics in a way different from us. For someone with

---

[1] See Reisz (1953), an article which should be read with some caution; and Pauline Kael's more clear-headed 'Morality Plays Right and Left' in her (1965). It is of interest that the McCarthy-ite films I instance, have now become camp favourites among audiences in sophisticated American cities.

no special interest in Japan, I seem to have gathered a great deal of fascinating information about Japan in the Middle Ages, especially court life, from watching Japanese costume films. Moreover, I suspect that the Japanese films, like those of Russia and Sweden, have a far better sense of the past than we have in England or America: they are more able to make pictures which recapture a little of what it was probably like, than we Anglo-Saxons are. This in turn leads one to reflect on cultural differences, the meaning of the past, etc. It can also lead into the intricate questions of the philosophy of history. Is there a past 'as it really was', or is each generation's and culture's view of what makes something 'real' different? Hollywood spends millions of dollars on background research for its more serious historical pageants, which yet remain unrelievedly artificial. Only in the films of the West and the Civil War does Hollywood succeed in displaying an historical sense. Swedish or Russian film makers appear to manage it effortlessly. When they try hard the British can do it, except that more often than not current social and class attitudes are projected back in silly ways. English and American reconstructions of the Knights of the Round Table, of the eighteenth- and nineteenth-century eras, tend to be absurdly hygienic and well-mannered. Attempts to film Brontë and Dickens have often been meticulous, yet remain stiff and unconvincing. This, too, gives us information about the producing societies and their relation to their past.

In a number of instances I have maintained that among the most exciting gifts learning the social sciences can give, is one of new insights into and ways of looking at our own society. Americans are much better informed about their own society than the British are about theirs, perhaps because of the self-consciousness – the exposé-consciousness – of American society. American society was created in a way English society was not. The British only began learning how to look at their society in a sociologically self-conscious way in the working class dramas of the late fifties (see my 1969b).

2 Slice of life or slice of cake

This is only, however, a part of the medium-at-large. Every social institution has its intended and unintended effects and ramifications throughout society. The institution is not to be identified with these effects since it can be independent of them. Having said this, I feel freer to go on and discuss what exactly the nature of the experience of cinema is, and especially to separate its subjective aspects, about which generalization is shaky, from its objective aspects, where the question of standards comes in. In neither case do I agree that what we call the content of the experience is something pure and given. There are always subjective factors involved: for example I am a passionate admirer of Audrey Hepburn and Monica Vitti, and their very presence on the screen is sometimes sufficient for me to be entranced. Others, differently disposed, might see nothing in the films at all. This is reinforced by the whole ritual of cinemagoing which serves to impress on one that one is somewhere special, going through a special confrontation; one is not allowed to forget the experience to come is to be out of the ordinary. Just as you do not mistake an art gallery for the display of advertisements in the subway, so you do not mistake the cinema for a slice of life.[2]

Which reminds me that cinema 'realism' is, therefore, a lost cause to begin with. Reality is not an entity to be captured, as truth is captured by a true statement. A sense of reality in connection with a film is an attempt to indicate that the characters and situations are clearly set out, and the logic of their interaction is coherent, consistent and convincing. One assents to what is shown and speaks (loosely) of it being 'real' or 'true'. One difficulty here is that any dramatic situation we know to occur, shown to us in detail for the first time, has a great impact which makes it disproportionately convincing. The murder in *Shane*, the first time a film showed a woman's face *in* childbirth, the use of strong dialects in dialogue, nude love scenes – all these when first seen were hailed as 'real', 'true': a breakthrough. There is something in the latter claim. But on re-seeing the English north country working class films of the late fifties, it is apparent that what faces us is a new set of conventions devised to expand the class coverage of films. Do they really expand the content, the truth of the medium? Is there any more truth in the ritually masked actors of *Antigone*, than in the broad accents of *Saturday Night and Sunday Morning*? Closely examined, these films expand the consciousness of the cinema very little, they merely act out tales in new settings, and rather Victorian tales at that. Let us make a tally.

In *Room at the Top* the success-drive causes the hero to lose, indeed indirectly kill, the woman who loves him. After a beating, he is married off to the doting little silly he made pregnant.

In *Saturday Night and Sunday Morning* the hero's determined rebelliousness involves him in an attempted abortion, a beating, and then marriage and the housing estate after all.

In *A Kind of Loving* a shot-gun marriage runs into mother-in-law problems, only solved by the hero getting some spine when his wife miscarries while they are separated.

[2] Hitchcock commented somewhere: 'the cinema isn't a slice of life, it's a slice of cake'.

126

In *This Sporting Life* the hero's brutish inarticulateness and frantic desire to evoke a response leads to a breakdown of his relationship with 'his woman', and his breakdown when she dies.

In *Alfie* the ruthless libertine causes a respectable woman to have an abortion and proves incapable of sustaining any relationship.

Not one of these stories grew out of their self-consciously adopted settings, although the film makers might have been hard put to realize them in alternative settings. Practically all of them could have been done in the setting of university student life. Result: it became, in fact, a butt of satire, this vogue for working class backgrounds, e.g., *Sparrows Can't Sing* and *Morgan*, enjoyable enough in themselves, culminated the trend, since the prole background becomes more or less decorative.

From realism to decoration. Only intellectuals confuse conventions with reality. Ordinary folk may see films as a dream world, but when a film pretends to realism, they are ruthless in picking at it and undermining its pretence. (This is also true of children, see Tavistock Clinic, 1952.) The true audience situation is that we know very well we are supposed to be giving our attention to the screen; that someone has made something for us and put it up there and that we are here to receive it as best we can. This already involves a high degree of expectation and interpretation. We know, for example, that a film will have a beginning a middle and an end: reality, whatever it is, does not.

So, besides our subjective responses, and besides our interpretations, does the experience also have aesthetic aspects which we can appraise? It seems to me that aesthetics enter only when we try to appraise the film in terms of our interpretation of it: we try to understand the experience. This is discussed below (Part Four). It suffices to say, that separating experience-interpretation from aesthetic judgment aids enormously in solving the problem of the objectivity of artistic appraisal. Standards can be separated completely from subjective responses to the experience.[3]

Films in themselves are a special kind of experience, then. They leave less to the imagination than a book on the visual and aural planes, but they leave more to the imagination in so far as the feelings and personalities of the persons portrayed are concerned. Special kinds of imagination 'fillers' have to be developed for the films. Just as the novel-reader has to accustom himself to imagining the scene described almost as a picture, so the cinema-viewer has to build the separate shots into a whole three-dimensional world. Untrained viewers first have difficulty with the third dimension; then they baulk at the convention of medium and close-shot when they imagine

[3] See my (1967a).

127

that the characters have had parts of their bodies cut off; then they are faced by the switching of viewpoint from shot to shot; and finally they can make no sense of continuity jumps, time lapses, and so on. We, the film-educated, are highly trained in all this. Such films as *The Secret Life of Walter Mitty* or *Billy Liar* (or *Morgan*) would be impossible without such sophistication. Both are films about men who have day-dreams in the middle of their working days, thus there is incessant flashing back and forth between the dream and 'reality'. In *Mitty* the cues are quite subtle: a funny look comes into his eyes and then we cut to his fantasy. In *Billy Liar* the director, John Schlesinger, dispensed even with that. For example, in an early scene where Billy's mother, father and 'gran' are all nagging him there is a quick shot of him shaving in his pyjamas, which cuts to him in uniform mowing them down with a submachine-gun accompanied by realistic sound effects, then a reverse shot of the three adults pottering normally as the sound of the machine gun and the flashes it makes continue. In a series of three films, a highbrow director – Alain Resnais – pushed this use of our film sophistication to the verge of mystery. In *Hiroshima Mon Amour*, he intercuts scenes from the heroine's memories of the death of her German lover and her own humiliation as a collaborator, with her present *affaire* with a Japanese. In *Last Year at Marienbad*, he presents a woman trying to remember from various hints that are dropped, what she did last year in this vast hotel: leaving it to the viewer to decide which scenes are in the present and which in the past. Or whether they are all in the mind. In still another variation he mixes, in *Muriel*, a chain of events: then lets us sort them out. The same technique has been used in amnesia films like *Mirage*, *The Third Day*, and *Mister Buddwing* (*Woman Without a Face*) where glimpses of the past are intercut with the present. Gregory Peck, in *Mirage*, gets only momentary recall at first, and then longer and longer memories as his mental block begins to crumble. In *Buddwing*, James Garner wakes in Central Park without the slightest idea of who he is: encounters various women and remembers scenes from his previous life with their faces instead of the face of his wife. It slowly transpires that he knows none of them, but is trying to avoid the memory of what happened by seeing them as his wife.

These are just a few examples of how specialized the experience of the film is in the non-subjective sense. Having been raised on films, we all know how to read cues and techniques with a high degree of sophistication. Thus, among hyper-sophisticated audiences, one will sometimes hear audible groans when time-lapse is indicated by blowing calendar leaves, or intercourse is symbolized by crashing surf or fireworks. Directors must be as sensitive to the audience's sophistication as possible. Knowing one's way around the language of the cinema is rather like knowing one's way around a library; and it is equally ritualized, and equally secular. The cinema is secular iconography: our film-star-saints are not saintly at all. But then we don't worship them, we admire them. They are gods, but not like Christian gods, more like the gods of ancient Greece. We are amused by them, irritated by them, tolerant and respectful towards them: but we don't pray to them or request their intercession with us as individuals. We do, however, at personal appearances and bazaars like to have them appear to sanctify the activity in some way or other. A little of the quality they bring to their films can be brought to their personal appearances.

3 The medium as the message

A few years ago, this is where I would have ended this chapter. I have discussed our subjective experience of the medium, our interpretation of it, and hinted at its similarities with mass religions. But now there has, as the result of Marshall McLuhan, to be discussed a further aspect of the experience the medium constitutes. McLuhan's thesis might be generalized like this: technology not only changes our environment, it changes our experience of it. Take writing. Before writing was invented, what was our sense of the past like? It consisted of memory. How did we know whose memory was good, whose bad? How short were memories? Did we envisage history stretching before and after us beyond memory and recollection? Were we fully aware of radical changes in the course of events and prepared for further ones? Frankly, even reading anthropologists, I don't know, although Peter Lawrence has given us some wonderful insights into the complexities of the problem.[4] Think now of the revolution producing by writing. Facts could be fixed, memories checked, or whole time-pictures changed.[5] But then writing – written speech – had its feedback, since it began to determine what was correct language and what not.

In his second book, McLuhan explores *The Gutenberg Galaxy*, the consequences the invention of printing had on the world, the world print created. Not just the dissemination of knowledge, and so forth, but the ways in which our manner of experiencing the world has been radically altered by printing. Print is a medium with certain

---

[4] *Road Belong Cargo*, London 1965; see also my paper 'On the Explanation of Cargo Cults', *European Journal of Sociology*, 7, (1966): 299-312.
[5] For a brilliant and seemingly unnoticed paper on this problem see Jack Goody and Ian Watt: 'The Consequences of Literacy', in J. Goody, ed., *Literacy in Traditional Societies*, Cambridge, 1968.

characteristics: it is private, direct, and cool (that is, it doesn't impose itself on you). It is a means of communicating extremes of subtlety to vast audiences very easily. Since so much of our time is spent consuming print, and since there is so much overlap between what we consume, new possibilities of experiential uniformities are released. We can now all read about love, war, death, foreign lands, strange people: things we could not do before printing.[*] Before Gutenberg we could only experience directly, indirectly by hearsay, or read if we were members of a small, privileged, literate class. One remembers how difficult it is to establish rapport with a person whose education and reading hardly overlaps with one's own. One considers how differently one responds to things and behaves because of that part of one's experience that comes from reading. Martin Green in *A Mirror for Anglo-Saxons* relates the sad story of how a grammar school education for English children frequently takes them out of their parents' world. That education is mainly reading. The difference between the educated and the uneducated has a lot to do with whether and what they read. Reading transforms. Ours is a society where we assume other people share vast swathes of knowledge with us. We wouldn't be able to conceive of building space rockets, if it were not widely understood that the theory that the earth is ovoid is well-tested and probably true. Because of shared experience the world is immensely richer: we have larger ranges of expectations and different sensibilities. Technology, says McLuhan, actually extends and develops our nervous system. With our five senses we can do only a certain amount. With writing we can extend our memories. With printing we can introduce a large measure of overlap in our memories. And since we are all products of our education and upbringing, we are all products of our technology. Leaving aside the senses of taste, smell, and touch, let us instead concentrate on how the new media have improved our sight and hearing.

The telephone enables us to hear people miles away. The gramophone enables us to preserve sound that would otherwise be lost forever (if only we had been able to record Bach!). Film enables us to see things we could never see, and also to order and select them for our convenience. And so on. It is against this background that in his third book – *Understanding Media* – McLuhan formulates his famous thesis that 'the medium is the message'. Obviously, in saying this he is speaking of the message for mankind rather than the message of the telegram, for example. It is a sloganeering way of putting the message of *this* book: the sociology of the cinema is what it has done to and for our society. Just as railways and cars permit the develop-

---

[*] A friend remarked truly that if one doesn't read *Time* the day it comes out, one gets a feeling of being out of touch.

ment of new kinds of cities; just as printing allows one to communicate with people you have never seen; just as electric media transmit messages faster than the messenger boy and thus create a village intimacy without face-to-face contacts; so the cinema, one of the electric media, is significant too. In *Upton Sinclair Presents William Fox* (1933) there is a nice illustration of this. In New York before the advent of the cinema, the focus of a neighbourhood had been a corner, a few shops, and especially a saloon bar. This was money-consuming, selective – since women and children were hardly encouraged – and not necessarily educative or socially valuable. Indeed, to drink because there is nothing else to do is terrible. Then the cinema became the new neighbourhood focus. It was cheap, classless, unselective, yet not altogether face-to-face; had social value (see above) in raising issues and purveying information, and it became a focus of family social life the way bars never could.

The 'message' of the film medium for our society was that a completely different set of interpersonal and community relationships were possible. Recreation could be harmless and cheap, but it required completely new mental attitudes. Interestingly enough, the 'message' of television is different again. It further reinforces family life at the expense of destroying neighbourhoods and neighbourliness (remember the stories when television came, of going to visit people who had just installed television and how they continued looking at it, waving guests to chairs?). It is cool, rather than hot, since normal activities can be continued with it as a background.

The 'hot' cinema experience is the centre of our book, the heart of the sociology of the cinema. The experience of cinemagoing is central to the medium-at-large. Producers produce, audiences assemble, critics evaluate, and all because of the confrontation of people and the screen. Films are a peculiar communication channel: only a few outlet points, only intermittently 'on' (mostly after the sun has passed its noon zenith), a cinema is more like a library than a water tap. The message is usually transmitted in a little over two hours. Darkness descends, the screen is lit, the film rolls and a world opens up.

X

The Sociology of the Screen World

1 *Film content and reality*

The question to be attacked in this chapter is the social content and structure of what is seen on the screen. In other words, the relationship between the societies that produce films and the societies created in films. Do films reflect accurately or inaccurately the societies they spring from? What messages do films contain? This is an enormous topic, known in the jargon as 'content analysis'. The most thorough examples of the genre are Wolfenstein and Leites (1950) and Jones (1955). There are also some interesting analyses in the Mead volume *The Study of Culture at a Distance* (1959). These are brief and fragmentary, and I have not been able to get at the original research from which they are extracted.

The topic first assumed importance for me when reflecting on two theories about the cinema experience which I had come across. The first theory was disclosed in a precocious reading of S. Kracauer's extraordinary book *From Caligari to Hitler* (1947). Kracauer's thesis is that the tendencies towards fascism, which were present in Germany before Hitler came to power, are symbolized in and can be analysed from many films of the period. Kracauer is not concerned with the popularity or the representative character of the films he analyses. He is concerned with them as the unconscious expression of hidden psychological propensities which revealed a developing predisposition to fascism. The book strikes me as very poorly argued and incredibly overrated. Arty expressionist films are analysed alongside cheap commercial products. One is expected to believe the same unconscious drives are revealing themselves in the works of both kinds of creators. Moreover, the whole question of symbolic readings is fraught with the dangers of arbitrariness and lack of testability.[1] The thesis itself is not seriously defended against the obvious charge that hindsight is being used, or that fascism is as much a social and political phenomenon as it is a psychological one. But most seriously, from my point of view, the entire argument is conducted by the accumulation of endless examples, most of the

[1] As another example, I would cite Rhode and Pearson (1961).

132

analysis of which is based on plot summaries and attitudes which could easily be detected by reading scripts, not necessarily seeing films. For my purposes there is a great difference between stories with an authoritarian cast and films like *Olympische Spiele*, the fascism and body-worship of which are displayed solely in the use of camera, editing, and music, and which would be unnoticeable in a script summary.

Much later (1960), Kracauer went on to develop a peculiarly conservative view of the essence of good cinema.[2] His theory is that physical reality, life as it is lived, can be captured on film in a way that no other medium can rival (he does not refer to Munsterberg (1916), who anticipates him). It is thus an extension of still photography, for the essence of that is catching the right moment. Again, this theory that film captures reality is expounded rather than critically discussed, and extraordinary attempts are made to evade counter-examples, like cartoons and musicals, by contorted arguments somehow connecting the best of them with 'real life'. The obvious objections that media do not have essences inherent in them, but only given or attributed to them, and that much of the greatest cinema resembles poetry in the intensity, ellipsis, and sophistication of its effects, and that the essence of poetry is not realism, are nowhere taken up.

Nowhere does Kracauer draw the crucial distinctions between reality and realism, or realism and naturalism. Granted for a moment that there is a reality to be captured – 'war is hell' or whatever – the attempt to capture it may or may not be based on the philosophy of realism. In *The Burmese Harp* we see hardly any combat, in *Paths of Glory* we see a great deal. Both strive to capture the reality of the experience of war, the first indirectly, the other by direct realism. A further alternative would be to 'show it as it was', to recreate in meticulous detail, actual occurrences, not even condensing the time sequence. Unedited newsreels are of this kind. There is a fallacy in the philosophy behind this – which we may call naturalism: to convey boredom or elation does not require that the audience be bored or elated; to convey that war is hell, it is not necessary to simulate war as hell.

The other big problem with Kracauer, which was pointed out by Franklin Fearing in a review (1947) is that, like J. P. Mayer, Hortense Powdermaker, and a great many others, he has a curious view of the cinema experience. Groups, i.e., cinema audiences, are uncritically treated as individuals – even to having a kind of collective unconscious or mass-soul for Kracauer. The audience is engaged in a

[2] See Pauline Kael's critical attack 'Is there a cure for film criticism' in her (1965).

133

'participation mystique' with the film. Aside from the gross character of the social psychology here, and the tendency to mystical utterances, it seems no sort of tool for film analysis, once it has done its job of reinforcing a Jeremiah-effect.

But the fascinated horror induced by Kracauer's absurd edifice of theory gets blunted by acquaintance with the quite widespread theory, taken for granted by a great many critics, namely, that Hollywood and Britain have inferior film industries because they are allowed to be no more than factories of escapism. The high point of the folly this theory represents is to be found in the film writings of the forties, when documentary films and later Italian neo-realism had an intellectual vogue. Here, too, the theory was that Realism = Truth = Goodness = Beauty = Morally and Politically Correct. The extraordinary tensions produced by systematically following this theory, even when it leads to critics trying hard to convince themselves, can be sensed in Richard Griffith's sequel to Paul Rotha's *The Film Till Now*, and in the short-lived but interesting career of the magazine *Sequence*. Griffith is unable to bring himself to praise even the Hollywood work of Orson Welles because he thought it lacked the serious realism and correct moral attitudes he demanded of films. The Italian neo-realists themselves proclaimed in their writings that they saw themselves as destroying the tradition of the glossy 'white telephone films' preceding them in the Italian industry. In *Sight and Sound*, Henry Raynor penned a humourless article called 'Nothing to Laugh At', in which he said the class-consciousness and snobbery of English comedies was a Bad Thing. That these films were being relatively realistic in the sense of capturing English social reality seems not to have impressed him.

I have explained earlier (Introduction, § 3) how a connection can be made between a position of this kind and the desire of intellectual film fans to make the object of their love respectable. In the age of stern Leavisite moralizing what else could be expected?[3]

From my first acquaintance with the idea The Film Captures Reality (or should), I knew there was something wrong with it. The fortunate accident of being born later than its authors may have disinclined me to accept the suppressed premise that the best films were the Russian silent films, the documentaries, and the various neo-realisms. I found it ludicrous when finally I saw the poetic fantasies of Renoir and Carné, that they had been applauded for their 'realism'. The Russian cinema of the twenties was a let-down when at last viewed; it seemed to be very cranial with little intuitive grasp of the dynamics of making films – despite all the teutonic theorizing of Eisenstein and Pudovkin. The German silent cinema

[3] The author who pointed out this connection is J. R. Taylor.

appeared on the whole more successful, especially the work of Pabst and Lang. One can attempt various explanations of this. Possibly, for example, after D. W. Griffith ceased actively to innovate, there was a certain faltering in the development of the medium, a question as to where it should go next. Hollywood itself, however, quietly went on without 'D.W.' to consolidate the entertainment feature form. The Russians and the Germans, convulsed by their social and artistic revolutions, had much of their film created by artists and intellectuals from the theatre and visual arts. It is perhaps not surprising that they tried to mould the cinema into new forms. To their contemporaries in other countries, their approach was intellectually flattering to the cinema and certainly a far cry from Hollywood – films with expressionist sets and no stars!

This intellectual appeal allowed the Russian and German silent cinema to become a Cause, and a useful canon against which to measure the mediocre films churned out in Hollywood and Britain. The coterie thus formed was, in some ways, the first generation of film intellectuals facing the first generation of intellectualized films. Young, literate and progressive, this generation soon had a monopoly of intellectual film writing. The ground was cut from beneath them and their theorizing by the arrival of sound. That generation never, it seems, got over sound (see Arnheim 1958). They had expended so much effort in theorizing about films as a visual medium that they persisted with this characterization in the face of sound, holding that film is *primarily* a visual medium.

Such a view is especially perverse to those of us raised on sound cinema. Silent films, far from being the purest form of cinema, were rather quaint – a primitive forerunner not of true cinema, but of cinema as we knew it. And, of course, in the forging of silent cinema entertainment it was directors like Ford in America, and Hitchcock in Britain, who were developing the economical and unfussy styles which were to find their culmination in the sound cinema. They were able to take sound in their stride. For the cinema is not 'primarily' visual or 'primarily' anything else. Sound has equal rights with the visual, and the attempt to rely exclusively on either unbalances the medium.

In the writings of the middle generation critic Roger Manvell (from the Second World War on), the strain can already be felt. He makes his obeisance to the Russians and to *montage* theory (the cinematic equivalent of *collage*), but at the same time eulogizes the richness and complexity of the sound cinema's achievement. In the magazine *Sequence*, edited out of Oxford between 1947 and 1952, the clash between the instinctive tastes of those formed during and by the sound era, and the obeisance intellectuals felt was owed to the

135

classical canon is everywhere manifest. We find there a high camp liking for musicals, cartoons, stars like Joan Crawford, alongside articles contrasting Italian and American realistic films with the escapist world of the average Hollywood or British product.

The final intellectual break away from the classics only came with my generation – weaned as we were on Disney, Danny Kaye, *Meet Me in St Louis*, Bogart, the whole bit. We went on from there to know and love current Hollywood and to re-discover Hollywood in the thirties, forties, and twenties (in that order). To us now, Russian and German expressionism is obviously a side-track which virtually failed to affect the mainstream of world cinema – as Hollywood, with its professionalism and glamour, its immense capacity to learn and absorb, had become. As long as the Russian and German silent film was an exciting experiment, high hopes could be held out for it. To us it is clear that the experiment led nowhere, was a failure, to be consigned to a side slot.

More positively, my own concern with the cinema grew and centred around individual artists, and not around abstract categories like 'realism'. Cartoons, westerns, and musicals have for long been favourite *genres*, and it was difficult to make sense of these in terms of realism. What was interesting was the personal style of Orson Welles, or John Ford, or Alfred Hitchcock, or William Wyler or Robert Siodmak. The important question was the artist and his vision. Neither Leni Reifenstahl nor Alfred Hitchcock were 'realists'; they were sure-footed *realizers* of total worlds of their own imagining; their control and clarity of vision fascinates us. This seemed to me to apply even more to the post-war artists I most admired: Robert Bresson, Ingmar Bergman, Michelangelo Antonioni and Akira Kurosawa. Perhaps the most exciting members of the Nouvelle Vague and of the school of British realism have been those with the most idiosyncratic personal vision: Truffaut and Godard; Clayton and Schlesinger; Donner and Losey. In Italy, too, among the younger men, Damiano Damiani, Bernaldo Bertolucchi; in America, Robert Aldrich, John Frankenheimer, Sam Peckinpah, Arthur Penn, etc. The work of these creators does not draw its power from any special relationship with 'reality', but rather from the coherence and consistency of the personal imagination which informs it.

Even where this was accepted as a general explanation of what stands for quality in films, there was a failure to detect it in the American cinema. This in its turn had much to do with the notion that fantasy is by nature frivolous and superficial. Certainly there was much fantasy in American films, indeed their three most distinct strains, the musical, the western, and the gangster, struck me as

136

completely unreal; tenuously, if at all, attached to what actually happened; worlds obeying conventions of their own; drawing their power and universality precisely from those elements which were fantastic conventions. To explain a little. *The Alamo* was not fought by John Wayne; *Cleopatra* did not resemble Elizabeth Taylor. The use of such stars is, however, an essential part of the dramatic conventions of the cinema. Or, to put it directly: drama and newsreel are different – even when drama is made to resemble newsreel. (To do that is just to adopt another convention.) We know that 2½-hour films, not 2½-hour newsreels, are shown in our local cinemas. As we buy our tickets, settle down, glance at the credits, we expect an experience *totally different* from what we would experience if we were there: an experience, I would claim, closer to that of the voyeur than to that of the participant. The voyeur wishes to watch because the actions enacted have for him a private meaning. In cinema, the meaning lies in the dramatic conventions: similarly indirect but dissimilarly no longer private. The thrill we get from watching Taylor and Burton on screen, is not what we would experience if we saw Cleopatra and Anthony.

It was refreshing then to find, when I came to read *Cahiers du Cinema* in the mid-fifties, that the French, under a cloud of metaphysical verbiage, had developed a theory that films had authors, and their worlds were what was interesting, and that the greatest gathering of film authors was to be found in the USA. In particular, they ignored Distinguished Figures and concentrated on commercial film makers with an outstanding command of the medium like Hawks, Fuller, McCarey, Tashlin, Walsh, Boetticher, etc. However, this view did not go far enough. The problem which bothered me was the decisive difference between the British and American cinema of the thirties and forties, i.e., the badness of most of the British output, the complete anonymity and lack of professionalism of the finished product. Only the master, Hitchcock, was able to impress himself on his films, and he emigrated at the end of the thirties. Not until the appearance of Lean and Reed did anything approaching a personal vision intrude into the British cinema. Whereas, in America, there was an abundance of creative artists whose vision had developed and matured over the years in fascinating ways.

However, apart from its tolerance of the personal vision, albeit the tightly disciplined and relatively unflamboyant one, there was something else that was vigorous and exciting about the American cinema, something deeply entwined in the relation it bore to its society: its ability to portray every aspect of American society with almost clinical accuracy: from the urban, rural, and negro slums, through suburbia, to its highest social and political realms: American film-men knew their society and put it on their screens. When I first visited America, I was staggered by how accurately it had been portrayed on the American screen, portrayed with a fidelity hardly ever achieved in Britain, and portrayed in a cinema with no pretensions to 'realism' whatsoever. Yet for all that, perhaps because of that, there has always been in the American cinema a vigorously critical attitude to society. It has criticized, condemned, satirized, and lampooned its home society quite mercilessly. This is a general truth about America: its best critics are Americans. Gangsterism, political corruption, lynching, prejudice (against Jews and negroes), fascism, witch-hunting (ancient and modern), war, and, recently, the Bomb, have been the object of critical films made within the mainstream of the American cinema. Even overtly political issues are taken up – not just *Advise and Consent* or *The Best Man*, but *Dr Strangelove*, *Fail-Safe*, *The Bedford Incident* and *Seven Days in May*, conducted frank discussions and criticisms of the military and its tactics in the modern age. My own astonishment surpassed itself, however, in the neglected satire *John Goldfarb Please Come Home*. This story of the U2 pilot, 'wrong-way Goldfarb', who fouls up a Middle Eastern oil deal; which shows the State Department populated by dithering and sycophantic ninnies prepared to go to any lengths to appease a capricious caliph; went to lengths one could hardly credit. If this is compared with the furore raised in Britain by the relatively innocuous *I'm All Right Jack*, one perhaps sees the difference between a critical and an uncritical society and the films they deserve. One of the most encouraging things to happen in the Eastern block has been the appearance in the sixties in Poland, Hungary, and Czechoslovakia of films which have something to say about their society which is not just slavish praise.

2 *Films and society in the Far East*

It is, perhaps, time to bring in the Far East. The two biggest film industries of the East are Japan's and Hong Kong's. I have some familiarity with the range of products of each. What is the relation between the society there and the films produced there? In Japan one finds many similarities with America. A tradition of films that is both accurate and critical. Japan is portrayed extraordinarily well by its great artists: Ozu, Kurosawa, Mizoguchi, Kobayashi, Ichikawa. Since the war, the strain of social criticism has been very strong and probably most highly developed in Kurosawa – whose *The Bad Sleep Well* indicts more than enough sections of his society. He has criticized in other films the impotence of bureaucracy (*Ikuru*), the conditions which produce crime and vice (*Stray Dog*,

High and Low), the nuclear age predicament (*Record of a Living Being*), and so on. He has also made many films in the great tradition of reconstructions of medieval Japanese society: but in these has shown us the ordinary peasants and market towns as well as the plush courts, princes, and samurai. Withal he is the richest and most brilliant creative mind presently at work in the cinema: possibly the greatest film craftsman the world has yet seen.

Other Japanese directors have criticized the police and the wildness of adolescents. Japan is an exciting and, I would suppose, fundamentally healthy society. One that is capable of change and growth to meet modern conditions. It is not perfect by any means, and there are disturbing things, but its marvellous film industry has roots in a rich social fabric.

Hong Kong is something of a contrast, filmically and sociologically.[4] Unlike Japan, Chinese society was hidebound as well as conservative, having developed no mechanisms for dealing with and absorbing change when it arrived. Or, at least, the traditional mechanism of swamping the changing forces and 'sinicising' them failed. First corrupt politics, and now a crushing totalitarian grip, have prevented a truthful and critical Chinese cinema from developing.[5] In Hong Kong, where the producers are free to make what films they please, they don't often set the stories in Hong Kong itself. The potential audience, overseas Chinese for the most part, do not know Hong Kong; they only know China (sometimes they only know of it). China, however, appears not to have the relation with its past that Japan has: firstly, the Japanese have a fairly plausible idea of what their society looked like then (whenever); secondly, they seem to have an abundance of historical stories involving individualism, justice, and other universal issues, not just fantasies and court intrigues. Moreover, they have a genuine interest in what actually happened; no exclusive interest in sweetening, modifying, or covering up. The Chinese cinema of Hong Kong, however, in contrast to the Japanese, but rather like the British and American historical cinema, is cosy and artificial. Films about the life of the fabulous, murderous, nymphomaniac Empress Wu, for example, are not exactly possessed of verisimilitude – although she would make a marvellous film character. Chinese musicals are merely filmed stage productions, with no concession to cinematic values at all. Other dramas and comedies, set in a nebulous interwar period, again are stagy and indifferently done. Why have no Chinese artists come to the fore to create their own imaginative world on the

---

[4] For material on Hong Kong, see Jarvie and Agassi (1969a) and Weakland (1971).

[5] Even an apologist like Leyda (1960) cannot find much to say.

screen? The explanation is institutional. China has been too poor and unsettled to support a high-cost industry, where young men have been trained to the point where they can create their visic n in screen terms. Moreover, the monopoly of production in the hands of a few studio machines in Hong Kong, leaves little room for the gifted individual to have his way. Hong Kong film magnates display little serious ambition to conquer world markets, despite what they say, but are quite happy with the millions they rake in at present. Yet Hong Kong is a vigorous and exciting society where exciting films (e.g., American and Japanese) do very well. (As do certain films from both Chinas, mainly for political reasons.) The market is too small, however, to sustain creative experiments which might flop elsewhere.

A propos of Professor Gans' ideas, mentioned earlier, about the subcultural pluralism of our society and the opportunity to make films for these sub-cultures. Sub-cultures exist in Hong Kong, but they are so small in absolute numbers, and so divisive, that they hinder rather than help production. Among Hong Kong Chinese, the sub-cultures follow dialect lines: Mandarin, Shanghainese, Amoy, Fukien, Hoklo, and the various branches of Cantonese. Some of these are scarcely mutually intelligible. Thus many Chinese films are subtitled – in Chinese! Amoy dialect films, e.g., do not lose money, but the need to fraction and tailor when the market is small anyway, seems to inhibit balanced growth. This is hard to explain, especially in light of the idea mentioned earlier that often the most culturally 'pure' and narrow of films, e.g., westerns, Ozu's films of Japanese middle class life, Statyajit Ray's films of Bengali peasants, have the broadest and most universal appeal. Ersatz 'international' or cosmopolitan films rarely so. This suggestion must be qualified. In communities where film is a new and dominant mode of entertainment, it cannot be expected that subcultural and cultural barriers will be easily crossed. It is only when the audience is sophisticated about using the cinema as one among numerously available modes of diversion, that the exotic-universal appeal of a film utterly steeped in the ways of another culture can get across.

To explain more fully. Gans' argument that films should be subculturally programmed, i.e., more consciously directed at an audience that is subculturally distinct, and not always for the across the board appeal, gains strength from the well-known view that films designed to reflect a society in its own terms to itself, and which might be expected to be baffling to the outside world, can often prove of universal appeal. However, subcultural programming is not possible when each subculture provides only a very small market; and market widening by appeal across subcultural boundaries is strongly inhibited when a change of language is involved. As audiences become more filmically sophisticated this becomes less of a problem (cf. the universal popularity of American films).

A further problem arises at this point, specifically about Chinese films produced for the domestic and overseas market – typically by the improbabable brothers Shaw, Run Run and Run Me, who operate from Hong Kong and Singapore. These films, from the Technicolor and Cinemascope epics which find their way into cinemas in San Francisco and New York, to the family life comedies in black and white shot in a week, are unrelievedly theatrical, artificial, and dull. Good, one could say, that is just an Occidental prejudice: judging by the box office returns the Oriental thinks differently. Brushing aside the notorious difficulties of interpreting box office returns,[6] there remains the problem of explaining the popularity of American films alongside this tedious *kitsch*. Hypothesis: the audience which laps up the Chinese language product is not the same audience which is avid for *The Guns of Navarone*.[7] The audience for the Chinese product, in my observation, is the middle class and family audience which in our culture is sucked into Disney and *The Sound of Music* – although a less intermittent audience in the Far East because cinemagoing is still the dominant habitual mass medium there. Granted the hypothesis, then the problem: what is the functional satisfaction gained by the Chinese audience from the artificiality and theatricality of Chinese films?

This is a specific version of the general questions, what function do cinematic conventions serve, and what do people look to films for? Conventions, as we have hinted, serve as a language in which to articulate meanings; people look to films for aspiration-fantasies of one sort or another (Gans 1959a). The young Oriental audience which loves American films, uses those films to serve virtually the same functions as does the British audience analysed by Gans (1959a). They are films which enshrine the outlook of the working class on the way up: industrial England, like industrial Asia, appreciates them. American films show a world where ordinary people can live lives of comfort and splendour almost undreamt of before this century.

What of the audience for the Chinese product? Who are they? A displaced peasant working class, disoriented, whether in Hong Kong or overseas – otherwise they would still be in China – possessed both by nostalgia and insecurity. They are presented with films set in a classical past, or in a vaguely interwar period, or, more generally, in

---

[6] To remind readers: box office figures do not measure potential audience lost; do not measure walk-outs and disappointment; do not discriminate habitual and unthinking filmgoers from those out to see *this* film, as opposed to attending this cinema.

[7] See Jarvie (1963).

a 'China that has ceased to exist, or even perhaps [in] a China which never existed, the mystical essence quite distinct from the territorial reality' (Jarvie and Agassi 1969a). The placing of the films in the past allows nostalgia and a sense of security (Chinese are culturally highly self-conscious, they take their identity from the collective culture, not from personal individuation); the conventions are taken from the classical theatre and popular comedy theatre and thus reinforce this purpose. An unsophisticated, moral world is created not unlike how the audience would like to think of the past. This completes my explanation.

The situation is not unique. A brilliant American film like *Meet Me in St Louis* crosses subcultural barriers easily, but its emotional tug has to do with nostalgia for a more gentle and secure age. This may well be mythical, but the Main Street in Disneyland, the decades of *Saturday Evening Post* covers, testify to its almost archetypal character. There are made in America and England, utterly crude, broad comedies, never shown to the critics, and, in the case of America's 'country comics', never shown in cities. Indeed, I would say the style and sentiment of country music and 'The Beverly Hillbillies' is very similar to the Chinese comedies, and performs much the same function.

3 *Identification and escape*

One of the commonest theories about why people like some films as opposed to others, or why they prefer films to other media, or why films have stars, or what is the main experience filmgoing provides, is that which says the audience 'identifies' with who they see or the situations they see. In this Identification Theory, it is maintained that the satisfaction gained from *identifying* with a character, or a star, or a person in a certain sort of situation, explains a great deal about our response. As I have indicated, perhaps it explains too much. The notorious commercial failure of nearly all naturalistic films up to the wave of British working class films beginning in the late fifties,[8] encouraged adding The Escapist Theory of Cinema to The Identification Theory. The Escapist Theory tells us that people go to films mainly in order to escape from the dreariness of their everyday lives. Whether, in fact, their lives are dreary, or whether they would acknowledge this, or would try to escape rather than cope is not discussed: judgment is handed down from on high. Yet the theory would presuppose that people find their lives, conditions, and

[8] If I am right, the intense romanticism of the English working class *genre*-film and its connections with sexual myths and trendiness, may explain this exception. See my (1969b).

problems, so insupportable that they must escape from them. One can see that this could be true of sections of the working class in industrialized countries during the depression of the thirties. But in general? And then, the middle classes are just as much filmgoers, and just as numerous a group – do they want to escape from unsupportable problems? Is their filmgoing explained as escape? Moreover, in detail, an impression one has of the early days of magnates like William Fox, is that the price, not the content, was what counted most towards films' popularity. Films were cheap entertainment – or does perhaps the Escapist Theory classify *all* entertainment as escape? This smacks too much of the Protestant ethic for my taste as, one must grant that there are plural motives for seeking out entertainment.

Since the 1950s, when the USA, the UK, and the common market countries began to think of themselves as 'affluent societies', some decline in cinemagoing was perhaps to be expected. Yet we do not explain the actual decline which took place by this factor alone, but by the important factor of the impact of television. Assume, for a moment, that films and television both provide escape routes for the alienated mass man, what do the citizens of the affluent society want to escape from? They still use the media in great quantities, despite their lives being on the whole pleasant and comfortable – *and their being aware of this*. Is the answer that they want to escape from *anomie* and boredom?

Here I must protest. Boredom is not part of the original Escapist Theory of the mass arts – except in so far as industrial jobs under mass production were grindingly boring, as well as frustrating, poorly paid, exhausting, deleterious to health, and so on. The boredom of the well-off is another matter. For this case we must substitute the Distraction Theory for the Escapist Theory. People want to be *distracted* from their problems or from their boredom and the fact that they have nothing to do.

These theories rest on a great many shaky psychological ideas. Are they dispensable? The cinema is a dramatic experience, and to establish our desire for this, and the many ways there are to gratify it, is sufficient as a starting point for sociological study. Moreover, these theories are indifferent as to the quality and cinematic virtues of the film. This is no accident. If you believe, as many critics of mass society do, that popular films are *kitsch*, then you are not inhibited by not having seen them. You know the content of *kitsch* without having to subject yourself to it. Even if you can discriminate *kitsch* from quality in films, the mass audience certainly can't: their cultural consumptions function as *kitsch* – witness the lurid publicity which sells even 'quality' films.

143

This highbrowism on the part of critics of the mass media is deplorable – especially as it is based on false premises. This is very controversial, but I maintain that the mass public *is* discriminating, and that they will pass over big stars and big escapist material if the word is around that the film is poor. Box office winners like *Gone With the Wind, The Guns of Navarone*, and *The Sound of Music* were made with an exhilarating professional polish. They are distractions, certainly; they even allow us to identify if we want to. But more significant is that they create a consistent and enthralling dramatic world, which we can enjoy for itself and for the wonder of its creation. None of these films is more than efficient, but the public's preference for them is understandable and not deserving of derision. Truly great films are more thorough, possibly more austere, informed by greater subtlety, sophistication, and intelligence, perhaps essentially more personal in the worlds they create. There is the flavour of the debased convention, the stereotype, in these three films which barely raises them above mediocrity if the individuality of their artistic imagination is in question. To most people, however, who do not see that many films nowadays, who certainly do not remember them or see them again, who are unaware of the creative intelligence responsible, who have not had their sensitivities trained to detect such fine points, these are satisfactory worlds. The test of a good critic is his ability to discriminate on this ordinary level, and not to lose the capacity for discussion on the more severe and demanding level.

4 *The film world*

This business of the films creating a world into which the spectator enters can be pushed a little further. It explains, for example, the appeal of conventions. To build up the world of southern gentility as in *Gone With the Wind* or *Raintree County* takes a lot of doing; to paint the decay of that society (*The Sound and the Fury, Baby Doll, A Streetcar Named Desire*) is also an elaborate task. But to establish that a film is taking place in the west, or gangsterdom, or spyland, or in terms of song and dance, takes only a few suggestive strokes which evoke the whole familiar set of conventions and free the film's writers and directors to explore diverse problems, using those conventions as a shorthand. At one time, the Japanese thought that their films depended so heavily on Japanese society, culture, mores, and sensibility, that it would be useless to try exporting them to the incomprehending West. Certainly the Occidental takes a long time to come to terms with the conventions of an exotic *genre* like Chinese opera films, since he has no background to which to anchor it.

144

Skill plays a part here; Demy's all-singing *Les Parapluies de Cherbourg* jolts and then enthralls us in a couple of minutes, because he gently pushes us into the convention. In fact, Western filmgoers latched on to the conventions of Japanese society and culture very quickly – their efforts mediated by Japanese film makers' use of universal film conventions.

This theory of films creating a world apart is sociological and not psychological – since this world is said to come into existence only when the film is shown to a *group* of human beings. This thought leads to a modification of the idea that the audience is an unstructured group. Certain demands of perception and education are required before any group of people can be described as an audience in quasi-interaction with a world on film. Primitive peoples shown films often cannot even 'read' the pictures as those of people and places. We, the film-trained, can not only do this effortlessly, but we can read the pictures and clues for a world suggested, not shown. Films have their own way of inviting the human imagination to fill in what is left out. Primitive peoples, i.e., those uneducated in film (e.g., the 1895 French audience which ducked when watching Lumière's *L'Arrivée du Train en Gare*), wonder where the feet are when they see a close-up, think a new scene is showing when the camera changes angle, and so on.

To a certain extent this world of the cinema must be connected with the self-images of a group. The characters in a samurai film must first and foremost be Japanese (unless the film is by J.-P. Melville!); gangsters must be American. Confronted with gangster pictures set elsewhere we are confused. To a certain extent the international conventions of gangsterdom are Americanized, where they are not, much time must be spent on explanation and exposition; the convention cannot be utilized as dramatic shorthand. Only if we know that the samurai are Japanese can we recognize them as samurai. If we saw people acting like gangsters without knowing they were in America, we might mistake them for men fighting a civil war; anything. This is most revealing when one looks at films with the conventions of another culture. It is fascinating to enter the world and conventions of the Japanese or American teenage sex film. What is taken for granted in these films, and what is explored in detail, is entirely a function of the culture or subculture they stem from. It is revelatory to enter the world of modern dress Chinese films out of Hong Kong. This is a world where either: everything takes place in an indeterminate interwar period, and the characters wear pyjamas and cheong-sam, old men have beards, fat husbands are figures of fun – as is lisping or stuttering – and where most problems are intra- and inter-family ones; or: the time is now and the characters dress in western-style, are similarly motivated, go around in fast cars and aeroplanes, flavour their speech with English words, and in the end, behave with as much propriety as in the other type. To outsiders like myself, even the most basic question as to what relation these conventions have either to the so-called real world or to the myths of their subcultures is unanswerable. One's lack of education can be exposed, too. In writing about British films in 1968, after seven years out of the country, I found a return journey and fieldwork essential even to make basic headway with the films' claims to realism, atmosphere, emotional and visual verisimilitude, etc. The advent of 'swinging London' while I was away, might have seen the appearance of new types of people with reactions, appearances, interaction rituals I did not recognize and therefore could easily overlook. In fact, I found that, far from reflecting a new world, these films were trying to create that new world – swinging London is a sort of hard-sell to itself.

Perhaps above all, this world into which the filmgoer enters is one which is inhabited by *stars*. Stars are not, as the educated public sometimes misconceives, *just* actors; often they are not even actors. There are stars who never could act, like Errol Flynn or Victor Mature. There are great actors who never became true stars (Peter Ustinov, Alec Guiness). On the other hand, stars are not just people who got there by luck. A common distinguishing characteristic referred to when a choice has to be made between aspirants to stardom is a 'something': people who have a certain something, call it glamour, an intense camera-presence, something that immediately catches the attention of the otherwise innured watcher. This quality cannot be fabricated, as the many unsuccessful 'star-building' campaigns testify; but, like the quality of being photogenic, is just something you have. Moreover, it appears that one cannot preselect those who have it or not. At the least a screen test, and possibly even a film role, is required to reveal the fact. This is extremely important in the popular image of 'stardom' – as the space in which the profession has its existence is known. Almost no one need feel they could not ever be a star, until they have made the attempt. Stardom is thus somehow egalitarian. Since obvious faculties like intelligence, discipline, and technique, are not essentially involved with it, the inequality between persons on those grounds is swept away. Of course, not everyone has 'star quality'; but that fact cannot be known about any particular person without a test; and getting a test is part of the whole process called 'getting the breaks'. Moreover, even poor reception of a test or a minor role may also be explained away as due to 'bad breaks'. Some have made the grade after falling at these hurdles. Thus the egalitarianism of the system cannot be challenged. One can quite easily cherish the illusion that one possesses the ineffable 'star quality', and is as good as any star. This is a comfort. One is in a sense as good as the admired star. Yet stars are also gods and goddesses. Enormously magnified; embodiments of pulchritude, articulateness, elegance, and what not; they make love only to each other, way up there on the silver screen. Paid immense salaries, heavily guarded, living in palatial accommodation, sweeping around the world for festivals, openings, romances, divorces, adulated everywhere by fans; the stars live a life that has become a fantasy of the Ultimate Fulfillment for many ordinary adolescents.[9] On the one hand, the star is a star because he or she has something anyone might have – 'star quality' and 'breaks'; on the other, he or she is rewarded for having the quality and the breaks by a semi-divine status, with its attendant rituals of luxury, adulation and flamboyance. So far from the tension between the admiration on the one hand and feeling that 'I could get there too', on the other, proving a problem, it is a source of the power of the myth: we are all potentially gods. Nothing is ever said of the neuroses, egomania, and strain of this way of life, the artificiality and basic futility of being adored for doing nothing but exist. And indeed, while it is true that 'star followings' are real enough, it should be noted that they are sufficiently small to indicate a neurotic rather than a normal mentality. This is indicated by the fact that the presence of stars is often not enough to save a bad film (I discuss this, and what a 'bad film' means in this context, with reference to *Cleopatra*, elsewhere).

Apart from their following, stars have a function in films which is seldom appreciated and has little to do with the numbers of people they draw past the box office. Stars are what one might call a point of stability in a transient and disconcerting medium. Let me give examples. When one sees laconic Gary Cooper in a film, one's reaction is intensified by dim memories of him in a whole string of previous films in which he played laconic heroes. Thus, to any particular film, the viewer brings a whole set of expectations which the film maker can satisfy or disappoint. But, more important, Gary Cooper metaphorically carried with him all of these expectations and was thus able to build his screen performances with considerable economy by playing on and with our expectations. Were John Wayne

---

[9] The fan magazines (another topic for an essay) tried in the heyday of Hollywood to make Hollywood an extension of the world on the screen, especially in that the stars were shown as hobnobbing and romancing largely with each other. Of course th: stars connived at this, even to living and loving in a style (*mores*, housing, etc.) which owed more to their screen worlds than to the rest of America. See Sisk (1955).

to sing and dance in a film, or play an evil villain, this would be most disturbing. When he is the solid hero, one's confidence in him, and one's belief that he will survive all danger, turns on that previous context of expectations provided by his long career as a star. Even Marlon Brando, a serious actor, has not managed to defy our having expectations of him – we expect him to mumble and be neurotic. Occasional departures from this pattern (Brando singing in *Guys and Dolls*, playing a mannered fop in *Mutiny on the Bounty*; and Shirley Maclaine, a suicide and a lesbian in *The Loudest Whisper*, is another example) do not destroy the expectations built up and reinforced over many films. This 'casting against type' is in itself a means of exploiting audience expectations.

This function of stars as part of the economical language of conventions available in the film maker, perhaps explains – as an unintended side-effect – the phenomenon of 'type-casting'. Type-casting is where an actor or actress is consistently given parts of the same general type – laconic good-guy, evil heavy, pure innocent, good-time girl, etc. Understandably, actors and actresses of ambition resent this treatment and fight it, because, aside from one or two basic types which are perennial, the passing from fashion of a type means unemployment. Then there is the tedium of basically playing only one part again and again. Type-casting, like other mass-production attributes of Hollywood, has declined with the big studios, although in so-called 'character acting' it is still quite common – as volumes like *The Heavies* and *Who is That?* testify.

In general, our expectations of male stars are much stronger than of females. We're never sure if Joan Crawford or Bette Davis is going to be the heroine or the villainess – although we do know Doris Day will be Goody Two-Shoes. This may be because the male screen career tends to be longer. Many female stars never graduate to matron roles but disappear; whereas men in their sixties can go on and on playing ageless romantic figures.

This stability of the expectations surrounding the star, our confidence in him or her, may even allow film makers to explore themes they would otherwise be unsure of. Alfred Hitchcock played on this in *Psycho*, when he had sexy Janet Leigh, a major star, brutally murdered a third of the way through the film. Antonioni, similarly, in *L'Avventura*, led us to believe a striking young creature (Lea Massari) was his star. She disappears after half an hour of the film and never reappears, but the audience remains absorbed because they expect that the mystery of such a fascinating girl will be solved – it never is. Another use of the star system, is to try out a new star by giving him a star-type role to see if he can carry it off, sustain expectations, etc., despite his not being established.

148

The star system, then, has its objective logic. However, the usual theory of stars is that they are someone to identify with. Gods and goddesses, heroes and heroines, they are what we would like to be – both in their work and in their play – and our attachment to one or another of them reveals the content of our fantasies and dreams. To put it briefly, this theory appears to lack general application. Its usual picture of silly shop girls escaping their dreary existence into the lush dream world of Elizabeth Taylor, is highly contrived and even repugnant. People are not that simple, and shop girls are people.

On one point, however, the Identification Theory does shed some light. Namely, the alleged tendency of young girls (and young men) to imitate the style of currently fashionable stars. Rita Hayworth, Betty Grable, Ava Gardner, Marilyn Monroe, Brigitte Bardot, Audrey Hepburn, Julie Christie, burst upon the world – and suddenly everywhere one turned there were copies of them. Sometimes one even wonders: how odd that when Hepburn began as a star, girls suddenly developed boyish figures and pixie-ish features. But, of course, this metamorphosis is easy to explain.

One function a star serves is to fix a type of beauty, to help a physical type identify and realize itself. So what happened when Hepburn arrived as a star, was that many girls at all resembling her took the hint and set out to exploit those features of themselves that she does. To this end they marshal clothes setting off their slim figures, crop the hair, and use eye make-up for the dewy effect. Again: men now look for and at girls who resemble Hepburn; she crystallized and popularized the sex-appeal of a certain physical type. This sort of thing goes on across subcultures too – arty girls playing up the Joan Baez look; models (real, aspirant, and imaginary) the Jean Shrimpton or Twiggy looks. It is not only that a lot of English girls, as I write, are trying to look like Julie Christie; or that many who look like Julie Christie have learned from her what to play up. It is that Julie Christie represents a 'look' among English girls that has been around for some time, but which no film star possessed. All these considerations need to be taken together to handle the problem of so-called identification with stars.

My own theory of stars, despite its superficial resemblance to the Identification Theory, is much more objective, and it is that stars in films, like stars in football or the academic world, are clearly correlated with talent. Now what constitutes talent in the films is almost intangible. But to say that it is hard to describe, is not to say that it doesn't exist; the sheep are not separated from the goats by chance. A disjunctive array of the factors included under 'talent in films' might be like this: striking photogenic looks, acting ability, presence on camera, charm and personality, sex-appeal, attractive voice and bearing. These qualities are in short supply, especially in combination, and are highly prized when discovered. The fan goes to see a star because he can have high expectations of him or her in some of these areas. But a star is only part of the total image the audience has of the film, and that image can be an off-putting one, whoever the star is. This is taken up in Part Four.

XI

The Western and the Gangster Film: The Sociology of Some Myths

> . . . something romantic about him. He lives
> on horseback as do the Bedouins; he fights on
> horseback as did the knights of chivalry . . .
> he swears like a trooper, drinks like a fish,
> wears clothes like an actor, and fights like a
> devil.   Webb (1931)
> (quoted in Allsop 1967, p. 77)

1 *Myths and their meaning*

Films, like popular fiction in any medium, can, for different purposes, be grouped into various kinds of categories, all of them overlapping, and none more than a convenience. Musicals, family pictures, romances, spectaculars, war pictures, westerns, and gangster pictures are some of these categories. To 'locate' a film in one of these groups says nothing about it, it merely helps an author to organize his material, especially when he wants to make comparisons. I would allege, although I cannot easily substantiate it, that many producers think about films in these categories. This would give the categories a little more significance since, as Herbert Gans (1959a) and Lawrence Alloway (1964) have asserted, it would justify our looking at cycles of films, as well as individual films.

What is interesting about westerns and gangster films is a certain ritualistic and mythical quality their stories and heroes seem to have taken on. It is not, certainly, a quality wholly developed by the cinema. Western novels and gangster stories were being published prior to the invention of films, although certainly not in such large quantities. Nevertheless, film westerns and film gangsters have enough special characteristics and thus interest of their own to effectively prevent me from looking much at the written forms.

It is interesting that the original events and persons out of which the legends and myths of the film cowboy and the film gangster have grown are so relatively recent and well documented. The period of

151

the western appears to run from the 1840s to the early 1900s. Little is shown of the west earlier or later. The gangster films are entirely concerned with the period from Prohibition to date. This documentation is interesting in that it gives us a unique opportunity to watch myth and legend in the making.

My thesis in this chapter will be that the simplicity, well-understood character, and (connected) ritualistic quality of these two types of story, is sufficient to explain their appeal both to creators and to the public. I shall argue that these two forms, and especially the western, are conventionalized simplifications or frameworks within the discipline of which authors can pursue the most outlandish, or profound, allegories and make ethical explorations which would never be industrially possible if they were made more or less 'straight'. These *genres* resemble nothing so much as epic poems in the style of Homer: they have heroes, trials, and ordeals. They bear some resemblance to the reality they are taken from, but are also distorted and exaggerated in the way of legends.

We have, in my opinion, the true moral drama of our time within these conventions (Rieupeyrout 1952); and it is significant that this drama should be enacted within the confines of the cinema – a popular art form.

The popularity of the western and the gangster melodrama lies in the formality and simplicity of their settings and action. As a consequence of this formality and simplicity, even quite complex moral issues can be boldly and simply presented.

The simplicity and strength of these dramatic conventions is to a large extent due to their familiarity, and their familiarity comes from their frequent use by the mass media. The so-called 'adult westerns' or 'psychological westerns', developed only after many decades of straight western stories. The 'serious' use of the gangster or crime story was pioneered in print by Dashiell Hammett and Raymond Chandler in the nineteen thirties – the latter raising the form to literature. Much the same thing happened at the time in the cinema. Almost from the beginning, the gangster form was used to explore and expose the conditions that were thought to have brought it about.

The western and the gangster film, far from being worn-out by over use, constantly increase and renew the possibilities of the film drama, and extend the range and depth which writers can explore in it. In earlier times, only an oral tradition of great strength could have familiarized so many people with such a remote locale, its personalities and its issues. In our abstract societies, the oral tradition of story-telling has almost entirely been replaced by the mass media.[1]

[1] The transmission of (dirty) jokes and scandalous gossip is something that still proceeds largely as an (underground) oral tradition.

152

The heroes and locales of the western and the gangster were to some extent legends in their own time. The opening up of the frontier, the incredible exploits of Chicago gangsters, these things were talked of at the time. For this the popular press was largely responsible, and in the reporting of crime, and the exposing of nefarious activities, the American press has a long and distinguished tradition.

Buffalo Bill, Davy Crockett, Jesse James, Wyatt Earp, Al Capone, Baby Face Nelson, Legs Diamond, Dutch Schultz, John Dillinger, Bonnie and Clyde have been folk 'heroes' of long standing in the English-speaking world; their exploits, real and imagined, being written about, sung of in popular songs and folk ballads, and chronicled in innumerable popular novels, from their own time onwards. How to explain why such a list mixes vicious criminals with Robin Hood types? First of all, of course, Robin Hood was a criminal: an outlaw. Attitudes to these figures seem to be mixed. There is the simple Robin Hood appeal: the man who undertakes to right injustices in a world where the laws and authorities are unjust. Many of the heroes of westerns are of this cut: from *Shane* backwards. Then there is the anti-hero appeal: the man who gives one a vicarious pleasure by doing and relishing doing something we might secretly like to try ourselves. There is a third, rather crude Marxist theory, which has been put forward by Richard Whitehall (1964a), that capitalist society was rotten during the first gangster cycle and the gangsters ruthlessly carried through its injunction to pursue self-interest and profit at all costs. They, so to speak, showed the truth about the free-for-all society, and they prospered while millions suffered during the Depression – millions who only wished they dared imitate the gangsters.

The interesting point about the anti-hero explanation is, that it is quite unbelievable that most people would like to beat-up saloon keepers, push women around, throw bombs, launch machine gun blasts, arrange 'hits'. When the opportunity for doing some of these things in war presents itself, Western man very often cannot – at least without a shudder. Unless one accepts Bertrand Russell's theory that man has an inborn quantity of aggression which must be released, then I do not see how the explanation can be maintained. I think we must modify it and say that some of the elements, like taming horses, shooting villains with a fast draw, being the rich head of a criminal gang, give us a vicarious pleasure to contemplate.

I think the third explanation – Whitehall's – is suggestive, but can be criticized. It would explain why gangster films were popular in the Depression: but not their continuing popularity; nor the popularity of western villains – like the James Brothers, or Billy the Kid.

To return to the simplicity. Clearly, in the real west, if there was such a thing, and in real life, if there is such a thing, the issues and the men were not necessarily simple; and one of the more interesting developments that has taken place over the years has been 'hat, as the *genres* became more familiar, the makers of films could draw on more and more background knowledge of the locales and heroes, and thus paint ever more complex pictures of the issues and the people involved. Again, issues did tend to get simplified and blurred in the West and in Chicago too, because the people involved needed clear guides to action. On whatever side of the law people stood, they were in situations where actions counted most, and delay could easily be fatal. The idealizing and simplifying process, then, might be seen as beginning in the events themselves.

I call this whole tradition a 'folk' tradition because it has been carried, primarily, by popular art. Neither in Britain nor in America are the legends of the West or of gangster land taught in, for example, schools. The diffusion of information (or misinformation) about these matters has always been informal and popular. Popular, I suppose, because it dramatizes living issues in a simple way: the advantage of simplicity being that simple issues, unlike complicated ones, are easy to resolve. Whether the problems faced in the simple and direct form of western and gangster films have some bearing on contemporary people's lives, I must leave until later.

The issues dramatized in these *locales* strike me as being primarily moral and social. One can see a development from the early western novels, and films, to those of modern times. This development illustrates the incredible richness of the material. While at first, the western tales were simple ones of robbery and beating off the Indians (*The Great Train Robbery*, 1905, Griffith's *The Massacre*, 1912), the gangster stories told of the rise and fall of the criminal (*Public Enemy*, 1931; *Little Caesar*, 1932), both *genres* later became much more involved. *Broken Arrow* (1950) initiated a completely new cycle of western films in which the Indians were seen as hard done by. A year or two after this, I remember seeing several B-westerns whose names I cannot even trace, which centred much of their story on the machinations of corrupt Indian agents who practically drove the innocent Indians onto the warpath. Moderates versus extremists in both Indians and whites (*Run of the Arrow*, *The Searchers*, *The Unforgiven*), have been explored (*Taza*, *Son of Cochise*).[2] The morality of the Indian Wars has been chewed over again and again, from *The Massacre*, through *Fort Apache*, *Wagon-*

---

[2] 'Radical indeed is the change in attitude: redskins still bite the dust – but in no greater numbers than the White-eyes. Taza is no untamed, noble savage, but a high-principled, orthodox and democratic atheiete, tanned rather than red-skinned.' (*Monthly Film Bulletin*, 1954, 21, p. 91.)

master, to innumerable other westerns. The morality and psychology of honour and of being a gunman have been explored: there has been an entire film devoted to the thesis that shooting a man in the back is sometimes justified (*The Tin Star*). *Vera Cruz* begins with cynicism and anarchy, and ends on a high moral tone. *Guns in the Afternoon* is a brilliant study of the primitive gold mining camps and the conflict between two guards. The fight to establish law and order is a perennial theme: against timorous townspeople (*High Noon*, 1952); against organized criminals (*3.10 to Yuma, Day of the Outlaw*); against local big shots (*Law of the Lawless*); against criminal terrorists (*The Man Who Shot Liberty Valance*); against lynch-happy tyrants (*The Ox-Bow Incident*). Then there has been a chronicling of the so-called range-war, when the cattlemen fought to prevent the prairies being fenced in by the sharecropping farmers, and resorted to strong-arm methods to do so; examples are *Shane* – Alan Ladd the Saviour of the farmers, Jack Palance a black-clothed gun for the cattlemen – *Man Without a Star* (Kirk Douglas and barbed wire) and Samuel Fuller's splendid and unexpected *Forty Guns*, with Barbara Stanwyck as the cattlemen's boss. Apart from these, of course, there are the endless biographies of the major heroes and criminals (Earp and Holliday, *Gunfight at OK Corral*; *The James Brothers*; *Kansas Raiders* – the Quantrell gang – *Rancho Notorious*; *Johnny Guitar*, and so on).

But I have stated that Westerners were legends in their lifetimes, and legends in my view, are created. Why were those legends which were created consumed? Basically, I suppose, because America was a melting pot at the same time as it was a society with a lawless frontier, with a new, revolutionary, yet striving-to-be-stable political organization. It was a society with a future, but no past: yet it was a society that had to have a past or something to look up to it if was to survive. The lawless and the new arrivals had something in common: the need for an identity around which they could mould their lives and aims. It is an interesting point that America created its legends and its identity as it went along. The West, the frontier, and the gangster became legends while they were happening. They were a contemporary golden age, it might seem: but then, on closer examination, this turns out not to be true. Many films, for example, have treated the problem of the supply of women in the frontier West. First of all, women wouldn't go there: it was dirty, hard, dangerous and uncivilized. Yet without women to cook and breed, the men would die out. So at exactly the same time the West had a romantic appeal for men; and an unromantic lack of appeal for women. Those women who went West tended either to be floozies after the money, or a breed of tough, self-reliant women who faced the hardships with equanimity. In how many B-features has one seen the city-lady stepping delicately from the stagecoach into the dust of the boorish frontier town where she manages to be uncomfortable, unhappy, and, often, ridiculous? Similarly, I would tend to think, with gangsters. To live in Chicago, especially in the Capone suburbs, was not funny or romantic.[3] Yet Capone had a widespread Robin Hood-type appeal. He was an outlaw, but the laws he flouted were, initially, that outlawing drink, and, by extension, those outlawing gambling and girls. Most societies do not approve of their whore-house owners, or their publicans. But when the wet-noses try to outlaw every outlet, all outlets became equally respectable. Basically Capone and Co. provided a product; it was only when their ruthlessness and violence went beyond all imaginable limits (with, e.g., the St Valentine's Day Massacre), that they provoked a public revulsion.

2 Western myth and reality

So much on the general character of these mythic forms. I turn now to the western, and will leave the gangster for the subsequent chapter.[4] First, what is a western? Traditionally, the first western film has always been said to be Edwin S. Porter's *The Great Train Robbery*. A simple crime story (the robbery of a train), it is a western because of its *setting*, the American West. But the western is more than its setting: it is also the issues and the kind of men to be found facing the issues. Kurosawa's Japanese Eastern-western *Seven Samurai*, was with little difficulty turned into a western proper, *The Magnificent Seven*. The British have made westerns set in Australia (*The Overlanders*, *Eureka Stockade*) and South Africa (*The Hellions*). The Japanese, the Germans, and the Italians make their own 'cowboy' films. Now here we have a complete mix-up: westerns which take place in the West but with Japanese, German and Italian

---

[3] Kenneth Allsop (1961) says that Capone's marauding and extortion cost the State of Illinois $150 million annually (p. 281).

[4] I had the impression, when I began the research for this book, that a great deal had been written on the western. Yet, I found myself searching in vain through *Sequence, Sight and Sound, Film Quarterly* and *Film Culture* for definitive articles. There are one or two, of course, which are listed elsewhere, especially in *Films and Filming*, but the majority were in literary periodicals (like that by Warshow). Further checking revealed that a great deal has been written on the western, but almost all of it in reviews of single films. This made it a daunting task to sift the literature to see how much of what I say has been anticipated. I am prepared to believe it is quite a lot, and merely claim that it is here said for the first time in an extended form. On the gangster, there is almost no analytical writing whatsoever. Certainly no book comparable to Rieupeyrout's or Everson and Fenin's, and little attempt to take it seriously – with the exception of Warshow again.

creators; westerns which do not take place in the American West, with European creators; Eastern-westerns located in the East but nevertheless manifestly western in spirit and theme. All this indicates how vigorous a form the western is – it can get so mixed up, have endless variations played on it, and yet somehow still retain its universal and compelling character.

The figures of the western are: leathery scouts and trappers (*The Big Sky*); noble or ruthless Indians (Taza, Geronimo, *Apache*); strong, monosyllabic gunmen; powerful cattle barons; tireless bluecoated soldiers; single women – the waiting reward, sometimes replaced by 'saloons' and 'dancing girls'. The characters are plentiful.

Westerns have also covered every situation from the fight against the plains Indians during the drive West, to the Gold crazes of California and the Yukon. In 16 years of filmgoing I have seen more westerns – from Gene Autry, Tex Ritter, Hopalong Cassidy trash to the intricacies of Ford in *Wagonmaster* and *The Searchers*, the selfconscious psychologizing of Huston's *The Unforgiven* and Stevens' *Shane*, to the magnificence and high spirits of Wyler's seriously underrated *The Big Country* and Robert Aldrich's masterly romp *Vera Cruz* – than I have seen of any other film form, including war, gangster, and horror films. Westerns form far and away the greatest single *genre* of film output: they seem to exercise a permanent fascination for writers, directors, actors and audience alike. I believe that in seeing these films, one picks up an enormous amount of knowledge about the sociology of the West, as it was, and as it is interpreted by film makers. To give a few lighthearted examples: it appears that stage coach robbers always waited until the stage had passed them, before they gave chase. That convention has been dropped more recently, however. The ambush has been discovered at last. Another thing one 'learns', is that the best way to fight Indians is to draw up a circle, and then wait for the Indians to ride around it to get picked off. One also 'learned' that quite a few Indians are not keen on night attacks because if they were killed their souls couldn't find the Happy Hunting Grounds; and then one saw films like *The Unforgiven* where unsuspecting throats were slit, precisely, at night. One gets the impression that saloons were rather nice places where very pretty girls sang and showed their legs to appreciative gentlemen. One 'learnt' that no-one ever thought of shooting the villain's horse from under him: indeed horses came out of everything remarkably unscathed. One 'knows' that people chasing other people, would take aim with their pistols when still a good 100 yards behind. One 'knew' that they shot from the hip, that bullets kill quickly. One also 'knew' that to be tagged as a 'fast gun' was dangerous, since all the young punks in the territory liked to try their skill against one.

This kind of nonsense has been peddled, it is true. But we also know some things which are not quite so easy to dismiss. For example, it appears there were deep conflicts about the Indian wars and about fencing-in the range. We know that the establishment of law and order in new territories was a slow and hazardous business. Obviously, in the matter of the Indian wars there were at least two parties: the 'the only good Injun's a dead one', and the 'they were here first and, while they don't need all the land, they deserve considerate treatment', schools. These two schools battled both in Washington and the army, and among the frontiersmen themselves. One often sees pictures in which the Indian scout is looked on with deep suspicion by the new arrivals. Clearly, too, the cattle farmers needed vast spreads and unrestricted access to water holes and no wire against which cattle could hurt themselves. Then, Washington rode rather rough-shod over them in allocating land to dirt farmers in the heart of cattle country, providing little Federal backing in the form of soldiers to see that their rights were enforced. Obviously once either lawlessness, or summary justice, established itself in the new areas, it was extremely difficult to replace it with a more formal legal system. Apparently the whole tradition of drawing one's gun against another was a substitute for law and order. Disputes had to be settled and the easiest and cleanest way was to shoot it out. Once this became established, even trivial verbal insults became a shooting matter (witness the climactic scene in *Shane*). In a situation where a man was alone against the world, the imputation of his honour was something that could not be allowed. Just as a trivial theft like rustling or horse-stealing was punishable by death, because it so disrupted the economy and the society. A man without cattle was ruined, a man without a horse was helpless.

We have learned from western films a great deal about how the United States reneged on its reservation deals with the Indians, how the reservations were reduced, how armed whites were allowed to traverse them. We know that saloon keepers and merchants were often involved in gangs of stage and train robbers, being both providers of capital and fences for getting rid of the 'hot' money. We know that there were bitter feelings in the West after the Civil War was over, and even before, and that this led to quarrels and victimization (*Shenandoah*, *Invitation to a Gunfighter*, *Major Dundee*). We know that new land was occasionally distributed by means of a race to get there first (*Cimmaron*); that gold prospectors were preyed on by gunmen, who would kill them and stake the claim if gold had been found. We know that life was very rough in the West, that women were scarce and liquor was hard, and that there existed a class of gunmen-mercenaries who either would gun for whoever paid them, or who became sinister Bounty Hunters, that is, men who made a living by tracking down those on 'Wanted Dead or Alive – Reward' posters. We know that there were various kinds of Indians, some 'hostiles', others peaceable and innocuous; we also know the Indians fought each other as well as the white man. We know the West was a place where people could go to forget, or to bury, their pasts.

This list is already long, and perhaps boring to the non-fan of the western. However, I feel I have adequately made my point that there was a lot to be learned from watching the ordinary western film, that the legends they peddle had bases in historical fact and that some of these facts found their way to the screen. There was in the process of transfer a softening, a romanticizing, it is true. But boldly, I would say the westerns of the post-World War II period have, bit by bit, been discarding this protective shell and revealing to us a little more of what it was really like. Or, to be more philosophically precise, they have been showing us the real West in terms of our current strengthened concept of what that reality amounts to. I would cite the mining camp scene in *Guns in the Afternoon*: the makeshift and ill-lit bar, the hopelessly drunk miners, and the horrifying mockery of a marriage in a brothel with a whisky priest. The end of romanticism.[5]

So much, then, for the sort of thing we learned from westerns. Our education was never their makers' aim but, one thing which is interesting, is that from a few basic situations – the cowpoke, the Indians, the cattle wars, the cavalry – writers seemed to find plenty of scope for every kind of story line. Early westerns tended to be simple, and not especially western. *The Great Train Robbery*, for example, was a train robbery in western costume, no more. Similarly with much of the silent two-reeler westerns. In fact, the conventions of Victorian melodrama seemed to invade them. But in the twenties, and, especially after the revival of westerns in the sound era, around 1939, westerns increasingly came to have stories which would be meaningless outside the western situation. Attitudes towards women, corruption of Indian agents, cavalry manoeuvres, the range wars, protecting the gold and the Pony Express, these were all unique to the West.

More recently, there has been this reverse tendency to project anything from incest (*The Last Sunset*), to prostitution and rape (*Guns in the Afternoon*), into the western setting. This has done no harm, it tends if anything to enrich the western. All the more remarkable, then, that the West retains its separateness and identity as a situation and as a genre, despite these intrusions.

⁵ Cf. Woods (1959), on the reality behind the romance.

As to the absolute realism of what we see, and bearing in mind my earlier animadversions on the whole notion, my impression is that the early westerns were realistic as to setting and dress ('cl.aps' were big and flappy, guns were long and smoky, bars were crude and dirty), but that their stories were cursory and not very western. Later, as the stories became more realistic (better situated and motivated) and more western, it seems that setting and dress were glamourized and made much less realistic. 'Forties western conventions: clean clothes, elaborate shirts and pearl-handled six-guns, were absurd. Then, after *Broken Arrow*, a reaction set in and westerns became more sophisticated and more realistic in every respect (*Shane*, *The Hangman*, *Guns in the Afternoon*, despite romantic trimmings, were quite realistic), and at the same time more flexible. Nostalgia (*The Man Who Shot Liberty Valance*), and even satire, became possible (*The Pale Face*, *Red Garters*, *Ruggles of Red Gap*, *4 For Texas*, *Cat Ballou*).

Westerns can generally be 'located' in one of five rough-and-ready categories, which are in some sort of temporal sequence. The first, we might call Stories of the Pioneers. These are the hunters and trappers who explored the West, the wagon trainers who tried to cross it, and the cattlemen who ranched it. Here the themes tend mainly to centre on man versus nature: his natural hardships, including the country itself, and the marauding Indians.

The second category can be called The Opening Up of the Frontier. Here we have the stories of the stage coach and the Pony Express; the building of the railroad against physical and other hazards; and, of course, the conflict between the sharecroppers, sold land by Washington, and the cattlemen who thought they had the land preempted. It is at this stage we begin to meet the professional gunmen.

A third category I would single out, cculd be labelled The Coming of the Law. Here the stories centre on the differences between States and Territories; the problems of Marshals – understaffed with vast areas to cover; the anxiety of new towns to clean out their bad elements so that they can lead decent, orderly lives; the appearance of vigilantes and the bounty hunters; the driving of cattle to railheads for shipment; and the petering out of the Indian wars, the pacification of the occasional revolts.

Then one might invent the label The Law in Action: here the concern of the cinema is less with the physical and economic facts of the West, but with the moral and legal problems it entailed. Despite the pacification of the Indians, despite the arrival of the law, crime flourished in these wild times. A particular theme has been the good and the bad gunmen, and how they were played off against each other. In general, we have many examinations of the moral problem of sorting out the good from the evil. In *The Hangman*, the sheriff lets a suspect he believes is either innocent or reformed escape because he cannot expect a fair trial. In *The Tin Star*, a young sheriff learns that shooting in the back may be a necessity, if he is to survive and do his job. In *High Noon*, a newly-married marshal has to defend himself against four killers bent on revenge. The townsmen who have been so 'grateful' for what he has done, prove too cowardly to help him. His Quaker wife realizes that in the face of violence she will defend the man she loves. In the end the couple, thoroughly disgusted with the town, shake its dust off their feet. *Shane* shows how the forces of evil, when stronger than the forces of good, are overcome by a mysterious stranger.

A final categorization I would use is The Psychological Western. This is 'periodless', but was first produced only after World War II. Apart from relatively straightforward films with neurotic heroes or villains, there are also those entirely concerned with the psychology of the characters. In *The Searchers*, a father pursues, for years, the Indians who carried off his little girl, his neurotic loathing of the Indians becoming stronger all the time: when finally she is located as a domesticated Indian squaw he rejects her in disgust. In *The Unforgiven*, the discovery of the Indian blood of the heroine exposes neurotic attitudes in almost everyone, including a brother whose incestuous emotions turn to hate. While in *The Last Sunset*, the neurotic central character, discovering he wanted to commit incest, deliberately allows himself to lose a gun fight. Most westerns set in the modern or semi-modern period are heavily psychological, especially *Apache*, the story of the last Apache warrior, *Lonely Are the Brave*, the story of a man trying to maintain the western tradition of rugged individualism, and being defeated, and of course *Hud*, a modern western about the conflict of the generations.

The problem of why the West, in particular, lent itself to becoming the stage for these various kinds of drama is a difficult one to solve. My hypothesis would be this. America was a new nation, with ideals but without history. Ideals are difficult to envisage and be loyal to, but the exploits of one's fellow-countrymen are not. Could it be that, as soon as America had a history, her early period was glamourized for mass consumption? Then why was the revolutionary period not glamourized? This is a hard one: but I would trace the reason to ideology. The revolution was far less amenable to being given an individualist twist, unlike the West. And since rugged individualism was the keynote of the struggle to emigrate and then to make good, it found its echoes in those heroic days of the frontier and the West. A period that was quite short and soon over. What is interesting is the universal appeal of the dramatic form so developed. Englishmen, Frenchmen, Germans, and Japanese, all love westerns. Germans and Japanese have copied them, the Japanese have allowed their samurai films to be deeply influenced by them. Can this be less than the universality of individualism showing through? The grandeur of the form has produced some beautiful films from Japan: in particular Kurosawa's pair of masterpieces *Yojimbo* and *Sanjuro* in which a masterless samurai sets things to rights in corrupt towns; in Shinto's *Onibaba*, where the struggle for existence and love is reduced to basic essentials; and in the beautiful series of Zatoichi films, in which the blind masterswordsman Zatoichi fights single-handedly against evil and against those bent on destroying him. Zatoichi is a very western hero: he is a rough, simple man, who loves his *sake* and makes his living as a masseur and paid sword; he is a compulsive gambler. In *Zatoichi*, *Zatoichi Nidangiri* and *Zatoichi and the Chest of Gold* he creates a kind of Robin Hood swordsman, brilliant but vulnerable.

Although the simple basics of the West have this universal appeal, it should not be forgotten that much of the short history of the USA is glorified in films with a passionate intensity lacking in, e.g., British historical films. America's struggles, her wars, and her tragedies are living patriotic issues in a country not yet finished with forging her identity.

Television made a take-over bid for the western, and quantitatively it has made staggering demands on the conventions and settings. But I think the cinema western remains more sophisticated and exciting. Small screens cannot portray the romantic and evocative landscape of mesas, frame-built towns, and the tiny rider weaving among the scrub. Moreover, in their enforced confines of one hour and one half-hour television slots, which must be self-contained, they are unable to build much tension, or create an atmosphere as strongly as in the cinema; not to mention the lack of time for the writers to establish character and to develop their plots a little. The western is a great and moving story, and I believe a selection of the best westerns represents some of the finest work in the American cinema. Nearly all of Hollywood's great directors have 'been in the saddle', but the strength of the western is such that often the best come from the unknown or unimportant directors and writers,[6] who find a discipline and shape available to them in the western, which they could never achieve outside it.

[6] E.g., Walsh, Boetticher, Mann, Daves.

XII

The Gangster-Spy

1 The richness of formulae

Within the general category of crime melodrama films, in which policemen, private eyes, etc., can be heroes, there is a sub-category of films called 'gangster films'. In these the hero is either a gangster, or a policeman posing as a gangster. The plot formula is either the hero's rise and fall – if he is a gangster – or the hero's successful penetration of the organization and its destruction by him – if he is a policeman. The mood of the first formula is usually grim as we watch the brutalization of a youngster, and his development into a full-time mobster. The mood of the second is one of ever-present danger and threat. The first is the more interesting and characteristic – from *Little Caesar* to *The Rise and Fall of Legs Diamond*, they are almost Grecian in their certainty that the hero/villain's nemesis is to come. As in the western, the gangster milieu – overwhelmingly Chicago – has elements of folklore. Also as in the western, there is a streak of realism. How are these combined? By romantic use of the hero-cum-villain: no one doubts that gangland, like the real West, was a drab and dangerous place, that the individuals singled out by the folklore were in fact a good deal less charming than is implied. But this is a tolerable manipulation of reality. At its best, it goes only for sociological empathy, not sympathy. We are made to see the logic of the situation that made boy criminal, criminal vicious, policeman vengeful. We have here a general formula for the western, the gangster film, the spy film, the war film: they are semi-documentary in their choice of locales, plots and characters; they are romantically individualistic; they place emphasis on capturing an adventurous mood; and they stick to one or two basic plot formulas – sometimes even to certain stars to play stereotypes, and their popularity and strength gain greatly from this.

As Pauline Kael remarks (in her *New Yorker* column of 16 November 1968) of westerns, audiences go to them because however botched the job, there are the guaranteed pleasures of the background landscape, the relaxing stereotypes, and simple values. There is also the underestimated intellectual pleasure of being able to

163

compare it to others. These remarks apply, *mutatis mutandis*, to the other archetypal formulas of the popular cinema: the gangster film, the war film, the spy film, the musical – even the woman's weepie. One of the vastly underrated strengths of the popular arts, is their use of formulas. Entire television series are predicated on such formulas. Perhaps the most rigid ever was the Perry Mason series; more recently there has been the 'Mission Impossible' formula. The point about the Perry Mason formula is its irrelevance: nothing in the work of a criminal lawyer has such a formula as: first part groundwork, second part courtroom – with everyone kept in the dark until the final sleight-of-hand revelation by Mason in cross-examination. This is a superficial and magical picture of a lawyer at work. 'Mission Impossible' in its own way is equally impossible. The schoolboy tricks of briefing, and the perfectly timed ingenuity with which they defeat whatever cause they are against, are useful only to display machinery.

The whole point about the formulas of the western and the gangster film are their flexibility and their relation to universal human experience. Flexibility, in that the formula allows as true and realistic a film to be made as is desired, and yet remains within the formula. Universal, in that the formula can be utilized and varied to explore themes from those unique to the west, to those commonly found in every group of mankind. The stereotypes and rituals need not enslave the creator, they can be exploited to challenge or surprise the audience.

2 The rise of the gangster film

The career of the gangster in the cinema has been an altogether more self-conscious story than that of the western. Moreover, this story cannot so easily be explained as being the case of a legend which served a function in America's social melting pot, and found in film a natural vehicle to carry it. For one thing, gangsterism began with Prohibition in 1920, when the need for a melting pot was to a certain extent already over; for another, gangster films themselves began only in the late twenties – with *Underworld* (1927). They were an immediate success, a success immensely increased by the addition of sound – when the crack of gats and the chatter of tommy-guns could be reproduced in all their chilling horror.

As Kenneth Allsop so persuasively narrates in *The Bootleggers*, large scale gangsterism was born in the Chicago of the Prohibition era. The political cause was the attempt to prohibit the manufacture, sale, and import of all but the weakest beers into continental United States. The social cause was the active resistance of a large number of the public to this puritanical legislation. The economic cause was that this resistance was converted into an effective demand, since people discontented with the liquor ban were prepared to back their dissent with money. The demand came to be supplied by illegal organizations which gained public approval for their resistance to puritan legislation. The money to be made was large. Those gangs which learned to organize liquor-running, used their organizational expertise to take over other forbidden pleasures such as gambling and brothels, which could be conveniently streamlined by the already wealthy and powerful alcohol criminals. The money was so tempting that the criminals fought internecine wars over who 'controlled' what 'territory'; they also 'bought' public officials to turn a blind eye to their activities.

Now these men, while admirable when running booze to a thirsty public, and an amusing spectacle when killing each other off, were less admirable when, after Repeal, they continued to indulge in criminal activities, and in the corruption of public officials for the benefit of their prostitution, gambling and drug rackets. Moreover, the system of 'protection'[1], which had appeared during prohibition, continued after liquor was freely available. Thus, despite the public's initial amusement at men like Capone, so well described by Allsop, gangsters were not folk heroes for long. Then how to explain the popularity of the *genre*, and the concentration of film makers upon it?

I have several hypotheses: one is that gangster films are often films critical of aspects of American society – or even protests about it. The gangster form is an exciting and saleable formula in which to make the protest. The second hypothesis is that the gangster formula provides admirable opportunities for studying the individual fighting for himself against powerful odds. The carefully planned crimes, the betrayals and double-crosses, sometimes seen from the policeman's, sometimes from the criminal's point of view, tend to exaggerate what the individual is up against in society. Thus they constitute a framework in which writer and director can dramatize and reflect on these problems.

A third hypothesis would be of a more general character: gangsters are a secret society; a world in which the real world is mirrored and its values at times copied, other times inverted. This world has the appeal of all such worlds: the conspiracy theory of society.[2] If there are secret conspiracies which are held responsible for many of the ills of our society, but which also permit their members to do some of the

---

[1] 'Protection' – payment to criminals who ostensibly agree to protect the payer from others; in fact who agree not themselves to attack.

[2] See Popper (1962) for an explanation of this term.

things we might secretly like to experience ourselves, these conspiracies can expect to be the focus of a certain amount of curiosity and even romance. These remarks also apply to the recently-popular spy film cycle. Except that in the latter case, there are two conspiracies battling it out in the shadows: the good guys and the bad guys. This perhaps heightens, in our uncertain age, the romance and the thrill. Westerns, gangster films, have tended to revolve around certain simple and straightforward value attitudes. Spy films have rocketed to popularity at a time when established values are undergoing intense scrutiny and testing. Spy films appear to present issues in more subtle and involved ways, while in reality falling back on staid and old-fashioned values like love of country.

It would be as well to add that both westerners and gangsters have this in common: deeds count more than words. They are both peculiarly photogenic in that sense. I tend to agree with those who think a good plot and rousing action are ingredients in many of the most successful films. I don't accept the theory that action and visuals are the *essence* of the cinema, since I don't know what the essence is, and since there are many great films in which there is little action and a lot of dialogue. But as a generalization, characterizing much popular cinema, it seems to me true enough.

The first really important gangster pictures were *Little Caesar* (1930) and *Public Enemy* (1931). Their savage stories, use of locations and sound, and their introduction to two of the great gangster actors (Edward G. Robinson and James Cagney) mark them as a milestone. At that time, gangster films were mainly jazzed-up crime stories, putting forward the view that crime didn't pay. Or, at least, that was the overt attitude adopted by the films. In fact, there was an open invitation to enjoy vicariously the sense of power and excitement the gangster had at his peak, and then to watch him get his due deserts and be glad one is enjoying it in films and not in reality. Simply expounding and exploiting the milieu was the concern of these early efforts, and it was to be some time before Wyler, in 1936, examined how, in *Dead End*, the criminal was a product of a 'criminal environment' of poverty and contact with mobsters. It was still later that in his last great gangster role, Cagney was to participate in a film, *White Heat* (1949), in which the gangster is seen as a psychopathically disturbed and tormented personality.

The *genres* of the gangster and the mystery story were rather woven together in those early days, and it is difficult to classify the Raymond Chandler films, Huston's *Maltese Falcon, Key Largo* and *Asphalt Jungle*. In my view, the gangster is a special kind of crime and mystery film in which gangs are involved and usually there is little mystery: it is mostly a matter of excitement at who will win.

Perhaps one identifies these films best by their stars; Robinson and Cagney, were soon joined by Bogart, Raft and Widmark. Certainly other actors (like Muni and Steiger) have taken on gangster parts, but this first group made a speciality of it for a while in their careers, and the *genre* remains connected with them.

Most people think the thirties and forties were the great vintage era of the gangster film – and certainly many wonderful films of this kind appeared then.[3] But one should draw attention to the fact that, in the mid-fifties, a completely revived and revamped gangster film began to appear; the *genre* was injected with new themes and new life. Starting quietly with crime films like Quine's *Pushover* and *Drive a Crooked Road*; Karlson's *Five Against the House*; Lang's *The Big Heat*; Webb's *Pete Kelly's Blues*; rising through *Black Tuesday*, *Kiss Me Deadly* to Corman's *Machine Gun Kelly*, Witney's *The Bonnie Parker Story*, Lerner's *Murder by Contract*, Siegel's *Baby Face Nelson*, Wilson's *Al Capone* and *Pay or Die*, Karlson's *The Scarface Mob*, and thence to the splendid sixties when we have a positive rush: Wise's *Odds Against Tomorrow*, Boetticher's *The Rise and Fall of Legs Diamond*, William Asher's *Johnny Cool*, Sam Fuller's *Underworld USA*, Don Siegel's *The Killers*, Ralph Nelson's *Once a Thief*, Rene Clement's *The Love Cage*, Arthur Penn's *Bonnie and Clyde*, Roger Corman's *The St Valentine's Day Massacre*, John Boorman's *Point Blank* and Peter Yates' *Bullitt*.

The most immediately noticeable feature of this recent crop of films is the new directorial faces – especially Wilson, Nelson, Asher and Boorman – from television. They bring with them a new abruptness, an addiction to the bizarre and the vicious. Robert Aldrich's *Kiss Me Deadly* set both styles in motion. His hero is ruthless, even sadistic; the film is full of modern art, terrifying ellipsis and mordant humour.[4] In *The Killers*, the younger assassin plays with toys and giggles compulsively; in *Once a Thief*, one mobster, who always uses a sinisterly-plopping, silenced gun, is a nasty, heroin-addicted albino, permanently shrouded in tinted lenses.

But in many ways the most polished and satisfying of these films are *Johnny Cool*, *Underworld USA*, and *Point Blank* (enough has been said about *Bonnie and Clyde* by Pauline Kael [1968]). Cool's assassinations: of Jim Backus in a railway station, with a bomb

[3] For a brief survey, cf. French (1967).
[4] See my (1961a) for a detailed treatment of Aldrich up to that time. His subsequent films have been commercially more successful, but not quite so interesting (*The Last Sunset*, 1960, *Sodom and Gomorrah*, 1961, *Whatever Happened to Baby Jane?*, 1962, *Four for Texas*, 1963, *Hush Hush Sweet Charlotte*, 1964, *The Flight of the Phoenix*, 1966, *The Dirty Dozen*, 1967, *The Legend of Lylah Clare*, 1968, *The Killing of Sister George*, 1969).

thrown in a swimming pool, with a sub-machine through the double plate glass on a skyscraper penthouse, are spectacular; his nemesis – tortured in screaming agony suspended over his own coffin – is suitably grim. This is a film without social or moral pretensions of any kind. The hero is a killer and the girl is simply attracted to a remarkable man. *Underworld USA* is like a dramatized newspaper story. It opens with a boy watching his father beaten to death, it closes, after his revenge, when he crumples in a heap among some garbage cans: the final shot is blown up until it resembles a screened newsprint picture. The murder of the little girl on her bicycle, the getting up of Gela for his 'hit', and the final struggle beside a swimming pool are all memorable. *Point Blank* makes the best-ever use of the remarkable Lee Marvin. Tall, tough and unswerving, Marvin is out to get back some loot he was doublecrossed out of by his wife and partner. Time-juggling and bizarre elements show how the experiments of Resnais can find their proper home in a commercial film. Marvin's endless walk in Los Angeles airport (c.f. *The Graduate*), his wrecking a new car, the smooth executive-suite-respectable front of the man who double-crossed him, the executive mansion where Angie Dickinson turns on all the electric gadgets, the final confrontation while the villain is seducing Dickinson, the whole thing bathed in California sunshine, is compelling and intelligent. It is established that Marvin is a pro and the attempts of everyone to tell him he's out of date, or hopelessly outnumbered, wash off like raindrops. With *The Killers* and *Bonnie and Clyde* there is in *Point Blank* a most successful adaptation of colour to gangsterism.

The three films I have described hardly bring in the outside world, or 'the law' at all. They concentrate exclusively on the inter-criminal situation, and the characters of these people. One can speak no longer of heroes and villains because one is asked to follow and understand, not sympathize and forgive. Marvin receives no 'just deserts'.

3 *The emergence of the spy*

What of the broader significance of the gangster film? The modern gangster films are explicitly *not* socially conscious films with a message, or even a direct social comment. They portray an underworld, resembling, especially in its meticulous business arrangements, respectable American society, but with its own ruthless discipline and rules. Practically none of the films I have listed, is concerned with the gangsters' relationships with the public. Almost all are stories of intergangster conflict and bloodshed for revenge or whatever. I do not see any particular significance in the appeal this world has for cinema audiences. It would appear to be simple enough: we are all intrigued by disclosures of sensational things going on around us which we are practically unaware of. This is why the best gangster films have almost no external frame of reference. The underworld and its codes are complete and autochthonous.

What one might call the philosophy of the gangster has undergone an interesting evolution, which may parallel some increase in sociological depth. *Dead End* seemed rather to imply that slum living and bad example were at fault, and many thirties gangster films showed the good guy going wrong. In the forties and fifties, the emphasis turned to the psychological problems of the gangster, especially with his mother. Modern gangsters are neither slum kids nor neurotics, but members of an under-class with its own deviant norms. One sees a gradual improvement in what is called explanation by logic of the situation. The 'good boy gone wrong' theory, views the gangster more as a victim of his situation than a creator of it. The neurotic theory sees the gangster as psychologically crippled, and thereby creating or seeing his situation in a fundamentally distorted way. The modern view sees the gangster as in a special situation more or less of his own choosing, in order that he can realize certain aims. Sociologically, all three explanations are partial; but the latter is nearer to the truth.

It is this appeal of another world which would explain the fascination that spy films currently exercise on the public. No doubt Hitchcock made spy films long ago, but our modern breed are different and are mostly descended from 007, James Bond. Ian Fleming's novels, which began to appear in the fifties, became, around 1960, enormously popular in Britain and in America. Only then did someone take the plunge and film *Dr No*. Immediately this became a world-wide hit, and the Bond cult began. His imitators have been called 117, 017, x18 and so on; a great many of the imitations stem from France, and star Eddie Constantine or the hirsute Ken Clark. But Bond was followed by Napoleon Solo – the man from UNCLE – with three films to his credit; then we had Patrick McGoohan as Danger Man; Patrick McNee as John Steed, an Avenger; Len Deighton's nameless spy in *The Ipcress File, Funeral in Berlin, The Billion Dollar Brain*; then J. Le Carré's Smiley and Leamas (*The Spy Who Came in From the Cold, The Deadly Affair*); then Peter O'Donnell's *Modesty Blaise*; Matt Helm in *The Silencers, The Liquidator*, etc. Half parody, half sadism, was reached in *Our Man Flint, In Like Flint*, and *Licensed to Kill*, American and English respectively, and attempts to out-Bond Bond. Flint, besides flying his own plane, having immense wealth, being a karate and

169

ballet expert, has three mistresses and a cigarette lighter that will do anything. Vine, in Bond's wake, carries a pistol with an eighteen-inch silencer and a one-inch tie-clip gun. There are some very tense moments in his films, and the dazzling series of double-crosses at the end leave one gasping.

My feeling is that the spy should replace the gangster. If audiences now want more violence, sex, and an anti-hero who does not get his deserts, then the glamorous spy is perfect for the job. Practically anything he does can be justified as part of his work, including his women. In this respect, Fleming's increasing interest, in his last books, in bizarre villains was going in the wrong direction. Audiences seem to enjoy Bond for the pillow touches Fleming affected not to take seriously: his way with women, and his luxurious accoutrements. A curious obsession in spy films has been the gadgetry the hero carries, although Solo gets away with unashamed corn when he is, in one episode, strapped beneath a descending pendulum.

How do these two kinds of films illuminate my general ideas on the social structure of what is seen? The western is clearly a dramatic form which appeals to audiences and artists alike. The gangster-spy is nowhere as grand. They make jolly good yarns, extremely watchable, but there is little that is serious in them – and this is increasingly so now. They were made in response to a definite demand. In the thirties and forties they dramatized an insane historical period in the Chicago of the twenties. In the fifties they became increasingly an exploration of the *mores* of an alien world coexisting with the ordinary world. The spy is the final touch: the man who can live dangerously, act ruthlessly, and be admired for it. The films veer between the convincing and believable: *Pay or Die, Underworld USA, Once a Thief, The Ipcress File, The Spy Who Came in From the Cold*; to the utterly fantastic *Johnny Cool, Kiss Me Deadly*, Bond films and UNCLE films. Yet somehow the *genre* is all of a piece.

The sudden rush in supply can doubtless be explained by the industry's new hypersensitivity to what is the latest trend of fashion. Just as a certain style of design in advertising, or magazine layout catches on and is suddenly everywhere, so it is with films and bestsellers. But the existence of the most insatiable demand is harder to explain without reference to more general features of the society. Remembering Shils' (1961) warning that we cannot 'read off' anything about the audience from the films, can we use audience changes to explain taste changes and taste changes to explain changes in films? Many sociologists have suggested there has been a loosening, a diversification of the audience in the last twenty years. The decrease in puritanism, the increase in wealth, the siphoning effect of television, all indicate a new pattern. Perhaps they do. I am more nclined to reverse the sequence, and say that the plural and diverse character of the audience was always there but that the suppliers, the film makers, did not bother to diversify their product very much while the sellers' market persisted. The taste for the more sophisticated (and the more violent) film was built-in to the audience. In the new and more highly competitive situation of late, film makers have had the chance to reach out to this audience with the results noted. Of course, the increase in education and discrimination in the audience is an important secular trend, but the thirty-five years of the gangster film are too short a time for this to have had any effect as yet.

XIII

The Musical

1 *The rise of the musical*

Musicals[1] belong to a *genre* with many variants, e.g., operetta (Jeannette Macdonald-Nelson Eddy), comedy with music (Mae West), cartoon musicals (*Snow White and the Seven Dwarfs*), and the, for want of a better word, family child-star musical (*Bright Eyes*, Shirley Temple, 1934; *One Hundred Men and a Girl*, Deanna Durbin 1937; *Copacabana*, Gloria Jean, 1947). Not to mention straight opera and ballet, which are essayed from time to time – with as yet little solid box office success (*One Night of Love*, 1934; *Red Shoes*, 1948; *Tales of Hoffman*, 1951; *The Beggars Opera*, 1953). To restrict the scope of my inquiries, I shall declare my interest to be mainly in the musical considered as a film in which much of the story or theme is conveyed by singing and dancing. While components of it, like opera and ballet exist in high culture, and the music-hall exists in low, the form is a relatively new one. It is a folksy product of America, where Gershwin, Cole Porter, Irving Berlin, Rodgers and Hart, worked out a marvellously flexible *genre* allowing song and dance to be used not as interludes but as part and parcel of romantic, dramatic, and even satirical stories. The form came only slowly to maturity in the cinema, which inexplicably felt the need of an 'excuse' for song and dance. The first move was to film theatrical shows in a crude and unimaginative way, or to simulate such shows; of this kind were *Broadway Melody of 1929*, *Hollywood Review of 1929*, *Glorifying the American Girl* (1929) and the Marx Brothers *Cocoanuts* (1929). Perhaps the innovation of integrating song and dance into the development of the story can be attributed to Ernst Lubitsch and Rouben Mamoulian, whose respective efforts *The Love Parade* (1930), *One Hour with You* (1932) and *Love me Tonight* (1932) were highly advanced. In Germany, too, experiments along these lines were made with *Drei von der Tankstelle* (1930), *Congress Dances* (1931) and *The Threepenny Opera* (1931). However, with the marvellous exception of *Roman Scandals* (1933), most of the early musicals

[1]For critical suggestions in connection with this chapter I am grateful to a fellow student of the popular arts, Mr Brian Sanders of Lehigh University.

were of the back-stage drama trend. This did not preclude splendid numbers like 'Shuffle off to Buffalo' on the train in *42nd Street* (1933), or 'Dancing on the Ceiling' in *Evergreen* (1934), or the completely abstract dance-sequences of Busby Berkeley. Yet even in the very successful Astaire-Rogers musicals, it is rare that the song and dance is unconnected with show-biz somehow.

Standard histories of the cinema are confused on the relationship of the musical to its social context. Particularly puzzling is the coincidence of the first golden age of the musical with the Depression. Griffith and Mayer (1957) go so far as to claim that the Depression had killed off the early musicals by 1930 (p. 253), and then revived them again in 1933 (p. 302). These assertions can be rebutted by a casual glance at the evidence of stills printed in Griffith's and Mayer's own volume – there was no interruption in the output of musicals, or even of the 'all talking, all singing, all dancing' variety, e.g., they cite two in 1932, *Safe in Hell* and *The Kid From Spain* (with the Goldwyn Girls). These crude attempts to relate the popularity of a film *genre* to generalizations about 'Depression psychology', are opposed by our earlier critique of escapism (chapter X, section 3). The current example shows how escapism can be used to explain anything.

Musicals do pose a genuine problem, though. They are an artificial, conventional, frivolous, and yet highly popular form. For a time in the thirties, forties, and fifties, they were the major source of that most important item, hit parade songs. For many years they topped the Hollywood popularity polls. This was true in the depressed thirties, during the war, and in the late forties. How tempting to attribute the appeal of the most lighthearted of forms to the bad state of the world.

More plausible is the following: in the rush to capitalize on the innovation of sound, music, singing, and dancing were exploited to the hilt. After this first flush, there naturally came a phase of shaking down and sifting out. But the flow of musicals, although lessened, was uninterrupted, because, as we argue below, musicals appeal as a peculiarly full and pure use of the resources of the medium. The arrival of sound and the onset of the Depression overlapped by coincidence – but the slow-down in musicals is connected with the general fall in box-office figures in the early Depression, the approaching bankruptcy of several leading studios, bringing on a flush of caution. When revenues rose again there was an increased boldness. Musicals were also in jeopardy in the general rush towards the Hays code – as some of them were quite risqué. After the censorship clamp down, they were one of the few forms in which sexual suggestion could still be reasonably overt.

Cinema was well consolidated as *the* collective popular entertainment long before the Depression. It is intriguing that films showed a high inelasticity of demand – only comparable to that of shoes. But we don't need films the way we need shoes. Don't we? We need collective relaxation and pleasure certainly. In the Depression we needed more – because we had more time on our hands – and we needed it cheaply, and films were always that. There may be some component of escape or distraction in our general need for collective entertainment and relaxation, and this component may increase at times of social stress, but it is not a separate explanatory category.

In 1944, Vincente Minnelli made an innovation with *Meet Me in St Louis*. This utterly captivating musical was a nostaglic recreation of small-town life in America at the turn of the century – the locale now deep frozen in Disneyland's Main Street. Songs and dance numbers were used as naturally as could be, i.e., with no apology or 'framing' at all. Judy Garland's 'Have Yourself a Merry Little Christmas' is a lullaby to her sister (Margaret O'Brien); 'The Trolley Song' is just some exuberant kids rejoicing at a trolley ride; etc. Immediately after, Minnelli – who is the key figure in the American musical – made the extravagant, surrealist, and disjointed *Ziegfield Follies* – a dream-realization of what the lavish follies were like.

Several other MGM musicals were back-stage (*The Pirate, Easter Parade, Summer Stock* or *If You Feel Like Singing*), but his two other masterpieces were not. *An American in Paris*, which suffers slightly from an incongruence between the refined and sophisticated Minnelli, and the rather brash and showy Gene Kelly; and *Bandwagon* – the supreme example of the *genre* – the most sophisticated of all. *Bandwagon* is a backstage story which nevertheless integrates song and dance into the off-stage action. Fred Astaire's song 'By Myself' as he walks from the train in a continuous tracking shot and his *pas-de-deux* with Cyd Charisse in Central Park are both exquisite – perfect harmony between director and performers. While the climax, a pastiche Mickey Spillane ballet with Astaire and Charisse again, is one of the wittiest inventions of the whole *genre*.

Betty Grable, Doris Day, Virginia Mayo, Esther Williams, Jane Powell, Howard Keel, were all stars of the musical in its second golden age. This was a time when a great many directors, under contract to major studios, tried their hand at musicals. Here I want only to discuss the work of Stanley Donen, and especially his brief partnership with Gene Kelly.

On The Town was Kelly and Donen's version of Bernstein's stage musical about three sailors on leave in New York. It was brash, high-spirited, and fast, even if the music was unmemorable. Their second effort, *Singin' in the Rain*, was a triumph – the peak of the

Kelly musicals, it benefited from a sharp and witty script by Betty Comden and Adolph Green, vintage songs by Arthur Freed and supporting players – Donald O'Connor, Debbie Reynolds, Jean Hagen – as breezy as Kelly. The special fun and vivaciousness of the film may have had something to do with it being one of Hollywood's self-satires – about the coming of sound.

Donen went on to make the over-rated and over-done *Seven Brides for Seven Brothers*, and a final re-run with Kelly – *It's Always Fair Weather*, where the latter was joined by Dan Dailey and Michael Kidd as three soldiers on a spree. Kelly made an all-dance film in England, *Invitation to the Dance*, which was never shown in full. Donen's last musical was very romantic and wistful – *Funny Face*, with Fred Astaire and Audrey Hepburn. This was full of great ideas framed as a send-up of a high fashion magazine. There were sickly and unsuccessful things in it, but the best parts had style and distinction.

2 The end of the musical?

There, but for the stage, musicals almost ended. MGM, the company behind all the Minnelli and the Kelly/Donen musicals, began to fall apart as the big studio system was dismantled. The talented group of designers, writers, directors, and stars, by whom the best musicals were created disbanded. Kelly and Donen have done nothing since in musicals, Minnelli only pale, half-attempts (*Kismet*, *Bells are Ringing*, *Gigi*). Instead, with the rise of independent production, packaging resulted in only tired stage successes being filmed. *Gigi* had no dancing, and was by the *My Fair Lady* team. *My Sister Eileen*, *The King and I*, *Oklahoma*, *Guys & Dolls*, *West Side Story*, *My Fair Lady*, *Pajama Game*, *Damn Yankees*, *Funny Girl*, *Camelot*, etc., were all filmed with their inherent staginess and lack of true filmic poetry intact. The last attempt at a true film musical was Demy's *Les Demoiselles de Rochefort*, charming, but with no attack. An advantage of the big studio system was that they sought out and built up all kinds of talent, including singers, dancers and choreographers specializing in the screen. Since the break-up there has been none of this, and the trained talent just does not exist that can get out a filmically-conceived musical. *Star* (1968) is the first for a long time and looks like being a classic.

In their interesting book *Preface to Film*, Raymond Williams and Michael Orrom argued that the resources of the film medium were under-exploited in the matter of speaking, singing, and dancing – that all these could be directed to serious, expressive ends. My own feeling is that they seriously underrated musicals by ignoring them.

This is, of course, because they are well-meaning highbrows who Take Their Art Seriously.

In my view, the musical is among the purest and most enjoyable of all *genres* in the cinema, constituting the nearest the cinema comes to the pure sensuous delight of poetry. The musical is of sociological interest since to me it is the most refined and sophisticated of film *genres*, and yet it has on occasion been extremely popular. Naturally, it could not exist before the sound film. Naturally, too, it has connections with that tradition of stage folk-musicals from whence so many of our popular songs come.

Yet the magic blend of colour, sound, and movement of the best musicals could be done only on film (where there is time to get it right), and comes off best when lighting up the darkness of a theatre. It is musicals which divide the critical sheep from the critical goats. In Rotha's *The Film Till Now* they are barely mentioned. Some critics, who obviously love them, try to reduce them to something else – romantic escape, folk art, or even realism (Kracauer 1960). But truly they are *sui generis*, and response to them is a measure of response to pure film. Musicals cannot be looked at for their plot or their social comment: to do this is to make them seem impossibly thin. This is not to say the experience of them is very profound, although that word has philosophical overtones I dislike. I do think the *genre* is as subtle and as capable of expressing ideas as, say, opera or ballet. Musicals, however, are definitely simple and popular, usually being light romantic comedies. The critic who cannot respond to this use of film is, to me, insensitive to the medium in a fundamental way. To be insensitive to the medium might also involve insensitivity to the message.

Part Four

THE SOCIOLOGY OF
EVALUATION:
HOW DO WE LEARN ABOUT,
AND APPRAISE, FILMS?

In this part we take up the question of how learning and evaluation
take place. The answer, a trifle vaguely, is in all ways, all the time.
Evaluation is built into the making of films from the word 'go', even
though its institutionalization is not widely recognized. We learn, of
course, by trial and error, by making and matching. Putting these
two accounts together, we arrive at a theory about critical evaluative
traditions being accumulated, along with a vocabulary and syntax of
evaluation which is constantly self-enriching, allowing the cinema
full status as a mature art-form.

XIV

The Role of Evaluation in the
Medium-At-Large

1 *The unending process of evaluation*

Evaluation is a constant process which goes on throughout the life of a film, from its conception, through its production, to its first release, and even after that – when its age qualifies it for consideration as having 'classic' status and thus open to revaluation. As we become a culture more and more permeated by film, gaining much information from it, being familiar with its coding, or language, this constant process of evaluation grows commensurately in social importance. The notorious badness of most films on scientific, technical, or training subjects, not to mention films for schools (if I may be permitted so flat an evaluation), can be seen to be important when set against this background. People are expected to ignore a film's badness for the sake of an allegedly more important purpose which it serves. This is an implicit evaluation. The evaluation that goes on all the time is also perpetrated by several groups of people, not the same group, by any means: the cinema-going public; a specialized bevy of film critics; and people in the industry itself, both those involved in making the film and the jury of their peers.

The point of these arguments is to stretch the idea of evaluation to cover more than usual. The point of doing this, in turn, is to excise the preconception of filmgoers and film makers alike that evaluation comes up only when critics view films. Quite properly Gans (1957) emphasizes the great influence of evaluation and feedback involved in the creative process itself. So let us review the various stages of evaluation.

To begin with, the industry. We have already discussed how a project has in effect to be tentatively evaluated before it is made. However, this evaluation will be exclusively in commercial terms – or will it? It will be presented to the money men in those terms, certainly. But it is clear that producers like John Houseman, David Susskind and Stanley Kramer, whatever one may think of the end product of their efforts, sincerely seek out projects and people with

179

something to say and some prospect of excellence. How they come to their decisions and choices is a personal mystery. It cannot be that they go by reputation because occasionally they try out new talent. Though in the main, they know the talent involved and hope that it will gell into a good piece of work. In his important article A. H. Howe (1965), emphasizes that the real money men – the banks – do not evaluate the project at all. They evaluate the security of the loan. A producer with a project must approach a distributor, who evaluates. On the basis of this evaluation, he either stands guarantor for the bank, or agrees to stand guarantor once the finished print is ready. If the latter, the producer has to convince a third party (completion guarantor) that the project is feasible – evaluation and presentation are involved there too. Third parties and distributors are form-watchers, since a man whose previous projects have made money (at least recently) is preferred by them to a new man – other things being equal. The producers may take into account more intrinsic factors like the strength of the story, the quality of the script, the ability of the director and his suitability, and so on.

The industry goes on evaluating the film at every stage of production. The rushes are chewed over sometimes by the highest authority, sometimes by friends and others casually invited to give an opinion. When the film is being cut and finished, debate continues. After completion the distributors view it to make their sales evaluation. Sometimes the film's promise may have been such, that it was booked for showing before it was made. Otherwise, they are either deciding how best to market it or, if they have no financial interest, whether to market it at all.

A decisive feature of all evaluation up to the making of the final prints for showing, is that it can be *constructive* for the project. That is, what is said can *alter* the film as shown. Subsequently, of course, no amount of evaluation can change it (with the exception of limited re-editing which can be imposed on the final print). Can evaluation after the film is completed serve any purpose? Well, it can give pointers and lessons to the artists which they may care to apply in later work. Otherwise it is largely for the benefit of the audience.

After distribution has been arranged, the press shows are held for magazines and newspapers – special screenings for invited audiences. Here some of the audience resemble the distributors, in that they are looking for selling points which can be used to fill uncritical magazines. This will cause them to ignore films not to be widely distributed. Therefore, they are evaluating the films in terms of what they think will go down well at the box-office. Other critics, while not uninterested in this aspect, conceive their job more as one of giving a critical account of the film, from which their readers will be able to decide themselves whether or not to see it.

Finally, the film reaches the general public themselves. They do not evaluate when they go to the box-office; the box-office is mute, and while it sounds wonderful to say 'the public is never wrong', this may be deeply connected with their not saying anything. How can they? They haven't seen the film when they pay their money, and there are no mechanisms for refunding money to dissatisfied customers. No, the public surely evaluates the film and may remember and discuss it a little; but because this is decisively a *post hoc* process, do we find producers worrying about it? This is a problem; I know of no case where producers succeeded in getting a lot of people to pay and see a film, who were then bitterly disappointed and resentful. This may have something to do with the cheapness of the ticket relative to levels of tolerable waste of money. If the public were led by publicity to expect great things and were then let down, one would expect there to be an occasional outcry. Does its lack show how unimportant publicity is or the lack of a mechanism to make an outcry heard? My theory of the image, which I develop later, gets round this by showing that public evaluation is built into the image that sells the film, and that this image is not under the control of those selling the film. The theory of the image is a theory of co-ordination between film makers and film audience. Before I can explain this, I must explain the problem of co-ordination itself.

2 *Two theories of co-ordination*

Are cinemagoers getting what they want? Yes, say the film companies – look how much money we are making. No, say the highbrow critics – profits are no guide. It is easy to criticize both views. However, while I agree that all film industries can be criticized, I am less critical of Hollywood than of Moscow. Therefore, I come down slightly harder on the critics of Hollywood, than on Hollywood, for their lack of appreciation of Hollywood's superiority to Moscow.

To the companies, one could point out that some companies are making money, others are going out of business, so we cannot be sure that the public is getting what it wants all the time – if we are to go by profits. A possible reply to this would be that business is risk and obviously not all risks are going to pay off. In arguing this, the film companies would be changing their position slightly and indicating a partial co-ordination between what the public wants and what it gets, and that free market situations allow filmgoers to drive out of business the companies whose films they do not like. So some of the time they will be getting films that they don't want, and resources will be being wasted in producing these unwanted films.

To the highbrow critics it can be said, that if we canno. judge by returns or popularity, what can we judge by? The highbrow critic can reply that we could judge by returns if there were a perfect market – but there isn't. Since people have no real choice we cannot say what they want. To this we could respond, that in some places people do have an enlarged area of choice – a circuit books a highbrow film, or there is a cheap highbrow cinema in the neighbourhood. Why in such circumstances do people still show a preference for the lowbrow film? Here the highbrow can shift his position and attribute the public's failings to the corruption of their taste, the alleged conditioning or education of people to prefer the stereotyped and predictable. The position he might take is that it would not change things were producers to offer a different product, unless they (or someone) took steps to counteract the corrupt state of the audience – which somehow is no one's province.

These two opposite positions are those around which my discussions in this book have centred. In terms of these, the industry, the audience, the content and the criticism of the cinema have been considered. Both sides are guilty of exaggeration – the film companies oversimplify, the highbrows overcomplicate. But the opposition of their views may bring out what truth there is, and point the way for a more balanced appraisal of the situation.

I have made film companies argue that the public is getting what it wants; that suppliers are supplying what is demanded. To this it can be asked, if the suppliers are out to give the public what it wants, why do they not provide more salaciousness and lewdness, as these seem to be popularity-making attributes? They may reply that censorship, both by public authorities and by their own consciences, forbids them to exploit such tastes. If so, they would have shifted their ground again. The new position admits that the film companies deliberately do not always provide what they know the public wants and will pay for, but that they exercise restraint. Within these limits, they will provide the public with what it wants.

We have already come along an odd route. From the question of whether the film public gets what it wants, and the answers 'yes' and 'no', we have arrived at a position where it is held that the public is not allowed to have what it wants by the companies, and it doesn't know what it wants according to the highbrows. It is curious how both positions are highly self-reinforcing. The producer is saying he knows what's best and as he is making money he sees no reason to change. The highbrow is saying he perceives something most people are blind to and, because they are corrupt, cannot easily be made to see. The highbrow's conviction of his own rightness is as unshakeable as the producer's. The one judges by money, the other by his intuitive insight or intellect.

Clearly, both of these theories of co-ordination have some truth in them. The money is real enough and the sterling qualities [sic] of some wonderful films which have flopped are also clear enough. Wherein then does the mistake lie? It lies, I suspect, in a shared assumption: the corrupt character of the film audience.

The producer thinks the audience is corrupt and would be satisfied with a diet of sex and violence or even pornography – were he prepared to provide it. The highbrow thinks that education and upbringing have corrupted people to this state from an original distaste for such things. Both share a contempt for the tastes of their audience. One thinks they have to be checked, the other that they have to be 'corrected' (by re-education perhaps?). This is the fundamental assumption which I want to attack. I do not think people are natural lowbrows who have to be pandered to and controlled; I do not think people are natural highbrows who have to be educated to the realization of this. At the same time, I do not uncritically endorse the *status quo*.

Let us see what happens if we put our trust in, rather than have contempt for, the taste of the audience. Firstly, audience response cannot really be gauged by their entrance money – a lot happens after that act of payment or trust. Who has not sat through a send-up of a pompous or pretentious film by a shrewd 'local Odeon' audience, all of whom have paid to get in? If a film is popular, or runs a long time, then the word about it must have gone around, it might be said. This raises the little-discussed question of the cinemagoers' intelligence system – how knowledge about films is transmitted (by advertisements, by word of mouth, by star appeal), and what this knowledge consists of.[1] My own view is that every way open combines to produce and transmit an 'image' of a film in the advertising men's sense, and that it is this image which sells a film – which creates the expectations or anticipations which induce the audience to fork out their entrance money.[2]

---

[1] The single, but very good, text is Katz and Lazarsfeld (1955). Their whole book is on the flow of public opinion, and the crucial chapter is XIII where 'Movie Leaders' are discussed. There is a critique in Schulman (1965).

[2] *The Image* is already the title of two contrasting books: Boorstin's bemoaning of the power and influence of images and pseudo-events in a world of things and real events; Boulding's argument that our action is predicated on our image of how the world is, and that there may be some distance between how it is and how it appears in our image of it. Boorstin's is very much a pre-McLuhan book: he really has the picture of a real world of reading and seeing threatened by a

Now granted that audience response is important, and is not the same as box-office takings, we have to come to question our whole interpretation hitherto of the problem we started with: 'are cinema-goers getting what they want'? No one, I imagine, would seriously suggest that audiences only want good films, or that they resent paying for bad films. They can and do enjoy bad films, and they are perhaps even necessary to them as a canon against which to see, and recognize as such, better films. The quality of what the audience sees is irrelevant to why they go to the pictures. Box office returns are a general measure of the importance of the social institution of the cinema and not of the value of the films shown. Individual fluctuations between films, I take to be a function of the image-making. When a person pays his money at the box office he has, I think, two aims, one is to go to the pictures, the other is to go at a time when he can satisfy his curiosity about the image he has received of this one particular film he is about to see. If he doesn't like what he sees, his only redress is word of mouth. I know of no word-of-mouth campaign against a film, except for one or two organized boycotts by fanatical anti-communists in the high McCarthy years.[3] Mostly people are very uncritical of what their friends tell them about films and of trailers and critics – once the image has their curiosity roused they go in. My thesis is that when box-office returns of a film are poor, it has a bad or nonexistent image. When the market has a degree of freedom (places with fewer cinemas have more frequent changes and increase the week-to-week choice that way), such an image kills it. But when overall annual returns start changing, as they did with the advent of television, social change, not bad films, is the cause.

The highbrow view has to be reformulated as this: why does the public stomach so much trash? The answer is: (a) because the cinema is an important institution, the function of which is to pass time in a certain way and which cannot be killed by poor films; (b) that few people have the opportunity to develop their tastes. But people can develop their tastes – in this we trust them, we are optimistic. Is (a) really satisfactory? Maybe the public does not go to the cinema to see good films – good films, like the good life, may be something of a personal quest in which there is little co-ordination. Surely they do not go to see trash? By 'trash', I don't just mean

---

pseudo-world of media and images. Yet he sees the self-realizing character of images, and fails to go on to conclude that what he thinks in reality is constituted (Hayek 1955) out of the images he shares with others and acts out.

[3] The old Legion of Decency used to boycott and picket theatres showing films with a 'condemned' rating. This usually was only a threat, sufficient in itself to have the film withdrawn or cut. It is all *passé* now.

'ordinary' bad films, which again may be rather vague as a category. I mean, sheer incompetence – poorly shot and edited films without plot, sense, or acting. How do producers get by with this sort of thing? And is the producer of it showing contempt for his audience? Could it not be that the producer is a member of his audience and that he likes what he makes? Think of Cecil B. De Mille, he was perfectly sincere (see his 1960). But we are now referring to *really* incompetent trash, not to bad films. Material that the makers wouldn't lay any claim for. Does this show their contempt for the audience? My answer is 'no', because usually it is limitations of time and money which force them to make trash. There are few of these who produce trash without knowing it, or who, if given money and time, could not at least be competent. Then how do they get away with it? Possibly because of the cinema's social position, especially when it was the major mass-entertainment medium – and insatiable. Now that it has had a dose of competition, the real trash has changed. Inane serials and idiot westerns are now shown only at matinees for children, who are (mistakenly) thought not to pay any attention to technique. Also, much trash now appears on television where again it can scrape by because of the role of television viewing in the society. Television in its turn is now insatiable; it is desperate for material to fill its hours.

It is not my belief that either cinema audiences or children do not notice unadulterated trash. But they never receive such an unending stream of it that they are prepared to stop the cinemagoing habit altogether. Moreover, I have seen audiences refuse to be taken in or be impressed by a pompous biblical epic or a pretentious French film. When that happens, I can believe that if there were something like cinema-education, people's tastes could be developed. Why is there no cinema-education? Why do I state that people's intelligence about films is poor? Because the principal way in which education could be pursued, *via* critics, is defeated because the critics are highbrows. Instead of outlining the film story in simple language, and then why they think it is or is not good, giving examples and argument, critics prefer to be witty and clever about or at the expense of the film. Worse, when they see a film they enjoy which, reviewing all films and being highbrows, is rare, they more often than not write unintelligibly about it.

Intelligence from other sources, the advertisements, word of mouth, I judge to be poor both on experience and on the facts. The facts are that neither advertisements, nor word of mouth (nor the critics for that matter) can make or break a film. On the whole I think people are critical and on the look-out. Quite what they are on the look-out for I do not know. But it appears that huge audiences are mostly composed of people who do not go regularly to the cinema. The average takings and the average attendance indicate the importance of the institution not the quality, or lack of it, of the films. Seeing a film is only part of the sociological meaning o.' going to the cinema. In an effort to analyse the rest, I have written the other chapters of this book.

Does this lead us anywhere? Perhaps we don't know what there is in good art – but we recognise rubbish. Is the producer really corrupt – is he not a member of the public, shrewd to see what it likes, and that serving these likes would lead to his own destruction (by censoriousness and censorship)? Yes and no. Hammer Films know they are producing rubbish, but they do it with panache and get the Queen's Award for Industry. De Mille was sincere and thought his films were good. Neither produces really *incompetent* work.

However, we know rubbish is produced and we realize that people go to see it. Why? Because they go for social reasons. So we come yet again to whether they see what they like, or like what they see, or neither. It could be argued that public taste had improved. Certainly I think the average film these days, in the sixties, is in some sense or other better than in, say, the forties (*pace* Higham and Greenberg 1968). But the explanation of this is only indirectly connected with the public. It was a shift in social habits: the substitution of the television habit for the cinema habit that caused the shrinkage of the cinema market. The producers of the poorest films, Republic, Allied Artists, RKO, and the B-films of every company were squeezed out. Most of the big stars, writers and directors survived unscathed and went on to do good work. That this work has proved able to keep bringing in the customers, is an indirect tribute to the customers. With this rather optimistic view that films are getting better and that audiences are partly responsible, I may seem to be going too far. For example, there are those among the film critics who deplore the popularity of the James Bond films and the *Carry On* series. Now without taking up the cudgels for either – I find the Bond films quite entertaining, the *Carry On* films not that funny – one has to see a strain of puritanism in this criticism. The values of Bond are snobbish and violent and people enjoy this vicariously. The *Carry On* films are unabashedly vulgar, ritualistic, and corny. Yet I do not think one should moralize about either, that is not the place of anyone – critic, philosopher, or priest. Moralizing involves insufferable presumption: to judge other adults. One may argue that snobbery is to be deplored, that violence is to be deplored: it is a non-sequitur to say, therefore, films of snobbery and violence are to be deplored. Propaganda for snobbery and violence, yes. But that in a way is the nuance

186

of the Bond films; they mock snobbery, and their violence is quite unreal and unserious, no more advocated than a Chaplin comedy advocates kicking people in the seat of the pants. About vulgarity and corn, one can say no more than that these are special tastes, harmless, and carried off with some verve in the *Carry On* series (*Carry On Spying*, *Carry on Cleo* and *Carry on Cowboy* being good examples). If one compares these films with the witless inanities of the films of Abbot and Costello, The Three Stooges, or Old Mother Riley, one would admit some progress.

XV

The Structure of Promotion and Evaluation

1 *The image and box office success*

The first problem I want to take up here is why people go to see the films they do go to see, and then proceed to discuss the ways and means devised by the film industry to influence that choice.

It is a fascinating study, the study of film box office hits. So often they are quite unpredictable; so often they are quite predictable; so often predictions go wrong. One of the most striking instances recently of the latter was *Cleopatra*. Its phenomenal cost was only sustained because the studio expected the returns to be astronomical. They were very high, to be sure, but it took some time before the film even covered its cost, despite increased admission prices and a mammoth publicity campaign. Meanwhile, *Dr No*, or *West Side Story* or *The Sound of Music*, or *The Graduate*, not especially expensive films, using no really big names (roughly, those actors and actresses who command more than US $250,000 per film plus a percentage of the profits, e.g., Cary Grant, William Holden, Gregory Peck, James Stewart, Kirk Douglas, Elizabeth Taylor, etc.), have made many times more money than they cost. The biggest enigma remains, of course, *Gone With the Wind*. Although made in 1939, then re-released every five years, it remained the biggest box-office grosser of all time until very recently. Why? Why do people go to see any particular film? My examples already refute three theories that have been put forward: they go to see stars (what about *Dr No*, or, for that matter, *Birth of a Nation*?); they go to see films they know are 'colossal' (Griffiths' *Intolerance*, most colossal of all, was rather a flop); they go to see films which have been 'sold' with high-pressure salesmanship (all its publicity didn't make *Cleopatra* break even quickly, and the other box-office hits had good, but not special publicity). One can generalize and say: stars are neither necessary nor sufficient for success; not all colossal pictures are successes; and publicity may be necessary but it is not a sufficient condition for success.

188

What then explains it? My own hypothesis, which is vague and tentative, postulates what I call the film's 'image' in the public mind. I claim that people go to a film because it has an attractive image. This image can be that great stars give wonderful performances; or simply that the story is very absorbing; or that it is an exciting film; or that there has never been anything like this before; or that it is spectacular. An entire company, Cinerama, has been sustained for ten years on this latter image. Cinerama is enormous and overwhelming, and people have willingly paid to see unimaginative documentaries and inane features like *How the West Was Won*. Cinerama came of age with *The Battle of the Bulge* and *2001: A Space Odyssey*.

The Longest Day was successful because it had a marvellous theme: D-Day, lots of realistic action and excitement, and the fun of spotting the stars. Its image was excellent. *Psycho* was elaborately publicized, as other pictures have been, with a 'can you stand to sit through it' campaign. But, because the film had the touch of genius, those who saw the film found it lived up to their expectations and their incredulous reactions spread the word. *My Fair Lady*, *West Side Story*, and *The Sound of Music* filmed some of the most popular stage musicals of all time, and did it slickly to satisfy a pre-sold audience.

My thesis is that the image is not wilfully created, because it emerges from an interaction between the publicity, the film itself and the audience. Hard-selling a mediocre film will not create an image; stars are not enough, they must be somehow in a suitable story and locale. Certainly, I would contend that an image tinged with ideas of the colossal and a good publicity campaign, are necessary conditions for the success of many films.

The image seems to arise like this. A film is made or is being made. Certain elements in it are selected out for sales points, and certain elements *are* sales points (the degree of coincidence between these two sets might be called 'talent at publicity'). These begin to be put around in the press and mass media. The film is checked for response against test audiences. If the image is fulfilled by the film, publicity (including critics) and word of mouth combine to spread this image abroad.

The problem now is, what makes an image a selling image? This is very difficult to determine, but there is little doubt in my mind that moods and fashions are involved. War films were surprisingly popular during the war; surprisingly unpopular immediately after it; popular again during the Korean War; unpopular again after it; revived in popularity in the early 1960s. Musicals, again, seemed to go through a slump in the late fifties, but to revive again in the early sixties, although in a different manifestation. Westerns are perennials, but here we see the image particularly at work: the average western gets its average audience. Some westerns, however, like *High Noon*, *Shane*, *The Big Country*, *Cat Ballou* have something special about them: an exceptionally tense construction, an epic proportion, immense grandeur, and zanyness, respectively. As a result all were successful. In general, however, it would seem that the successful image is what one might expect it to be: an image of thrills, mystery, horror, enthralling story, etc. In the creation of this image, one factor ought not to be forgotten, and that is the often decisive importance of the title. The title should be compact but tempting, not obscure (cf. *Behold a Pale Horse*), although the recent spate of long titles has done their films no harm (*Dr Strangelove: Or How I Learned to Stop Worrying and Love the Bomb*, *It's a Mad, Mad, Mad, Mad World*). The very presence of certain stars can, combined with the title, suffice, e.g., Sellers was enough for *The Pink Panther*: a completely irrelevant title. The biggest image as I write is still James Bond: this image is so strong that it has made a minor actor, Sean Connery, into a big star; his straight films *Woman of Straw* and *The Hill* undoubtedly did better than they otherwise would because of him, and because the Bond image and its charisma had 'rubbed off' on him.

The role of stars in the image of a film is difficult to pin down. The first film, *Dr No*, was full of unknowns; any foreign film or Disney cartoon gets by without stars. So stars are not a necessary condition of a saleable image. Are they sufficient? Absolutely not: one could list dozens of expensive flops similarly bursting with stars. Neither a necessary, nor a sufficient, condition of success, the star's position is thus highly ambiguous. My guess would be that stars have their followings: those who make an effort to see the films of their favourites. But in aggregate this following is a small proportion of the audience needed for success – it is useful, but not enough. Looking at image-formation one requires a different concept than 'following'. Part of the appeal of an image will have to do with the appeal of the stars of the film. Here concepts like (the Spanish) '*simpatico*' and 'aversion' are needed. Cinemagoers become familiar with an array of stars, some of whom they feel *simpatico* towards, and still others they feel aversion to. Now, depending on which they feel towards the stars concerned, there is here a contributory factor to the emotional pull of the developing image. As the image is passed along to, or starts to be constructed by, an individual, his reactions to the familiar names of the stars will play a significant role.

One can argue, then, that stars function principally as fixed points of reference or familiarity for the filmgoer.[1] The image he has of the new film is, clearly, vague at best. But if there are stars in it, he will be able to narrow the range of his expectations considerably – at least he knows how the protagonists will look and sound. It should be remembered that stars were created by the public, in the teeth of industry resistance. Even in the Soviet Union, where opposition to the cult of personality in the cinema has a longer history than opposition to the cult of personality in politics, the public has focused on certain admired players. The star-system is a feature of all the dramatic arts, and I would suggest that this general function it performs in the cinema applies to these too.

Zany comedy is in revival now in a way not seen since *Hellzapoppin*: one reason being the teenage fad for 'kookiness': *Cat Ballou, What's New, Pussycat?*, the bikini beach comedies, etc. A tendency detected in these last few years, is that of pushing against the limits of what is dared to be shown. Gone are the settled days of production codes and the captive audience. With palates whetted by the almost overpowering violence of the murders in *Psycho*, the explicitness of the sexual scenes in *Liaisons Dangereuses, Bambole, The Servant*, we are witnessing creators striving ever harder to shock and titillate. Certainly *Repulsion* combined horrible murders and extraordinary sexual detail (the sounds of intercourse clearly heard, male underwear smelt), going as far as, for that moment, could be devised. When a film manages to go a little further and still has entertainment values independent of this, then that seems to become part of its image, and often a very saleable one. Ingmar Bergman's pessimistic and searching study of loneliness, despair and frustration *The Silence*, was seen by many because there was so much detailed public discussion of the sexual scenes, including how much the censors felt compelled to cut out in various countries, and so on. *The Dirty Dozen*, and *Bonnie and Clyde*, took the level of violence a stage or two further. On ground thus prepared, Sam Peckinpah was able to base his masterly meditation on violence and morality, *The Wild Bunch*.

2 How the image is formed

The problem now to be considered is that of the structure of image formation. This is done mainly by a publicity machine. These machines are entirely separate from the usual advertising agencies

---

[1] 'The importance of stars in forming expectations is related not only to their intrinsic popularity, but also to the type of role in which they are usually cast and the type of film in which they are usually featured.' (Federation of British Film Makers (1963), p. 46.)

which are used by other industries. In the first place, there are a large number of specially developed outlets for the publicity machines. In big studios these are special departments, in the case of independent productions the publicity is usually worked out between an officer of the production company and the publicity department of the distributor-exhibitors. The special channels available are: trailers (that is, short excerpts from the film interlaced with commentary and shown in cinema programmes up to the day before screening); fan magazines (that is, monthly magazines devoted wholly or largely to gossip, interviews and 'previews' of film industry product – gossip concerns stars mainly, but also producers and studio executives; radio and television also have magazine programmes of this kind); the general press (that is, interviews, serializations, and feature articles can be placed in ordinary newspapers and magazines, sometimes written by the professional publicists, sometimes written by staff writers or freelancers of the magazine with the production company's co-operation); 'sneak' and 'gala' previews and premieres (special showings of the film to typical or special audiences); critical writing by the multitude of critics of newspapers and magazines; and finally, books of the film, or novels adapted from the film's script, and sound track records. In all these ways publicity is spread. To a certain extent most of these can be manipulated. Even critics can be flattered, cajoled and by other means influenced. Their influence in general being so small, however, there is not much effort expended on this. Last but not least, there is poster advertising in every medium and on special billboards, anywhere. Which of these many channels is utilized, and how, is a matter for the ingenuity of the individual publicity man and his staff. Trailers and posters are always produced. Stanley Kramer flew journalists from all over the world to Hollywood to preview his *It's A Mad, Mad, Mad, Mad World*. Simultaneous premieres are held in different capitals of the world. Illustrated brochures are given away, 'oscars' are awarded (contrary to popular belief, these accolades are mainly of publicity value), film festivals are entered, parties are given, and so on.

One structure, however, is quite unintended and more or less out of the publicist's control, and that is simple word of mouth. As I have said, I think a film gets good word of mouth publicity provided that it has good entertainment value and good promotion and that it fulfills expectations. This last factor seems to me important, because however well sold a film is, if it disappoints people generally they will hardly commend it to their friends; rather the contrary: they will speak of it as over-rated or not very good. I know of few cases of word of mouth selling a film which has not been publicized or given a good image. There are some, and the trade calls them 'sleepers'. Usually what happens is that a minor film gets such enthusiastic public response that it becomes worthwhile to cultivate its image and make money where little was expected. The methods of publicity are understood well enough from other industries: sales campaigns are created and paid for, etc. But the process of evaluation of films – where the critics come in – is not well known at all. Firstly, 'sneak' previews have nothing to do with it. A sneak preview is not sprung on an audience expecting something else. Rather, on a marquee is marked 'major studio preview tonight'. Gala premières, oscars, and festivals too have little to do with the 'trade'. The first are celebrity and often charity occasions; the second are voted by the industry which tends to appraise by box office returns as much as anything else; the latter are, it is true, adjudicated by juries, often of critics. However, the preselection process is controlled by the industry or the festival authorities, whose motives are decidedly mixed. The critics, on the other hand, are an especially privileged breed. For them are staged late morning 'press shows', when severally they sit in a half-empty cinema, their hands clutching wads of publicity material, trying to make up their minds about the film that will open tomorrow. Sometimes they are primed with drinks afterwards, and must seek to evade the pressing invitation of their hosts': 'what did you think of it?' Most national newspapers and many magazines employ a specialist full-time to write their film criticism. If they have integrity, they will let him or her write what he thinks without concern for advertising revenues lost or gained. What is extraordinary is that these shows are staged by an industry which firmly believes that the critics have little or no effect on the box office success of a film. Moreover, I personally believe that the industry is right in this supposition. There are so many films, so many film critics writing on so many days in so many periodicals, that no member of the public not a specialist could be expected to be influenced by them. Those that are influenced are likely to be followers of one or two critics they find they have an especial affinity with. Magazines like *Time* and *Newsweek*, of course, wield some little influence; yet their film critics are often uncompromising highbrows and seem incapable, however savage their treatment of some film, of directing public taste.

Yet if the cinema is a medium of artistic expression, as well as a major social institution, criticism is of the greatest importance. For the function of criticism is to explain why works are good or bad; it is thus educational and enlightening. We seek to develop discrimination and standards, for otherwise the film cannot be taken seriously. This is a study in sociology and not in aesthetics, so no serious discussion of the film's claims to be taken seriously can be entered into. However, I have some points of a sociological character to make about film criticism, its history and development, and its objectivity. They would seem to be appropriate to end the volume, since they stake a claim for serious recognition of the medium which is still sorely needed when one sees how little about film is as yet taught in our academies to children and undergraduates.

XVI

Towards an Objective Film Criticism

The history of film criticism is that of a late developer. It hardly seemed appropriate to spill ink in discussing the actualities[1] of primitive short films in the early days. Although serious writing about films began on some sort of regular basis in the teens of this century, it received its first real injection of vigour from the writings of the Russian theorists and directors, Eisenstein and Pudovkin. These great directors also wrote a great deal on their theories of film aesthetics. Not long before this time, in the twenties, regular film columns began to appear in newspapers and magazines, becoming almost universal in the thirties. It is curious that *reviewing* and *criticism* seem to have developed at about the same time. The distinction is an easy one to make, and to overlook: the aim of *reviewing* is to provide promptly a reasoned answer to the question of whether the film is worth seeing or not; the aim of *criticism* is to evaluate the film by more rigorous standards, by some more interesting test. The critic tries to explain wherein the merit of the good film lies, and why the flawed film is flawed.

1 The evolution of critical theory

One of the encouraging things about the development of reviewing is its gradual acquisition of the standards developed by critics. The best film reviewers in the English speaking world, operate with very high standards derived from critical discussions. Therefore, I shall discuss the evolution of critical theory and not deal particularly with the extent to which it has influenced reviewing. Early reviewing, and poor reviewing even now, barely operates with standards at all.

Early film critics had two problems to tackle at once: to stake a serious claim for the cinema medium, and to develop that claim by expounding its standards. This mixture of the two problems not unnaturally created confusion. Answers to the first problem were mistaken for answers to the second and left at that. Thus we find an entire argument which runs: film is an art because it can capture

[1] i.e., films of real events.

195

reality; because reality should be taken seriously, film must be taken seriously.[2] The more plausible argument: such and such a film is clearly a masterpiece of world art, therefore, the medium in which it was created should be taken seriously – this argument was distorted when attempts were made to say: such and such a film was a great work of art *because* it captured reality. Naturally, there were all kinds of other questions mixed up in this as well, for example, the confusion between truth and reality, etc.

But this was the first serious critical theory of the film: that film was unrivalled in being able to reproduce life as it is lived: here was its claim to artistic truth. However, realism did not consist simply in a recording and observing camera. Already Eisenstein noticed that, by editing, reality could be selected and emphasized: he felt the function of selection and emphasis was to reproduce the feeling of the moment and to reveal what was not visually apparent. The vividness of a horse falling off a rising drawbridge could be reproduced by slowing the shot down and otherwise prolonging it; the overthrow of established institutions could be shown by the collapse of statues and a shot of a church upside down; Kerensky's rise could be shown as he walked up a flight of steps.

Certain assumptions such as that the film is an essentially visual medium, and that it should therefore strive for visual realism, were contained in this theory. Both assumptions were ruined by the introduction of sound, which the theorists at first attempted to ignore.[3] Cinema has, for more than thirty-five years now, been aural *and* visual. Yet there are arguments against its essence being realism, quite independent of this. The place of cartoons, horror films, historical romances, and musicals has to be accounted for somewhere. Clearly it is not too satisfactory to be told that these are not *essentially* cinematic. This is just arguing by convenient definitions and the victory is merely verbal.[4] Moreover, let us take as counterexamples Czinner's films of great operas and ballets, and Cantonese opera films. These are very stagey and boring to my taste: they do extremely good business. Moreover, they are faithful visual and aural reproductions of real stage performances. Now these real stage performances are part of the real life people live; no more real and no less real than their family relationships, their jobs, their

[2] See section 1 of chapter X above.
[3] Cf. Raymond Spottiswood's book, and those of Rotha (1963), Eisenstein (1943, 1949), Manvell (1944), Kracauer (1960) and Montagu (1964). Some of these books barely acknowledge the existence of sound; others explicitly denounce it as an irrelevance.
[4] Cf. Pauline Kael's review of Kracauer's *Theory of Film* (1960) in her (1965).

struggle to exist, etc. Why then are not these films the epitome of screen art?

The demand for realism, moreover, has unfortunate consequences. For example, it leads to emphasis being placed upon sincerity or integrity in the creator. Being a state of the creator, it is in a sense irrelevant to the work of art; the creator's intentions, for example, are by no means necessarily a way of appraising or even interpreting his work. Moreover, a camera and a tape recorder are as much selections of what they are recording as a pen or a paint brush. And yet ... despite all these obvious arguments the theory was: realism.

2 *The mirror up to nature*

While I could not agree with those theorists who maintain that films have any special intimacy with reality, I do think there is interest in the way they hold a mirror up to society. It has always puzzled me as to why films have been continually subject to critical attack for showing violence, sex, wild college parties, etc. For these things are real, and are exposed in other media – like the press. The standard argument for making the cinema a special case says, that the attacks are mounted in the belief that films are abetting the tendencies they portray. It is as though what is being said is, that films are focusing on, recording, and thus permanently fixing certain, things the critics would rather were not happening. This fear that showing something will reinforce it, is rather akin to word magic. To talk of a thing, especially to name it, is to fix it, make it concrete, make it accessible, unavoidable. To ignore it, not to talk of it, on the other hand, allows the half-hope that it doesn't exist. In our culture 'death', 'sex' and 'cancer' are words that are treated like this. When we read in Stephens (1926), of how dreadful it is that films show petting parties, it is clear that really petting parties and not films of petting parties are what he dislikes. True, films may spread news of petting parties, but so will other media and word-of-mouth. No, by showing petting parties films help to strengthen if not endorse their reality, and thus to be guilty of working their evil magic on society. This is how they are a mirror up to nature. They can reflect, magnify, and even create. Films not only reflect society in its own image, they can cause society to create itself in the image of the films.

The theory which succeeded realism, and which was developed in the context of the actuality or, as it came to be called, documentary film, was one which called for the cinema to be 'the creative interpretation of reality'. This theory dealt with the 'the camera is selective' argument. But it persisted with the view that there is something called 'reality' or 'real life', which can be captured on film, and that film is peculiarly, especially or essentially equipped for this task. However, as soon as creativity is admitted, new difficulties accumulate for this theory. The great pro-Nazi documentary pictures of the thirties, *Olympische Spiele, Triumph des Willens, Blitzkrieg im Westen*; the great pro-Communist Russian films of the twenties, *Strike, Potemkin, October*; the patriotic propaganda films of the Second World War, all these became admissible as art, since they were all creative interpretations of reality. Their makers, probably quite earnestly and sincerely, wanted to portray reality as they (or their cause) saw it. For some reason this consequence was not relished; the progressivist bias of much writing about the film is difficult to explain. It persists in France, where one whole journal is more or less explicitly Marxist (*Positif*), in England, where the Free Cinema movement of the mid-fifties was part of the left-wing syndrome that developed after Suez, and in America where Richard Griffith has for long been its High Priest.

It may have been in response to these difficulties, that in the fifties yet another realist theory developed: films should be *committed* to reality. These theories, it should be explained, were intended to explain why the acknowledged masterpieces of world cinema were masterpieces. However, whether one could take the theory seriously for a moment, seemed very much to depend on one's selection of examples for explanation. My own personal test cases are: does the theory explain Griffith's *Birth of a Nation*; Keaton's *The Navigator*; Welles' *Citizen Kane*; Milestone's *A Walk in the Sun*; Kurosawa's *Rashomon*; Bresson's *Journal d'un Curé de Campagne*; Cocteau's *Orphée*; Minnelli's *Bandwagon*; Antonioni's *L'Avventura*; Bergman's *The Silence*? But I have to hand other awkward cases than those mentioned above: certain cartoons, horror, gangster, spy, and western films. The trouble is, the theorists seem to calculate their views by starting with D. W. Griffith, the Russian silents, British documentary, and Italian post-war neo-realism as their paradigms. This is all very well, but these films are already of a piece, in that a principal aim of each of them, was the Capturing of Reality. My list contains films that aspire to truth, but their Reality or lack of it is an involved matter.

To return to the fifties and the theory which came forth: the theory of commitment. This, which seems to have obscure origins in Sartre's obscure theory of *engagement*, evaluated films in terms of whether or not they were *engagé*. It seems to have been developed in reaction to the *Cahiers du Cinéma* theory of the *politiques des auteurs*. This latter contended that what counted in the cinema was the creative artists who shaped the whole. Now in the cases I have cited above, this *auteur* is pretty easy to identify. But the *politiques* was

applied to the American cinema, and threw up heroes such as
Samuel Fuller, Budd Boetticher, Raoul Walsh, Howard Hawks, Leo
McCarey, Nicholas Ray, Frank Tashlin and so on. In particular, it
practically deified the impish Alfred Hitchcock. On discovering him
to be a Roman Catholic with a fascination for blondes (Madaleine
Carroll, Ingrid Bergman, Grace Kelly, Kim Novak, Eva Marie Saint,
Tippi Hedren), a penchant for the serious (*I Confess*), and his being
given to such comments – baffling and profound for French film
critics – as 'the cinema isn't a slice of life, it's a slice of cake', he
became for them the profound metaphysical scrutator of the medium.
The *politiques* decreed that any film of an *auteur* was more interesting
than a worthy effort by a nonentity. Thus time was wasted on
inanities like Howard Hawks' *Hatari* and Nicholas Ray's *King of
Kings* and *The Savage North*, while anything by Wyler or Zinne-
mann was '*inutile de se déranger*'.

The commitment theory went to the opposite extreme and
measured films by their commitment. Curiously, no commitment
critic would ever answer the obvious question: commitment to
what? Yet, from the pantheon of commitment heroes, one could
deduce that commitment meant commitment to the poor, the
oppressed, the simple, the peaceful, etc. Even within its own terms
this theory led to absurdities: it was such a strong preconception (for,
after all, a script or plot summary will usually indicate what a film's
commitments are) that the amateurish films of the Free Cinema
movement were lauded, and their inadequacies overlooked: while a
film like Lewis Milestone's *Halls of Montezuma* was dismissed as
jingoistic; the Bond films were scrutinized for fascist tendencies; as
was *On the Waterfront*. This was a fun game, a sort of McCarthy-ism
in reverse, but hardly an enlightening theory. What were the commitments of Minnelli or Walt Disney, for example? Again the persuasive definition could be used, but the theory did not explain the
counter examples.

Wrapped up in this theory was another, that there were no purely
formal standards of excellence in any art; that good technique no
more implied a good film than mastery of rhyme implied good
poetry. There was some truth in this view, to be sure; but the fact
remained that while empty stylistic exercises and incompetent but
passionate pleas were equally bad, the former were the less boring
and irritating. Here a cleavage of sensibilities seems to occur: one
temperament appears to forgive inadequacies of presentation if the
cause is good; another temperamental type maintains that incompetent or inarticulate artists have no right to make a claim on
our time. Yet, even so, there is surely a blind spot in someone who

can dismiss *Olympische Spiele* as an artistic experience. Here concentration and consistency, the beautiful articulation of a point of view, however uncongenial that point of view, triumph over personal taste. One can no more sensibly blind oneself to this work than one can to, say, Aristotle or St Thomas Aquinas just because one thinks their philosophy was bad or mistaken. One can often read a book on philosophy and lay it aside with complete admiration for a consistent presentation of a clear and well-developed point of view, even though one thinks the point of view mistaken in all its particulars.

The beauty or wonder of a work of art is not dependent on its content being true, anymore than the truth of its content entails that it be great art. A work of art, like a stone, is not a moral agent, therefore it can itself be neither good or bad, true or false. What it says can be morally true or false, or factually true or false quite independently of its artistic value. Works of art dealing with subjects favoured by the Marquis de Sade are not *ipso facto* bad art, any more than works of art explicitly portraying sexual encounters are *ipso facto* bad art, as anyone who has seen Japanese Shunga will testify. Does it matter whether *The World of Suzie Wong* was or was not true about Hong Kong? There were certain facts in it about the economics and the social structure of prostitution which were quite true; there was also a shallowness in its psychology, and a false picture of the emotions of those engaged in prostitution. Do we not have to argue that there must be an autonomous aesthetic sphere, where works of art can be judged with only a glancing reference to what they portray? Do we not have to say that a mastery of form is a necessary condition of good art, although it is not a sufficient condition? Does not the same apply to a rich content, although not to an acceptable, or true, or appealing one? Humanity and understanding are desirable in human beings: I do not see that they can be demanded of works of art.

To be honest, I don't quite believe the argument I have just made, and I don't know how to modify it. Some people are blind to Fascist Art as I am blind to Hegel or Wagner: I can't even manage a grudging, 'one for trying: nought for achievement'. Art cannot logically be divorced from its moral and political dimensions and I sometimes fear that my ability to enter into the spirit of the masochistic Roman Catholicism of *Le Journal d'un Curé de Campagne*, or the rituals of Fascist films is a warning sign of how near the surface sympathy with these repugnant ideas is in me.

Now, after being subjective and autobiographical, I shall try to rescue film criticism from the morass.

3 *Towards a rational tradition of film criticism*

'Towards' because a short section at the end of a short book cannot create a tradition. I shall argue here that film criticism can only be rational and objective within a tradition of *critical discussion*, a rational tradition. I shall be rebutting the idea that film criticism cannot escape being *mere subjective reaction*; and trying to show that there is a definite sense in which *film criticism can be considered objective, viz.* in such a tradition within which we learn.[5]

In 1961, intellectual film buffs in Britain were in the grip of a revival of the commitment debate of 1956–7, which had grown out of a dissatisfaction with the existing state of film criticism. While agreeing the premise that there was something wrong with a great deal of film criticism, one must regret the way discussion of it quickly ran off into the sidetracks of form *versus* content, commitment *versus* uncommitment.

The following is a rational reconstruction of how the whole commitment theory muddle arose. The idea that there are true and discoverable critical principles in the arts, has to be rejected when the fact is faced that all candidate principles prove highly contentious. From this failure to *discover* true principles, it is invalidly inferred that there are no true principles and that subjectivism and relativism have to be accepted. All that legitimately, can be inferred is that the true principles are not manifest. Not unnaturally, there are those who are appalled at this yielding to irrationalism and who seek a way to escape it. They try to overcome relativism by accepting the subjectivist argument that no critical principles are *demonstrably true*, which they (mistakenly) interpret as meaning that none are *true* and therefore, whichever one chooses to accept is a purely arbitrary personal decision. This decision to commit oneself to a set of principles appears to ameliorate subjectivism, because once adopted they can be applied in a purely objective way. But the irrational subjective decision has merely been shifted back – it still lurks in the background. Because it is still there, and because it has been irrationally overcome, we find moral and political prejudices aired in film criticism with a fanatical sense of their unassailable rightness (cf. Lindsay Anderson's 'Stand Up! Stand Up!').

However, the subjectivist is right in thinking there is no *recipe* for good film criticism (or good film making), it is essentially an individual affair and therefore commitment to any particular side, or the lack of it, cannot be a necessary ingredient of this recipe. On the other hand it does not follow from there being no demonstrably true critical principles, that all principles are equally untrue.

[5] For a more technically philosophical statement of this view, see my (1967*a*).

Let us make a fresh start on the premise that something is wrong with present day film criticism. As I see it, there are three main faults: it is romantic, oracular, and literary. I shall develop my view of what it should be, in the course of criticizing what it should not be.

4 *The romantic rejection of reason*

The romantic believes in the film maker as a very special person possessed by a mysterious 'inspiration', whose flashes he rushes to set down. This view of the artist is at least as old as Homer – who virtually invokes the Muse to speak through him – and has obvious connections with the idea that unusual, holy, and mad people are inhabited by spirits (whence 'inspiration'). Unfortunately for the romantic, modern rationalists feel they can do without belief in both muses and spirits in trying to understand and criticize films. After all, the poet who dashes off perfect poems without thought or revision, is as rare as the philosopher who writes books straight off (Russell), or the film maker who works off-the-cuff (Godard). Generally, the process of creation is a much more thoughtful and considered process than the romantic allows, involving the rational use of knowledge of the medium's possibilities and, even more, its limitations. A film is not a direct personal statement, but the result of several people combining their talents and compromising with each other under a more or less powerful chairman (the director), to make a coherent piece of film. Film is a language which can only be written down by several people working with a number of pieces of equipment. This limitation is at least as important as the chairman's 'inspiration'.

Many people get ideas in a revelatory flash, but some have more and/or better ideas than others. The film artist is noted for what he is able to make of his ideas, when he tries to transpose them into a partly non-verbal medium. This 'creative' process normally proceeds by trial and error, draft and revision. How things turn out, not the intrinsic merit of the original idea, is what counts. Many attempts have been made to show how social pressures affect love, a noble and important theme. But only one *Muerte di un ciclista* and only one *L'Avventura*, has appeared. Why? Because it takes a Bardem or an Antonioni to succeed with such a theme. These two films show up bad criticism very well: a plot summary would conceal their marked resemblance; a description of their theme (how social pressures affect love) would suggest more similarity than there actually is. Only criticism which concentrates on their special style as films, would be able to answer the real problem they present the critic: why are these films among the greatest ever made?

If creation is a rational process then we can abandon the pernicious romantic idea that art is self-expression on the part of the artist. This theory is normally held *contra* those Communists and others who hold art to be merely subtle propaganda. As Wind has shown in his Reith lectures (1963, p. 57, 62ff.) the notion that art should be purged of ideas and express only artists' feelings is very recent. A primary function of art before the romantic revolution was to clarify and portray 'non-artistic' ideas. Wind has also argued convincingly that this mistaken divorce of art and ideas is a product of the romantic revolt against reason, which tried to replace ideas with emotions and feelings. But all artists and, therefore, the art they create is impregnated with non-artistic ideas (even if only with the meta-artistic idea that art should steer clear of non-artistic ideas). Films especially are not self-expression – like Isadora Duncan dancing – but are the result of transposing many kinds of ideas into the medium using imagination and a knowledge of its possibilities, effects and, more important, limitations. In those limitations we have, surely, the refutation of the self-expression theory. The limitations of his medium *force* the artist to compromise, to adjust, and even to change his original ideas so that the final product never much resembles the original 'inspired' blueprint.

Making a film is far more like making a building than it is like the conventional image of the painter dashing off an 'inspiration'. A building is originally an architect's idea, true. But before that idea can be realized there must also be land, money, materials, workmen, machines, etc. The film director, like the architect, has to compromise. To imagine, as some critics do, that a director is responsible for everything is extremely naive. Even rich amateurs are constrained by the limitations of their equipment, the talent of their friends, time, weather and luck. A film, then, is a compromise between ideas and circumstances. The artist seeks the best way to solve his problem: how to put *this* idea into film; how imaginatively to overcome or even use circumstances to this end. He may arrive at his solution purely intuitively, but his aim of solving a problem as best he can is rational. Credit for that much rationality is the least he can expect from a critic, and if from this compromise there comes a beautiful, coherent and moving film, then its whys and wherefores should be analysed with due respect for a triumph of the human spirit over circumstances.

5 Oracles and sages

Film critics too often tend to write as oracles, ultimate repositories of truth to whom two questions are put: what does this film mean (or, what is it about); and, is it any good? Then, like oracles, they pronounce their answer and there is no more to be said. The fact that other oracles make different pronouncements can be explained: either as (1) because the whole matter is simply one of opinion (so there are no oracles after all); or (2) that the other oracles are fakes. Let us take the second, *ipse dixit*, attitude first. (2) Not only does this view expose itself to the *tu quoque*, but it is also deplorably immodest and utopian. Immodest in assuming that the truth has been revealed to 'me' alone. Here we find no intellectual humility, no willingness to learn, no sense of the difficulties of talking about a complex and mysterious creation of the human spirit – a work of art – in a clumsy, verbal language. Only the bland assumption that 'I' know once and for all the truth about its meaning and value. This assumption is utopian because it is a mistake to believe that even were the final truth accidentally come upon we should recognize it as such; neither a lifetime nor an eternity is sufficient to complete the search for truth. We know from the history of thought how we learn more and more every day; and this is as true of films and works of art as it is of the world science studies. We find more and more meaning in great films (although, at the same time perhaps, time erases other meanings) and, by discussion and reflection, we come to a better appreciation of their value. Sometimes we teach ourselves to learn about these things by arguing out our judgments with ourselves. Sometimes we let others teach us by reading and reflecting on how they see the meaning and value of a film. But there are *no* oracles. There is only trying to learn about films by the rational method: critical discussion, which, when sustained over time, I call a *critical tradition*. These traditions work, e.g., just as literary critics agree on who the greatest English poets are, by and large; so also do film critics tend towards a common centre, when taxed to draw up the films they consider greatest. At the same time, because it is a tradition which challenges people to attack judgments and interpretations, we are not imprisoned by it. We can criticize and try to overthrow a widely accepted judgment or interpretation; but we cannot try this with all judgments at the same time. This way lies chaos and the breakdown of the rationality of the tradition.

Only by the free exchange of ideas within an institutionalized tradition of discussion, can we preserve the advance of learning. Just as in science we propose theories to solve our problems, and then discuss and even refute those theories, so in film criticism we should suggest interpretations of meanings and judgments of value and give arguments to back them up, and then listen to criticism and counter-arguments, *and try to learn from them.*

Although I think we can learn about the meaning and value of films in some objective sense, it would be a mistake to suppose that I am suggesting there is a formula which, when known, will give the correct results. There is *no* critical recipe. There is no set of principles in the sense that they can be learned and used like a machine, into one end of which you feed films and out of the other end of which they appear marked alpha, beta, gamma, delta, etc. This is as mistaken as to expect an induction machine in science. Criticism, like art and science, cannot be programmed, for it is an intensely human and fallible activity. However, we do seem able to arrive at some form of agreement within a critical tradition so that, from this lack of specifiable principles, it does not follow that there are no principles. Indeed, in learning to judge, and agree in judgment, these are probably what we are learning.

(1) Now to oracular subjectivism – all one does is express one's personal, subjective tastes. But if we can learn about the meaning and value of a film we are learning something, i.e., something external to us, something objective. But if we are learning something objective, then oracular subjectivism is false.

6 *The literary vice*

It might be argued that the curse of *all* criticism of the arts is that it has to be in words, while most of the arts are nonverbal. You can no more explain what Bardem did in *Death of a Cyclist*, what Antonioni did in *L'Avventura*, in words, than you can adequately say wherein lies the meaning and greatness of Bartok's Fourth String Quartet using words. Unfortunately, films are misleading: they contain dialogue and they have synopses. The critic using words finds it easier to talk of these other words than of the cinematic realization of the ideas: like the literary critic who prefers discussing the inconsistencies of Shakespeare's plots, to discussing his expressive and structured use of language to manipulate ideas and feelings. It is easier to bring a ready-made and arbitrarily committed set of principles to bear on a film, than it is to struggle to learn about the true principles of criticism. It is easier than trying to write better and better reviews knowing that you cannot succeed, that the perfect review is a chimera.

There is no finality, because there are no critical revelations or, if there are, we can never know who has them, *because learning both about the meaning and the values of a film is a slow, thoughtful process of mutual interaction between suggestions and criticism.*

Appendix

Appendix

Film and the Communication of Values[1]

Viewing a film can often be a powerful experience, leaving a deep impression. Particularly when the experience is worrying or upsetting, it may challenge people's values. This leads one to question what values films have, where they acquire them, and whether they are (e.g. inadvertently) making propaganda for violence. Other questions follow: is the film industry geared to churning out worthless and possibly corrupting distractions for money; is filmgoing an encouragement to apathy and passivity, favouring *anomie* rather than community; do films deal in idealization, stereotypes and oversimplification almost exclusively; is it the case that film publicity debases taste and blurs discrimination between good and bad? Because mass media impact on so much of society, should the society exercise some control over the injected values of the films? My argument is that films are not at all special, we know very well where their values come from and how they are introduced. In so far as they make propaganda, and that question is full of pitfalls, not control but a pluralism is the solution.

To organize my argument I shall treat separately of values in the *industry*, the *audience* it creates, the *experience* it gives them, and the *evaluation of the end-product*.

1 Values in the film industry

In *Picture*, Lillian Ross's acid account of the making of John Huston's film *The Red Badge of Courage*, there are only two encounters with the legendary studio head Louis B. Mayer. On each occasion in a cream-panelled office, with cream furniture and trimmings, Mayer histrionically outlines his values. *Ninotchka*, he explains, was a critic's delight full of smart alec values; while the sincere and lovable Andy

[1] Revised version of a paper given to the Centre for Culture and Technology, University of Toronto, March 1968. I have benefited from the comments of Joseph Agassi, John O'Neill and the members of the Centre.

Hardy series made money but gained no critical praise. It would not, I think, be unfair to say that during Mayer's reign MGM films reflected such sentimental and homely values. However, Hollywood made a lot of films in its day and if they had all truthfu'ly reflected the rather harmless outlook of the executives, there would be little controversy about the social value of Hollywood films or any worry about the lessons they teach in sex and violence. Since this is where queries have been raised, our discussion must range wider than the character of the executives.

The problems of values in the industry come down to these: whether people with particular value orientations are in a position to foster them in the industry; and whether the industry as a whole embodies values, regardless of whether these are the values of its personnel. On the first matter, one asks if the industry's management and workers have any socio-economic, ethnic, religious, political or establishment connections.

The cinema was and is a large industry: for a time in the forties it ranked third in the whole of the USA, and it is very big there today, if television filming is included; it is considerable in Japan, Egypt, Hong Kong, India, and Italy in relation to the gross national product of those places. What sort of values does the industry embody? There are several ways of looking at this. Who, for example, is the industry: where do its personnel come from, what are the values they hold? I can only answer these questions for the United States and Great Britain, but I have no reason to suspect that other countries differ greatly except perhaps for Cambodia, where one of the penances diplomats have to perform is watch films made by the head of state, Prince Sihanouk.

The cinema industry has always been, in an important sense, a classless industry. Indeed, its recruits are significantly concentrated in the lower socio-economic strata. Many of the most powerful executives in the big American studios arose out of that amazing immigrant ghetto that was New York at the turn of the century. The heads of 20th Century Fox, MGM, Columbia, Paramount came up from nothing. They were self-made men, usually Jewish, who got into the industry when it was wide open, and survived the various contractions, mergers and take-overs. Some of the battles were rough.[2] Indeed, one reason for the re-location of the industry from New York to Los Angeles was to escape patent infringement suits by Edison and others: Hollywood had the advantage of being a three or four days train ride from New York and only hours from the

[2] See William Fox's story of how he was deposed in *Upton Sinclair Presents William Fox* (1933).

Mexican border – it also happened to have good weather and low rent.[3]

What experience these early executives had of show-business was mainly in travelling road shows and vaudeville. In the early days, films were produced by the camera manufacturing companies, but the supply and the quality were soon found to be unsatisfactory, as was also the practice of selling copies of the films outright: audiences were bored by repeats long before the copies were physically worn out. When permanent show places found audience attendance slacking off, they got the bold idea of offering new programmes. But money was tied up in copies that had outlasted their drawing power. The solution was to circulate prints, not sell them. Capital was scarce, however, and films were produced fast and cheap for quick sale to release the money invested in them in order to make more films. If theatres wanted to hire and producers to sell, an intermediary was bound to appear – the distributor. One other solution was vertical integration of production and theatre chains.

The whole image of nickelodeon cheapness of the early picture shows was amply justified. Yet in little over ten years, the reorganized industry was so rich that Chaplin received a contract for more than $600,000 in 1916. Soon after, perhaps by the end of the First World War, the cinema's image was becoming somewhat more respectable. In explanation of what constituted the cinema's approach to respectability, I would offer Chaplin's work and D. W. Griffith's film of the Civil War, *Birth of a Nation* (1914). This was quite expensive to make, but grossed very well. Both Griffith and Chaplin reached a wide audience with works that demonstrated films could be sophisticated, even works of art. (Incidentally, in the case of both of them, increasing self-consciousness about Art was their downfall.)

Over the years, the film companies gradually found finance for permanent studios, stocks of back-log films, and so on, in the New York banks. Unlike production, this source of film finance did not move, and continues to be New York based. This need not concern us because, high risk or not, what came to be called 'the New York money boys' left production virtually completely in the hands of the Hollywood moguls. Overlords like Adolph Zukor, Louis B. Mayer, Sam Goldwyn, Harry Cohn, Spyros Skouras, Irving Thalberg, Jack Warner, etc., were for a long time adept at showing overall profits. New York did not begin seriously to intervene until the late forties and early fifties, when television and other circumstances made profits harder to come by.

[3] The tale is best told in Ramsaye's (1926a).

Mayer's scale of values as described by Lillian Ross was perhaps more frivolous than these others, but one's impression is that Goldwyn and Zukor and Skouras were not that different. Warner and Cohn were bolder and less philistine, and this certainly showed in the fact that their studios, Columbia and Warner Bros., consistently made more films that got away from the values of Andy Hardy praying at his mother's bedside. As is clear from the biography of Cohn (Thomas 1967), the personal influence of these men was immense. Where they chose to employ good film makers the result was often extremely good films.

Commercialism at the top is to be expected; more difficult to analyse is the attribution of sinister political motives and values to these powerful men. They are, after all, part of that military-industrial power élite which is credited with everything from pre-determining our consumer choices to pre-selling the Vietnam war. One crucial episode, the response of Hollywood to the attentions of the House Un-American Activities Committee, is a sorry tale of compromise, betrayal and blacklist. The record is bad, but not unique; the universities went through their shabby loyalty-oath convulsion at about the same time.

Whatever the values at the top – and we might be justified in defining it as the role of the top to be sensitive to commercial and political matters – to be of interest to us as filmgoers they must be shown to seep down into the typewriters, studios and cutting rooms, which turn out the product. This is tricky because people are inclined to cite what is *not* produced as evidence of the permeation of commercial and political values. It is true that Hollywood has yet to produce a film preaching Communism, vivisectionism, or flat-earth-ism. Why should it? There is no obligation here; Communist countries specialize in Communist films. If Hollywood or America try to prevent Communist films from entering the market, that is a different matter.

Another problem to do with how far the values at the top seep down into production, is the myth that while books are made by one person, films are of necessity made by several. Thus, the role of the co-ordinator who turns those several people into a team is essential, and that co-ordinator can be subject to executive pressure to co-ordinate in certain ways – ways which will favour a pattern of value preferences. However, it is a falsehood that films *must* be collective products; one man can today make a film unaided. There is, then, relative ease of access to the means of production in the film medium. Although one man with a special camera *can* make his own films, generally speaking in professional production this isn't done, since films, like most of the dramatic arts, can benefit from the division of

APPENDIX

labour. A brilliant director may have no talent for writing realistic dialogue; a man who is a genius at getting the photographic quality he is asked for, may not be able to instruct actors for toffee. But all this is a matter of degree. Where does division of labour stop and wilful tampering and alteration begin? It amuses us now to look at Rembrandt's 'Night Watch' and wonder over the stir it caused among his patrons, who pressured him to paint something more to their liking. Rembrandt was one of the first artists to consider this sort of pressure illegitimate and to be resisted in the name of integrity. We shall never know if Huston's *The Red Badge of Courage* was bad, as its preview audiences maintained, because they caused it to be re-edited, considerably shortened, and to have a commentary added – all this after Huston had departed for Africa to shoot *The African Queen*. A few directors have disowned work that has been tampered with in this way, but in my opinion, these were primarily problems confined to a phase in the development of the industry: it hardly happens today: the directors' union has helped to clarify legally the extent (or lack of it) of their control of the final product *before* a job is accepted. Ostensibly, when films are altered it is to render them more commercial – but that is often a smokescreen. When that most commercial of producers, Joseph E. Levine, was producing that most commercial of films, *The Carpetbaggers*, from that most commercial of novels of the same title, he gained a lot of publicity because Carroll Baker was playing a nude scene. In the final version distributed to all countries, this had been snipped out. The explanation offered was that it didn't add anything. That is not, in my view, an unmixed commercial judgment.

Perhaps the key problem here, is who should and who does co-ordinate the division of labour in films? Intellectuals assume that the co-ordinator is the director, and where it is not, it should be. In the industry, credit is often given to the producer. There is nothing in the nature of the process that makes the director the natural or the right co-ordinator, and if the industry is structured so that the producer always has the final say-so, then we see the director's complaints about art and integrity versus commercial values, for what they are: moves in a power-struggle or for a structural change in which the director will gain command of the co-ordinating role. What senior directors often do is become their own producers; but they have to have been successful, i.e., commercially adept, before they can achieve this.

What is the director after in this struggle? Freedom from commercial and political pressures, perhaps? But this is naive: whatever the structure of production is, no artist can reasonably

213

demand control of millions of dollars of his community's wealth-resources, and at the same time declare that he does not want to be either commercially or politically accountable. No, it might be said, all he wants is that decisions on resource allocation be made on the basis of aesthetic considerations, not money-making or political end-serving. Here the presupposition is that artistic considerations can be neatly divorced from money questions, and then re-married when allocations are considered. It is not clear how this translation can be effected; and if it is effected it can work in reverse, money decisions can be made and translated into artistic ones. What is there to choose between these methods? The very separation is suspect. The artist is countering the man who wants to decide all questions, including aesthetic ones, commercially, by proposing to decide all matters, including commercial ones, aesthetically. Both forget the community, which might step in and say that since *it* produces and owns the resources *it* shall decide their allocation – politically. No film industry has, so far as I know, resolved these problems to everyone's satisfaction, so it would ill behove me to pronounce where justice lies.

In addition to drifting down from the top, values can well up from below.

Producers, directors, writers, photographers, actors, etc., have diverse social backgrounds, although almost none come from the higher strata of society. Peculiar among these creators are the actors, whose neuroses are almost a defining feature, and the writers, who are usually well-educated by industry standards. So long as actors, in Hitchcock's immortal phrase, were cattle, penned by seven-year contracts inside the big studio, their neuroses hardly showed through in the product. Now that so many produce and own their films, indeed with the growth of so-called independent production generally, films have become much less homogenized. Such things as 'MGM gloss' are a thing of the past. But actor control gives rein to actor's values. Those endless close-ups of Marlon Brando in his recent films, where he has a lot of control, are a thing of the present. Is such narcissism the decisive refutation of the theory that good or true art has anything to do with self-expression?

Apparently the most bitter and dissatisfied creators in the film colony are the writers: their status is low, but their self-estimation is high.[4] Is it because the writers are so bitter that every film about Hollywood, almost without exception, is very bitter? Why were eight of the Hollywood ten, blacklisted by the HUAC, writers?[5] Apart from their general grumbling, now much muted, is there any

[4] See that mine of information by Rosten (1941), chapter 14.
[5] For their story see Kahn (1948).

214

real evidence that Hollywood pre-selected stories for their political or valuational aspects? It depends on the studio, compare MGM with Warner Bros.[6] If we refer to Hollywood as a whole, then from all periods there have come biting, bizarre, explosive films. If attempts at pre-censorship were being made they were singularly unsuccessful.[7]

Does the glamorous and extravagant image of the industry as a whole have any value significance? Does it corrupt? Does it instill false values? Is it an escape? These questions are disingenuous. Certainly for a time, instant stardom replaced the dream of log-cabin to White House as the fulfillment of the American dream. Less so nowadays, I would say, with the passing of that whole night-life-of-the-gods bit, and the general loosening up of American and British puritanism. Cutting a hit record, or being a model or photographer is much more of today; the drug-store racks of fan magazines have an old-fashioned air.

2 Values and the audience

The advent of the cinema, considered from the audience point of view, resulted in the rapid restructuring of patterns of leisure behaviour. William Fox remarks that when he was starting to build his chain of cinemas in New York before the First World War, the social centres of districts were the corner saloons. These were an exclusively male province, and resulted in men wasting money, and quite a few other socially deleterious habits: the splitting of men from their families, drunkenness and violence. Fox said that over the years he was to see the focus change, and the neighbourhood cinema become the social centre of the district: the twice weekly visits, with wife and children, involved limited spending, no splitting of the family, no drunkenness and no violence. How the patterns have changed! Family cinema outings are rare nowadays. The bulk of the regular attenders is unmarried young people.

There are various irreplaceable things about cinema-going: the insides of cinemas are faintly reminiscent of rather vulgarized church

[6] This fact about MGM, the lightweight character of its product, perhaps the most important fact about the studio, isn't even mentioned in Bosley Crowther's hagiographical *The Lion's Share*, the story of an Entertainment Empire (1957). If not the book itself, then this omission should have jeopardized Crowther's authority as a critic (for the *New York Times*) much more than it did. When one remembers Lillian Ross was banned forever from MGM because of *Picture*, one can guess how independent Crowther was able to be. See by contrast pp. 149f of Paul Mayersberg, *Hollywood The Haunted House* (1967).

[7] e.g., they did try and were awful at it. See Karel Reisz, 'Hollywood's anti-red Boomerang', *Sight and Sound*, 1953, for the story of their attempts to be anti-Communist. See *op.cit.* in note 5 for the consequences of war-time attempts to be pro-Russian. Even in Eisenhower's 1950s some critical films appeared.

architecture, and what of those cinema organs that used to rise up magically from the ground? The whole ritual of the lights going down, a hush descending, then ads, shorts, trailer, and a feature, virtually adds up to a liturgy. One might think the object of worship was the film stars, or even the values and ideas put over by the films. But the cinemagoing process itself may have been at the centre: if memory serves me, 'what's on at the pictures' was a dominant topic of conversation in those halcyon days of the thirties and forties. Cinemagoing ritual is a pure form of what Durkheim called collective representations: its only ideological content is itself. Significantly since television displaced films as a dominant conversation topic the rituals at local cinemas have been drastically simplified and curtailed. . . .

Cinema audiences are a radical case of the medium is the message. What the audience actually sees on the screen is subordinate to the social values implicit in the act of cinemagoing. Nowadays more than ever, since alternative channels of entertainment, distraction, and stimulation are plentiful. Like the theatre, the cinema is a collective experience away from home; unlike the theatre it is not necessary to feel oneself on show, e.g., in dress or companions; unlike the theatre too one can eat there, or neck and pet, or simply go in out of the cold, rain, or heat; unlike the theatre it is cheap; unlike the theatre it is classless. The theatre is decidedly middle and upper class. Vaudeville and pantomime is lower class. Even the ritziest cinema is classless.

This is to simplify a little, no doubt. True, the double feature has gone, but the long film, and the high-priced film, have come. Prices once found only in the première cinemas in the centres of large cities, where the intention *was* to copy the theatrical occasion, these prices are now attached to certain films wherever they are shown. In the other direction, jeans and an open-necked shirt are no longer frowned upon at live theatre performances. The class identities of both media are happily being eroded.

It follows from this that the usual explorations of the effects of the cinema on its audience, especially children, are utterly misdirected and beside the point. My McLuhanism is radical enough to incline me to dismiss out of hand all juvenile delinquents and others, who claim they did it because they saw it in the films. It is much more to the point to notice that pre-existing street gangs may go to a cinema and ruin other patrons' enjoyment of the film by noise, comment, and possibly, interference. The cinema is the sort of a social institution where they can carry on some of their pre-established deviationist *mores* – until the police arrive. The television outlet is usually in households, and is harder in any case to disrupt – witness its popularity flickering away in the corners of bars. Films are hot and harmless. What content gets through are things like the fashions in *Bonnie and Clyde*, and they are put over in stills, posters, and magazine promotional tie-ups, just as much as in picture-houses. This is not to say that Lenin and the Nazis were wrong in rating film very highly as a propaganda medium. But our exposure to film is sporadic and diverse, the message of one is wiped out by the next. Only a long and sustained single message set of films could seriously be considered to have any effect of the kind propagandists seek.[8] There are examples of these, and none is deliberate: one would be the presentation of the life of the ordinary American as sun-filled, secure, and problem-free; another would be the persistent slurring over of the reality of violent death in war, western, crime, and accident. This sort of thing is counteracted by the odd critical or questioning film; but the tendency of some people to avoid 'disturbing' or 'unpleasant' films, ensures that there is a group which preserves fond illusions about life and death if they are guided solely by movies.

Propaganda assumes an audience as being acted upon. However, there is an element of positive self-selection in audience groups, and this raises the vexed question of whether the audience gets what it wants or likes what it gets. I think the problem is solved now because we have seen the cinema deal with competition from television. Only this year (1968), the last American cinema newsreel ceased production and it is about time: this is a case where television completely worsted the cinema. The film industry has had to contract and restructure itself; but, this over, it is doing as well as, or better, than ever. Some of the biggest box office successes of all time have been made in the last eight years or so.[9] This appears to me a strong *prima facie* argument for saying that people are, by and large, seeing what they want. If they are not, I know of no way to find this out. In a market place people vote at the cash register. Two worries often raised over this point can perhaps be dispelled. One can argue that the cash register is a measure of demand, and demand does not decide whether resources are ill-distributed. But films, like bread, are cheap, and therefore the box-office should not be maligned as an approximate indicator of public taste. It is sometimes said that we do

---

[8] Studies of propaganda connect its success with the primary reference group. If that buttresses the values under attack the propaganda is relatively ineffective so long as the primary group structure remains intact. See Riley and Riley (1959). See also R. K. Merton, *Social Theory and Social Structure*, Glencoe (The Free Press) 1957, pp. 509–28.

[9] See the useful table in *Cahiers du Cinéma*, vol. 24, no. 150–1, December 1963–January 1964, at pp. 236–40. *The Sound of Music* has taken in more money than *Gone with the Wind*, but since its production costs were greater its profit ratio is not as high.

not know whether, *if* there were better quality films on offer, and *if* people's taste was carefully nurtured, *then* they might not choose any differently than now. Such hypotheticals are rarified, especially as there is a wide range of choice in the market for the time that the education of taste bears fruit. This is evidenced by the growth of art houses and re-run cinemas where the discerning may go.

It is instructive to compare the industries in Great Britain and the USA on this matter of adapting to changes in public taste. Despite its size, the American industry has proved more successful at regenerating itself in the face of competition than the British. Both had injections of fresh talent: in the USA from television, in Great Britain from the renaissance in the theatre. Yet the style and diversity which characterize today's Hollywood product, are nowhere near matched by the British product. Some of the most exciting new people in Britain are idle for long periods, while endless streams of dud films are still made. This, despite the break-up of the old big studios of Rank and ABC. The talent is there: my explanation is the hidebound conservatism of British society which, in face of competition, leads to demands for protection, by contrast with the competitiveness and adaptability of American industry. The regeneration in America was done at the cost of a great many people losing their jobs, firms being taken over, closed down, etc. In Britain, the same people seem to be running the industry as fifteen years ago, and all one ever hears from them are new devices for government subsidies and protection. Of course, 'hidebound conservatism' is a superficial explanatory category in sociology. My aim is merely to connect the British film industry with the general ills of British industry and society in responding to change and new conditions.

In the long run the industry will have to adjust itself. These adjustments indicate the impact of films on what McLuhan calls the sensory profiles or biases of cultures. Indeed, there may be such things, but films learning to co-exist with television, inclines me to saying what happens is that we acquire more sensory possibilities with each new medium, rather than that we are dominated by one sense. It is true that literacy, and then printing, decisively affected the sensory apparatus, and I am sure films did too. But I would be cautious in summing up the sensory bias attributable to films in their heyday from about 1914 to 1950. Moreover, films are not a one-sense medium: they are two: sound and vision, although those brought up with silent films are inclined to regard sound as an irrelevant accretion. This is a mistake: the conventions of the sound film are quite different from the silent film. Think of the stars which sound killed: nowadays a star has to be a voice as well as a face. The combination, moreover, of the two is greater than the sum of the parts. Among the most sensually thrilling of aesthetic experiences are those moments in the great film musicals, for example, where dancer, music, and the camera sweep one along into an exhilarating number: a sensation not to be gained from any other medium.

3 Values in the content of the experience

Earlier, I stated that I am of the film generation. How did films affect our sensorium? Films are a linear medium of course, but in both the senses of sound and of sight. They are hot, high-definition, high-involving, low-participation. What else? Once upon a time, people thought they were the ultimately real. There is an entire, utterly misguided, school of film theory and film making which conceives the essence of films as being 'the creative interpretation of reality'. This was why the Russians were so excited about films: they seemed, for a mad moment back there in the twenties, to be a history-sent answer to the demand for social realism in art. In retrospect, the Russian silent films and the English documentaries look like beautiful side-tracks, fundamentally alien to the cinema. The cinema's greatest expressions are to be found in highly formal, conventionalized species like musicals, cartoons, and the special conventions of the western, gangster and horror epics. The point of these is their strict use of conventions to do or say what they aim at. They are the opposite of the philosophy of films summed up in Isherwood's 'I am a camera with its shutter open'. It took a while, but it has finally been realized that cameras are not recording machines any more than computers are thinking machines. Both are machines which perform carefully assigned, and strictly circumscribed, tasks. These tasks reflect *our* interests and values.

When we see the grimacing and posturing in Eisenstein films, it is hard not to laugh, and still harder not to laugh when one realizes all this was once claimed to be real and true. What we are amused at is the conventions. *The Great Train Robbery*, the first western, made in 1905, is also ludicrous; perhaps in fifty years *Shane* will be too. As of now, it is splendidly sinister when Jack Palance rides into town dressed in black; the mud street and lowering sky convince us that that is how it must have been. Or are we being simplistic and naive? How real is *Bonnie and Clyde*? Or, again, how unreal is *Bonnie and Clyde*? Or are the categories of real and unreal as much red herrings with *Bonnie and Clyde* as with other works of art?

As I have said, I think film is a medium on its own, more than the sum of its parts, and that its strength lies in its use of well-defined conventions. It is these conventions which McLuhan mentions when he discusses the reaction of Africans to films. When we notice a loose end in a novel it bothers us: McLuhan mentions that Africans want to know where the body of someone shown in close-up has gone. The film is a language, very much like print, although not prose print, rather poetry print. The way connections are unsta:ed, and the way concentration is used in film, is in a literal sense poetic: as is the adoption of strict rules for the handling of structure, pace, time lapse, etc. McLuhan argues that what a medium does to us is more or less independent of its content. For him it is much more significant that the cinema is a hot medium, high definition, and concentrated, rather than low definition and involving a good deal of participation, as is television. I accept this. The cinema, I believe, is a total environment medium, and the wider the screen and louder the sound, the more sense one has of being swallowed up in it. It is a medium in which we talk of identifying with those who appear, and what happens to them on the screen. This is less the case with television and never the case with a single programme on television, which is why, in a decisive sense, old films on television are a different kind of experience to going to see them at a cinema. Having seen enormous numbers of old films on television, I yet, when I am writing about films, continue in a strange way to think I haven't *really* seen them and cannot write about them with the same authority as those viewed and reviewed in cinemas.[10] This also explains why television has favoured the series: 'Dr Kildare', 'Coronation Street', 'The Avengers', 'Star Trek'.[11] The medium is cool; it takes repeated doses to familiarize us with people and situations that will grip.

Many things follow from these ideas.[12] Film is clearly best-suited to use in education only where the subject is dramatic and involving, and where feedback and audience participation are unimportant. I can remember little of those Encyclopaedia Britannica science films we were shown every week in my grammar school. Yet, the American army training films and films about VD are said to be most effective, but then their subjects are dramatic. Maths lessons would, one suspects, be more suited to television considered in the abstract. But almost all educational television is simply films being shown on television. This is not a play on words. A film of a man lecturing is excruciating; even filmed opera and ballet can be deadly dull. Yet

---

[10] There is an important article on this by America's master-critic Pauline Kael: 'Movies in TV', *New Yorker*, 3 June 1967 (reprinted in her (1968)).

[11] I am grateful to Michael Burrage of the London School of Economics for the suggestion that series are also relied on because there is no previous criticism of upcoming programmes, far fewer trailers, and no street or newspaper advertisements. All of this is done, but on such a small scale as not to make any overall difference.

[12] For another attempt to get at them, also sympathetic to McLuhan, see Barry Day (1967).

television opera and ballet, and television lectures – like those of A. J. P. Taylor – can work very well indeed.

McLuhan's ideas also raise the question of whether, talking about films is 'rear-view mirror driving'. The answer is yes: mine was the last movie-formed generation. Nowadays, children are as much formed by the sensibility of television as we were by that of films. When television first arrived it was for a while like a continuous and hypnotic film show in a corner of the living room. By now we have it in better perspective, and the younger generation already take for granted their entire Saturday morning cartoon show, just as we took for granted our regular Saturday morning trip to the local cinema 'club'. Even the beginnings of the global village were present in our time. Jean-Luc Godard, perhaps the most brilliant young French director, dedicated his film *A Bout de Souffle* to Monogram Pictures, a long defunct Hollywood company which in the forties specialized in western second-features. I share with Godard his sentimentality for Gene Autry and Tex Ritter westerns, for the B-film à la Monogram, Republic, etc.: perhaps even for that almost forgotten medium Cinecolor.[13] When he refers back to that shared experience he sets up a special resonance in those of the movie generation.

However, the very hotness of the film medium does allow me in good conscience to try to analyse not only the message of the medium, but the message the medium manipulators are putting through it. The immense influence of the cinema on fashions, dating habits, manners of speaking, senses of humour, *mores* generally, everywhere in the world it has penetrated are due to it being hot. One can observe people in Hong Kong behaving like, e.g., lovers in American films. The visitor to the USA, can come across an insoluble chicken and egg problem: are the waiters, waitresses, taxi-drivers, etc., behaving like their film counterparts, or are their film counterparts modelled on the so-called real thing? Not only Japanese gangster films, but Japanese gangsters are modelled on American gangster films. The extent to which America is reflected *and moulded* by its films, is not yet matched by a parallel effect from television.

How this comes about, how the message of the medium is decoded in practice, could be a summary of what follows.

The experience of films, due to their being hot, is the opposite of Brechtian alienation, detachment or endistancing. It is not escape either – in the cinema one does not daydream or fantasize: one is gripped and carried along – made to involve and experience. A horror film is a way of rehearsing a basic ambivalence towards thrills,

[13] I can't stand films in sepia.
And about films in Cinecolor
I am even cynicaller – Ken Tynan

danger, fear. But we don't identify in any simple way – films do not offer us the chance to feel like a killer, a vampire, a cowboy, There are elements of that, to be sure. To watch Fred Astaire and Cyd Charisse dancing is to experience something quite different from what one would experience if one were out there leaping about oneself. Film is essentially a third-person medium, most attempts at the subjective camera fail. Even where we follow one character exclusively, it is as if we are his companion, not him. In films about amnesia there are always meaningful views of objects, or of the villains approaching, which the hero does not have. Closeness the films do give us, but not identification – much more, perhaps, voyeuristic. The thrill of watching hero and heroine in bed is that of the voyeur, not a member of the wedding.

It is doubts about voyeurism that encourage me to rate conventions so highly. Musicals, e.g., are usually simple and delightful romantic comedies. Their value lies entirely in the expressive power of the dancing and the songs. About the gangster convention I will say little – mostly it has been a vehicle for social criticism and clean-up crusades. The heights of absurdity are reached in exultant close-ups of Eliot Ness smashing beer barrels with an axe.

Westerns are perhaps the richest set of conventions the cinema has developed – so potent are the conventions that they are toyed with the world over. Everyone knows there are Italian, German, even Yugoslav westerns; but how many know there are Japanese ones as well? And Japanese sword fight films draw conventions from the western film. The American West was a short-lived but archetypal era of new land, harsh conditions, profound social change, and great stress on the individual. A perfect framework for dramas about:

> the unity of mankind
> the place of violence
> the rule of law
> the crime of passion
> the loneliness of man
> friendship
> sacrifice
> the redemption of cowards
> conflict of loyalties, etc.

4 Evaluating films

To conclude this brief overview of films, I want to discuss briefly their status as art, and especially questions concerning popular taste, highbrow taste and art. Strangely in films there is no real distinction between highbrow and lowbrow. Some of the finest films from every point of view are immensely popular with all kinds of people: for example, the western *Shane*, which was a box-office 'hit'. Moreover, some self-consciously cultured films, like those of opera and ballet on stage, are unbearably dull and unfilmic. Of course, quality and success do not correlate 100%: Orson Welles is a film maker of genius who has yet to make a box-office 'hit': whereas Hitchcock, who is equally a filmic genius, has had only one or two flops in fifty films. Indeed, it seems almost impossible that there is *a* film audience, there must be several: how else can one explain the success of pure treacle like *Sound of Music*, and pure astringent like *Bonnie and Clyde* – in successive years?

Of course, most intellectuals have frightfully snobbish and puritanical views about popular taste and art generally. They think that television drama is good, and television soap opera is bad; they like Olivier in *Richard III*, but not Lana Turner in *Imitation of Life* or Joan Crawford in *Mildred Pierce*. These attitudes involve misunderstanding and ignorance. To draw a few comparisons: take painting. Painting includes everything from Calendar Art, through middling and 'serious' art, to indisputably high art. Within Calendar Art there is good, bad and indifferent. In dime store mystery novels there are poor, middling, serious and even great ones. So it is in films; there is everything from skin flicks, through B-pictures, through serious and on to art films. In each category there is good and bad, and the *cognoscenti* of that category can discriminate between them; as to whether the categories themselves can be ranked, I am dubious. Clearly, however, it is an error to slide from disapproval of a category to distaste for the medium; that is like denigrating prose because of a distaste for who-dun-its.

Just as the lighter poet and the lighter poem have their place in writing, so do the series, quiz shows and soap operas in television, the great star vehicles, tear-jerkers, skin flicks, and others in the cinema. What can be said critically about popular taste and the mass media, is not that they cover such a range, although on the whole they do so rather well, but that the *audience* tends to concentrate on one *genre* or the other. In principle, a reader of detective stories can learn to discriminate good from bad ones, just as a follower of Joan Crawford vehicles gets to know the better from the worse. We should not criticize those who declare no interest in other *genres*. Moreover, to denigrate what they like is an alienating move. My own view is very optimistic. I think that there is tangible evidence that popular taste is broadening and becoming more discriminating: television viewers in England startled everyone by watching appreciatively a Pinter play inserted between their usual diet of quizzes and westerns. This, less than ten years after there had been an outcry when *1984* was televized. The range of films on display in our big cities seems to me to leave virtually nothing to be desired, except perhaps some very specialist historical interest. Television is in not such a good way, but the reason is simple to find. Television, like films twenty years ago, is still in a sellers' market where the competition is not fierce. There will come a time when competition gets tougher, and the programmes will diversify again as when television was just beginning and the audience had to be built.

Why defend the cinema against the charges levelled against it by highbrows? For fairness sake, really. Highbrows don't complain that of the novels published each year, a vast percentage are trivia, because a lot of highbrow material gets published too, including a good deal that is worthless. I maintain that films are much the same. With some exceptions, all active film directors are making films and these are being shown. In a way, the success of superb films like *Bonnie and Clyde* is hardly paralleled in the world of books, where great art rarely equals best-seller. It is amazing how much creative freedom there is in films, given the very high costs of production. And now, when it is easy to make films oneself, we see in the awful warning of the new form of Underground film, the spectre of what happens when almost all obstacles to so-called creative freedom are removed. Like any art medium, film is one that requires craftsmanship – and this cannot be gained by introspection. The creator must learn to be self-critical by interacting with his peers and thus indirectly with his audience, and finding out how to put over what he wants. But, of course, I am shouting into the wind, because the theory of art as self-expression on the part of the artist, or real living as self-expression on the part of the individual, grows more popular every day.

A few ideas now about why some films are successful and others not. The theory that the public is manipulated by the publicity machine is refuted by the poor showing of *Cleopatra*. The theory that the public likes what is bad is refuted by the success of such films as *Shane, The Apartment, Psycho, Bonnie and Clyde*. The theory that there is a constant in public taste is refuted by the boom in spy films followed by a tailing-off. A plodding film like *Goldfinger* was a success, while the far superior *Ipcress File* was only a moderate success.

Like fashion, success in films is attributable to an image which happens to grip the public at the time. Gangsters were popular for a year or two in the early sixties, as were horror films; the reaction was the spy and the spoof and sometimes the two together. This can only be stated as hindsight, of course, and possibly *The Sound of Music* refutes this theory. I am inclined to think not, because there is evidence that the audience of *The Sound of Music* was swollen by many people who never otherwise go to films – the same group Walt Disney cashes in on – schools, family outings, nuns, etc. And this audience is not the one most susceptible to fashion. What happens is that a film develops something called an image and that it is sold primarily by word of mouth. Notoriously, the critics have little influence. The content of the image may or may not include values, if it does these will usually be its values as a film, i.e., moving, exciting, horrifying, etc. This returns again to my point that the cinema is self-feeding – what everyone is concerned with is not a message in the conventional sense, but its message as a film – what kind of film is it?

In summary, what about films and the communication of values? Theories which attribute a corrupting influence to films are mostly humbug: people don't do what they don't want to do, even under hypnosis; and all imaginative art can give ideas to those already looking for them. Those who claim they get bad ideas from films, could equally well obtain them from any number of alternative sources. People are not receptacles whose contents can be changed; they are transmitter-receivers growing and adapting through their technology. Media do not corrupt man, they change man. Films as a means of communication operate on unstructured groups. The group that constitutes a film audience is relatively unstructured, as is the group that made the film. The film creates or brings together both groups and gives them a sense of identity and common experience. The audience gets a curious satisfaction from being and experiencing together, which is demonstrated by the uncomfortable feeling one has in an empty cinema. Such general propaganda as is transmitted to these groups by films, is of the kind related in this anecdote in *Understanding Media* (p. 294).

> Since the best way to get to the core of a form is to study its effect in some unfamiliar setting, let us note what President Sukarno of Indonesia announced in 1956 to a large group of Hollywood executives. He said that he regarded them as political radicals and revolutionaries who had greatly hastened political change in the East. What the Orient saw in a Hollywood movie was a world in which all the *ordinary people* had cars and electric stoves and refrigerators. So the Oriental now regards himself as an ordinary person who has been deprived of the ordinary man's birthright.

Bibliography

Bibliography

When I began seriously to research this book, I knew very well that there was a wealth of material scattered in all kinds of unlikely places, if only one could dig it up. To claim that I have succeeded in digging it all up would be silly; I hope that anyone coming across items they think should be included will send them to me, hopefully for future editions. In addition to the bibliographies listed below, I found useful lists in the following: Bluestone (1957), De Fleur (1966), Hall and Whannel (1964), annotated, Jacobs (1939), Klapper (1961), Kracauer (1947, 1960), Manvell (1944, 1966), annotated, Mayersberg (1967), annotated, Rosenberg and White (1957), Schramm, Lyle and Parker (1961), annotated, Stephenson (1967), White and Averson (1968).

For the rest, I have listed all the items I refer to, and all other items I have come across which seem to bear on the subject of the book. Where it has been possible, I have provided a guide through this literature in the annotations. Absence of annotation, however, should not be construed as indicating that an item lacks interest. Square brackets are used to indicate interpolated comments.

BIBLIOGRAPHIES

American Library Association and Warner Brothers, *The Motion Picture: A Selected Booklist*, 1946.
Bibliographie Internationale Cinéma 1966, 1967, Bucharest.
Blum, Eleanor, 1962, *Reference Books in the Mass Media*, Urbana.
British Film Institute, The, 1945, *Book List*, London.
Danielson, W. A., and Wilhoit, G. C., 1967, *A Computerized Bibliography of Mass Communication Research, 1944–64*, New York.
Denney, Reul and Meyersohn, M. L., 1957, 'A Preliminary Bibliography on Leisure', *American Journal of Sociology*, 62: 602–15, esp. 612–4.
Fearing, F., and Rogge, G., 1952, 'A Selected and Annotated Bibliography in Communications Research', *Quarterly of Film, Radio and Television*, 6: 283*ff*.
General Bibliography of Motion Pictures, 1953, Rome: Edizioni dell' Ateneo, Capitolo V 'I Problemi sociali e morali', Capitolo VI 'I Problemi giuridici ed economici'.
Hansen, Donald A., and Parsons, J. Herschel, 1968, *Mass Communication: A Resesarch Bibliography*, Santa Barbara.
International Film Bibliographie, 1952–62, 1963, Zurich: Rohr.
International Film Bibliographie, 1963–4, 1964, Zurich: Rohr.

Jackson-Wrigley, M., and Leyland, E., 1939, *The Cinema*, London.
Peterson, Wilbur, 1960, *Organizations, Publications and Directories in the Mass Media of Communication*, Iowa City.
Price, Warren, 1959, *The Literature of Journalism: An Anr. ?tated Bibliography*, Minneapolis.
United Nations Educational, Social and Cultural Organization, 1954, *Bibliography on Filmology as Related to the Social Sciences*, compiled by Jan C. Bouman, University of Stockholm, Paris.
United Nations Educational, Social and Cultural Organization, 1961, *The Influence of the Cinema on Children and Adolescents*, Paris.
United States, 1936, Library of Congress. *Motion Pictures in United States and Foreign Countries: Selected List of Recent Writings*, Washington.
United States, 1940, Library of Congress. Bibliographies 222. *Motion Pictures in the United States and Foreign Countries*, Washington.

BOOKS AND ARTICLES

ADLER, MORTIMER, 1937, *Art and Prudence*, New York.
Subtitled 'A study in practical philosophy', this is a massive and devastating critique of the Payne Fund studies (q.v.) of four years earlier. He defends films as a form of popular poetry, against the do-gooding moralizers, educationists and sociological researchers, showing that they load their premises and rarely meet the canons of good science. A rather Aristotelian view of the relation between morality and artistic purity.

AGEE, JAMES, 1949, 'Comedy's Greatest Era', *Life*, 27: 70–82.
Denny and Meyersohn: 'A study of the dramatic roles assumed by Chaplin, Langdon, and others in the American custard-pie period, by an outstanding writer and movie critic.' Reprinted in Agee (1958).

— 1958, *Agee on Film*, two volumes, New York.
One volume has five scripts, not in scenario form; the other is a collection of his criticism for *The Nation*, *Time*, etc., which was enthusiastic, biting and unpredictable. He displays a sensitive feeling for the medium and its stars, although traces of literary bias show through.

AGEL, H., 1963, *Romance Américaine*, Paris.
Essay on the American cinema with analysis of selected films and of 'Un Héros de Notre Temps: Humphrey Bogart'. 'Combien faudra-t-il de temps pour que le haut fonctionnaire, le juriste, le membre de l'Université qui avouent leur préférance pour le cinéma d'outre-Atlantique cessent d'être une exception? J'ose affirmer qu'il y a dans cette méconnaissance de la grandeur de Hollywood un symptôme assez inquiétant non point seulement d'affaiblissement du potentiel vital mais de dégradation culturelle. L'humanisme, le tragique, le lyrisme, le sens du sacré, sont en Amérique brassés, éclairés, redécouverts à travers le dynamisme et la curiosité d'un

peuple qui n'échappe certes ni au vandalisme ni à la schématisation intellectuelle, mais qui détient – contrairement à la plupart de nos metteurs en scène de l'ancienne ou de la nouvelle vague – une does appréciable de naiveté, un don de jaillissement, une réserve créatrice.' pp. 175–6.

ALBERT, R. S., 1957, 'The Role of Mass Media and the Effect of Aggressive Film Content Upon Childrens' Aggressive Responses and Identification Choices', *Genetic Psychology Monographs*, 55: 211–85.
Among eighteen conclusions are that: conventional cowboy films decrease aggression in all subjects; unconventional films produce no change; removing the ending decreases the aggression; the lower the IQ of the subject the more likely to be affected; the younger the more affected; high and low aggression subjects identify similarly with conventional films, differently with unconventional films.

ALLEN, K. S., 1955, 'Golden Anniversary', *Films and Filming*, 1: September, 10.
About the first Nickelodeon, 1905.

ALLOWAY, LAWRENCE, 1964, 'Critics in the Dark', *Encounter*, 22: February, 50–5.
A review of Agee (1958), Talbot (1959), Hughes (1962), Morin (1960), develops into a superb essay on the poverty of writing about films. On p. 53 he suggests attention to the establishment of cycles of films as a unit of analysis which 'provides the audience with a flexible, continuing convention and a body of expectations and knowledge on which the film-maker can count'. Morin is justly cut to pieces as unexportable French verbiage. 'The basic assumption of . . . Hughes, is that there are, scattered around the world, honest film-makers . . . and that there is, scattered around the world, an audience of sincere people waiting for their messages . . . The idea is that creative work, independent of business or too many machines, will spontaneously win a sympathetic response from the pure in heart, whatever colour their skin. Shadows fall on this ideal of communication because audiences keep going to the wrong films. Is the audience passively accepting trash or is the audience itself corrupt? . . . Perhaps only in film criticism would it be possible to assume that capacious O.K. words like "honesty" and "reality" provide a general critical standard', pp. 54–5. Exact and pungent, this article is essential.

ALLSOP, KENNETH, 1961, *The Bootleggers*, London.
Chicago in the twenties.

— 1967, *Hard Travellin'*, London.
The hobo and his history.

ALPERT, HOLLIS, 1956, 'Sexual Behaviour in the American Movies', *Saturday Review*, 39: 9–10.
The Production Code, and timidity, make it very difficult to treat sex honestly. Stevens did in *A Place in the Sun* – everyone else uses candles,

fireworks, waves, fountains, and Lana Turner's nostrils. The top female stars in a way embodied the feminine ideals of the studio heads.

— 1962, *The Dreams and the Dreamers*, New York.
A fascinating series of essays on stars (e.g., Marlon Brando, J an Seberg), producers (Hecht-Hill-Lancaster, Ross Hunter), directors, etc. 'Film and Theatre' argues that perhaps the film is the best form of drama. He is convincing and he delivers some good thrusts at theorists with nostalgia for silents and at Eisenstein's 'gobbledygook' (p. 243), and convincingly itemizes the limitations of theatre on imagination.

ALTENLOH, EMILIO, 1914, *Zur Soziologie des Kino*, Die Kino-Unternehmung und Die Sozialen Schichten Ihrer Besucher, Jena.
Part I is on production, part II on the public. In a series edited by Alfred Weber. Dated, naturally, but none the less of interest.

AMBLER, ERIC, 1949, 'The Film of the Book', *Penguin Film Review*, 9: 22–5.
Writers can be impressed by a producer expressing good intentions. But high hopes are gradually whittled away (based on Ambler's personal experience).

ANAST, P., 1964, 'Self-Image, a Determinant of Vicarious Need', *Psychology*, 1: 8–10.
Hypothesis: the more highly one esteems oneself, the less one's need for vicarious experience. The less favourable one's self-image, the more operative the mechanisms of identification. Tests were statistically significant for men, not for women. Mass media function differently for each, perhaps because of man's greater available range of activities.

— 1967, 'Differential Movie Appeals as Correlates of Attendance', *Journalism Quarterly*, 44: 86–90.
He tested and confirmed the idea that frequent film goers: 1) rank higher in their interest in the erotic and interpersonal violence, 2) perceive greater similarity between film life and reality, 3) are more hero and heroine oriented. Those with a high action potential, involving adventure and achievement correlate with very low cinema attendance.

ANDERSON, H., 1924, *Filmen i Social og Okonomisk Be lysning*, Copenhagen.

ANDERSON, J. L., and RICHIE, D., 1959, *The Japanese Film*, Tokyo and Rutland.
The authoritative study in English of the development of the industry in Japan. Includes a 'genealogy' of directors.

ANDERSON, LINDSAY, 1952, *Making a Film*, London.
Observer's diary of the making of *The Secret People* by Thorold Dickinson from script conferences to editing. Book published simultaneously with film première, thus preventing the author from throwing light on the strengths and weaknesses of the film in so far as they can be related to

production circumstances and decisions. This makes it less valuable than Ross (1950) and Kael (1968).

ANGER, KENNETH, 1965, *Hollywood Babylon*, Phoenix.
Compendium of Hollywood gossip, most of it prurient, much of it doubtless true, written in a perfect pastiche of fan-magazine style.

Annals of the American Academy of Political and Social Science, 1926, 'The Motion Picture in Its Economic and Social Aspects', ed. Clyde C. Kunz and Frank A. Tichener, **128**: Philadelphia.
Many of these papers are uninteresting – dealing with equipment, technical matters, fire hazards, newsreels, classroom pictures, etc. But the worthwhile ones are: Ramsaye (1926), Johnston (1926), Young (1926) and Stephens (1926).

— 1947, 'The Motion Picture Industry', ed. G. S. Watkins, **254**: Philadelphia.
Sub-heads: Development of Motion Picture Industry; Business and Financial Aspects; Sources and Production of Motion Pictures; Effects of Motion Pictures; Motion Pictures and the Public; Censorship and Self-Regulation; Areas of Research.
Denny and Meyersohn comment: 'Interesting to compare this issue with a similar number in 1926: the present pessimism, seriousness about the power of the industry; sophisticated sociological material.' Every paper is abstracted below under the name of its author.

ANONYMOUS, 1950, 'The Art of Our Age', *Sight and Sound*, **19**: 89*ff*.
The artist is swamped by the industry and the people have no voice in what is made or seen.

— 1963, 'An International Survey on the Film Hero', *International Social Science Journal*, **15**: 113–19.
Report on a conference at Sestri Levante, to do a comparative study of the hero. French, Yugoslav and Polish data are analysed: 'it would appear that film themes and the traits of film heroes undergo change much more quickly than one might think', p. 118.

Arab Cinema and Culture, 3 volumes: 1964, 1965, 1965, Round Table Conferences Under the Auspices and with the Participation of the UNESCO, Beirut, October 1962, 1963, 1964.
Nuggets among much dross include 'Viability of a Cinema Born Weak *versus* a Television Born Gigantic' by F. Mazzawi in the third volume.

ARNHEIM, R., 1958, *Film as Art*, London.
Mostly a reprint of his *Film*, 1933. In 'A Personal Note', dated 1957, to this edition, he comments: 'the reader of this book will find that film is, to me, a unique experiment in the visual arts which took place in the first three decades of this century. In its pure state it survives in the private efforts of a few courageous individuals; and occasional flares, reminiscent

of a distinguished past, light up the mass productions of the film industry, which permitted the new medium to become a comfortable technique for popular story telling. Correspondingly, the author ... has changed ... to a stray customer, who gratefully enjoys – a few times a year – the screen performances of intelligent artists', pp. 11–12. See also Rotha and Griffith (1963).

ARVIDSON, LINDA (Mrs. D. W. Griffith), 1925, *When the Movies were Young*, New York.
Charming and anecdotal memoir of a San Francisco ingenue who met and married 'D.W.' and then entered with him the Biograph company in 1908 where he acted, then, from mid-1908, directed. She chronicles the other actresses and people around, the moves to Los Angeles for the winter and finally D.W.'s break with Biograph and move to Mutual. The book ends with the completion of *Birth of a Nation*. [Reprinted in 1968, this is one of a whole series of valuable studies of the silent era: cf. Ball, Balshofer, Brownlow, Lahue, Pratt, Ramsaye and Wagenknecht.]

ASHEIM, LESTER, 1947, 'The Film and the Zeitgeist', *Hollywood Quarterly*, 2: 414–16.
Reply to Houseman's comments on *The Big Sleep* (1947).

— 1949, 'From Book to Film', Ph.D. thesis, University of Chicago, unpublished.

— 1953, 'From Book to Film', in B. Berelson and M. Janowitz, eds., *Reader in Public Opinion and Communication*, Glencoe, 299–308.
Section from his Ph.D. thesis (1949). Film versions of novels are usually comparably descriptive, more careful about the unities, less violent, brutal, and sadistic, and retain the original title.

ASHLEY, W., 1934, *The Cinema and the Public*, London.
Not at all what the title leads one to expect, but, in the words of its subtitle, 'a critical analysis of the origin, constitution and control of the British Film Institute'.

Australia. Parliamentary Papers, 1928. *Report of the Royal Commission on the Moving Picture Industry in Australia*, Canberra.

AYDELOTTE, W. O., 1949, 'The Detective Story as a Historical Source', *The Yale Review*, 39: 76–95, reprinted in Deer (1967).
Its popularity due to conventions. By studying this literature one can describe the readers it is intended for, in terms of their unsatisfied desires (p. 134). The detective story presents life as agreeable, reassuring, simple, understandable, meaningful and secure. The problems are simple, with simple solutions. They glamourize the everyday, e.g., the city. They portray a secure universe subject to fixed laws. The detective always wins. By showing death they minimize the fear of it. Occasionally the victim's death is all for the best. The solution releases everyone from guilt. The

reader is passive – as indeed is everyone in the story except the detective. [Wolfenstein and Leites (1950*b*) find the detective passive: things happen *to* him.] They describe daydreams of dependence and aggression, i.e., totalitarian. The villain could be anyone, i.e., paranoid suspicion. The detective simplifies life, gives it meaning; is strong, conservative, but a dictator, a superman.

BABITSKY, P. and RIMBERG, J., 1955, *The Soviet Film Industry*, New York. The classical and authoritative study.

BAECHLIN, PETER, 1947, *Histoire Economique du Cinéma*, Paris. Well-researched, Marxist, history-critique of the cinema industry, with no simple solution, only the conclusion that the capitalist system realizes, with few exceptions, none of the possibilities of cinema.

BAILYN, LOTTE, 1959, 'Mass Media and Children: A Study of Exposure Habits and Cognitive Effects', *Psychological Monographs*, 73: 1–48. Investigates stereotyping, belief in a general threat, self-image and preference for passive activities as coloured by exposure to the media. Mass media function as escape for certain children under certain conditions. They may also be thought of as functioning as supplementation: they widen horizons, supply information, offer relaxation. This escape function is found in children with psychological problems, extrapunitiveness (seeking external causes for their troubles), rebellious independence, and high exposure. The same children stereotype. The rebellious have self-image affected by media. Passivity is related mainly to high exposure, but is not to be interpreted as lack of initiative or desire to be on the receiving end in social situations: high exposures enjoy exposure, but this high exposure does confine their occupational ambitions. The media do not appear to have much effect on the sense of a general threat. The groups involved are small: 3% are highly exposed, the figure for high exposure plus problems is 12%, for high exposure plus extrapunitiveness is 11%, for high exposure plus rebellious independence is 9%. None of this applies to girls. Why? There is a low incidence of rebelliousness and extrapunitiveness.

BALABAN, CARRIE, 1942, *Continuous Performance*, New York. Autobiography of A. J. Balaban, founder of the theatre chain of Balaban and Katz – later to merge with Zukor's Paramount Publix Corp. – as told to and by his wife. Standard story of the frantic scramble in the beginning (Chicago this time), the nearly ruinous set-back, and finally the rise to unimagined heights. Paints himself as a public benefactor providing entertainment. The crucial elimination of vaudeville from the programmes seems to have happened almost accidentally when movie profits were very good. Nothing on the sociological significance of exhibition, nor on the relation between the exhibitors and Hollywood.

BALAZS, B., 1952, *Theory of the Film*, London. 'The art of the silent film is closed, but its place was taken by the mere technique of the sound film which in twenty years has not risen and evolved into an art'. His earlier volume *Der Geist des Films*, 1930, Halle, argued that film comes into its own only by serving revolutionary ends.

BALCON, MICHAEL, 1950, *Film Production and Management*, London.
A sketch of how films are produced stressing the differences from ordinary manufacturing and business practices.

BALDELLI, PIO, 1963, *Sociologia del Cinema*, Rome.
No sociological analysis at all. Cinema is a modern folk art.

BALL, R. H., 1968, *Shakespeare on Silent Film*, London.
Twenty years of research have produced case-study in how to piece together from fragments an episode of film history. Prints don't exist, or are unavailable in dead storage; serial runs have gaps; scripts are copyright and cannot be examined. Withal a phenomenal effort.

BALLANTINE, W. M., 1945, *Discussion Circle No. 4*, London.
In a pamphlet entitled *If I Owned a Factory and Other Topics* is contained N. Wilson's: 'Do We Get the Films We Want?' Not enough. Because of: low standards in the audience; industry pressures; the double feature system. The answer is not nationalization, but education.

BALSHOFER, FRED F. and MILLER, ARTHUR C., 1967, *One Reel a Week*, Berkeley and Los Angeles.
Two veteran cameramen reminisce.

BANDURA, A., ROSS, D., and ROSS, S. A., 1963, 'Imitations of Film-mediated Aggressive Models', *Journal of Abnormal and Social Psychology*, 66: 3–11.
Taking the sequence: real people, films of people, cartoons of people, as points on a scale of descending reality and increasing fiction, it was predicted that 'the more remote the model was from reality, the weaker would be the tendency for subjects to imitate the behaviour of the model' (p. 3). '. . . strong evidence that exposure to filmed aggression heightens aggressive reactions in children' (p. 9). No significant difference between effects of live models and film models, or between film models and cartoon models. The crude and sweeping conceptions behind this research come out clearly in Bandura's popular article for *Look*, reprinted in Larsen (1968), pp. 123–30.

BANTON, MICHAEL, 1965, *Roles*, London.

BARDECHE, MAURICE and BRASILLACH, ROBERT, 1938, *History of Motion Pictures*, New York.
Translation of the classic French history written by a prolific team. English liberal critics are always detecting 'fascist bias' in their volumes.

BIBLIOGRAPHY

BARISSE, RITA, 1955, 'New Life – New Films' and 'The Chinese Way', *Films and Filming*, 1: March/April, 5, 8–9.
Outline of the Red Chinese film industry.

BARKER, W. J., 1955, 'The Stereotyped Western Story', *Psychoanalytic Quarterly*, 24: 270–80.
The cowboy hero is the eternal son compulsively acting out an archetypal fantasy, as in dreams. The villain is the bad father, the weak sheriff the good father, the horse the phallus, the ranch the mother, the gunfights threats of castration. In an extreme repressed form, they are an account of a boy's love of mother and desire to kill father. 'One is justified in believing that these legends serve an integrative educational function, especially for the young child, and they are by no means entirely a passive, regressive, or purposeless pastime. Like the military commander who engages his troops in tactical manoeuvres with an imaginary or simulated enemy, the boy utilizes the 'western' to anticipate difficulties, to experiment, and to seek socially acceptable and tolerable answers to his most urgent and pressing unconscious emotional conflicts. Toy pistols and a cowboy costume help him to act out the story in play', p. 278.

BARNOUW, ERIC, 1956, *Mass Communication:* Television, Radio, Film, Press; the Media and their Practice in the United States of America, New York.
Widely cited authority.

BARNOUW, E., and KRISHNASWAMY, S., 1963, *Indian Film*, New York.
Highly informative and sociologically angled account of the history of film making in India, and its contemporary situation. Details the extended family basis of much production, and the extreme popularity of stars and song-writers. It does not essay deeper structural explanations of these phenomena themselves, although the material is perhaps present.

BATESON, GREGORY, 1943, 'Cultural and Thematic Studies of Fictional Films', *Transactions of the New York Academy of Science*, Series 11, 5: 72–88.
Analysis of *Hitlerjunge Quex* showing the way Nazism is built into the film and how Nazism means the destruction of the family. The alternation between dirt and self-contempt and cleanliness and self-respect is dangerous.

BATTOCK, G., 1967, *The New American Cinema*, New York.
An anthology of criticism, little of it critical.

BAUER, R. and BAUER, A., 1960, 'America, Mass Society and Mass Media', *Journal of Social Issues*, 16: 3–66.
Problem: what is the relationship of society to its system of communications? Thesis: the theory of mass society, mass media and of the omnipotence of the mass media in mass society is contrary to the evidence on

the effectiveness of the media. Mass communications by no means pave the road to totalitarianism as the pessimists fear. First consider their *non-recreative non-cultural impact*: 1) Primary group communication has far from atrophied in 'mass society'. 2) Far from being 'atomized' by the media, interpersonal relations 'control' use and consumption of media. 3) There is no simple connection between content and effect. The audience is not 'captive'; also not exclusive. The effects on us may be miniscule in the short run, greater in the long run. *Recreational and cultural impact*. After an initial fall-off-due to television, there is now a return to the cinema. Escape? Vicarious? Sense of reality? Americans are not more passive, more criminal, more mentally ill. In mass society artists are élitists. Intellectuals are social pessimists. Society is homogenizing, and homogenizing permits more deviation than previous folk-societies. The theory of mass society is a statement of alienation from our society. (In a comment on this paper in the same issue of the journal, Parsons and White say that television competition made films better and audiences more receptive.'

BAUER, R., 1963, 'The Obstinate Audience', *American Psychologist*, 19: 319-28.
The audience is influenced partly by what it selects from what is presented to it (and what is presented to it, is presented to it because it is thought it will be selected), and partly is involved in the communication as a form of problem-solving activity (e.g., ego defence, interpersonal relations, maximizing returns).

BAXTER, JOHN, 1968, *Hollywood in the Thirties*, London.
Extremely intelligent survey, socially conscious (e.g., in noting the class-images of a studio's films), and rejecting the old orthodoxy of treating Hollywood directors as a bunch of hacks. Rates Curtiz very highly as do Higham and Greenberg (1968).

BAXTER, R. K. N., 1948, 'The Structure of the British Film Industry', *Penguin Film Review*, 7: 83-90.
An all-too-brief account of the organization of production, distribution (renting), and exhibition in Britain.

BAZIN, ANDRE, 1959-62, *Qu'est ce que le Cinéma?*, I-IV, Paris.
Posthumously collected pieces of the leader of the Young Turks among French critics. Vol. III, called 'Cinéma et Sociologie', is mostly film reviews grouped under headings like Childhood and its Myths, Eroticism, Myths and Society. Most notable is the section on westerns, and the very high rating given to Boetticher's *Seven Men from Now*. Balanced review by Quéval, *Sight and Sound*, 1961, 30: 153. English selection *What is Cinema?* appeared in 1967.

BELL, DANIEL, 1962, 'Modernity and Mass Society: On the Varieties of Cultural Experience', *Studies in Public Communication*, 4: 3-34.

General sociological answer to the critics of mass culture, showing that the attack on midcult uses sociological categories to make aesthetic judgments. Complement to Shils (1961).

BELL, OLIVIER, 1939, 'Sociological Aspects of the Cinema', *Nature*, 144: 520.
Report of a British Association meeting at Dundee on 31 August, calling for more research on audience, tastes, motives for going, effects.

BELLOUR, R. and BRION, P., 1966, *Le Westerns*, Sources, Thèmes, Mythologies, Auteurs, Acteurs, Filmographies, Paris.
This *tour de force* has four introductory essays, fifty-seven descriptions of mythic paradigms (Indian [*sic*] Attack Caravan, Hold-Up, etc.) without by any means exhausting the possibilities, then adds an encyclopaedic reference section on directors and actors, and an alphabetical index (of nearly 40 pp.) of westerns, and lists of the ten best by more than a dozen critics.

BENEDICT, RUTH, 1946, *The Chrysanthemum and the Sword*, Boston.

BERACHA, SAMMY, 1947, *Le Miracle du Cinéma*, Paris.
Subtitled 'an introduction to an aesthetic and to a sociology of the seventh art', this is a journalistic 'social' treatment of the question 'is the film an art?' Argues it is universal and not simply a vehicle of Americanization. State should subsidize.

BERELSON, BERNARD, 1961, 'The Great Debate on Cultural Democracy', *Studies in Public Communication*, 3: 3–14.
A dialogue between academic critics of the media, empirical researchers into the media, and the practical media-operator, on the value-impact of the media. Concludes that each can checkmate the other because they are all striking attitudes. None is really interested in compromise, in learning, in genuinely refining their ideas in the light of experience, in truly grappling with the problems.

— and JANOWITZ, M., eds., 1953, 1966, *Reader in Public Opinion and Communication*, Glencoe.
Excellent reader containing Asheim (1953) in the first edition but not the latest, and Wilensky (1964) in the latest only, and a long bibliography.

BERGMAN, INGMAR, 1960, *Four Screen Plays of Ingmar Bergman*, New York.
Scripts (not shooting scripts) of *Smiles of a Summer Night*, *The Seventh Seal*, *Wild Strawberries*, *The Magician*.

— 1967, *A Film Trilogy*, London.
Scripts of *Through A Glass Darkly*, *Winter Light*, *The Silence*.

239

BIBLIOGRAPHY

BERKOWITZ, LEONARD, 1962, *Aggression: A Social Psychological Analysis*, New York.
Chapter 9, 'Violence in the Mass Media' is a review of the topic which argues that media violence can teach violent acts, instigate behaviour by morally justifying hostility. But other factors determine what happens – how 'aggressive' the subject is, how hostile the media make him, how much he associates the story he is seeing with situations in which he learned hostile behaviour and with the situations he confronts after his exposure to the media, and the intensity of guilt and/or aggression anxiety aroused by the media-exposure. While the media incite anti-social conduct only in a few, a heavy dosage increases the probability of subsequent aggressive behaviour in some members of the audience.

— CORWIN, R., and HEIRONIMUS, M., 1963*a*, 'Film Violence and Subsequent Aggressive Tendencies', *Public Opinion Quarterly*, 27: 217–29.
'The findings . . . offer little comfort to those who contend that fantasy aggression necessarily has socially beneficial effects . . . film violence may well increase the probability that someone in the audience will behave aggressively in a later situation (soon afterwards). If . . . the fantasy aggression appears socially justified . . . the consequence may be a weakening of constraints against hostility . . . angered audience members . . . may be more likely to believe it is permissible to attack the "villains" in their own lives . . .' (p. 229).

— and RAWLINGS, E., 1963*b*, 'Effect of Film Violence on Inhibition Against Subsequent Aggression', *Journal of Abnormal and Social Psychology*, 66: 405–12.
A male graduate student insults (or not) a group of students; a female graduate gives a plot summary either justifying (or not) a prize fight scene, which is then shown. Subjects then rate the male graduate student. So far from the justified aggressors having their emotions purged by the fight, they had their inhibitions lowered and had heightened overt hostility to the male graduate student.

— 1964, 'The Effects of Observing Violence', *Scientific American*, 210: 35–41.
A criticism of The Theory of Catharsis, claiming that general distraction and dissipation is the more likely explanation of the soothing effect of films. Violent films are potentially dangerous: especially if the observer is angry to begin with, the filmed violence will increase the chances that such a person will attack someone.

— and GEEN, R. G., 1966, 'Film Violence and the Cue Properties of available Targets', *Journal of Personality and Social Psychology*, 3: 525–30.
Another group of students shown the fight scene from *Champion* (cf. Berkowitz *et al.* (1963*a*, *b*) and given a shock, and allowed to shock their shocker 'Kirk', did so more than those who thought he was 'Bob' or who saw a non-aggressive film. 'Observed aggression . . . does not necessarily lead to open aggression against anyone. Particular targets are most likely to be attacked, and those are objects having appropriate, aggression-eliciting cue properties' (p. 529).

240

BIBLIOGRAPHY

BERTRAND, DANIEL, 1936, *The Motion Picture Industry*, Washington.
See United States Government, Office of National Recovery Administration, Division of Review, Industry Study Section, February 1936.

BERTRAND, DANIEL, with EVANS, W. D., and BLANCHARD, E. L., 1941, *The Motion Picture Industry – A Pattern of Control*, Washington.
A lucid analysis of the pattern of monopoly control of distribution and exhibition built up in the USA: asserts that these restraints of trade are not to lower costs but to eliminate competition.

BESSIE, ALVAH, 1966, *The Symbol*, New York.
This best-selling novel by one of the Hollywood ten (see Kahn (1948)) most closely follows the career of Marilyn Monroe.

BEUICK, M. D., 1927, 'The Limited Social Effect of Radio Broadcasting', *American Journal of Sociology*, 32: 615–22.
Radio does not involve congregation and therefore cannot compete with theatre, concert, church, or the cinema.

BLESH, RUDI, 1966, *Keaton*, New York.
Authoritative biography of the greatest genius of silent comedy, but technical rather than critical, chatty rather than analytical.

BLISTEIN, E. M., 1964, *Comedy in Action*, Durham, N.C.
His own suggested alternative title is: 'A Modest Inquiry into the Nature of the Comic and the Laughable, with Some Animadversions on the Pretensions of the Comic Theorists, and Some Appreciation for the Creators and Actors of Comedy'. Comedy is Truth. Ranges over theatre, literature, movies, radio. Like most books on humour, this one is not funny.

BLOOM, S. W., 1956, 'A Social Psychological Study of Motion Picture Audience Behaviour: A Case Study of the Negro Image in Mass Communication', PhD thesis, University of Wisconsin, unpublished.
The Negro image in films has improved over 45 years: is Hollywood following or leading? Following. *The Birth of a Nation* image was replaced by that of the Negro as a childish clown. As in the film *Lost Boundaries,* which is studied in detail, serious films smooth over or skim the problems in order to spare white feeling and in search of a neutral realism without preaching. The film is ambivalent.

BLUESTONE, GEORGE, 1957, *Novels Into Film*, Baltimore.
A balanced and liberal study of the adaptation of *The Informer, Wuthering Heights, Pride and Prejudice, The Grapes of Wrath, The Ox-Bow Incident* and *Madame Bovary* to the screen. Allows that, film being a separate art form, its proper approach is to treat a novel as just another piece of raw material.

BIBLIOGRAPHY

BLUMER, H., 1933, *Movies and Conduct*, New York.
Moley (1938) comments: Blumer regrets that 'motion pictures do not attempt to determine and guide forms of conduct', p. 36.

— 1936, 'The Moulding of Mass Behaviour Through the Motion Picture', *Publications of the American Sociological Society*, **29**: 115–27.
Mass behaviour can involve people from any stratum of society and is to be seen as a species of behaviour different from familial or cultural behaviour, etc. 1) Mass behaviour stands in opposition to local folk life, the preparation for a new social order; 2) the behaving mass consists of detached, alienated individuals, with no culture, no established rules or forms of conduct, no system of expectations or demands, so the control of behaviour must be by direct appeal; 3) a mass behaves as a congeries of individual lines of action, it may be irregular, capricious, foolish, or quiet, deliberate and deep-seated. Mass behaviour is basically selective. The cinema audience is a mass. Films are vivid and the use of close-up reduces physical distance and also social distance, so intimate identification and participation becomes possible. 'To induce this absorption or identification on the part of the spectator is the avowed purpose of the producer; to have the experience is the desire of the average movie-goer', p. 123. The general influence of motion pictures is a '*reaffirmation of basic human values but an undermining of the mores*', p. 124. Also widens horizons, creates stereotypes and allows reverie. '. . . movie-goers, by reason of being a mass in an undefined area have no culture which might interpret and order their cinema experiences, and integrate them with those of local life. Instead the experiences remain alienated with no-scheme to bridge them. It is this absence of an intermediate defining culture which makes motion pictures a matter of moral concern', p. 125. '. . . folk tales reinforce the folk culture by reason of being closely integrated with it whereas motion pictures are integrated with no culture', p. 126. 'One might interpret the shifting play of motion pictures in response to the selective acts of the mass, as unconscious experiments in feeling out the developing tastes and aspirations of the people and helping to mould them into a consistent pattern of life', p. 127.

— 1946, 'Collective Behaviour' in A. M. Lee, ed., *New Outline of the Principles of Sociology*, New York, 167–222.

— and HAUSER, P. M., 1933, *Movies, Delinquency and Crime*, New York.
Moley caustically speaks for them: 'We have set out to determine the effects of motion pictures upon criminals. We did not get much material and most of it is worthless, but it proves that the motion picture is a factor in causing delinquency. But in any event, if it does not prove that, it does prove that the motion picture did not keep delinquents from becoming delinquents' (p. 22).

BOLL, ANDRE, 1941, *Le Cinéma et son Histoire*, Paris.
Part IV treats of 'the social importance of the cinema'. The cinema creates myths, its influence is incommensurable. Some films succeed (réussis), some misfire (ratés). What cinema achieves (avenir) depends on how men use it.

242

BIBLIOGRAPHY

BORDE, R. and CHAUMETON, E., 1955, *Panorama du Film Noir Américain (1941–1953)*, Paris.
Exhaustive, authoritative and elaborately sub-divided French survey of *film noirs*, criminal psychology, costume criminal films, gangsters, police documentaries, and social tendencies. Typical of the love affair of the French critics with the American commercial cinema, re-discovered when it flooded back on their screens after the Occupation.

BORNEMAN, ERNEST, 1946, 'Rebellion in Hollywood. A Study in Motion Picture Finance', *Harper's*, **193**: 337–43 (October).
Explains how high corporate and personal taxes gave incentive to: independent production and the one-picture company, the growth of film finance corporations specializing in end money, and the new financial arrangements including public stock companies and some very complex deals.

— 1950, 'United States versus Hollywood', *Sight and Sound*, **19**: 418*ff*.
Account of the legal proceedings initiated under the Sherman anti-trust act to force the big motion picture companies to sell their theatres.

BOSE, A., 1963, 'Mass Communication: the Cinema in India', *Indian Journal of Social Research*, **4**: 80–2.
Unremarkable description of films in Indian society. Study of 60 Hindu films and 400 adult males. Audience selection is mainly on the basis of word-of-mouth recommendation and stars. Films set mostly in urban areas; audience too. Average of 7·2 songs per film!

BOUGHEY, DAVIDSON, 1921, *The Film Industry*, London.
Popular account of how films are made.

BOWER, DALLAS, 1937, 'Film in the Social Scene' in Bower, Herring and Bryher (1937), 23–31.
On the one hand: '. . . the modern entertainment film is mental dope, very often of a singular perniciousness' (p. 27); on the other the American entertainment film is preferable to documentary: 'the "actuality" of the contemporary American scene is quite familiar to the average European, and this has come about entirely due to the incidental indigenously American surround with which every American film is mounted' (p. 31).

— HERRING, R., and BRYHER, W., 1937, *Cinema Survey*, London.
Critical essays by non-experts. The most interesting by Bower (1937).

BOX, F. S., 1937, *Film Publicity*, London.
About using the film *for* publicity, not the principles *of* publicizing film.

BOX, K., 1947. *The Cinema and the Public*, London.
32% of the adult population go once a week or more. 13% go more than once. 24% do not go. 65% of children of school age go once a week. 5% do not go. Older people go more than younger, women more than men.

243

Higher working class adults and children are the most frequent attenders. 70% of cinemagoers (defined as those going once a month or more) go regularly, one to three to the same cinema, two to three choosing their cinema.

— and MOSS, L., 1943, *The Cinema Audience*, London. Results of the Wartime Social Survey, the results the same as Box (1947) – large population groups are better represented in the cinema audience than in the newspaper and book audience.

BRADY, ROBERT A., 1947a, 'Monopoly and the First Freedom', *Hollywood Quarterly*, 2: 225–41. Highly critical review of Ernst (1946) arguing that size is no guide to the extent of the threat to democracy. What is threatening is a small, irresponsible, owner-manager clique. He recommends public ownership of films and other parts of the economy.

— 1947b, 'The Problem of Monopoly', *Annals* (1947), 125–36. While it is not a text-book monopoly, the motion picture industry has a definite 'semicompulsory cartel'. Big producers co-operate with each other, not with independents. Distributors divide territory and show each other's films *quid pro quo*. The instrument of co-ordination is the MPAA. It is an ideal monopoly because: 1) of monopoly control of the natural monopoly of the unique star; 2) each film is unique; 3) public appeal tends to go together with expense, i.e., highly paid stars have their monopoly reinforced; 4) the appeal of the product is short lived and therefore priority in vending is important; 5) copyright is also a monopoly; 6) each vending outlet vends only one product at a time. The divorcement decrees apply only to distribution and exhibition. A production monopoly was not found by the court.

BRANCH, DOUGLAS, 1926, *The Cowboy and His Interpreters*, New York. Chapter 14 discusses the way westerns evolved from preposterous stage shows and cheap novels, and deviated ever more from reality. 'The screen-epic of the West developed its curiosities innocently and unintentionally. Many were borrowed from literature; many were the improvisations of directors who had graduated from back-stage in musical comedies and provincial stock companies', p. 232. H. S. Drago, in his introduction to the 1961 reprint is much nastier: 'The Western motion-picture was trash, acknowledged as such by the producer, made according to a long-established formula and outrageously profitable. It could be, and was, made over and over with only a change of place and character names and a new feminine interest for the star. It was self-perpetuating, and what we have on Western television shows today is its shoddy but legitimate off-spring. Its plot, characters and wanton disregard for anything approaching historical fidelity are the same', p. ii.

BRAUN-LARRIEU, ANDRE, 1938, *Le Role Social du, Cinéma*, Paris. Covers hastily cinema and children, international influences, cinema and tourism, cinema and workers.

BIBLIOGRAPHY

BRECHT, BERTOLT, 1964, *Brecht on Theatre*, trs. J. Willett, New York.

British Film Academy, 1950, *The Film Industry in Great Britain*, London.
Reviewed in *Sight and Sound*, 1950, 19: 175 by 'James Morgan'.

British Intelligence Objectives Sub-Committee, 1947, *German Scientific Films*, London.
Subtitled 'report on the use of educational, medical and industrial films in Germany', this post-war reconstruction sketches how centralized was film production under the propaganda requirements of the Third Reich.

'British Youth Dislike Love in the Movies', 1931, *Literary Digest*, 3: 22–5.
Denny and Meyersohn: 'Unimportant investigation of the likes and dislikes of movie-going British children deploring the lack of education received from the movies.'

BROD, MAX and THOMAS, R., 1930, *Liebe im Film*, Giessen.
Way ahead of its time (cf. De Beauvoir (1960), Lo Duca (1957, 1960, 1962)).
Marvellous stills and captions, already has 'Der infantile Typ, dis Girl nach dem Gesmack Amerikas' and 'Der schwache Körper des Kind – Mädchens, von Liebe uberwältigt'. Very amusing and sharp.

BRODBECK, A. J., 1955, 'The Mass Media as Socializing Agents', paper read to the American Psychological Association, September 1955, San Francisco.
Abstracted in Schramm, Lyle and Parker (1961). Recently remimeographed.

BRODSKY, JACK and WEISS, NATHAN, 1964, 'The Cleopatra Papers', *Esquire*, August, 33–41.

BROGAN, D. W., 1954, 'The Problem of High Culture and Mass Culture', *Diogenes*, 5: 1–13.
Rebuttal of the paper by Dwight Macdonald (1954).

BROOKER, FLOYD E., 1947, 'Motion Pictures as an Aid to Education', *Annals* (1947), 103–9.
Films are not only useful in the classroom and army, but cheap, despite the initial lump sum. Also a new language with access to historical events and time-lapse processes, etc., hitherto unavailable.

BROOKS, RICHARD, 1952, *The Producer*, London.
One of the most authentic 'insider' novels of Hollywood.

BROWNE, MICHAEL, 1951, 'Survey of the Hollywood Entertainment Film During the War Years 1941–1943', MS thesis, unpublished, UCLA.
Concentrates on the use of propaganda. Too few pictures were concerned with the issues of the war. The level was that we are fighting for Mom's blueberry pie, hot dogs and ice cream sodas at the beach, remember Pearl

245

Harbor. [In American war films the question often is not, why are we fighting, but what would we have to give up if we stopped.]

BROWNLOW, KEVIN, 1968a, *How it Happened Here*, London.
Amusingly written story of the vagaries surrounding the ambitious amateur film on the Nazi occupation of England: *It Happened Here*.

— 1968b, *The Parade's Gone By*, New York.
Magnificent panoramic survey of the silent, primarily in America, based on extensive interviews. Packed with information, love and many rare stills, this is among the handful of essential books. Its thesis, that the silent era was the pinnacle, and that everything since has been a falling-off, is none the less quite absurd.

BROUWER, MARTEN, 1962, 'Mass Communication and the Social Sciences: Some Neglected Areas', *International Social Science Journal*, 14: 303–19.
Criticizes the assumption of the atomized audience and the neglect of European work. 'It would be wrong . . . to consider the homogenizing influence just a disturbing factor . . . [it] may be held to belong to the very characteristics of audience experience, Moreover . . . some audiences should tend to be more heterogeneous instead of less, e.g., when low status members want to show reactions opposite to those of high status members . . . the individual no longer appears as an obvious unit', p. 308. He claims Kurt Baschitz anticipated both Lazarsfeld's two-step flow of communication hypothesis, and Festinger's cognitive dissonance theory!

BRUNER, J. and FOWLER, G., 1941, 'The Strategy of Terror: Audience Response to *Blitzkrieg im Westen*', *Journal of Abnormal and Social Psychology*, 36: 561–74.
One-third of the audience felt the futility of resistance during the film, less after. Clearly counterpropaganda is called for.

BRUSENDORFF, O. and MALMKJAER, P., 1965, *Erotik I Filmen*, Copenhagen.
Companion to Brod and Thomas (1930), Osten and Lundkvist (1950), and Lo Duca (1957, etc.). Being published in wonderful Copenhagen (not quite Sam Goldwyn's), it includes sections and stills which most countries would classify as pornographic.

BUCKLE, G. F., 1926, *The Mind and the Film*, London.
Amateurish 'psychological' study of how film technique is used to aid following story and arousing emotions.

BURNETT, R. G. and MARTELL, E. D., 1932, *The Devil's Camera*, Menace of a Film-ridden World, London.
Dedicated to 'the Ultimate Sanity of the White Races', this tract opens with a knife-killing blamed upon films, but hastily declares, 'We object not to the film camera but to the prostitution of it by sex-mad and cynical financiers'. Calls for censorship.

BIBLIOGRAPHY

BURTON, HOWARD A., 1953, 'High Noon: Everyman Rides Again', *Quarterly of Film, Radio, and Television*, 8: 80–6.
Analysis of *High Noon* as a version of the morality play *Everyman*.

BYRNE, R. B., ed., 1966, *The Film Issue, Arts in Society*, special issue, 4, no. 1: Madison (Wis.).
Rather confusingly edited collection of articles, interviews, and reviews, attempting to give an overall view of the film world today.

Cahiers du Cinéma, 1951 to date, Paris.
The French monthly journal. Scholarly, indefatigable, eccentric, over-whelmingly enthusiastic and lavish. Articles and reviews frequently impenetrable or bizarre. Most famous for its introduction of André Bazin's principle of the 'politique des auteurs'.

CAHUDHURI, ARUN, 1951, 'A Study of the Negroes' Problems in the Post-War Movies', MA thesis, USC, unpublished.

CALDER-MARSHALL, A., 1937, 'The Film Industry' in C. D. Lewis, ed., *The Mind in Chains*, London, 57–79.
A volume dedicated to the view that the mind is in chains 'forged by a dying social system' (which later made the editor Poet Laureate) but that these have been broken in the Soviet Union (p. 17). The film piece is a manic compendium of theses about extravagance, fantasy-escape, Big Business as Bogey Man, how wonderful and true and human and real Russian films are compared with the false, artificial, star-ridden, sinister American and British capitalist films. Full of gems like: 'The charge made against socialist films, that they are propagandist, can be returned with double force against capitalist films. The socialist interpretation of society takes full account of the facts and explains them without distortion. A film based on socialist ideology is, of course, propagandist in the same way that a film based on capitalist ideology is propagandist. The difference between them, however, is the difference between truth and falsehood' (p. 75).

Canada, 1931, *Investigation into an alleged combine in the motion picture industry in Canada:* report of commissioner, Ottawa. See White (1931).

CANTRIL, HADLEY and ALLPORT, GORDON W., 1935, *The Psychology of Radio*, New York.
Movies are intensive experiences, more vivid, more personal more glamourous than radio, identification is easier. Their stars have visual as well as vocal dimensions. 'Since the audience watching a picture is in-evitably a congregate assembly, it is bound by traditional convention in respect to its conduct. Although neither the radio audience nor the patrons of the talkie are in direct circular relation with the performer, more of the conventional social influences are present in the picture theater. Both are less personal, less human, and more mechanical than the ordinary theater audience and the face-to-face assembly', p. 15. The talkie provides an

escape from the restraints of the home and so is less of a 'moral' agency. Radio appeals to practical interests, talkies to repressed desires and fantasies. 'The social conventions of the theater are more numerous than those of the radio. Entering the theater we subscribe to an unwritten code obligating us to conform to certain rules of behaviour. Since we desire to give our complete attention to the film, we accept the obligation cheerfully, not expecting to sing, read, or play bridge before the silver screen as we do before the loud-speaker. As members of an audience, we are conscious of other individuals sitting around us. Their strained attention and expressions of emotion enhance our own and cause us to conform to the spirit of the occasion. This social facilitation makes our own reactions seem less artificial, less banal, less unsocial than they would appear to us if we were alone', p. 261. Radio is direct and fresh, movies preserved and out of date.

'The outstanding psychological characteristic of the talking picture is its power of providing hundreds of spectators at a single time with a standardized daydream. Vaguely aware that his neighbours are likewise losing themselves in the adventurous and amorous exploits of the actors, each member of the audience feels protected and justified in his own artistic absorption. It has often been pointed out how extraordinarily antisocial are some of the attractive exploits on the screen. Paradoxically enough, conventional sanctions have grown up to protect the spectator from feeling guilt in such antisocial fantasies. With multitudes of his fellow citizens to keep him company he can indulge in outrageous daydreams whose theme is not ordinarily admitted into his socialized consciousness. The radio seldom invites such an extreme degree of identification of the auditor with the actor, and its programs, furthermore, are limited by the conventions of the home. In short, it might be said that the type of social participation encouraged by radio is the type that is well integrated with conscious standards of morality, whereas the talking picture permits expression of the deeper, less socialized portions of the spectator's unconscious mental life', p. 261.

CARMEN, IRA H., 1966, *Movies, Censorship and the Law*, Ann Arbor.
History of censorship in the USA (cf. Hunnings, 1967).

CARPENTER, E. and MCLUHAN, H. M., eds., 1960, *Explorations in Communication*, Boston.
A selection from the defunct McLuhan journal *Explorations*, mostly short and very McLuhan-ish.

CARTER, EVERETT, 1947, 'A Short Inquiry Into a Form of Popular Poetry', *Penguin Film Review*, 4: 52–68.
A beautifully executed send-up of learned and footnoted commentaries on poetry and literature, and at the same time a good analysis of some major themes in pop songs, and with many gem-like quotations.

CARTER, HUNTLY, 1930, *The New Spirit in the Cinema*, London.
Subtitle: 'An Analysis and Interpretation of the Parallel Paths of the

Cinema, which have led to the present Revolutionary Crisis forming a Study of the Cinema as an Instrument of Sociological Humanism.' Problem: the Fall and Redemption of the Cinema. Thesis: 'the Cinema truly considered is primarily an organic part of social and human life . . . a highly sensitive instrument of representation and interpretation by means of which man may play with, understand and illuminate his experience in quest of a tolerable system of human life' (pp. xvi-xvii). Aim: to suggest the path from the Over-lordship of Money to the Over-lordship of Sense and Human Purpose. Cinema's Fall and Redemption is elaborately paralleled by the fall of man. Huntly's own summary tells how Good Purpose (true and decent movies) and Bad Purpose (the Demon is the Box Office) struggle to marry the Magician in the little Black Box. Bad Purpose is slain by her own cupidity. Huntly is violently anti-American and considers the U.K. and Germany as wings of Hollywood. He finds the New Spirit affirmed in Russia – because they have a synoptic vision of national organic unity. Replace mechanical power by Subject-power, Eisenstein *et al.*; double the quota, etc.

CARTER, S. B., 1945, *The Films*, WEA topics no. 6, London.
An early version of his (1948).

— 1948, *Ourselves and the Cinema*, WEA topics no. 17, London.
The cinema as escape. (Superficial, well-meant discussion topics on the film for WEA audiences.)

Cartoons and Animation, 1956, special issue of *Films and Filming*, 3: November, 6–12.
Articles by John Halas (the versatility of the medium), R. Manvell (history of cartoons); B. Kiesling (on Hanna-Barbera); and B. Orna (on Trnka).

CARVER, MARY VIDA, 1967, 'The Critical Evaluation of Films by Repertory Grid: Value-patterns of working and middle class youths compared with those of professional critics', PhD thesis, University of London, unpublished.
She had fifteen critics, thirty sixth-formers and thirty apprentices to rate ten films of their choice on a twenty-point scale to test perception and evaluation. Concludes that taste differences turn neither on differences or perceptual skills, nor on different critical evaluation, but on a complex interaction of the two. The responses to the most-mentioned film – *Goldfinger* – are carefully analysed in the key tables at pp. 123 and 183. Critics concepts (constructs) are richer – 'like real life' has many more resonances and discriminations for them. So learning the language of discrimination is the first step on the road to good taste. Good bibliography.

CASSADY, JR., RALPH, 1933, 'Some Economic Aspects of Motion Picture Production and Marketing', *Journal of Business of The University of Chicago*, 6: 113–31.
Outline of the economic and industrial structure, placing emphasis on monopolistic tendencies. 'In this exceedingly unorthodox industry,

the production system of lowest cost is not necessarily the most economical' (p. 127). At p. 120 there seems to be a confusion between block-booking and full line forcing.

— 1958, 'Impact of the Paramount Decision on Motion Picture Distribution and Price Making', *Southern California Law Review*, 31 : 150–80. This is the most careful documentation of how the Paramount anti-trust decision in America, which forced producing and distributing companies to sell their theatres, operated. It was a principal cause of the ruin of the seller's market (the other cause was television). Cassady finds that a varied and largely open market condition now prevails, with flexible leasing arrangements, and general compliance with the law. [This paper is among a handful which go in any detail into the labyrinthine intricacies of motion picture economics.]

CASTY, ALAN, 1968, 'The New Style in British Rebels and their Films', *Midwest Quarterly*, 9: 139–53.
From *Look back in Anger* to *Alfie* British films portray various attempts to rebel. Recently, there has been a shift of emphasis from overt rebellion to the cultivation of inner consciousness.

CATRICE, P., 1961, 'Problèmes Juifs à Travers le Cinéma', *Revue de Psychologie des Peuples*, 16: 391–416.
Study of the problems of whether the cinema helps us to know and understand the Jews, their civilization, religion, and the contemporary drama of their lives. Can it help us realize Judeo-Christian amity? Covers: films on the Catastrophe, on anti-Semitism, on Judeo-Christian amity, a long (and irrelevant) excursion into Biblical films on the grounds that the characters involved are Jews, Israel. Concentrates on the 'human' aspects of the films rather than the aesthetic aspects. Curious section on Hollywood conversions to Judaism. Concludes that films do help us to know, and they promote amity. But understanding is another, more complicated, matter. [Useful, if incomplete survey although some of the films were obviously not seen.]

CATTON, W. R., 1960, 'Changing Cognitive Structure as a Basis for the Sleeper Effect', *Social Forces*, 38: 348–54.
While selective perception and primary group mediation may inhibit the influence of the mass media, there is the sleeper effect and the way the effects of primary interaction on personal attitudes are mediated by mass communications. An experiment (involving the film *Neighbours*) showed that a film can change the cognitive structure, while not necessarily changing at the same rate the actual opinions. This latter change may come about later and may be the sleeper effect.

CAULIEZ, A.-J., 1956, *Le Film Criminel et le Film Policier*, Paris.
Defence of the *genre* plus some of the usual impenetrable French metaphysics.

BIBLIOGRAPHY

CAWELTI, J., 1962, 'Prolegomena to the Western', *Studies in Public Communication*, 4: 57–70.
Westerns are *art*. Their patterns or formulas for shaping material are their key. Warshow suggests that the westerner has a moral clarity corresponding to the clarity of the bare landscape. We must also ask, in what situation is the experience apprehended, and what are the relations between creators and audiences? Smith's (1950) study was a success. The western is an aspect of our endeavour to give meaning to our experience. Popular forms have a relatively rigid conventional pattern comprehensible and meaningful to large groups – unlike more complex individual works.

CERAM, C. W., 1965, *Archaeology of the Cinema*, New York.
Some reviewers claim this book should have been called '*Mythology of Pre-Cinema*'.

CHAMBERS, R. W., 1947, 'Need for Statistical Research', *Annals* (1947), 169–72.
Research is needed on theatres, films and audiences, and foreign business. It is beginning.

CHANDLER, RAYMOND, 1945, 'Writers in Hollywood', *Atlantic*, November, reprinted in Gardiner, D., and Walker, K. S., eds., *Raymond Chandler Speaking*, London, 1962.
Writers are the employees of producers, yet without them there would be no films. How little of worth are the talented allowed to achieve. 'The best things in any picture, artistically speaking, are invariably the easiest to leave out, mechanically speaking'. '. . . if we think bad television shows are apt to corrupt the youth of this country, take a look at what goes on in the high schools' (p. 125). [The acerbic tone is sustained:] 'It took a certain amount of effort to go to the movies. Somebody had to stay with the kids. You had to get the car out of the garage. That was hard work. And you had to drive and park. Sometimes you had to walk as much as half a block to the theatre. Reading took less physical effort, but you had to concentrate a little, even when you were reading a mystery or a western or one of those historical novels, so-called. And every once in a while you were apt to trip over a three-syllable word. That was pretty hard on the brain. Radio was a lot better, but there wasn't anything to look at. Your gaze wandered around the room and you might start thinking of other things – things you didn't want to think about. You had to use a little imagination to build yourself a picture of what was going on just by sound.
'But television's perfect. You turn a few knobs . . . lean back and drain your mind of all thought. And there you are watching the bubbles in the primeval ooze. You don't have to concentrate. You don't have to react. You don't have to remember. You don't miss your brain because you don't need it.' p. 125.

CHAPLIN, C., 1964, *My Autobiography*, London.
A trifle pretentiously written, Chaplin is more interested in reminiscing

251

about the famous than in explaining clearly the nature of his art, or going deeply into the reasons for the impact of the cinema.

CHAPLIN, LITA GREY, 1966, *My Life With Chaplin*, New York.
One of Chaplin's wives gets her own back after being ignored in his autobiography. It is in the keyhole-of-the-bedroom style, but contains interesting information on early Hollywood and the role of mums (cf. Moore [1968]).

CHARTERS, W. W., 1933, *Motion Pictures and Youth*, New York.
1) Motion pictures are a potent medium of education; 2) for children the content of motion pictures is not good. There is too much sex and crime and love for a balanced diet; 3) the motion picture is one among many influences. How powerful it is compared with others was not studied in the Payne studies.
This summary of all the Payne Fund Studies is also abstracted in Schramm, Lyle and Parker (1961). Fearing (1950) comments: 'Many of these studies seemed to reflect the widely held attitude that motion pictures are potentially "bad" in their effects and need some form of restriction ... Extensive controversy resulting from publication of the Payne studies was reflected in the detailed analysis made by Mortimer Adler, 1937. Professor Adler's critique was summarized and popularized by Raymond Moley, 1938.'

CHERRY, COLIN, 1966, *On Human Communication*, Cambridge (Mass.).
'A review, a survey, and a criticism' is the subtitle. This is one of the classic, basic, authoritative works.

CHEVALLIER, J., et al., 1963, ed., *Regards Neufs Sur le Cinéma*, Paris.
Hodge-podge anthology on the nature of the film, the industry, individual films, theoretical and technical matters, etc. Most of the selections are absurdly short.

CHEVANNE, A., 1933, *L'Industrie du Cinéma: le Cinéma Sonore*, Bordeaux.
Useful survey of production in 1933, compares the industries of several countries.

CHIATTONE, A., 1949, *Il Film Western*, Milan.
Elaborate historical survey of actors, directors, costumes, etc., of the real and the movie West.

CHIMET, IORDAN, 1966, *Western*, Filmele Vestului Indepartat, Bucharest.
Small booklet on the *genre*, heavily indebted to the sources cited in the bibliography, even the stills seem to have been duped off. Illustrative of just how universal the western is.

CHURCHILL, W., 1929, 'Peter Pan Township of the Films', *Daily Telegraph*, 30 December.

A travel article in which, touring down California, W.S.C. describes the queerest factory in the world, just recently converted to sound.

Cinéma Fantastique, 1963, L'Epouvante, special issue of Bizarre, no. 24/25, Paris.
J.-C. Romer writes interestingly on Tod Browning and James Whale, also included are surveys of the careers of Bela Lugosi and Boris Karloff.

Cinema 1950, 1950, R. Manvell and R. K. Nielson-Baxter, eds., Harmondsworth.

Cinema 1951, 1951, R. Manvell and R. K. Nielson-Baxter, eds., Harmondsworth.

Cinema 1952, 1952, R. Manvell and R. K. Nielson-Baxter, eds., Harmondsworth.
An annual successor to Penguin Film Review (q.v.) containing articles of some depth and scholarship. The mid-fifties were a low point for film books and magazines which were to proliferate again in the mid-sixties.

CIRLIN, B. D. and PETERMAN, J. N., 1947, 'Pre-testing a Motion Picture: A Case History', Journal of Social Issues, 3: 39ff.
Describes the use of Cirlin Reactograph making audiences press buttons to indicate their liking or disliking of a particular scene. These reactions are then charted.

CLARENS, CARLOS, 1967, An Illustrated History of the Horror Film, New York.
A definitive chronology and survey, with some rare stills.

COCTEAU, J., 1950, Diary of a Film, London.
Production notes on La Belle et la Bête.

— 1954, On the Film, a conversation recorded by André Fraighean, London.
Cocteau questioned about his films up until Orphée (1950), his utterances are as profound or mystifying as ever.

COHEN, ELLIOT, 1947, 'Letter from a Movie Maker', Commentary, 4: 344–9.
An exchange with Doré Schary à propos the encouragement to anti-semitism that might be given by an anti-anti-semitic film like Crossfire.

COHEN-SEAT, G., 1946, Essai Sur Les Principes d'une Philosophie du Cinéma, vol. I, Introduction Générale, Paris.
Socio-psychological, even phenomenological, analysis of the experience of films. 'Le film, en dernière analyse, propose à la sympathie une réalité objective, absolue, distincte des espirits qui étaient entrés par avance ou qui entreront en communication avec elle. Le fait filmique représente un trunchement entre une sorte moderne d'Idée platonienne, et la matière

des "ideés" qui doivent lui correspondre – comme une classe des choses à un type exemplaire – dans les espirits humains' (pp. 184–5).

COLLARD, CHARLES, 1919, *La Cinématographie et la Criminalité Infantile*, Bruxelles.

Commission on Educational and Cultural Films, 1932, *The Film In National Life*, London.
'Being the report of an enquiry conducted by the Commission . . . into the service which the cinematograph may render to education and social progress.' Recommends the setting up of what later became the British Film Institute (cf. Ashley, 1934).

Commonwealth Club of California, 1913, *Public Recreation*, Transactions, 8: no. 8: San Francisco.
Pp. 250–72 are on films.

— 1921, *Censorship*, Transactions, 16: no. 6: San Francisco.
'Is censorship of motion pictures necessary?' Films are erotically suggestive, low, show crime: 'Too many pictures exhibit as proper such features as a woman of good morals going unaccompanied to a man's apartment to meet him, as if this were done in daily life', p. 94. In general a bit stuffy as they rant on about the cinema. Part of the whole twenties outcry which brought about the Hays Office and the Production Code.

— 1925, *Motion Pictures and the Public*, Transactions, 20: no. 3: San Francisco.
'What is the Matter with Motion Pictures?' is discussed on p. 90.

The Community and the Motion Picture, 1929, Report of National Conference on Motion Pictures Held at the Hotel Montclair, New York City, September, 24–7, 1929.
A conference, organized by Hays, of community leaders from all over the USA to exchange ideas about the cinema – they themselves choosing the topics. The outcome – suggestions for a handbook, a list of suitable films for children's matinees – hardly seems to justify all the talk.

CONANT, MICHAEL, 1960, *Antitrust in the Motion Picture Industry*, Berkeley and Los Angeles.
History of trusts and anti-trust moves in the film industry.

Confédération Nationale du Cinéma Francais, 1954, *L'Industrie du Cinéma*. Paris.
Official analysis and statistics of the industry.

CONRAD, DEREK, 1959, 'Two Feet in the Air', *Films and Filming*, 6: 11–13, 28, 35.
About Fred Astaire.

BIBLIOGRAPHY

CONSIGLIO, ALBERTO, 1937, 'Le Rôle Intellectual du Cinéma', in *Role Intellectuelle du Cinéma* (1937), 167–93.
Film is a language. 'Le Cinéma est capable lui aussi d'assumer la fonction la plus élevée du langage verbal et qui jusqu'ici était à celui-ci exclusivement réservée: la pensée philosophique', p. 169. P. 177: 'Le cinéma est, en effet, la plus parfaite, la plus réaliste image de la vie . . . Seul le cinéma parvaient à réaliser une fiction extrêmement proche de la réalité. Si parfaite qu'il n'y à qu'un oeil exercé qui puisse distinguer un passage documentaire d'une scène composée'. The rest of the essay concentrates on the mutual influence of the cinema and its public, making some political and sociological points, including that the cinema crosses class barriers and can function to reconcile classes' *mores*.

COOKE, ALISTAIR, 1940, *Douglas Fairbanks: The Making of a Screen Character*, New York.
Son of a lawyer, he tried his hand at a great many things before becoming a minor Broadway star and accepting the call to Hollywood in 1915 at $2000 a week. Cooke analyses the relation between the athletic, extroverted real man and the character 'Doug' – first a light and satirical figure, later a swashbuckler. Suggests the change was due to the war and the desire to escape the present either into the future or the past. Fairbanks 'solved as early as anybody in the game the problem . . . of mating audience and actor, so that a movie seems to be . . . an actual creation of the audience, a copy of their liveliest impulses', p. 31.

COOPER, EUNICE and DINERMAN, HELEN, 1951, 'Analysis of the Film *Don't Be a Sucker*: A Study in Communication', *Public Opinion Quarterly*, 14: 234–64.
Much evidence of boomerang effects. The Fascist danger and anti-German message failed: people do not transfer to American experience from Germany; German was cast glamorously. Generalized and nonexplicit messages do not get across.

COUGHLAN, ROBERT, 1951, 'Now it is Trouble that is Supercolossal in Hollywood', *Life*, 31: 102–14, 13 August.
Describes the effect on the film business of the spread of television. Written at a time when there was 15 million television sets in the US, but the film business was tailing off even in areas not yet covered by television. Presciently predicts that Hollywood will survive, partly by selling its film libraries, partly by selling its skill as television goes in for more pre-filming, but that the big studios will not survive.

CRANSTON, MAURICE, 1949, 'The Pre-Fabricated Day-Dream', *Penguin Film Review*, no. 9: 26–31.
Films do not involve peoples' imagination but present mythologies – 'the true folk entertainment of our time'.

CRESSEY, P., 1932, 'The Social Role of Motion Pictures in an Interstitial Area', *Journal of Educational Sociology*, 6: 238–44.

BIBLIOGRAPHY

Report on a study to be undertaken among a Boys Club by the New York University researchers.

— 1934, 'The Motion Picture as Informal Education', *Journal of Educational Sociology*, 7: 504–15.
Children are exposed to many films and gain a great deal of information from them. Unlike schools they are not compulsory, but are freely chosen. What is absorbed is absorbed solely because of the industry's skill at catching and holding attention. Moreover, the childrens' and adolescents' play worlds are full of film characters, stars, situations, endorsed products, etc. Adolescents and assimilating immigrant's children are peculiarly susceptible to influence. If a film influences a delinquent, that is because of special factors in his background and situation. Films are here to stay, so the hostility of schools to them is out of place.

— 1935–6, 'The Influence of Moving Pictures on Students in India', *American Journal of Sociology*, 41: 341–50.
A questionnaire study of 233 Indian college students, shows their chief interests in the cinema to be recreational and educational. Foreign pictures have given them a better understanding of Europe and America, but have only a superficial influence of their general attitudes and behaviour. Women students are somewhat less influenced than men, even when attending films frequently. The type of pictures in which the students are interested and the extent of film influence, are directly related to the frequency with which they attend the cinema. Cultural differences and a sense of social distance tend to limit the general influence of foreign pictures.

— 1938a, 'A Study in Practical Philosophy', *Journal of Higher Education*, 9: 319–28.
Review of Adler (1937). Noting that Adler argues for artistic freedom and for censorship only at the stage of audience reception, and that films are cathartic, Cressey complains that Adler's criticisms of the Payne Fund Studies (q.v.) alternate personal abuse, citation of St. Thomas Aquinas as an authority, and unappreciative discussion of the sociological interpretation of the findings. Because the results are qualified and tentative, Adler dismisses them as useless to the prudent man. Yet despite his tone, most of the studies come out of his scrutiny of them rather well. 'The theatrical motion picture has, to some extent, been demonstrated to be an agency of informal education of rather high potency', p. 328.

— 1938b, 'The Motion Picture Experience as Modified by Social Background and Personality', *American Sociological Review*, 3: 516–25.
Picture-going is an extrasocial situation, neither wholly social nor nonsocial. Instead of social interaction there is imaginative participation, i.e., just like social participation or role playing, Projection, introjection and displacement mechanisms are all used. Psychic distance must be maintained, films must be neither too fantastic nor too painfully close to home. Cinema only adds to the complex web of social background, personality, and previous experience. The audience is not passive. Cinema involves suggestion and imitation. [This article is sane and critical.]

256

BIBLIOGRAPHY

— and THRASHER, F. M., 1933, *Boys, Movies and City Streets*, New York.

CRICHTON, CHARLES, 1948, 'Children and Fantasy', *Penguin Film Review*, 7: 44–9.
Children's ability to enter into and enjoy a fantasy, helped greatly in the shooting of the film *Hue and Cry*.

CRIST, JUDITH, 1968, *The Private Eye, the Cowboy, and the Very Naked Girl*, New York.
Collection of the criticism (1963–68) of a sharp, knowledgeable, but basically rather lightweight newspaperwomen. Contains no longer pieces. In general her condemnations read well but rarely say why the film is no good, her praise also tends to be slightly off the mark.

CROW, DUNCAN, 1954, 'The First Golden Age', *Sight and Sound*, 23: 149*ff*.

— 1954, 'The Advent of Leviathan', *Sight and Sound*, 23: 191*ff*.
Two articles narrating how sound made an impact on the British industry, and formed it into the 'oligarchy' which it has remained ever since.

CROWTHER, BOSLEY, 1946, 'The Movies', in J. Goodman, ed., *While You Were Gone*, A Report on Wartime Life in the United States, New York, 511–32.
Surveys feature and documentary production, the war activities of Hollywood denizens, and even the major scandals. More people had more money, and the box office reached unprecedented grosses. So Hollywood played it safe [a *non-sequitur* in a sellers' market unless they were complacent], p. 513. Hollywood films 'did not give a consistent or reliable impression of the wartime world', p. 519.

— 1957, *The Lion's Share*, New York.
Company history of MGM; hagiographical.

— 1960, *Hollywood Rajah*, New York.
Biography of Louis B. Mayer; see comment on previous item.

CUIJPERS, P. M. H., 1967, *Sociologie van de film*, Utrecht, unpublished MSS.
Uses the standard communications model with feedback to attempt a systematic sociology of the film.

CUNNINGHAM, R., 1954, 'A Sociological Approach to Esthetics: An Analysis of Attitudes Toward the Motion Picture', PhD, Iowa State University.
Taste is related to social and psychological factors. The reason the audience is lost when it matures is because adolescents and young people go mainly for status reasons and as they mature they come to orient towards other status factors.

CUTTS, JOHN, 1963, 'Bye Bye Musicals', *Films and Filming*, 10: November, 42*ff*.

Points out that the heralded 'revival' of musicals – *Gigi, West Side Story, My Fair Lady* – are stagey and derivative, quite different from the élan of Astaire or Kelly vehicles.

DADEK, W., 1960, 'Der Gegenwartige Stand der Filmsoziologie', *Koelner Zeitschrift Fur Soziologie und Sozialpsychologie*, **12**: 516–33.
There are three problems for the sociology of the cinema: 1) production; 2) the public; and 3) a theory of the film medium which should comprise a film aesthetic, a film psychology, and a film sociology. The highly divided process of production and use of different types of labour should be examined. The organization of co-operation in making a film should be studied, as well as the style of art produced by individuals. The antagonism between artists and management personnel is interesting. Studies of the audience have so far been empirical, statistical and functional. There has been little work done on the influence of content on opinion. Reviews the literature, i.e., Mayer, Lazarsfeld, PEP, Powdermaker, Durand.

DALE, EDGAR, 1933, *How to Appreciate Motion Pictures*, New York.
Proposes: reduction of production and longer exhibition periods; abolition of profit motive; some form of subcultural programming; training schools for motion picture workers.

— 1935a, *Children's Attendance at Motion Pictures*, New York.
A typical film audience had 2·8% under 2; 11·8% between 7 and 13; 22·1% between 14 and 20; and 63·3% over 21. 53% of children in the 4th to 12th grades attend at least once per week, 22% never go. Boys go to films more than girls, one-third of their attendances are in the afternoon, two-thirds in the evening. They go more frequently with friends than with parents.

— 1935b, *The Content of Motion Pictures*, New York.
Criticizes the vicariousness and escapism of films. Jones (1942) comments that his results lack scientific validity because of their infusion with value judgments, and because the classification of content was based on literary digests rather than actual viewings of the film. The films were viewed, but only the better to fit them in.

DAVIDSON, BILL, 1962, *The Real and the Unreal*, New York.
A lot of 'inside dope' on Hollywood and its denizens.

DAVIS, BETTE, 1963, *The Lonely Life*, London.
Intelligent and readable autobiography, with some information on just how the Hollywood contract system worked.

DAVISON, W. P., 1959, 'On the Effects of Communication', *Public Opinion Quarterly*, **23**: 343–60.
'Communications serve as a link between man and his environment and their effects may be explained in terms of the role they play in enabling people to bring about more satisfying relationships between themselves

and the world around them', p. 344. 'For our purposes ... it may be most useful to mention four aspects of the environment, as it is experienced by human beings: the physical, the social, the expected, and the imagined', p. 346. 'A given situation exists in the environment; this situation is reported by a communication that comes to the attention of the individual; the individual then adjusts his behaviour in a manner calculated to help satisfy some want or need', p. 353. The communication may tell us something new, remind us of something, or suggest new ways of patterning our relationship to the environment (e.g., as in religious conversion). 'The communicator's audience is not a passive recipient ... [it] is made up of individuals who demand something from the communications to which they are exposed, and who select those that are likely to be useful to them', p. 360.

DAWSON, A. H., 1948, 'Motion Picture Economics', *Hollywood Quarterly*, 3: 217–40.
In business volume, films ranked forty-fifth in 1937, thirty-fifth in 1944. Total assets invested are around 2 billion. Prognosis: 1) excess supply of labour will continue; 2) anti-trust suit decision imminent; 3) trade agreement with UK will come about; 4) trade barriers will be encountered; 5) so will political discord; 6) labour power will decrease; 7) banks will loan further. Drawing on the usual sources (Hampton, Klingender and Legge, Huettig, Temporary National Economic Committee) he sketches the spiral from monopoly to vicious competition, to more monopoly. The industry is more stable than the economy as a whole; most stable element is wages which are now at a peak. [Fails to predict US embargo to counter UK tax.] See also his comparison on British and American wage rates in the industry at 3: 241–7.

— 1948a, 'Hollywood's Labour Troubles', *Industrial and Labor Relations Review*, 1: 638–47.
Hollywood is wracked by union disputes and weaknesses, high rates both of pay and of unemployment. An overall union for the motion picture trades is clearly called for.

— 1950, 'Patterns of Production and Employment in Hollywood', *Hollywood Quarterly*, 4: 338–53.
Important figures and analysis of the pattern of production week by week 1937–40 and 1945–8. First three months of the year show lowest output. Annual meetings take place, and 31 March is California tax date when production is at its lowest. Discusses the need for centralization and decasualization.

DAY, BARRY, 1967, 'Too Hot Not to Cool Down', *Sight and Sound*, 37: 28–32.
Sympathetic presentation of McLuhan's ideas.

DEARDEN, BASIL and RELPH, MICHAEL, 1966, 'Two on a Tandem', *Films and Filming*, 12: 26–33.
What it is like to work for umpteen years as a production-direction team.

BIBLIOGRAPHY

DE BEAUVOIR, SIMONE, 1960, *Brigitte Bardot and the Lolita Syndrome,* London.
An essay in praise of nature's child-woman who cuts through false inhibitions and deceptions.

DE BECKER, RAYMOND, 1959, *De Tom Mix à James Dean,* Paris.
As a counterweight to that ignoring of the sociology of the cinema which goes on in so many volumes, here is one of those French exercises in reading in significance, which sees in screen images portents of things to come.

DEER, I. and DEER, H. A., 1965, *The Language of the Mass Media,* Boston.
A set of essays without interest to our concerns here.
— 1967, *The Popular Arts.* A critical reader, New York.
Contains items by Aydelotte (1949), Warshow (1962), Highet (1957), Hunt (1964), Agee (1958), and a bibliography.

DE FLEUR, MELVIN L., 1966, *Theories of Mass Communication,* New York.
Useful little handbook. Chapter on film rather disappointing, fails to take film seriously, breaks off abruptly. Summarizes theories well enough, and argues for viewing the media as social systems.

DELCOL, GUY, 1967, *Essai de Bibliographie Belge du Cinéma (1896–1966),* thesis for graduate diploma in bibliographic science, Bruxelles.
A professional work exhaustively listing all works published in Belgium or by Belgians.

DE MILLE, C. B., 1960, *Autobiography,* London.
Bulky but detailed story of 'the founder of Hollywood', pulling his punches here and there, but very absorbing. Filmography.

DE MILLE, W. C., 1939, *Hollywood Saga,* New York.
Reminiscences of a popular Broadway playwright persuaded by his brother Cecil B. to go to Hollywood in 1914, only to stay on for twenty years. Chatty and evocative, leaving the political and financial complications explicitly to Ramsaye and Hampton. Strong for the view that moviegoers vote with their feet, the glamour of stars is mysterious, and that producers mean by 'loyalty' a one-sided emotion. Writer-director conflicts began in 1914. Also, out of 10,000 uncommissioned MSS only a handful were worth the expensive sifting process. Later became a director. Interesting stories about the impact of sound.

DENNEY, REUEL, 1964, *The Astonished Muse,* Chicago.
This is a rambling and sometimes obscure book on the mass media, with many flashes of insight, such as the distinction between the Participative Purist, the Spectatorial Purist and the Reality Purist. Denney accepts the following as a summary: 'the productions of popular culture . . . deserve . . . to be discussed in terms of the artistic or conventional forms that make it possible or even probable that they will have this or that effect upon

260

their audiences . . . almost every aspect of American popular culture suffers from attachment to a particular form or style, that is, a prevailing literalism . . . the book also tries to investigate themes of activity and passivity in the consumption of objects of leisure enjoyment ranging from fiction to the graphic and plastic arts', pp. 255–6.

DEXTER, L. A. and WHITE, D. M., 1964, *People, Society and Mass Communications*, Glencoe.
Extremely useful reader, companion to Berelson and Janowitz (1966). No pieces deal directly with films, but contains Fearing (1962) and Katz (1960).

DICKINSON, THOROLD, 1950, 'The Filmwright and the Audience', *Sight and Sound*, 19: 20–5.

DISNEY, WALT, 1937, 'Le Cinema et ie Public', in *Rôle Intellectuel du Cinema*, Paris, 243–9.
Morkovin reports a few well-known facts about the cinema, its public and its organization. Vague and hopeful.

DOOB, LEONARD, 1948, *Propaganda and Public Opinion*, New York.
Fearing (1950) comments: 'interprets the results of the studies of the Army films as indicating that knowledge is more readily affected than attitudes, and that the latter may be only "pre-action responses", although action does not necessarily follow.' Pp. 498–527 on films.

DOSCHER, LUELYNE, 1947, 'The Significances of Audience Measurements in Motion Pictures', *Journal of Social Issues*, 3: 51–7.
Reviews difficulties in interpreting results such as Cirlin and Peterman (1947). Too much pre-testing might standardize the motion picture product; it oversimplifies reactions; ignores behaviour outside the theatre: 'the significance of the film includes the extent to which the basic orientations of the members of the audience, or their life spaces, as restructured by the films', p. 55. Is the film really a product like breakfast food?

DRINKWATER, JOHN, 1931, *The Life and Adventures of Carl Laemmle*, New York.
Biography by a British writer of the German immigrant to America who became an exhibitor, then a distributor, and who made the crucial decision, when he was the biggest in the country, to fight the monopoly set up by the Motion Picture Patents Company in 1908. After a protracted and bitter campaign the government filed anti-trust suits in 1912, which finally resulted in the defeat of the trust in 1915. Meanwhile, he had gone into production on his own in order to have some product to distribute and exhibit. His Independent Film Co. became the Universal Film Co., which in the fullness of time was to become today's Universal International. Pp. 176: Critic Winthrop Ames argues that good taste in patronage comes after the weaith that makes the patronage possible, and he expects the mass patronage of the cinema to take the same course. The book climaxes with the

production of Lewis Milestone's masterpiece *All Quiet on the Western Front.*

DURAND, JACQUES, 1958, *Le Cinéma et son Public*, Paris.
Economic and statistical treatment of supply and demand, frequency of attendance, choice and preferences. 'Questions fondamentales': 1) pourquoi va-t-on au cinéma?; 2) quels facteurs incitent à y aller plus ou moins? 3) quels facteurs incitent à aller voir plutôt tel ou tel film? The market is peculiar because the public doesn't contact the seller, but only an intermediary, the exhibitor, who doesn't even sell films, but the right to see them. The number of seats has a limit. So supply and demand are measured by different units and so cannot be equalised. This means demand depends less on supply than other factors and supply is in a situation much less favourable (except where there is vertical integration). Elasticity of demand cannot be measured by price because of fixing. Theories that the cinema came to meet a demand or that a demand met a supply are equally criticisable. It is spontaneous. The nature of the thing as well as human factors structure the situation.

DURGNAT, R., 1951, 'Ways of Melodrama', *Sight and Sound*, 21: 34*ff.*

— 1963, 'Epic', *Films and Filming*, 10: 9*ff.*

— 1964, 'Vote for Britain', *Films and Filming*, 10: April, 9*ff*; May, 10*ff*; June, 38*ff.*
How the British portray themselves in their films. Cf. Jarvie (1969*b*).

— 1965–6, 'Raymond Durgnat's World of Comedy', *Films and Filming*, 11: July, 8–13; August, 10–15; September, 8–12. *12;* October, 16–20; November, 14–19; December, 42–8; January, 40–6.

— 1966, *Eros in the Cinema*, London.
Rewrite of his articles in *Films and Filming* 1961–2. Elaborate run-through of various erotic themes as they have been treated in films. Occasionally a wry wit. Cf. Knight and Alpert (1965–9).

— 1967, *Films and Feelings*, London.
Collection of articles, some acute, some obscure, occasionally pretentious and silly verbiage, like a lot of talk about art.

DUVILLARS, P., 1950, *Cinéma, Mythologie du XXe Sièle*, Paris.

DYER, P. J., 1957, 'Censored', *Films and Filming*, 3: 11–13, February/ March, 9–11; April, 11–14.

— 1957–9, 'Patterns of Cinema', *Films and Filming*, 4–6: various pages, indexed in 6: December 1959.
A twenty-one-part historical survey of the cinema, a good deal of it clearly taken from secondary sources and thus largely, although not entirely, orthodox in interpretation.

BIBLIOGRAPHY

DYSINGER, W. S. and RUCKMICK, C. A., 1933, *The Emotional Responses of Children to the Motion Picture Situation*, New York.
Moley (1938) summarizes: 'The realistic portrayal of lifelike scenes has an emotional effect on those who see them, and . . . this effect may or may not be important', p. 33.

EATON, WALTER, 1915, 'Class Consciousness and the "Movies" ', *Atlantic Monthly*, 115: 48–56.
Films are a proletarian institution because quality live theatre is too expensive; films thus foster revolutionary class-consciousness amongst the proletariat. Live drama should be cheaply available to all, as libraries and museums are, if the debasing effect of bad films is to be countered.

EDWARDS, ROY, 1953, 'The Fifth Columnists', *Sight and Sound*, 23: 21*ff.*
Some films reveal children as anything but innocent darlings.

EISENSTEIN, S., 1943, *Film Sense*, London.
— 1949, *Film Form*, New York.

ELKIN, FRED, 1949, 'God, Radio, and the Movies', *Hollywood Quarterly*, 5: 105–14.
Content-analysis of *The Next Voice You Hear*. Points out the film's complacent, middle-class, passive view of religion and of society's ills, and relates its popularity to the felt complexity, danger, and imperfections of the world in 1948.

— 1950, 'The Psychological Appeal of the Hollywood Western', *Journal of Educational Sociology*, 24: 72–86.
[Written just before the 'psychological' or 'adult' western vogue.] 25% of Hollywood features are westerns. Christian values: Good = Right; Evil = Wrong. Only in its not portraying life as sacred is the western un-Christian. In conflicts of law and justice, westerns side with justice. Wealth and power are acceptable if within the law, but not for the hero. Individualistic. Problems are seen to be due to evil men, not social and economic forces. Victory is attributable to struggle and merit, not magic or luck. They have an egalitarian ethos and beautiful landscapes. The western hero is sober and respectable: heroines are either dutiful or independent. Villains are either city slickers or brutes. Comic figures are teased by villains and befriended by heroes.
An identifying child is relieved to escape to a world where everything is simple and clear cut, where threats can be overcome, where there is space and freedom, aggression has socially approved outlets, wins love and admiration, salves guilt, and where there are non-parental heroes. Horse as symbol of power and a loving pet. The comic is an adult to laugh at, feel superior to and aggression towards. The wily villain can be identified with the child's adversaries. Rural audiences love westerns because they glorify them and put down the city-villain. The influence of westerns depends more on what the child is, than what the western is, as well as on context.

BIBLIOGRAPHY

— 1951, 'A Study of the Relationship Between Popular Hero-Types and Social Class', PhD thesis, University of Chicago, unpublished.

Heroes may embody the values of a society, 'Most motion picture stars have achieved their fame not because of their professional ability as actors, but because of the symbols they represent', p. 11. Betty Grable is the girl next-door, simple but sexy. Greer Garson is not American, a cut above the common man level, cultured, takes her profession seriously (yet had three husbands). Bette Davis is a professional woman of the upper middle class, serious about acting, blunt, energetic, opinionated. Rita Hayworth is sexy, feminine, smart-set – an image derived largely from publicity, not from her roles. Katherine Hepburn is individual, even eccentric, upper class New England. Lauren Bacall is a masculine-feminine type in her roles and in life. Clark Gable is the virile, nice common man. James Stewart is a small-town, middle class, ordinary and unsophisticated type capable of leadership and bravery, who never pursues girls. Humphrey Bogart is crude and rough but more in the manner of an upper class rebel. Errol Flynn is romantic, adventurous, a satyr. Van Johnson is a simple, ordinary boy, young and fresh like the lad next door. James Mason is an upper class gentleman, independent, rough with women, but attractive. Star preference varies with class and with class image of star.

— 1954, 'The Value Implications of Popular Films', *Sociology and Social Research*, 38: 320–2.

Implicitly, films give us all kinds of social and value information. This raises many problems about how others see us, how they function as social control, etc.

— 1955, 'Popular Hero Symbols and Audience Gratifications', *Journal of Educational Psychology*, 29: 97–107.

Under the assumption that positive and negative reactions to stars are functional, responses of women to nine groups of stars and their images reveals how they are attracted to those who symbolize and reinforce their values, do not threaten, and how they tend to dislike the others.

— 1966, 'Censorship and Pressure Groups', *Phylon*, Spring, 71–80.

Censorship is always present; it is a matter of degree, a means of social control to prevent threat and damage to core values or to the group itself. It is premised on the theory that without stimulus there can be no effect.

EMERY, F. E., 1959, 'Psychological Effects of the Western Film', *Human Relations*, 12: 195–232.

Carver (1967): 'found differential recall among children required to write the story of a western one month after seeing it, notes . . . typical memory distortion in the direction of convergence towards a stereotyped "western film" plot'. See Emery and Martin (1957).

— and MARTIN, D., 1957, *Psychological Effects of the 'Western' Film*, A study in television viewing, Melbourne.

1) Appeal due to *latent* themes (good versus bad, super-ego versus id)

264

and not to *manifest* themes; 2) viewing involves selective processes (of identification and interpretation) as defence against anxiety-arousing aspects; 3) certain temporary changes may be brought about in the way an individual sees himself in relation to his social environment, but no systematic changes in aggressive drives; 4) the viewer will adopt the posture or prose of the hero. Viewing is primarily consummatory.

Encyclopaedia of the Social Sciences, 1933, 'Motion Pictures – Industrial Development and Social Implications', **11**: 58–69.
See Lewis (1933*b*) and Orton (1933).

ENGLAND, LEONARD, 1951*a*, 'The Critic and the Box-office', *Sight and Sound*, **20**: 43*ff.*
'The taste of cinemagoers is far less divergent from that of the critics than is commonly believed . . . where there is divergence this is often due to a different standard applied in judging the film, and does not mean that, within these limits, the public shows lack of discrimination', p. 44.

— 1951*b*, 'Popular Taste in the Cinema', in R. Manvell, ed., *The Cinema 1950*, 115–23.
The Director of Mass Observation on the relation between public taste and box-office receipts, with special reference to stars, etc. Concludes that there is less disparity between critical preferences and box office winners than is thought, instances the high box-office successes of some critical favourites and suggests better audience research would prevent film makers insulting the audience's taste and intelligence.

ENNIS, P. H., 1961, 'The Social Structure of Communication Systems: A Theoretical Proposal', *Studies in Public Communication*, **3**: 120–44.
A programmatic paper [read after this volume was sent to press] indicating the reasons for the individual-centred bias of communications research, and the fruitfulness of a reorientation towards group theory, which will break down the mass-minority dichotomy, and study audiences as social systems, as potential and sometimes actual groups, and point up the relations between producers, distributors, audience, content and critics. [In many ways the present volume carries out Ennis' programme so far as that has been possible with the existing data on movies.]

ERNST, MORRIS L., 1946, *The First Freedom*, New York.
Chapter VI criticizes film monopolies.

— and LINDEY, ALEXANDER, 1940, *The Censor Marches On:* recent milestones in the administration of the obscenity law in the United States, New York.
Chapters V and VI review the development of censorship, suggest it should be abolished and those interested publish lists of films recommended for children.

— and LORENTZ, PARE, 1930, *Censored*: the private life of the movies, New York.

BIBLIOGRAPHY

Amusing, anecdotal survey of US censorship and its regional quirks ('banned in Pennsylvania' is a recurring motif).

— and SCHWARTZ, ALAN U., 1964, *Censorship*: the search for the obscene, New York.
Chapter 22 on the cinema has extensive quotes from Warren, C. J., dissenting from the Supreme Court's decision to uphold the censorship of films.

— and SEAGLE, W., 1928, *To the Pure*: a study of obscenity and the censor, New York.
Only a few pages on films.

ERVINE, ST JOHN, 1934, *The Alleged Art of the Cinema*, London.
Virulent expression of loathing for the cinema as a drug for the horrid masses. Its pretensions to art are dismissed because it is made by several people.

ESCUDERO, J. M. B., 1958, *Cine-Social*, Madrid.
Comparative study of the 'social film' – The author apparently is unaware that all films are social films.

EVANS, PETER, 1968, *Peter Sellers: the Mask Behind the Mask*, New York.
Popular biography interested mainly in the contradictions, complexity and insecurities of the actor's character rather than his art, which is not discussed. No list of Sellers' parts, not even an index.

EVERSON, W., 1953, 'The Stock-Shot Habit', *Sight and Sound*, 22: 183–4.
Classic article detailing how sequences are 'lifted' from one film to another, and sometimes even constitute whole films.

— 1963, *The American Movie*, New York.
Informal and enthusiastic celebration of the American film by a British-born fan.

— 1964, *The Bad Guys*, New York.
Picture book on the villains.

EYLES, A., 1967, *The Western*, London.
Alphabetical list of the main westerns, with casts and production credits.

FABREGAT CUNEO, R., 1957, 'El proceso del cinema en el mundo yen la cultura y la deformation de los temas culturales al traves del cine', *Revista de Mexican Sociology*, 19: 387–404.
Analysis of the deformation which cultural themes undergo when presented through films; interpretation of their relation to the public's interests.

— 1958, 'Principales influencias del cine sobre el publico', *Revista de Mexican Sociology*, 20: 27–55.

266

Theoretical analysis of the influence of the cinema in terms of suggestion, imitation, educational consequences.

FADIMAN, WILLIAM J., 1947, 'The Sources of Movies', *Annals* (1947), 37–40.
20,000 items are sifted annually by story departments, purchasing some 40–75 and making 20–50 films. They are written and tailored for the stars. Stars are studios' principal asset.

— 1960, 'The Typewriter Jungle', *Films and Filming*, 7: December, 8, 36, 42.
The position of writers in Hollywood – how they are assigned to categories for types of pictures and types of 'script doctoring' on a picture.

— 1964*a*, 'Cowboys and Indies', *Films and Filming*, 10: March,51–2.
Clear exposition of the Hollywood 'independent' structure of production and their method of 'packaging'.

— 1964*b*, 'The Talkies', *Films and Filming*, 10: July, 48*ff.*
Hollywood's denizens, despite containing in their number many brilliant and accomplished people, are appallingly dull conversationalists.

— 1965, 'But Compared to the Original', *Films and Filming*, 11: February, 21–3.
The most resented kind of film criticism is that which compares the film with its source in novel, play or story. This is unfair to the medium itself.

FALEWICZ, J., 1964, 'Effect of Film Criticism on Urban Film Tastes', *Polish Sociological Bulletin*, 1: 90–5.
Both stars and critics are low on influence in Poland compared with word of mouth and film *genre*. Whereas in a 1958 survey in France, stars were top. Box office is no guide to appreciation. The more educated and the more geared to films people are, the more their tastes (appreciation) agrees with the critics' opinions. Leaders of opinion mediate between critics and people. This affects appreciation, not box office.

FARBER, MANNY, 1952, 'Movies Aren't Movies Any More', *Commentary*, 13: 560–6.
Very confused attack on films whose slow pace, overbearing technique and emphatic significant symbolism betrays the influence of Welles' Theatrical [*sic*] *Citizen Kane*.

— 1957, 'Underground Films', anthologized in Talbot (1959).
A panegyric to the neglected, unpretentious, action directors of Hollywood: early Ford, Hawks, Kieghley, Mann, Walsh, Wellman – 'masculine' film makers.

FAURE, E., 1963, *Fonction du Cinéma*. De la cinéplastique à son destin social, Genève.
Chapter V – 'Introduction à la mystique du cinéma' – is extremely interesting. 'Le film, comme le temple, est anonyme. Comme le temple, il tire

son principe collectif de moyens financiers dépassant la capacité de l'individu, de la multitude des figurants qui font songer aux maçons et aux manoeuvres, de ses acteurs qui répondent par leur mimique, après huit siècles, au geste des imagiers, de ses metteurs en scène et techniciens succédant aux maitres d'oeuvres, des procédés standardisés et mécaniques qui trouveraient aisément leurs répondants dans le principe unique de la croisée d'ogive et les charpentes du vaisseau, et des foules mêlées et déferlantes pour qui l'un et l'autre sont faits', pp. 48–9.

FEARING, F., 1944, 'The Interpretative Process', in *Writers Congress* (1944), 508–23.
'... man seeks occasions where, through the utilization of all the symbolic strategies available to him, he may give and receive communications regarding all that puzzles him. He does this in an effort to maintain constancy, stability and continuity in his world, and to identify his line of action with respect to it. This is a process of coming to terms with reality', p. 516.

— 1947, 'Influence of the Movies on Attitudes and Behaviour', *Annals* (1947), 70–9.
The film-goer uses the film in the course of coming to terms with the larger environment; his aims, dispositions, and problems in that enterprise decisively effect what he gets out of pictures. Other views are: 1) that films are mere entertainment – but anything which holds the attention is entertainment; 2) that films have measurable effects on attitudes and these effects are in the direction indicated by the film; 3) films reflect audience needs and stresses; 4) films reflect the collective unconscious. None of these views so much as tells us why people go to the cinema. Conclusion: 'it is probably impossible to construct a series of audio-visual images involving human action and interaction without at the same time presenting an attitude or ideological position toward that action', p. 78. The films assist the individual in structuring his world.

— 1947a, 'Films as History', *Hollywood Quarterly*, 2: 422–7.
Review article on Kracauer (1947). Very critical of treating groups as individuals; and of the mystical character of the resulting insights. Stresses that Kracauer (like Mayer (1946) and Powdermaker (1950)) relies on Lévy-Bruhl's 'participation mystique' – an inadequate tool for film analysis.

— 1950, *Motion pictures as a medium of instruction and communication: an experimental analysis of the effects of two films*, Berkeley and Los Angeles.
Report of tests of effectiveness of two service training films, one to modify cavalier attitudes to VD, the other to inform about malaria. A significant effect was found.

— 1950a, review of Wolfenstein and Leites (1950b) in *Hollywood Quarterly* 5: 101ff.
... concerned with the same problem and utilize essentially the same method as that of Siegfried Kracauer in *From Caligari to Hitler*. The

problem is concerned with the relation between the content of films and existing patterns of culture. The method consists in the analysis of the manifest content of films for the purpose of detecting recurrent or typical themes. The assumption is that in these themes will be found reflections of the daydreams, and conscious and unconscious wishes, of the mass audience, and that somehow the producers have tapped this material'.

— 1951, 'A Word of Caution for the Intelligent Consumer of Motion Pictures', *Quarterly of Film, Radio and Television*, 6: 129–42.
Research showed the impact of films to be slight. Prejudiced people revised the content of *Home of the Brave*, and saw in it or selected from it what they wanted to see. 'My point is that because the audience for the mass media is large it is not amorphous and faceless, ready to accept anything projected on it', p. 139.

— 1953, 'Towards a Psychological Theory of Human Communication', *Journal of Personality*, 22: 71–88.
Need-value systems result in instabilities and disequilibrium when interacting with the environment and these co-ordinate with increase in tension in the individual. Cognitive-perceptual processes structure the environment so as to reduce tension. Extremely important but highly technical paper.

— 1954, 'Social Impact of the Mass Media of Communication', in N. B. Henry, ed., *Mass Media and Education – Fifty-third Yearbook of the NSSE*, Chicago, chapter VIII.
Contrasts the one-way with his own two-way theory involving perception *and* the situation. Perceptual response is a process through which the individual comes to terms with his environment. He is seeking meaning, seeking to place or structure experience in his cognitive 'frame'. 'Clarity' does not make the message come through – all communication content is to some degree ambiguous. Thus propaganda may completely boomerang. Media can be used for reinforcement or value-transmission, as in the daydream theory. Also for problem-solving and the acquisition of new experience. Boomerang effect is explained as the interpreter trying to alter his cognitive frame as little as possible.

— 1962, 'Human Communication', *Audio-Visual Communication Review*, 10: 78–108, also in Dexter and White (1964).
A communication situation involves: 1) the purpose of shaping or steering behaviour, or establishing a relationship; 2) items responded to in terms of what they stand for; 3) a relationship of shared meaning; 4) dependence on the totality of culture and personality factors; 4) refutes the transmission theory of communication; 5) communication situations are those in which human beings enter into certain strategic relationships with each other and the environment; 6) they use signs, symbols, and symbolic acts centrally, 7) by means of 2) they provide the maximum opportunity for shaping experience, achieving goals, gaining insight and mastering the environment; 8) the sign and symbol material is subject to the perceptual processes. A symbol is a sign standing for a sign.

BIBLIOGRAPHY

Federation of British Film Makers, 1963, *Cinema Going in Greater London*, London.
An elaborate, sponsored, study of attitudes and behaviour intended as a guide to what was happening to audience patterns. Comparable to, if not better than, Handel (1950).

FELDMANN, ERIK, 1962, *Theorie der Massenmedien*, Press. Film. Funk. Fernsehen, München/Basel.'
A collection of important essays including one on the place of film in the system of the sciences, towards epistemological foundation of the science of film, the film as culture factor, the film viewing situation, etc. By a professor of Philosophy and Education at Bonn. Suffers only from not touching on Fearing and Gans.

— and Hagemann, Walter, 1955, *Der Film als Beeinflussungsmittel*: Vorträge und Berichte der 2. Jahrestagung der Deutschen Gesellschaft für Filmwissenschaft, Emsdetten.
Contains Feldmann on 'Der Film Als Kulturfaktor'.

— and MEIFR, ERNST, 1963, *Film und Fernsehen im Spiegel der Wissenschaft*, Gutersloh.
Collection by various hands and including A. Silberman on 'Die Soziologischen Untersuchungsfelder des Massenkommunikationen'.

FENIN, G. N., 1955, 'Motion Pictures and the Public', *Film Culture*, 1: January, 15–18.
Hollywood wants money and in a crisis it ignores the public. Even if films are to be treated as product, there should be research and product development and improvement. Usual ranting about commerce.

— 1956, 'The Western – Old and New', *Film Culture*, May–June, 7–11.

— and EVERSON, W. K., 1962, *The Western*, from silents to cinerama, New York.
Ostensibly a history of the western, in fact a paean in praise of William S. Hart. The authors lose interest after the silent period and the treatment of the best westerns (made post–1940) is cursory indeed.

FERNOW, D. L., 1952, 'The Treatment of Social Problems in the Entertainment Film', MA thesis, USC, unpublished.
'... purpose of unveiling any relationship between the social, economic and political temper and conditions of the times and the appearance of films concerned with vital social topics', pp. 2–3. Mainly looks at story and thematic content. When times are bad there are more social films and they are more realistic. When times are good we are not interested. This is due to the prevailing social philosophy.

FEYERABEND, P. K., 1967, 'The Theatre as an Instrument for the Criticism of Ideologies', *Inquiry*, 10: 298–312.

FIELD, MARTIN, 1948, 'Type-Casting Screen Writers', *Penguin Film Review*, **6**: April, 29–32.
Hollywood type-casts writers, i.e., chooses them to write pictures just as it does actors: there is no 'players directory' for writers, so they are typed on the basis of previous credits either by content or by the structure of their specialization (cf. Fadiman (1960)).

— 1949, 'Hollywood Report on a "Trend" ', *Penguin Film Review*, **9**: 100–2.
The 'trend' is for writers to become directors: Sturges, Huston, Odets, Seaton, Nichols, Hecht, Daves, Wilder, Brackett, Rossen, Mankiewicz, Krazna, Trotti, Nunally Johnson, Welles. It is still the exception rather than the rule, despite the publicity.

FIELD, MARY, 1945 (?), 'The Child Mind and the Screen', typescript, unpublished.
Account of cinema clubs and children's pungent criticisms of films which are unreal or silly.

— 1952, *Good Company*, London.
Story of the production of special children's films in the UK and the overcoming of suspicion and mistrust.

— 1954, *Children and Films*: a study of boys and girls in the cinema, Dunfermline.
Elaborate visual study of children's reactions, scene-by-scene, to selected cartoon, serial, interest and feature films, taken by infra-red camera. No disturbing results. The author is primarily concerned with drawing conclusions relevant to the production of films for children.

— 1958, 'Children in the Cinema', *Films and Filming*, **4**: April, 9–10.
A pure diet of fantasy in children's films is not indicated because by age seven, children are becoming reality-oriented. But film must be learned like a language – too complex a construction and material are no use. Their attention span and foci of interest are different. The borderline between demonstrating social responsibility and peddling propaganda is a fine one.

FIELDING, R., 1959, 'Mirror of Discontent: the "March of Time" and its Politically Controversial Film Issues', *Western Political Quarterly*, **12**: 145–52.
Description of the controversy surrounding 'Inside Nazi Germany – 1938' – perhaps the most censored film ever as people argued whether it was pro or con.

The Film in National Life, 1943, Being the proceedings of a conference held by the British Film Institute in Exeter, April 1943, London.
Level-headed, but hardly shattering discussion of adolescents; slightly snobbish coverage of the psychology of cinema-going – the public gets the films it deserves, tut-tut, let's change the public. Well meaning, but superficial.

Film Quarterly (formerly *Quarterly of Film, Radio and Television,* formerly *Hollywood Quarterly*), 1947 to date, Berkeley and Los Angeles.
Once far and away the best of the film journals, with long, scholarly and thoughtful articles on social aspects of film, in its latest incarnation this journal has become no more than a very good journal of film criticism.

Films and Filming, 1954 to date, London.
Beginning shakily, and uneasy about its level, this monthly has gradually become an indispensable mine of information and comment. Always barely literate, atrociously designed, it nevertheless has its place.

FISHER, DAVID, 1953, 'The Saint in the Cinema', *Sight and Sound,* 23: 93*ff.*
Why are there so few good religious films?

FISKE, M. and HANDEL, L., 1946, 'Motion Picture Research: Content and Audience Analysis', *Journal of Marketing,* 11: 129–34.
Reviews research of Dale, Peters and Jones, comments on paucity of data on audience size and composition.

FITZGERALD, F. SCOTT, 1949, *The Last Tycoon,* London.
Novel: unfinished but tormented

FLETCHER, J. G., 1929, *The Crisis of the Film,* Seattle.
'The American film has served as propaganda for the emotional monotony, the naive morality, the sham luxury, the haphazard etiquette and the grotesque exaggeration of the comic, the sentimental and the acrobatics that are so common in the United States'.

FLOHERTY, J. J., 1935, *Moviemakers,* Garden City.
An illustrated popular account of how movies are made, culled from a visit to MGM studios. No one is clearly identifiable in the pictures and the tone is one of awe-struck gratitude.

FORD, CHARLES, 1964, *Histoire du Western,* Paris.
Scholarly history with a list of real western characters and their main appearances in films.

FORD, RICHARD, 1939, *Children in the Cinema,* London.
British volume covering the same ground as the Payne Fund Studies (q.v.) and the summaries of Charters and Forman (q.v.). Collates British facts and figures because there are different patterns and social habits as well as different censorship systems as compared to the USA. Conclusions similar to Payne; but the emphasis on children's matinees and clubs is different. The more centralized effort in the UK to stage genuinely suitable shows taking account of what children like as well as what is good for them is described. Up to age ten to twelve children are bored, not 'corrupted', by 'love'.

BIBLIOGRAPHY

FORMAN, H. J., 1933, *Our Movie Made Children*, New York.
Popular summary of the Payne Fund Studies (q.v.). While admitting that many influences play on children and that some good movies are made, this volume deplores the sex, crime and tawdry life-goals depicted in most movies. Children remember the bad things, get disturbed sleep, can have their attitudes manipulated, blame movies for their delinquency (imitation) and benefit from moral and religious uplift.

Fortune, 1937a, 'Paramount Pictures, Inc.', 15: 86–96, 194–212.

— 1937b, 'Warner Brothers Pictures, Inc.', 16: December, 110–13, 206–20.

— 1939, 'Leow's, Inc.', 20: August, 25–31, 104–6, 110, 114.
Elaborate and witty studies of the major picture corporations emphasizing in Paramount's case the bankruptcy and reorganization, in the cases of Warners and MGM detailing their emergence unscathed from the depression.

— 1946, 'Movies: End of an Era?', 34: April, 98–102, 135–50.
Prophetic examination of the fall in box-office figures which was to come in 1948-9.

— 1947, 'Paramount: Oscar for Profits'; 35: June, 90–5, 208–21.
Sketch of the rise of Paramount from its bankruptcy; and studies Balaban and Ginsberg its bosses, Griffis who put its finances in order, and an outline of how the East Coast-West Coast production co-ordination works. In 1945 profits were $17·9 million, in 1946 $44 million, compared with Fox $22 million, Warners $19 million, MGM $18 million, RKO $12 million.

— 1949, 'End of an Era?', 39: April, 99ff.
With the b.o. down, foreign revenues cut, critics pained, older fans dwindling, reorganization at hand and television looming, the motion picture industry may be turning a historic corner. Eric Johnson demurs.

FOX, C. D., 1925, *Mirrors of Hollywood*, New York.
One of several popular volumes on Hollywood by this author. It begins with a descriptive portrait of the town and a tour of several studios, written in an ooh-ah-look-who's-over-there style. Ends with a section on the Significance of the New Language of the Cinema and Its Responsibilities. Tacked on are hundreds of *Who's Who* entries on stars. Estimates that 10,000 people are employed in Hollywood, which produces a product valued at $75 million, a payroll of $40 million, $20 million spent on supplies.

FRANKLIN, ELIZA, 1952, 'Westerns, First and Lasting', *Quarterly of Film, Radio, and Television*, 7: 109–15.

— H. B., 1927, *Motion Picture Theatre Management*, New York.

FRENCH, H., 1955, 'How Films Work', *Films and Filming*, 1: April, 6–7; May, 8; June, 12.
Detailed study of the British film industry.

FRENCH, PHILIP, 1967, 'Incitement Against Violence', *Sight and Sound*, 37: 2–8.
Survey of the gangster cycles, taking off from *Bonnie and Clyde* and *The Valentine's Day Massacre*, and returning to them.

— 1969, *The Movie Moguls*, London.
An informal history of the Hollywood tycoons, done from secondary sources and written in a concise, relaxed manner. Chronicles their rises and falls and looks to some explanation of it all. Too brief. Useful thumbnail biographies and an annotated bibliography.

FREOUR, P., SERISE, M., and COUDRAY, P., 1954, ' "La Possession" par le film: Préliminaire à une Etude Psychologique du cinéma', *Hygiene Mentale*, 48: 289–307.
The total absorption of attention – 'possession' – by films accounts for their impact on the development of values and behaviour. The relative isolation and passivity of the viewer contribute to this as well.

FREWIN, LESLIE, 1955, *Blond Venus*, London.
A lightweight life of Marlene Dietrich

FRIEDSON, ELLIOT, 1952, 'An Audience and Its Taste', PhD thesis, University of Chicago, unpublished.
Attempts to show the relationship of content, medium, personality, social definitions and the social situation of contact on the response of preference for specific contents or types of content and how these factors participate in the process of developing taste. Emphasizes social situation of media use and thus non-comparability of media and content. Movies mainly a peer-group situation, noise and comment must be taken into account as much as the show. *None* of those who usually go in a family situation *prefer* to do so. They see media in terms of definitions of peer and other groups – the peers are for, family, school, church, are against, and this structures response, the opinions of those who are more important having more effect than those of the less important. 'From the second grade on the opinions of adults steadily lose their potency in affecting taste. By the fourth grade the majority has begun to prefer content condemned by adults and by the sixth grade most children's favourites violate expressly condemning adult opinions', p. 113. Adults argue morally, peers socially and aesthetically. Taste has no relation to personality. 'Taste is a response to past experience directed towards recalled and anticipated content', p. 190. Taste is independent of personal definitions. Content is not important to fantasy-gratification since selection is social. Content responses depend on overt responses.

— 1953a, 'Adult Discount; an Aspect of Children's Changing Taste', *Child Development*, 24: 39–49.
Adult discount means less excitability, greater response to overall development of plot, ability to predict it, and an attitude of detachment. This explains children's changing tastes, shifting from action, to surprise,

to spookies and comedy. '... adult discount seems to place a definite stricture on the extent to which the spectator is able to use dramatic material as fantasy – to the extent that he adopts a critical and detached outlook in attending to drama, to that extent the spectator is not sufficiently involved in the drama to be able to use it as an emotionally charged fantasy and thereby obtain emotional release. Whenever we speculate about or investigate the effects or even the character of mass media experiences, if we seek accuracy these considerations must be taken into account', p. 49.

— 1953b, 'Communications Research and the Concept of the Mass', *American Sociological Review*, **18**: 313–17.
Lazarsfeld, and Blumer (1936) are wrong to see the audience as a mass. National audience versus local audience – only the former is a mass. But the explanation must go to local audience. That is where individuals have their situations. '... audience behaviour ... takes place in a complex network of local social activity. Certain times of day, certain days, certain seasons, are the socially appropriate times for engaging in particular activities connected with the various mass media. The individual is frequently accompanied by others of his social group when he is engaged in those activities. The individual participates in an interpersonal grid of spectators who discuss the meaning of past experience with mass communications and the anticipated meaning of future experience', p. 315.

— 1953c, 'The Relation of the Social Situation of Contact to the Media in Mass Communication', *Public Opinion Quarterly*, **17**: 230–8.
An audience: 1) has preconceptions about the context and the act of being a member of the audience; 2) is an immediate setting. Films are a peer situation, television a family situation, comics solitary. While preferences for films to television do change as expected as a child becomes less family-oriented and more peer oriented, there is no similar trend with respect to comics. This suggests that over and above the situation, the medium is also defined by its inherent characteristics. The act of attending to mass communications is an integral part of organized social life.

FÜLOP-MILLER, RENE, 1931, 'Das Amerikanische Kino' in *Das Amerikanische Theatre und Kino*, Zwei Kulturgesichtliche Adhandlungen, ed., J. Gregor and R. Fülop-Miller, Zurich.
Beautifully illustrated.

— 1938, *The Motion Picture in America*, New York.

FUNK, A., 1934, *The Film and Youth: An Investigation of the Psychological Effects on Film on the Life of the Young*, Munich.
Strong role of identification inferred from the constant use by youths of phrases meaning 'to be carried along', 'participate in everything', and 'to consider oneself as the hero of the piece'. Technical details largely explain the power of individual films.

GANS, H. J., 1957, 'The Creator-Audience Relationship in the Mass Media: An Analysis of Movie Making', in Rosenberg and White (1957), 315–24. Ticket buyers 'belong' to several publics, films appeal to several publics. Film makers anticipate or expect audience reaction, in making both creative and financial decisions. Every creator's audience image differs because of his unique life history. Ross (1950) can be rewritten as a series of audience image conflicts. The tenuous connection between audience images and the actual publics, accounts for the acute insecurity of all but the top few film makers.

— 1959, *American Films and Television Programmes on British Screens*: A Study of the Functions of American Popular Culture Abroad, unpublished report of the Institute for Urban Studies, University of Pennsylvania, Philadelphia. This short book is so rich that I can only lament the fact, and hope that one day its author will see fit to publish it. Roughly speaking, he establishes that American material is more popular with the working class and the young segments of the audience who are, by far the majority. He suggests that whereas American popular culture is oriented to working-class aspirations and fantasies, British domestic production is middle-aged and old middle-class oriented. This is sustained because the 'quota' gives no special incentives to change, and because there is a complex of traditions and beliefs involving those who feel their middle-class culture threatened, to those who believe the audience would not accept the reality distortions of action, pace and excitement in domestic films [*vide* Bond]. Whereas Hollywood is close to its audience and part of it, British producers are a peer group which is metropolis-oriented and staffed. Films do not *feed* anti-Americanism, they *need* anti-Americanism in order to be used as aspiration-fantasies and then pride is retained by rejecting them. Better American propaganda would do no good since the audience is uninterested in such films. American films do not intrude – they are used to fill a gap in English culture. The anti-Americanism of the middle class is different, not from pride but because *threatened*.

— 1959, 'The Social Structure of Popular Culture', unpublished. Society is composed of several subcultures ranked because of status and snobbery, but each possessing principles of judgment. Taste-level being a minor variable in the health of social systems there should be more emphasis on producing for subcultures and of evaluating with respect to intended subculture.

— 1960, 'The Relationship between the Movies and the Public, and Some Implications for Movie Criticism and Movie Making', unpublished. Audience: 1) The hypodermic theory – the audience is passive and can be anaesthetized by the film maker; 2) selective perception theory – we select or see to reinforce our beliefs, experience, aspirations. Film maker: 1) Implies the power of the film maker to uplift or manipulate the audience; 2) implies that film is primarily governed by the audience, film makers must give the audience what it wants. Films are more a diversion than an escape. The hypodermic theory is being superseded. Gans' theory: the audience cannot produce films, therefore, film makers have some influence since they fix the range of choice. Subcultures. Product-centred versus audience-centred evaluation – emphasizing the film as an end in itself or the film considered good by the audience. High and low levels of aesthetics use each film to add to their experience. 1) Evaluation should take account of the viewers' educational opportunities and achievements; 2) high culture is better than low, educated better than uneducated – this needs further research.

— 1961, 'Pluralist Aesthetics and Subcultural Programming: A Proposal for Cultural Democracy in the Mass Media', *Studies in Public Communication*, 3: 27–35.
At all levels of education and sensitivity, we should assume that adults make *aesthetic* choices and then should programme the media accordingly. The simple highbrow/lowbrow distinction can be split into at least five levels: lowbrow, lower, middle and upper-middlebrow, and highbrow. These subcultures are reference groups for programming. Box office statistics are uninformative as to satisfaction re content. Highbrowism is undemocratic.

— 1962, 'Hollywood Films on British Screens: An Analysis of the Function of American Popular Culture Abroad', *Social Problems*, 9: 324–8.
What function do US films serve that makes them popular? 1) The economic weakness of the UK industry compared to the US; 2) Hollywood peddles middle class life-style to working class. Action film is adolescent aspiration and working class in ideals. UK films are middle class, nineteenth century and middle-aged. Because U.K. industry is dominated by middle to upper-middle types, the lower class responded to *Room at the Top* and *Saturday Night and Sunday Morning*; significantly, American money was behind them. Maybe the UK industry will respond to the newly affluent working class.

— 1964, 'America's New Sexual Idols', *Twentieth Century*, Autumn, 86–92.
America's changing image of Britain reflects changes in the US. Courtly gentleman image is giving way to sexy, sceptical, working-class image which preceded new sexual freedom, the discovery of the poor, and new political critique in the US. British influence in USA can circumvent the power politics dimensions.

— 1964, 'The Rise of the Problem Film: An Analysis of Changes in Hollywood Films and the American Audience', *Social Problems*, 11: 327–36.
Four principal myths dominate the formula film: the individual succeeding in obtaining justice for himself or his cause; youth overcoming evil or age to get its reward; love conquering all; and being successful without getting corrupted. All four used heroic but shy males, erotic but good females. The fifties saw the problem film treating of delinquency, family conflict, McCarthyism, atomic war, etc. Meanwhile both the formulas and the public personalities of the stars who played in them became more

277

complicated and flawed. But still the hero magically intervenes; social problems like segregation and the conflicts of everyday living are not shown. Changes in the audience are the explanation, not television or the access of college-eduated film executives – the latter were b.ought in to cope with new audience demands. The old audience was poor, immigrant and lowbrow, hence formulas which reflected the realities and the values of that audience. The new audience is lower-middlebrow, high school educated, and likes pictures about the problems of other classes than their own, but only if they involve no institutional or moral upheaval. The upper-middlebrow and highbrow audience is new, and it likes foreign films on the problem of identity and the inability to love. In films for the adolescent audience, the problems of adulthood and sex are seen. More spectaculars are now made, and more novels filmed, this has much to do with the decline of the studios. Film makers do no market research and cannot distinguish standards from choices in box office figures. Using his (1957) argument, there is a lessening gap between the makers and the audience. Whereas the neglected highbrows have foreign films, the neglected lowbrows have neither films nor criticism. Integrity, diversity of product and market research are needed, for the problem film makes Hollywood an important source of social commentary.

— 1965, 'Some Changes in American Taste and their Implications for the Future of Television', in S. T. Donner, ed., *The Future of Commercial Television, 1965-1975*, Stanford.

Patterns of taste are more stable than taste fashions (fads) because the former are part of a taste culture (subculture) shared by a taste group. Taste groups are stable because they are formed by income, education, class, etc. Patterns of taste are shifting upwards because of the relative and absolute growth of the higher taste groups and the shrinkage of the lower.

— 1966, 'Popular Culture in America: Social Problem in a Mass Society or Social Asset in a Pluralist Society?', in H. S. Becker, ed., *Social Problems: A Modern Approach*, New York, 549–620.

The critique of mass culture is an ideology developed to defend the high status and power of the high culture élite by universalizing its values and tastes, and denying that high culture is just one subculture among others in our plural society. Gans repeats his (1959b) analysis of taste subcultures. In a democratic society either equal economic and educational access must be given to the higher subcultures, or else they must all be granted equal status and treatment. This would allow that those really entitled to complain are not the highbrows but the lowbrows who are neglected by the media and are not given any means of public expression of their standards and tastes.

— 1967, 'Audience Preferences for "Reality" or "Fantasy" in Mass Media Fare: Some Attitude Data From East Harlem Residents', unpublished. Does the audience aim to be entertained or educated? Harlem data do not show a preference for 'escape'.

BIBLIOGRAPHY

GEDULD, HARRY M., 1967, *Film Makers on Film Making*, Bloomington.
Interviews and statements by directors only, very uneven, compiled largely
from journals. Artists, need it be said, are not necessarily even coherent
interpreters of their own work.

GEEN, R. and BERKOWITZ, L., 1966, 'Name-Mediated Aggressive Cue
Properties', *Journal of Personality*, 34: 456–65.
After electric shocks and a showing of an 'aggressive' film in which a
person connected with their tormentor by name is fighting, subjects were
allowed to shock their shocker as a way of grading his work. Those shown
the film with the name-connection gave more shocks, than those shown
the film without the name-connection and those who didn't see the film.
'The persons most likely to be attacked by someone who has recently
witnessed violence are those people having appropriate aggression-
eliciting cue properties', p. 463.

GENTILE, T., 1963, *Cinema e Societa*, Rome.

Germany, 1953, [Allied Occupying Powers, 1944–53. US Zone] Office of
the US High Commissioner for Germany. Office of the Executive
Secretary, Historical Division. *Press, Radio and Film in West Germany,
1945–1953*, by H. P. Pilgert, Bad Godesberg-Mehlem.
Eight years after the war deconcentration of UFA proceeded glacially,
the industry was very unstable and HICOG gives gloomy prognosis for it
developing along approved lines.

GERSON, W., 1963, 'Social Structure and Mass Media Socialization', PhD
thesis, University of Washington, unpublished.
Mass media socialize those who are poorly integrated into their family and
school or who are well-integrated into their family but poorly into their
school.

GESSNER, ALEXANDER, 1928, *Film und Wirtschaft*. Versuch einer umfassenden
theoretischen Grundlegung, Koln.

GESSNER, ROBERT, 1968, *The Moving Image*, A guide to cinematic literacy,
New York.
An attempt at a cinematic aesthetics using shooting scripts as the basis.

GILBERT, EDWIN, 1949, *The Squirrel Cage*, London.
Novel about films, see *Cinema 1950*, 205.

GLADSTONE, GABRIEL, 1955, 'Hollywood, Killer of the Dream', *Dissent*, 2:
166.
Curious analysis of *It's A Woman's World*, arguing that Hollywood is
against The American Dream of an open and mobile society, in that this
film attributes a mysterious x-plus quality to the natural superiors.

GODFREY, LIONEL, 1967a, 'A Heretic's Look at Musicals', *Films and Filming*, **13**: March, 5–10.
Music and dancing are what count and the big theatrical transfers (*My Fair Lady, West Side Story, The Sound of Music*) don't match up to *Bye, Bye Birdie, Kiss Me Kate, Bells are Ringing*.

— 1967b, 'It Wasn't Like That In the Book', *Films and Filming*, **13**: April, 12–16.
Studies the relation between book and film in *A Fine Madness, The Moving Target, A Patch of Blue, Inside Daisy Clover, The Blue Max*, etc.

— 1967c, 'A Heretic's View of Westerns', *Films and Filming*, **13**: May, 14–20.
There are too many westerns and most are bad. Character and ideas are as important as action. John Sturges is better than John Ford.

GODWIN, H., 1931, 'Sociology, Fate, Form and Films', *New Republic*, **67**: 72–3.
Discussion arising out of the Russian film *A Shanghai Document* which had been dismissed, along with other 'sociological' Russian films such as *Cities and Years* (wherein the hero executes his best friend), as propaganda. Godwin says of *A Shanghai Document*, that it all seems unstaged and factual. In America things like the mutilation of Dreiser's work in the transfer to the screen, the stress on actors, the *deus ex* businessman, have deep sociological truths for the US contained within them. [Good example of the identification of 'sociological' and left-radical.]

GOLDBERG, A., 1956, 'The Effects of Two Types of Sound Motion Pictures on the Attitudes of Adults Towards Minorities', *Journal of Educational Sociology*, **29**: 386–91.
A dramatic film had a significant effect on attitudes, a documentary none whatsoever.

GOLDEN, MILTON M., 1960, *Hollywood Lawyer*, New York.
An excuse for a barrage of scandal, under disguised names except for the Tone-Payton-Neal fracas.

GOLDMANN, ANNE and LEENHARDT, JACQUES, 1967, 'Essais de Sociologie du Cinéma: *Morgan* ou l'impossible Révolution. *Blow-Up:* Essai d'Analyse', *L'Homme et la Societé*, **6**: 171–9.
The sociological analysis of films is a new method. *Morgan* can be interpreted thus: the hero is a conquered revolutionary, conquered not only by the petit bourgeoisie, but also by fellow revolutionaries, who have been corrupted by power and/or the strong forces of the status quo and reaction. *Blow-Up* is about the powerlessness of the hero in the face of the sinister and callous indifference of society, resigned to continue a life of appearance and facade; his discovery and truth are rendered irrelevant by the unconcern of the outside world.

BIBLIOGRAPHY

GOMBRICH, E. H., 1960, *Art and Illusion*, New York.

GOODE, J., 1963, *The Story of 'The Misfits'*, Indianapolis and New York.
A diary account of the making of *The Misfits* by a non-too-well-informed author (e.g., 'Director Huston resets the camera for one of the longest continuous scenes ever filmed, a five-minute dialogue . . .'). The film goes smoothly, way over schedule, and before it is released Gable dies and Monroe separates from Arthur Miller.

GOODMAN, EZRA, 1961, *The Fifty Year Decline and Fall of Hollywood*, New York.
Recollections of a journalist for *Time*, etc., writing when it looked as if Hollywood was on its last legs. Good material on D. W. Griffith and Marilyn Monroe, many crumbs from the notebooks of a *Time* cover writer. Old fashioned in judgment.

GOODMAN, WALTER, 1955, 'How Not to Produce a Film', *New Republic*, 133: 12–13.
Story of an aborted film on Youth Workers among juvenile delinquents to be written by Arthur Miller, but dropped because of politicians' dislike of his dubious past.

GORDON, J. E., 1951, 'There's Really No Business Like Show Business', *Quarterly of Film, Radio and Television*, 6: 173–85.
A plea for more individualized, more honest film advertising in conjunction with the ad agencies.

GOUGH-YATES, KEVIN, 1965–66, 'The Hero', *Films and Filming*, 12: December 11–16; January, 11–16; February, 25–30; March, 25–30.

— 1966, 'The Heroine', *Films and Filming*, 12: May, 23–7; June, 27–32; July, 39–43; August, 45–50.

GOW, GORDON, 1966, 'Novel Into Film', *Films and Filming*, 12: May, 19–22.

— 1967, 'Thrill a Minute', *Films and Filming*, 13: 5–11.

GRACE, H. A., 1952, 'Charlie Chaplin's Films and American Culture Patterns', *Journal of Aesthetics*, 10: 352–63.
Hypotheses: 'reflect the American culture patterns at the time of the film's release'; 'the American culture is strongly concerned over matters of sex and economic occupation'; 'American woman are portrayed as being apparently but not actually helpless, and as responding with pity rather than with love'; 'the behaviour pattern of the lower economic class is portrayed as violent, vulgar, and aimed more directly against authority symbols than that of the middle class'; 'the American climax pattern is portrayed as that of the American dream or the vanishing man'.

— 1955, 'A Taxonomy of American Crime Film Themes', *Journal of Social Psychology*, 42: 129–36.

281

Cinema 'offers one source of insight into the social dynamics of our culture' and transitions in themes 'parallel very closely the major changes in the American culture over the last half century'.

GRANT, CARY, 1961, 'What It Means to be a Star', *Films and Filming*, 7: July, 12–13 and 42.
Or 'random thoughts of a star'.

GRIFFITH, H., 1932, 'Films and the British Public', *Nineteenth Century*, 112: 190–200.
British writer recounts how his heroine was made pure, and his ending happy, in a quota quickie. Instead of London setting the tone, he regrets, as it does in theatre and fiction, Wigan and the suburbs call the tune.

GRIFFITH, RICHARD, 1959, *Anatomy of a Motion Picture*, New York.
Descriptive, not analytical, photo-journalism on the production of Preminger's *Anatomy of a Murder*: must have been a bit Augean for the author of 'the gospel according to Iris Barry' as his 'The Film Since Then' supplement to Rotha (1963) is known.

—and MAYER, ARTHUR, 1957, *The Movies*, New York.
Ostensibly an illustrated volume – in fact, a highly sophisticated and informative text, full of bite and wit and very well organized. Almost exclusively American in emphasis.

GUNDLACH, RALPH, 1947, 'The Movies: Stereotypes or Realities?', *Journal of Social Issues*, 3: 26–32.
Variety of pressures tend to provide escape pictures of conventionalized fantasy. Idealization; vicariousness; cathartic. But a growing number of pictures are more realistic and objective.

HAFEEZ, M. A., 1950, 'Psychology of Films', *Journal of Educational Psychology*, 8: 14–22.
It is difficult to combat this twentieth-century evil because, lulled by publicity, gregariousness, and semi-hypnotic lighting into a trance-like condition, the public is overwhelmed by sex, leading to sex offences, child rebellion and criminality; they drown their cares, leaving them insensitive and thick-skinned. The cinema should be educational and nationalized. [This trivial and naive piece portends the appalling India (1951). The remarks on sex should be set in the context of Indian censorship, which doesn't even allow kissing.]

HAGEN, RAY, 1966, 'The Day of the Runaway Heiress', *Films and Filming*, 12: April, 40–3.
The frivolous films which coincided with the Great Depression.

HALEY, JAY, 1952, 'The Appeal of the Moving Picture', *Quarterly of Film Radio, and Television*, 6: 361–74.

This interesting article summarizes itself thus: 'Whether in moving pictures, radio, or television, dramatic programs appeal to people not because they take them into some other world, but because they make their own world more bearable. They are an up-to-the-minute guide which people use to find their way in an increasingly complicated environment. By creating order for the individual they help maintain order in society, just as religion did when society was much simpler many long wars and economic crises ago'. P. 374.

HALL, STUART and WHANNEL, PADDY, 1964, *The Popular Arts*, London.
A well-meant handbook for school teachers and adult educators, attempting to be serious, reasoned and discriminating. Utterly orthodox and pedestrian in outlook and preferences, the book epitomizes the owlish humourlessness of the usual courses in popular culture.

HALLIWELL, LESLIE, 1967-8, 'Merely Stupendous', *Films and Filming*, 13: February, 5-12; March, 49-56; April, 44-52; also 14: January, 11-15; February, 39-44; March, 43-7; April, 49-53.
Revaluation of the films of the 'thirties'.

— 1967, *The Filmgoer's Companion*, London.
An indispensable reference book.

HALSEY, EDWIN, 1951, 'The Defective as Movie Hero', *Commonweal*, 55: 445-6.
A Place in the Sun, *A Streetcar Named Desire* and *Death of a Salesman* have central characters who are unreal and unconvincing. They are defective, stupid, or sick; victims, rather than responsible agents. Such dramas provide no catharsis.

HAMPTON, BENJAMIN B., 1931, *A History of the Movies*, New York.
To the *cognoscenti* this is *the* history of the early pictures, especially strong on disentangling the corporate and financial aspects. Denny and Meyersohn comment: 'Good early history of films. Should be read in the context of the beginnings of psychological insight into films'.

HANDEL, L. A., 1947, 'The Social Obligations of Motion Pictures', *International Journal of Opinion and Attitude Research*, 1: 93-8.
A summary of Inglis (1947).

— 1948, 'A Study to Determine the Drawing Power of Male and Female Stars Upon Movie-Goers of their own Sex', *International Journal of Opinion and Attitude Research*, 2: 215-20.
One hundred people were questioned; three-quarters of the men and half of the women preferred stars of their own sex, listing identification, emotional affinity, and the better acting of their own sex as principal reasons.

— 1950, *Hollywood Looks at Its Audience*, Urbana.
An account of Hollywood's audience research. [And very thin it is.]

HANSEN, HARRY L., 1945, 'Hollywood and International Understanding', *Harvard Business Review*, 25: 28–45.
How can Hollywood avoid giving offence to foreign audiences and succeed in giving foreign audiences a balanced portrayal of the USA? The McMahon Report suggests that the Production Code needs more staff. More research. The notion of 'balance' is vague, but at least offence could be avoided and some liaison with the State Department may be desirable.

HARDING, U. E., Evangelist, 1942, *Movie-Mad America*, An utterly frank and revealing expose of the American film, Grand Rapids.
'We are defaming our morals, corrupting our youth, inflaming our young people, exciting passion, debauching our children, making prostitutes and criminals through picture-going!', etc.

HARLAN, VEIT, 1966, *Im Schatten Meiner Filme*, Gutersloh.
In his autobiography, the director of the infamous *Jew Suss* tells what a good German he was all along.

HARLEY, J. E., 1940, *World Wide Influences of the Cinema*, A study of official censorship and the international cultural aspects of motion pictures, Los Angeles.

HARLEY, NEIL P., 1968, 'Using Motion Pictures to Aid International Communication', *Journal of Communications*, 18, 97–108.

HARRINGTON, CURTIS, 1952a, 'Ghoulies and Ghosties', *Sight and Sound*, 21: 157ff.
A classic study of the horror film, paying especially careful attention to the silent period when so many of the conventions were laid down.

— 1952b, 'The Erotic Cinema', *Sight and Sound*, 22: 67ff.
The definitive survey of types of eroticism in the cinema, giving due space to Stroheim and Dietrich. Subsequent accounts like Lo Duca, Durgnat, and Knight and Alpert are deeply indebted.

HARRIS, T., 1957, 'The Building of Popular Images: Grace Kelly and Marilyn Monroe', *Studies in Public Communication*, 1: 45–8.
In building a star-image, the on- and off-screen personage must be consistent with each other; and the image-building stories, in the two cases under review, relied to a remarkable extent on fidelity to the facts of their background.

HAUSER, ARNOLD, 1938, 'Notes on the Sociology of the Film', *Life and Letters Today*, December, 80–7.
The cinema audience is not a discriminating *public*: it reacts to impressions through which they feel reassured or upset as to their conditions of life. Only a young art can be popular, as it develops it becomes esoteric. Films are social romanticism, i.e., glamourizing social climbing.

BIBLIOGRAPHY

— 1948, 'Can Movies be Profound?', *Partisan Review*, **15**: 69–73.
Not psychologically, no; but there is a lot of great art that is not profound.

— 1951, *The Social History of Art*, London. Vol. 4, chapter II of the paperback edition (1962): 'The Film Age'.
His absurd Marxism (e.g., 'Film production owes its greatest success to the
realization that the mind of the petty bourgeois is the psychological meeting place of the masses', p. 239) notwithstanding, there are good insights:
film as a collective art [requiring planning, as if we didn't know] and the
audience as unstructured group. Film techniques invented in Russia
spread everywhere, illustrating how film conventions take on an autonomous existence which allows their use elsewhere 'without the ideological
background from which it has emerged', p. 242.

HELLMUTH, W. F., 1950, 'The Motion Picture Industry', in W. Adams, ed.,
The Structure of American Industry, New York, 360–402.
Sandwiched between 'The Cigarette Industry' and 'The Tin Can Industry'
– both of which it has been accused of resembling – is an economists survey. Investment estimated at $2·8 billion. The history has four phases:
1896–1908: 'almost perfect competition prevailed'. Beginning of distribution was Miles Brothers Exchange 1903. By 1907, 125–150 'exchanges'.
Nickelodeon was to attract larger audience, by 1908, 10,000 in USA.
1908–30: 'a battle for control'. Motion Picture Patents Cc. (MPP Co.)
formed 1909, first vertical integration. Trust wiped out everyone but Fox
and distributors. Independent producers improved films, publicized stars,
gave credits to fight trust. Shift to Hollywood. It was the independents who
introduced features, after seeing how well foreign ones did. MPP Co.
unimportant by 1914. Others tried to get control. Features needed more
plush theatres. In 1917, Paramount introduced block booking. Cinemas
combined into circuits to strengthen their power. In 1921, Paramount
bought 303 theatres. Motion Picture Producers and Distributors of
America founded in 1922. Sound made Warners rich and forced reluctant
majors to follow. RCA's sound system was blocked by AT and T control
of the market, so RCA set up RKO, completely integrated, then sued for
unlawful restraint of trade. Settled out of court in 1935. By 1943, 60% of
sound equipment was RCA. 1931–48: 'A mature oligopoly industry'.
1948: 'change and trouble'.

HENDRICKS, GORDON, 1961, *The Edison Motion Picture Myth*, Berkeley
and Los Angeles.
Scholarly attempt to correct Ramsaye (1926a) and show that W. H. L.
Dickson deserves the credit as the inventor of the motion picture, traditionally credited to Edison.

HERZOG, HERTA, 1941, 'On Borrowed Experience', *Studies in Philosophy
and Social Science*, **9**: 65ff.
Three types of gratification are offered by radio soap-opera: 1) emotional
release; 2) wishful remodelling of drudgery; 3) ideology and recipes for
adjustment.

BIBLIOGRAPHY

HEUER, FEDERICO, 1964, *La Industria Cinematograficana Mexicana*, Mexico City.
Seemingly authoritative economic and statistical survey of the Mexican industry.

HEUSCH, LUC DE, 1962, *The Cinema and Social Science*: a survey of ethnographic and sociological films, Paris: UNESCO.

HIGHAM, CHARLES and GREENBERG, JOEL, 1968, *Hollywood in The Forties*, London.
Superb and evocative critical study of the heyday of Hollywood. Judgments often contentious. It does the long overdue job of revaluing directors like Curtiz, Goulding and Farrow. In a series with Robinson (1968) and Baxter (1968).

HIGHET, GILBERT, 1957, *Talents and Geniuses*, New York.
Includes 'History on the Silver Screen': Hollywood lacks a sense of history, a feel for research and shows a contempt for the audience.

HILDEBRAND, H. P., 1967, 'We Rob Banks', *Mental Health*, 26: 15-17.
Psychoanalysis of *Bonnie and Clyde*.

HILL, DEREK, 1955, 'Napoleon '55', *Films and Filming*, 1: March, 10-11.
Film Napoleons from 1906 to 1955.

HIMMELWEIT, H., OPPENHEIM, P. and VINCE, P., 1958, *Television and The Child*, London.
Basic study of the impact of the media, which failed to reach any alarming conclusions.

HODGKINSON, A. W., 1964, *Screen Education*. A Critical Approach to Cinema and Television, UNESCO Reports and Papers on Mass Communication, No. 42: Paris.
Herbert Read's idea of art as the basis of education is expanded to include film. A Leavis-Hoggart-Williams view is taken against processed experience and for making art serve society.

HOGGART, RICHARD, 1957, *The Uses of Literacy*, London.

HOLADAY, P. W. and STODDARD, G. W., 1933, *Getting Ideas from the Movies*, New York.
Moley: 'Those children remembered motion pictures best who were mentally more able and generally better at learning . . . Children did not remember bootlegging, drinking and business incidents so well as the things that were familiar to them in everyday life. Children remembered better than adults what they saw in motion pictures', p. 38.

HOLLAND, N., 1964, 'The Puzzling Movies: Three Analyses and a Guess at their Appeal', *Journal of Social Issues*, 20: 71-96.

Why are puzzling highbrow films (i.e., those that evoke an 'and what was *that* all about?' response) popular? *The Seventh Seal, La Dolce Vita* and *L'Année Dernière a Marienbad* are analysed. 'In effect, the puzzling movies are an intellectual's version of the old De Mille Bible epic, where we gratify our sexual desires by watching the . . . grand pagan orgies', p. 91. 'The puzzling movies hold out to their intellectual audience the possibility of mastering childish puzzlement by the defenses of the adult intellectual', p. 94. Why do people feel film is 'passive'? – it is no more so than reading or theatregoing. Maybe because the actors can't fight back, or because the audience no matter what it does can't alter their experience even by switching off: [what about walking out?]. Like all art, the puzzling film is a comfort and *that* pleases us. These films are regressive.

Hollywood Reporter, 1947, *Facts About Hollywood, USA*, Hollywood. Of 1,235 people surveyed, 30% were executives, 16% actors, 14·3% producers, etc. 71% went to college, 35·5% graduated.

HOLMES, J. L., 1929, 'Crime and the Press', *Journal of the American Institute of Criminal Law and Criminology*, **20**: 6–59, 246–93. Section VII at p. 266*ff*: 'Do the Moving Pictures Incite to Crime?' Most of his respondents (judges and policemen) thought not. Juvenile audiences were not large and no sympathy was shown with evil characters in the films.

HOLSTIUS, E. NILS, 1937, *Hollywood Through the Back Door*, London. Holstius, a writer and business-man, went to Los Angeles to try to break into films. He decided to go incognito, live in the slums and get to know the place, then offer to work for nothing to ascertain whether he was worth paying. Despite promises, introductions, and the friendship of many stars and executives, he got the Hollywood run-around. They were always friendly and interested – and they never called back. The system decreed that notice could not be taken of those without screen credits, but screen credits could only be had if someone first took notice. His hanging around, his naive honesty about what he was up to, his lack of ballyhoo, ensured that doors remained closed. At the end of the book he realizes what the reader seems to have known all along: that Hollywood is a social system with rigid channels of approach and entry. Yet Holstius seems not to have twigged in time to decide his whole scheme was hopeless and to try another. With his contacts there is little doubt he could have sold himself, but only by playing it big. The system is designed to make entry selective and difficult; it is also designed to protect executives from the hordes of people trying to 'break in'. By putting himself among those, and not cashing in on the fact that he already knew enough 'in' people to consider himself in, Holstius got demoralized and went back to England.

HOMANS, P., 1961, 'Puritanism Revisited: An Analysis of the Contemporary Screen-Image Western', *Studies in Public Communication*, **3**: 73–84. Westerns are myths with hidden meanings – for the easterners, not the westerners. The hero draws last to put the responsibility for the destruction of the evil threat on to that threat. 'Here is the real meaning of the western: a puritan morality tale in which the saviour-hero redeems the community from the temptations of the devil', p. 83. Are periods of popularity of westerns the same as those of religious revivals? Tries to set up ideal-type western.

HONIGMANN, J. J. and VAN DOORSLAER, M., 1955, *Some Themes from Indian Film Reviews*, University of North Carolina, Institute for Research in Social Science, Studies in Pakistan National Culture, No. 2: Chapel Hill.
Analysis of reviews in *Screen* (Bombay). [The *reductio ad absurdum* of studying our sort of questions without seeing the films.]

HORTON, DONALD and WOHL, R. R., 1956, 'Mass Communication and Parasocial Interaction', *Psychiatry*, 19: 215–29.
Extremely important article. Media give an illusion of face-to-face relationship. We respond as though the performers were in our primary group, but we cannot in fact interact, only withdraw. Radio and television are alternatively public platforms and theatres. They create media personalities or 'personae'. The performance of a persona is open-ended, calling for a rather specific answering role to give it closure (p. 219). These roles are learned over time, as the performer develops his part and 'what for youth may be the anticipatory enactment of roles to be assumed in the future may be, for older persons, a reliving and re-evaluation of the actual or imagined past' (p. 222). 'The function of the mass media, and of the programs we have been discussing, is also the exemplification of the pattern of conduct one needs to understand and cope with others as well as of those patterns which one must apply to oneself' (p. 222). Stars may be heroes or vicarious experience – but they are surely para-social. 'There is no such discontinuity between everyday and parasocial experience as is suggested by the common practice, among observers of these media, of using the analogy of fantasy or dream in the interpretation of programs which are essentially dramatic in character. The relationship of the devotee to the persona is, we suggest, experienced as of the same order as, and related to, the network of actual social relations' (p. 228). The audience is not passive.

HOULTON, BOB, 1966, 'Hollywood: The New Dream Merchants', *The Sunday Times*, 11 November, 33.
Narrates the corporate changes, mergers and take-overs that have fundamentally wiped out the old Hollywood system: there are no leaders left.

HOUN, Z., 1957, 'Motion Pictures and Propaganda in Communist China', *Journalism Quarterly*, 34: 481–92.
Despite nationalization and reorganization, in the five years to October 1954, China produced only 108 feature films, sixty of them in 1950. Apparently, *The Biography of Wu Hsün*, which portrayed a man who spent

his life begging for the poor, after initial praise, was found to be ideologically in error, and all connected with it and those who had previously praised it, confessed their errors and underwent self-criticism. As a result writers became very reluctant to write stories, and feature production fell off sharply. Films are closely ideologically controlled. The production units must have suggestions approved by the Bureau of Cinematic Arts of the Ministry of Cultural Affairs, and then when produced they cannot be shown until they have been reviewed by the Bureau and the Ministry. More important ones must be reviewed by the Department of Propaganda of the Central Committee. Films, as a result perhaps, are dull and poorly attended, despite the expansion of exhibition facilities. American and British films were suppressed, and Russian films encouraged.

HOUSEMAN, JOHN, 1947, 'Today's Hero: A Review', *Hollywood Quarterly*, 2: 161*f.*
A curiously unappreciative analysis of *The Big Sleep*, and detective heroes. See reply by Asheim (1947) and reply by J. H. in 3: 89–90.

— 1950, 'The Lost Enthusiasm', *Harper's*, 200: 50–9 (April), and 'Hollywood Faces the Fifties', and 'Battle Over TV', 200: 51–9 (May).
The current crisis generates less panic than in 1946: the strikes of 1945 and the imminent HUAC hearings in 1947 were morale injuries, on top of which came the UK tax of 75% along with a decline in grosses. 'During the winter of 1947–8, there appeared on the books of an American motion picture company that ghastly relic of the past, that almost forgotten evil – a movie that actually lost money' (p. 52). Hollywood's search for the universal film, displeasing nobody, may court disaster when special release patterns have proved successful. Television and the divorcement (of theatres from production and distribution) will have its effects, Hollywood will have to come to terms with the new medium, and its human, technical and copyrighted assets are considerable.

HOUSTON, PENELOPE, 1950, 'Mr Deeds and Willie Stark', *Sight and Sound*, 19: 276*ff.*
Hollywood does make critical, sociological films, but the demands of business impose a comforting solution, a happy ending.

— 1963, *The Contemporary Cinema*, Harmondsworth.
A breathless rush round world cinema since 1945, all of a piece, but less interestingly illustrated than Manvell's (1967 and 1968). See my severely critical review where I document poor argument, unexamined assumption and skew emphasis: Jarvie (1964*b*).

HOVLAND, CARL I., LUMSDAINE, A. A. and SHEFFIELD, F. D., 1949, *Experiments in Mass Communication* (Studies in Social Psychology in World War II, vol. III), Princeton.
Elaborate report on the effectiveness of Second World War film propaganda on troops in motivation, information, and teaching, showing variation due to prior state, intellectual ability, degree of participation, and drawing out some conclusions of use to makers of these films.

— 1954, 'Effects of the Mass Media of Communication', in Gardner Lindsey, ed., *Handbook of Social Psychology*, vol. II, New York. Rather pedestrian review of the literature, with an extensive bibliography on the experimental study of effects.

HOWARD, JACK, 1952, 'The Film in India', *Quarterly of Film, Radio, and Television*, 6: 217–27. Sketch of the film industry in India.

HOWARD, LESLIE RUTH, 1959, *A Quite Remarkable Father*, New York. A personal biography of her father, by his daughter.

HOWE, A. H., 1965, 'A Banker Looks at the Picture Business', *The Journal of the Screen Producer's Guild*, December, 9–16. [Howe was at the time Vice-president of the National Division, Los Angeles Headquarters, Bank of America, with twenty years experience of film financing, and in charge of it since 1959. This article is of the greatest importance and the most unchallangeable authority.] Two myths about financing that just aren't so: 1) there are no bankable stars. Top stars mean high costs too. 'Each new picture is a new venture, and a loan must be so arranged that it will be repaid even in event of a disaster', p. 10. 'The banker does not even try to influence production decisions as to what pictures are made. His effort is directed to insure the repayment of the loan; *he lets the people in the business pick the packages* ... the producer needs to be associated with success.' 2) bankers do not control the industry unless it is bankrupt – even investment bankers are advisers. The risks and who takes them: not the banks. Costs are up ten to one hundred times in the last fifteen years, the risks are higher, the losses severe, have even become a matter of course since the consent decrees. But the occasional film makes more than ever it did. But there is a better than 50/50 chance of loss. Banks do not make investments for profit (that is illegal), their interest is in interest and repayment. The same credit tests are applied as to other loans: collateral. *For fifteen years the assumption has been that each picture would not return any of its production cost: i.e., the banks refuse the risk.* 90% of the risk is taken by distributors: *they* dictate ingredients. The other 10% is producers and miscellaneous investors. The bank gives cash backstopped by the risk takers. How to go about financing a picture: with big company guarantee the rate is 1% above prime interest rates. A risk-taker might agree to pick up the tab upon delivery of a satisfactory picture. Then you need a 'completion guarantee'. This is expensive, comes from private sources, and may include bonuses and a part-ownership guarantee. No company which specializes in risk taking in the USA has made a success of it. If the company is not big, collateral is needed. If the completion guarantor has low liquidity, then a cash completion fund of say 15% of the budget in bonds or securities is needed. Loan maturity is normally two years after first borrowing. Producer must provide: proof of ownership of the 'property'; a detailed budget; distribution agreements; financial statements of guarantors. Bank then: writes a mortgage, pledge and assignment, giving it first lien on producer's share of receipts; agrees with distributors to pay the producers share directly to the bank and to limiting advertising expenses; various agreements subordinating all other claims to the bank's; laboratory agrees to hold the physical properties for the bank; sees that there is a completion guarantor where the distributor refuses to be; loan payments are contingent on progress reports. Advantages and handicaps of foreign production: it is a higher risk, but completion guarantees are easier to obtain in the UK because of the subsidy system.

HUACO, GEORGE A., 1965, *The Sociology of Film Art*, New York. Weirdly misleading title. Studies the emergence and decline of three homogeneous waves of films which attempted to come to terms with reality. The German expressionist film of the early 1920s (where ' "reality" is the subjective emotional experience of horror, fear, degredation, sadism, masochism, oppression', p. 16. In such films as *The Cabinet of Dr Caligari*, *The Golem*, and ending with *The Blue Angel* and *M*.) The Soviet expressive-realist film of the 1920s (where ' "reality" is the transformation of the human and nonhuman environment from an undesirable to a desirable state by the application of human will, rationality, and revolution', p. 17. In such films as *Strike* and *Mother*, and ending with *The General Line* and *Earth*). The Italian neo-realist film of the 1940s (where ' "reality" is poverty, unemployment, hunger', p. 17. In such films as *Open City* and *Shoeshine*, ending with *Love in the City* and *The Roof*). Believing, with Marx and Smelser, that film art is ultimately dependent on nonartistic structures and forces (or at least its waves are), i.e., 'the necessary conditions for the emergence and duration of film waves will be found among historically specific social resources, modes of social organization, political and legal norms, and the artistic traditions of the society in question' (p. 19), he argues as follows: 'this study will give a causal account of the rise and fall of three stylistically homogeneous waves of film art in terms of the presence or absence of four structural factors: a cadre of film technicians, the required industrial plant, a favourable mode of organization of the industry, and a favourable political climate. The character of these factors will be established independently by the use of historical data. We will then examine the ideology implicit in the film plots of each wave and show for each period whether the organization of the film industry and the political climate were favourable to the development of a particular ideology. Next, we will explore the larger artistic-literary-dramatic cultural context for clues as to the genesis of the style of each wave. Finally, we will examine the social characteristics of each group of directors and link some of these social characteristics with specific ideological or artistic aspects of each film wave', 22.

Limitations: 'we know nothing about the audiences' (p. 22); the study of individuals and heterogeneous waves is sociologically unrewarding (p. 2); 'the ideology of a film wave . . . has to be established . . . by a content analysis of film plots (p. 20).

HUETTIG, M. D., 1944, *Economic Control of the Motion Picture Industry*,
Philadelphia.
Good, clear summary of the industrial history. Critical and lucid, an
excellent guide to how things stood in 1944. Discussing high salaries, she
gives these figures for the combined compensation paid to L. B. Mayer,
A. Rubin and I. Thalberg at MGM 1927–37.

Salary	$ 4,292,500
Share of profit	14,470,900
Value of stock options	2,696,078
	$21,459,478

But these remunerations were part of the price of an earlier company
merger, and the company was clearly profitable and their share in the
profits was a high incentive to see that it continued so.
  She believes there is competition in the industry for talent, etc. There is a
sellers' market in distribution, but in theatres there is competition, although
the majors do co-operate with each other. 'The outstanding economic fact
about the motion picture industry is this: that by means of the ownership
of a relatively small number of theatres, five firms have achieved within
less than twenty years apparently stable control over an industry consisting
originally of thousands of independent units, operating as three fairly
distinct branches of the industry, scattered geographically, and quite
unorganized', pp. 5–6.

HUGHES, R., ed., 1959, *Film: Book 1, The Audience and the Film Maker*,
New York.
A couple of articles by Kracauer (see his (1960)) and Knight, some replies
to a questionnaire (mostly sensible, cf., Kazan, Lean, S. Ray) and then
some irrelevant filler articles about Flaherty, etc.

— 1962, *Film: Book 2, Films of Peace and War*, New York.
Useful articles on the uses of war films in America (Young) and Eastern
Europe (Morris). Also interesting interviews, especially with Huston about
his great documentaries *The Battle of San Pietro* and *Let There Be Light*
(a full scenario of the latter is included).

HULETT, J. E., JR., 1949, 'Estimating the Net Effect of a Commercial Motion
Picture on the Trend of Local Public Opinion', *American Sociological
Review*, 14: 263–75 and 550–2.
How did *Sister Kenny* affect public attitudes to polio treatment when it
was shown in Champaign-Urbana? Not much: 1) the film appealed only
to a small group; 2) its arguments were not intrinsically convincing; 3)
'propaganda sophistication'. At pp. 550–1 Seisel tries to show from
Hulett's statistics that the effect *was* great, while Hulett replies that he
includes in his calculations the 'drift' effect.

HUMMEL, R. E., 1964, 'A Study of Motion Picture Production Management
in the Major Studios', MA thesis, UCLA, unpublished.

Study of the unit managers and all other production functions and organization. Good analysis.

HUNNINGS, N. M., 1967, *Film Censors and the Law*, London.
Technical, lawyer's comparative account of film censorship in several jurisdictions. Excellent bibliography.

HUNT, ALBERT, 1964, 'The Film', in D. Thompson (1964).
Critique of *Guns of Navarone* (crude and immoral), *The Young Ones* (corrupt), and *The Angry Silence* (gloats over violence). These films simplify experience; conform to prejudices; borrow from the other mass media. 'This tendency to reduce experience to a formula which fits our most commonplace assumptions can only contribute in the end to the fixing of sharply defined limits of taste and awareness. Anything which questions the commonplace or challenges the imagination is likely to be discouraged.' The conventional film's response to human experience is 'inadequate'. Mass market makes taking risk difficult. Goon show proves minority taste can become popular.

HUNTER, ALLAN A., 1947, 'A Clergyman Looks at the Movies', *Annals* (1947), 95–7.
Suggests there is a tension between the overt moral preached by many films and the hidden propaganda of the film, and what its stars *are*. Also, foreigners get a distorted picture of the USA.

India, 1928, *Report of the Indian Cinematograph Committee 1927-8*, Calcutta.
Gives the history of Indian production. By 1928, there are only 300 cinemas in British India and a further 60 in the Indian States. Women rarely attend the cinema, and very few children. Twenty-one producing concerns in India. A stigma is attached to film acting. Production should be encouraged by a quota. Rebuts vigorously the Grundy-ish attempts at control.

— 1951, *Report of the Film Enquiry Committee*, New Delhi.
This authoritative report gives the following figures for Indian film production:

1939	167	1947	283
1940	171	1948	264
1946	200	1949	289

Brings history of the Indian film up-to-date since the 1928 Report. Ambitiously surveys the legal, social, reproduction, distribution, exhibition, raw material and industrial aspects of films. Leading to a long list of recommendations for reorganizing the industry to rectify: 'In brief, the haphazard growth of the industry under the full blast of *laissez-faire* except for the fortuitous but erratic control during the war, lack of careful and proper planning, decentralization and dispersal, the absence of a godfather in government departments, overmuch reliance on individual rather than collective initiative and effort, too little regard for art and too much emphasis on wrong notions of entertainment, the burden of taxation, the presence of misfits and 'unfits' in key positions, 'professionalism' rather than 'contractualism' among the artistes, the strangle-hold of finance, lack of organization and co-operation, the absence of any policy on the part of Government in regard to the direction, purpose and regulation of the industry, the multiplicity of authorites which have a say in its affairs, the confused attitude of State authorities and Ministers towards the very claims of the industry to exist, its dependence on the foreign market, and competition with foreign film incorporating a different approach to life and containing different ideas of moral and spiritual values but possessing superior organization and commanding wider markets, better talent, richer resources and less strict censorial attention – all these have been important factors which have affected the industry during its progress to its present stage of development . . .', p. 171. [The horror of the tidy-minded socialist bureaucrat at the sprawling, thriving, chaotic world of films is expressed here clearly. One's heart warms to him until the part about 'unfits' and the Government giving purpose to the industry reveals what it is all about.]

INGLIS, RUTH A., 1947, *Freedom of the Movies*, A report on Self-Regulation from the Commission on Freedom of the Press, Chicago.
Reviews the history of the industry and the development of self-regulation. Recommends 'improved' self-regulation, including solving the 'problem of monopolistic control', p. 193. Reviewed in *Penguin Film Review*, No. 7, 125ff, by R. K. Nielson-Baxter.

— 1947a, 'Need for Voluntary Self-Regulation', *Annals* (1947), 153–9.
In 1942, the Production Code Administration fine was dropped for exhibitors so quietly that some producers did not realize it – until Hughes released *The Outlaw* (given a seal and then withdrawn because of lurid advertisement). PCA has been in restraint of trade, the fine was used to bully independents to submit to the PCA to get release. What is needed is a voluntary, liberal and flexible advisory body.

INKELES, ALEX, 1950, *Public Opinion in Soviet Russia*, Cambridge.
Chapter 19 is a factual survey of the history, organization, technical base, audience patterns, and political control of the Russian movie industry. This study forms the jumping-off point for Rimberg (1959).

Institute de Sociologie Solvay, 1960, *Le Cinéma fait social*, Bruxelles.
Report of a conference, with papers and discussions. Includes Morin's second thoughts on stars ('je dirai que le phénomène "star" est carrefour du phénomène suivant: l'industrie au XXe siècle entrepit de coloniser l'âme humaine, et alors se sont créés les "usines de rêves" ', p. 94), Davay on myths, Dumazedier on popular culture ('les psychologues et les sociologues admettent généralement que le spectacle cinématographique provoque la passivité du publique. Mais qu'est-ce que la passivité et qu'est-ce que l'activité? Pour certains le spectateur de cinéma est passif, le spectateur

de theatre actif; mais c'est une définition à priori', p. 194), and the closing remarks of Cohen-Séat.

Instituto 'Agostino Gemelli' Per Le Studio Sperimentale Di Problemi Sociali Dell Informazione Visiva (ISPSIV), 1965, Milan.
A filmology document taking a psychologistic view of the film as experienced, the spectator identifies, his mind sinks into a dimmed twilight and exposure to traumatic stimuli is possible because normal defence mechanisms do not work (pp. 27-9). Other papers are mostly technical psychology, some with English summaries.

International Educational Cinematographic Institute, 1934 (?), *The Social Aspect of the Cinema*, Rome.
One of the series of IECI – League of Nations – volumes, this one is in response to a questionnaire. Enthusiastic reformist, defensive, humourless, curiously nineteenth century feel to it. Not even any nuggets of real interest.

IRVINE, KEITH, 1955, 'The Film You Won't See: Unofficial Censors at Work', *Nation*, 181: 109-10.
Wages of Fear was cut by twenty-two minutes by the timid distributors to remove all critical, social and political ideas that were controversial.

IRWIN, WILL, 1928, *The House that Shadows Built*, Garden City.
Useful popular biography of Adolph Zukor and his principal associates, appears to have had the collaboration of the subject. Reports Zukor's yearning to supervise films but his inability to avoid looking after finance. Interesting section on the US seizure of control of the world market during First World War, suggesting that the narrative talent, universal acceptability of US physical types, the huge domestic US market and wealth, indicate that 'even if Europe had met us, during the period when the motion picture was finding itself, in equal and unfettered competition, we might have swept the world just the same', p. 240. 'Unconsciously, those fur workers, small salesmen, clothing operators, and vaudeville performers who brought the moving picture out of the back streets, were creating the first universal language of mankind', p. 243. The talking film will put an end to this.

JACOBS, L., 1939, *The Rise of the American Film*, New York.
Authoritative and scholarly history of the American film with the conventional American intellectual's penchant for stressing those films with social significance or radical views as the most important. Much less extreme than Griffith, however.

— 1960, *Introduction to the Art of the Movies*, New York.
A useful anthology of mainly formal analyses.

JACOBS, N., ed., 1961, *Culture for the Millions?*, New York.
Contains pieces by Shils (1961), Lowenthal, Arendt, van den Haag,

Handlin, Rosten (1961), Stanton, Sweeney, Jarrell, Berger, Baldwin, Hyman, Hughes and Schlesinger. At the end there is a vigorous set-to discussion between the participants.

JACOBSON, HERBERT L., 1953, 'Cowboy, Pioneer and American Solder', *Sight and Sound*, **22**: 189*ff.*
The Western has helped preserve America's military tradition through the principle that the good hero wins if he holds out long enough. Westerns revived in 1939, and again in the early fifties, in each case a time when America was girding herself. More people died of dysentery than of Indian arrows on the frontier, which was closed in 1890.

JAIN, R. D., 1961, *The Economic Aspects of the Film Industry in India*, Delhi.
Extremely detailed facts on the film industry of India, with many of those hidden gems seemingly so ineliminable from Indian works – listing the difficulties of finance – spread need, low profit, conservatism, long-run losses – gives us this: 'Producers, in majority, do not keep on investing their profits earned out of the motion picture industry. In some cases, profits are invested in other enterprises, while in many others, they are spent on the race-course or on similar activities', p. 93. Fundamentally he thinks the industry is over-equipped with labs and studios and careless of cost – this has the result of permanent uncertainty.

JANOWITZ, M. and SCHULZE, R., 1959, 'Trends in Mass Communication Research', in *World Congress of Sociology, Transactions*, **3**: 129–49.
Brief history of mass communication research, using Laswellian headings: who, what, to whom, and with what effects? Notes the oligopolistic tendency in the media, and the persistent discrepancy between popular views of the dire effects of media and research findings that these effects are almost negligible. Suggests the discrepancy is a topic for research. Mass communications are means of social control.

JARVIE, I. C., 1961*a*, 'Hysteria and Authoritarianism in the Films of Robert Aldrich', *Film Culture*, **22-3**: 95–111.

— 1961*b*, 'Towards an Objective Film Criticism', *Film Quarterly*, **14**: 19–23.

— 1963, 'Hong Kong Notes', *Sight and Sound*, **33**: 22.

— 1964*a*, *The Revolution in Anthropology*, London.

— 1964*b*, 'The Celluloid Revolution', *The Bulletin*, **86**, Feb. 1: 41–2.
A review article on Houston (1963) and Taylor (1962).

— 1966, Review of Shickel (1966) in *The Bulletin*.

— and JOSEPH AGASSI, 1967, 'The Problem of the Rationality of Magic', *British Journal of Sociology*, **18**: 55–74.

— 1967*a*, 'The Objectivity of Criticism of the Arts', *Ratio*, **9**: 67–83.

— 1967b, 'On the Theory of Fieldwork and the Scientific Character of Social Anthropology', *Philosophy of Science*, 34: 223–42.

— 1969a, *Hong Kong: A Society in Transition*, London and New York.

— 1969b, 'Media and Manners', *Film Quarterly*, 22: 11–17.

— 1969c, 'The Logic of the Situation', in *Critical Essays on Sociological Explanation*, ed., G. K. Zollschan, Santa Barbara.

JENNINGS, G., 1963, *The Movie Book*, New York.

JOBES, GERTRUDE, 1966, *Motion Picture Empire*.
History of motion picture companies in the USA to 1960. Of 372 pages only thirty-nine given to the era 1934–60. All the signs of an old manuscript dusted off, without the energy to up-date it. Not as good as Ramsaye (1926a) or Hampton (1931).

JOHNSON, IAN, 1964, 'Merely Players' *Films and Filming*, 10: April, 41ff.
About Shakespeare in the cinema.

JOHNSTON, ALVA, 1937, *The Great Goldwyn*, New York.
Disappointingly anecdotal survey of Goldwyn's career, not analyzing his success and staying power – despite his cantankerousness – at all.

JOHNSTON, E., 1947, 'The Motion Picture as a Stimulus to Culture', *Annals* (1947), 98–102.
Films, a popular art like Greek theatre, have wiped out provincialism in the USA and help international understanding.

JOHNSTON, W. A., 1926, 'The Structure of the Motion Picture Industry', in *Annals of the American Academy of Political and Social Science*, 128: 20–30.
Surveyor of production, distribution and exhibition. Of the production dollar, costs are split as follows:

Actors	0·25
Directors, cameraman, assistants	0·10
Scenario and stories	0·10
Sets	0·19
Studio overhead	0·20
Costumes	0·03
Locations, rents	0·08
Raw film	0·05
Total	1·00

JOHNSTON, WINIFRED, 1939, *Memo on the Movie*, War Propaganda 1914–39, Norman (Okla).
Argues that peace-loving peoples are saturated by film war-propaganda engineered by Wall Street, and the film trusts and aimed ultimately at Russia.

BIBLIOGRAPHY

JOHNSTONE, J. W. C., 1959, 'Social Context and Mass Media Reception', *Studies in Public Communication*, 2: 25–30.
There is more than one context or level of social pressures: 1) Level of social aggregates (of age, sex, job, educational level, class). While not real groups, these aggregations are significant – young children prefer television, older children (10–12) films. Television is home-centred, films peer-centred. Adolescents have to show interest in pop music. In addition to being a source for learning roles, the mass media are tied up with the role-expectations of aggregates; 2) level of secondary groups. High school children subdivide into which pop singers, or which sport, they like. At both levels the media serve to define identity. Also to maintain status; 3) level of primary groups – see Katz and Lazarsfeld (q.v.); 4) level of the mass.

JONES, DOROTHY B., 1942, 'Quantitative Analysis of Motion Picture Content', *Public Opinion Quarterly*, 46: 411–28.
'... studied 100 Hollywood feature films of all types released between April 1941, and February 1942. The difficulty of the task is clearly illustrated by the fact that this painstaking study can be considered only a small first step in the direction of adequate classification of content', (Fearing, 1950).

— 1945, 'The Hollywood War Film: 1942–1944', *Hollywood Quarterly*, 1: 1–19.
Of 1,313 films, 374 concerned with the war. Highly critical content analysis, generally arguing that Hollywood was slow to grow up and fell back a great deal. It has gained in social responsibility

— 1950, 'Quantitative Analysis of Motion Picture Content', *Public Opinion Quarterly*, 14: 554–8.
Not only are you only as good as your last picture: people don't remember any more. The entire product of an unnamed major studio from 1917–47 was analysed, comprising 1,026 feature films. Whom are the films about? Men to women 2:1. Three out of five were 'independent adult' characters (rare in real life). Half were well-off, a third moderately so, 17% destitute. Two out of five were either wealthy or poor, 8% were élite, 11% déclassé. Seven out of ten single, two out of ten married. Four out of five were Americans. What are the films about? Boy meets girl. Four out of five wanted Safety, Income or Deference. 68% wanted love; 26% fame, reputation, prestige; 18% safety; 14% a way of life; 10% money or goods; 9% to do their duty. 61% get it; 10% do not; 14% get some not others.

— 1955, *The Portrayal of China and India on the American Screen, 1896–1955*, report of the MIT Center for International Studies.
Extremely important content analysis of hundreds of films. An appendix (II), is said to have been deleted from the original report for this publication.

JOWETT, GARTH, S., 1969, 'Acceptance of the Motion Picture in America, 1895–1910', unpublished.

298

BIBLIOGRAPHY

There are two problems: the innovation, and its acceptance. The problem
of getting living pictures was important because of the economic limitations of peep shows, and because the limits of stage realism were being
reached. Movies were cheap, universal, and easy to master.

— 1970, 'The Concept of History in American Produced Films: An
Analysis of the Films made in the Period 1950–61', *Journal of Popular
Culture*, forthcoming.
Analysis of distributed films by historical periods and by main drift of
treatment. They reinforce current American values. The Revolutionary
War and the Civil War are curiously neglected. The western Period
1865–90 collects the biggest group of films.

JUNGERSEN, F. G., 1968, *Disney*, Copenhagen.

KAEL, PAULINE, 1956, 'Movies, the Desperate Art', anthologized in D.
Talbot, ed., *Film: An Anthology*, Berkeley and Los Angeles, 1959, 51–71.
A bitter attack on Hollywood and the *avant-garde*, written in the nadir of
the fifties, but absurdly out of proportion even so. Rightly not included
in her two anthologies (1965, 1968).

— 1965, *I Lost it at the Movies*, New York.
Pugnacious and provocative, easily the most closely argued of film writing.
Judgments are usually dead-on; when off (e.g., Antonioni) very off indeed.
Contains her usual love-hate pieces on Hollywood and those reflecting
healthy distrust of European pretensions ('Fantasies of the Art House
Audience'). Also included are her devastation of Kracauer (1960) ('Is
There a Cure for Film Criticism?'), and a superb analysis of propaganda
('Morality Plays Right and Left').

— 1967, 'Movies on Television', *New Yorker*, 43: 3 June, 120–34.
Why are our reactions to old films on TV different from our reactions
when first we saw them? Answer: loss of sympathy with the culture they
formed and expressed and which we grew up in and out of, failure of highbrow films to come across, the home-oriented rather than outgoing viewing environment. To young viewers films are an undifferentiated stream
like traffic, they live in and with what the older generation passed through.
Reprinted in her (1968).

— 1968, *Kiss Kiss, Bang Bang*, New York.
A second collection containing immense riches including her masterly
'The Making of *the Group*' which is better than Ross (1951). Also (1967).

— 1969, 'Trash, Art and the Movies', *Harpers*, Feb., 239, 1425: 65–83.
Trash movies have wonderful moments of enjoyment, these are closer to art
than middle class, respectable, serious, highbrowism. We use movies to
enjoy ourselves. Don't ask whether the director succeeds in his aim, but
rather his skill at finding something acceptable. Trash is honest, not pretentious. But kids are intellectualizing their response to trash. They have no
memories, haven't seen it all before and thus are less demanding. Those
who have seen it all before are a minority – that's why the old and the

critics stop going – it is also how trash gives an appetite for art, i.e. 'what we have always found good in movies only more so. It's the subversive gesture carried even further, the moment of excitement sustained longer and extended into new meanings' (p. 76).

KAHN, GORDON, 1948, *Hollywood on Trial*, New York.
Story of the indictment of the Hollywood Ten who refused to collaborate with the HUAC. Much fun is had with Ginger Rogers' mother.

KALLEN, H. M., 1930, *Indecency in the Seven Arts*, and other adventures of a pragmatist in aesthetics, New York.
'. . . interferences are not healthy policy but the activities of sick minds', p. 50.

KATZ, E., 1960, 'Communication Research and the Image of Society: Convergence of Two Traditions', *American Journal of Sociology*, 65: 435–40.
The atomized anomic image of society had to be given up because the mass media have been found to be far less potent than expected, and this has turned out to be explainable by the network of inter-personal relations. Rural sociology always took this for granted – maybe urban and rural sociology are not all that different.

— and FOULKES, D., 1962, 'On the Use of the Mass Media as Escape: Clarification of a Concept', *Public Opinion Quarterly*, 26: 377–88.
Analyses and clarifies the concept of 'escape', showing that it is used glibly – there are various routes of escape – drugs, alcohol, suicide, sleep – the media is only one. There are various successes of escape – it is not necessarily bad to want not to face things for a while.

— and LAZARSFELD, P., 1955, *Personal Influence*, Glencoe.
Classical study of patterns of influence in society, the role of opinion leaders and their special structural place, the two-step flow hypothesis and the decisive importance of primary interactions and groupings.

KAUFMAN, STANLEY, 1966, *A World on Film*, New York.
Collected criticism of a rather dull critic. Parts worth reading.

KEIR, GERTRUDE, 1949, 'Psychology and the Film', *Penguin Film Review*, 9: 67–72.
Interesting criticisms of Tyler's Freudianism, and of Kracauer and Mayer.

KELEN, H., 19, 'Hollywood in India', *Travel*, 62: 36–8.

KELLY, T., *et al.*, 1966, *A Competitive Cinema*, London.
An economic and industrial report prepared by the Bow Group and published by the Institute of Economic Affairs, directed at suggestions to enhance competition in the British film industry.

BIBLIOGRAPHY

KENNEDY, JOSEPH P., ed., 1927, *The Story of the Films*, New York.
Kennedy in his introduction gives amusing thumb-nail sketches of Hays, Lasky, Zukor, Kent, Cochrane, Giannini, Fox, Leow, Warner, Katz, DeMille, Hammons, Sills. Says motion pictures fourth largest industry with an investment of $1,500 million. They were a series of lectures given at Harvard and have excellent question and answer session after them. Giannini describes the origins of bank financing by making personal loans, fighting against loan bonus sharks and the general indifference of the banking world. In 15 years, 'at no time have I sustained a loss in this business', p. 83.

KERR, A., 1945, 'The Influence of German Nationalism and Militarism Upon the Theatre and Film in the Weimar Republic', unpublished typescript on file at the BFI, London.
Right-wing influence gradually eliminated liberal ideas from film and theatre. 'The militarized mind of the German ... will not change if the ideas of misunderstood Christianity and humanity will be the fundamental basis of a re-education programme'.

KEZICH, Tullio, ed., 1953, *Il Western Maggiorenne*, Trieste.
Articles on various aspects and an eleven-page bibliography.

KLAPP, O. E., 1954, 'Heroes, Villains and Fools as Agents of Social Control', *American Sociological Review*, 19: 56–62.
1) '... they operate within personality as norms of self-judgment and roles for emulation or avoidance'; 2) organize and simplify collective response – non-rational consensus, scapegoat, hero, strengthening morale; 3) rituals of solidarity and norm-affirmation; 4) 'help in the perpetuation of collective values, nourish and maintain necessary sentiments'.

KLAPPER, J. T., 1958, 'What We Know About Mass Communication: the Brink of Hope', *Public Opinion Quarterly*, 21: 453–74.
The problems of the effect of violence, the effect on taste, and the persuasive effect of the media are puzzling since research confirms every view. Among factors found relevant to effects are pre-dispositions; self-selection; selective perception; contextual organization in the medium; audience image of the source; the passage of time; the group orientation of the audience member and the value he sets on group membership; the activity of opinion leaders; the social aspects of the situation during and after exposure and the degree to which the audience member has to play a role while exposed; the personality pattern, social class, and level of frustration of the audience member; the nature of the media under free enterprise and the existence of social mechanisms for implementing action drives. So rich are the factors that 'almost every aspect of the life of the audience member and the culture in which the communication occurs seems susceptible of relation to the process of communicational effect' (p. 455). Replacing the hypodermic theory of mass communication with a situational theory locating them as one influence among others

sharpens the analysis. Conclusions: 1) mass communications are neither a necessary nor a sufficient cause of social events, but function among and through other factors; 2) these others render mass communications a reinforcement of existing conditions rather than an agent of change; 3) where mass communication does aid change either other factors are inoperative and the media make a direct effect or other factors, normally reinforcing, will also be impelling change; 4) mass communication in residual situations has direct effects and serves psycho-physical functions; 5) efficacy governed by media context, channels for action, etc.

— 1961, *The Effects of Mass Communication*, Glencoe.
The authoritative study of this question. Summarized in the preceding item. Exhaustive bibliography.

— 1963, 'Mass Communications Research: an old road resurveyed', *Public Quarterly*, 27: 515–27.
Functional rather than dichotomous studies look promising. Get away from 'media violence perverts' yes or no dichtomies. Psychologists (Bandura, Berkowitz, Lovaas) will in the end conclude: 'some *types* of *depicted violence* will be found to have some *types* of effects on the *aggression levels* of *some* types of *children* under *some* types of *conditions*', p. 518. People don't ask if hospital shows encourage children to perform appendectomies, but we also don't know why they hold the audience. What element provides the gratification? The content, the process, or the concept-of-the-medium? A suggestion is a function only when its consequences are shown to be functional. What the media do to people may turn out to be inseparable from what people do with the media. How about an experiment in altering children's media tastes?

KLINGENDER, F. D. and LEGGE, S., 1937, *The Money Behind the Screen*, London.
An exposé of film finance in the UK. No clear statement of the aim of the exercise but this is perhaps revealed by the choice of left-wing publisher, and Grierson's militant introduction about shedding the odd tear if Arabian nights-type entertainment is swept away; but getting on with the work we want to do: 'our concern is the concern of creative workers for the medium in which they must work', p. 8.

KNEPPER, MAX, 1950, 'Hollywood's Barkers', *Sight and Sound*, 19: 395*ff.*
Caustic look at the fan magazines.

KNIGHT, ARTHUR, 1949, 'The Two-Reel Comedy – Its Rise and Fall', *Penguin Film Review*, 9: 39–46.

— 1953, 'The Reluctant Audience', *Sight and Sound*, 22: 191*ff.*
Roadshow selling techniques made *Henry V* pay off. Hollywood's mass audience is a mass minority of one-third of the population.

— 1956, 'Myths, Movies and Maturity', *Saturday Review*, 39: 7 April, 7–8 and 38–40.

'Harassed by "family audiences", rising costs, aging stars, code and censorship restrictions, and the menace of pressure groups of every class creed and ideology, it is a miracle that Hollywood continues to produce as many meritorious pictures as it does' (p. 40). Of the ten highest grossing films, seven have been released in the past four years. No one knows how the word gets around about a film – publicity campaigns notwithstanding.

— 1959, *The Liveliest Art*, New York.
A very lively modern history of films.

— and ALPERT, HOLLIS, 1965-9, 'A History of Sex in the Cinema', in *Playboy*, as follows:

Part I, April 1965, 12: 127*ff*, pre-1910.
Part II, May 1965, 12: 134*ff*, 1910–20.
Part III, June 1965, 12: 155*ff*, USA in the 20s.
Part IV, August 1965, 12: 114*ff*, Europe in the 20s.
Part V, September 1965, 12: 170*ff*, Sex Stars of the 20s.
Part VI, November 1965, 12: 150*ff*, USA in the 30s.
Part VII, February 1966, 13: 134*ff*, Europe in the 30s.
Part VIII, April 1966, 13: 142*ff*, Sex Stars of the 30s.
Part IX, August 1966, 13: 120*ff*, USA in the 40s.
Part X, September 1966, 13: 172*ff*, Europe in the 40s.
Part XI, October 1966, 13: 150*ff*, Sex Stars of the 40s.
Part XII, November 1966, 13: 162*ff*, USA in the 50s.
Part XIII, December 1966, 13: 232*ff*, Europe in the 50s.
Part XIV, January 1967, 14: 95*ff*, Sex Stars in the 50s.
Part XV, April 1967, 14: 136*ff*, Experimental Films.
Part XVI, June 1967, 14: 124*ff*, The Nudies.
Part XVII, November 1967, 14: 154*ff*, The Stag Film.
Part XVIII, April 1968, 15: 138*ff*, USA in the 60s.
Part XIX, July 1968, 15: 130*ff*, Europe in the 60s.
Part XX, January 1969, 16: 157*ff*, Sex Stars of the 60s.
Part XXI, November 1969, 16: 168*ff*, Sex in Cinema 1969.
Part XXII, December 1969, 16: 206*ff*, Sex Stars of 1969.

This literate and well-researched mammoth series is mainly a chronicle of fashions in pulchritude and exposure. Some marvellous stills, very little about directors.

KOBAL, JOHN, 1968, *Marlene Dietrich*, London.
A serious attempt to get at the legend.

KOCH, HOWARD, 1950, 'A Playwright Looks At The Filmwright', *Sight and Sound*, 19: 210–14.

KOENIGAL, MARK, 1962, *Movies in Society* (sex, crime and censorship), New York.
Incredibly inaccurate, naive, ill-written attack on the cinema and a call for UN censorship. Films should be censored because juvenile delinquents

BIBLIOGRAPHY

might see them! Samples: 'If we look at the latest statistics on mental levels [sic] of the world's population, we will be greatly surprised because we will see that 25% of the total consists of mentally unbalanced individuals . . .', etc., p. 51. 'Many are not worthy of being shown ɔn our screens – especially the Tarzan, Western and thrill film groups. Many of them have no artistic quality and instead of instructing do more [sic] harm to adolescents, and even adults', p. 189. Tarzan arouses the special wrath of this Brazilian gentleman.

KRACAUER, S., 1943, 'The Conquest of Europe on the Screen: The Nazi Newsreel 1939–40', *Social Research*, **10**: 337–57.
Explains how, from the Polish campaign, the Nazis began to organize newsreels. Using little commentary, and only when the pictures cannot tell the story, they always start the commentary after the pictures have begun. Such devices, including contrapuntal sound create a newsreel not of unrelated fragments but of scenes orchestrated into an overall effect. The allies need to catch up.

— 1942, *Propaganda and the Nazi War Film*, New York.
Reprinted as an appendix to his (1947).

— 1946, 'Hollywood's Terror Films', *Commentary*, **2**: 132–6.
Hollywood's sadistic terror films suggest a condition of mental disintegration – they go together with a cycle of psychiatrist-priest 'healer' films. Dangers of Fascism.

— 1947, *From Caligari to Hitler: A Psychological History of the German Film*, Princeton.
Mysterious rumblings of Fascism (and the desire to return to the womb) are detected and exposed in the German cinema before Hitler. Also mysterious, the seriousness with which this book has been taken. Denny and Meyersohn: 'Psychological history of German film, 1919–1933, to determine the dominant influences. Use of film as index to study of mass behaviour. Fascinating, if overextended'. Vesselo (1947): German films 'mirrored a fatal schism in the collective mind of the German nation . . . between opposing psychological forces. These forces the author characterizes as the urge to chaos on the one hand and authority on the other. With Hitler, complete submission to authority finally won the day'. Fearing (1950): 'His thesis is that the films produced in Germany during this period contain evidence of the existence of forces that eventually manifested themselves in the form of Nazism. His basic assumption is that the mass media of communication express the unconscious needs and fantasies of those who see it. This is essentially a Freudian interpretation and analyzes the film as Freud analyzes the dream, that is, as possessing a manifest and latent content. Although Kracauer's analyses of German films are shrewd, he supplies no objective evidence that the meanings he finds in these films actually reached the audiences that saw them. Indeed, there is no objective evidence that these films signified what Kracauer believes they did for their producers. Kracauer's study, however, is important, since it is a thoroughgoing attempt to understand motion pictures in the context

of a specific cultural setting. It is marred by the difficulties implicit in the Freudian method and theory, especially when applied to the interpretation of a cultural manifestation. In the present instance it is necessary to assume that the unconscious forces operating in the minds of the producers result in films containing hidden meanings, which in turn affect the unconscious minds of the mass audience' (p. 107). See also Fearing (1947a).

— 1948, 'Those Movies with a Message', *Harper's*, **196**: June, 567–72.
In *Crossfire, Best Years of Our Lives, Farmer's Daughter, Gentlemen's Agreement*, liberals and liberalism are on the defensive. The common man is portrayed as indifferent to thought; liberals as wordy. Whereas *Paisan* is peerless 'in its grasp of the humanly essential', p. 571. The disoriented average individual shuts his eyes. Dangerous.

— 1949, 'The Mirror Up to Nature', *Penguin Film Review*, **9**: 95–9.
A sketch for (1960)?

— 1950, 'National Types as Hollywood Presents Them', in *The Cinema 1950*, 140–69.
Begins with his classical argument that Hollywood cannot be thrusting unwanted material down the audience's throat because in the long run the profit motive forces it to pander to people's desires, acute or dormant. So, if audiences receive what Hollywood wants them to want, in the long run, what they want them to want must be determined by their desires. Mentions the dearth of films with German subjects in the thirties, the similar dearth of films with Russian subjects after the war. When it became clear the Nazis would have to be stopped, when US public opinion had hardened onto a tough line with Russia, then films on Nazis and Russians appeared. What then about the lack of films with British subjects after the war? *Ad hoc* explanation that the Labour government presented a controversial challenge to the American way of life. US films portray the Britisher as snobbish; German films, by contrast, emphasize British ruthlessness and hypocrisy. Market necessities are the cause, and they express subjective opinions. Objective views are hard to come by and belie intentions: both *Ruggles of Red Gap* and *Mrs Miniver* were inaccurate. There were few prewar films of Russia, the one or two are satires; lot of pro-Russian films during the war; anti- after. Films can help change audience attitudes if they have already begun to change. The industry must divine the audience's feelings.

— 1960, *Theory of Film*, New York.
Kael's review in her (1965), which exposes the absurdities of this last-ditch attempt to refurbish a theory of cinema based on its ability to capture reality, is accurate. Kracauer's saving grace is that he loves films so much, he wriggles around frantically trying to get his theory to allow them all as legitimate.

KUNZ, CLYDE C. and TICHENER, FRANK A., 1926, *The Motion Picture in Its Economic and Social Aspects*. See: Annals of the American Academy of Political and Social Science (1926).

LAFFAY, ALBERT, 1964, *Logique du Cinéma*, création et spectacle, Paris.
Existentialist view of cinema: 'Le cinéma construit donc sous nos yeux un monde quasiment réel, c'est-à-dire de pseudo-objects interdépendants qui, à la manière des véritables, se définissent par exclusion réciproque et semblent résister chacun à sa place de toute la force d'une existence mutuellement empruntée. D'une ombre de rapports spatiaux ils tirent une ombre de réalité', p. 31. 'Le cinéma set ainsi la poési de l'étendue. Son kaléidoscope nous permet de contempler ce que l'enterprise de vivre ne nous laisse pas le loisir de goûter à distance de vue, la servitude d'espace où s'appuie précisément notre liberté. Mais nous ne pourrions ressentir cette *dureté* du monde (aux deux sens du mot) si nous y adhérions de trop près. Point de vérité pour qui colle à la vérité. La conception de "l'état théologique", chez COMTE, revient à ceci . . . que l'homme doit d'abord *décrocher* sa pensée grace au mythe. Le fable est ce qui sépare l'homme de l'animal. "Il importe plus, dit quelque part WHITEHEAD, d'avoir des idées intéressantes que des idées justes".' Pp. 170–1.

LAHUE, KALTON, C., 1964, *Continued Next Week*, a history of the moving picture serial, Norman, Oklahoma.
History of the American serial.

— 1966, *World of Laughter*, the motion picture short, 1910–30, Norman, Oklahoma.
Elaborate scholarly history of the comedy short in America.

— and BREWER, TERRY, 1968, *Kops and Custards*, the legend of Keystone films, Norman, Oklahoma.
Elaborate study of Keystone, producer of many of the early comedians, Chaplin, Arbuckle, the Keystone Kops, etc.

LAKE, BERYL, 1959, 'A Study of the Irrefutability of Two Aesthetic Theories', in W. Elton, ed., *Aesthetics and Language*, Oxford.
The appearance of talking objectively in the aesthetics of Croce, Collingwood and Bell is false, because no possible instance could count against them.

LAMARR, HEDY, 1966, *Ecstasy and Me*, New York.
Astoundingly 'frank' autobiography, confessing fecklessness and nymphomania. Has all the signs of being hastily ghost-written. The author has denounced and denied some of it, and filed various suits.

LAMBERT, GAVIN, 1950, 'A Line of Experiment', *Sight and Sound*, 19: 444*ff*.
Study of the new gangster realism in American films.

— 1952, 'Further Notes on a Renaissance', *Sight and Sound*, 22: 61*ff*.
Thoughts on Italian postwar cinema.

— 1959, *The Slide Area*, New York.
Stories of Hollywood, displaying the Englishman's very sharp response to the bizarre-ness of Southern California.

BIBLIOGRAPHY

— 1963, *Inside Daisy Clover*, New York.
Novel about a Hollywood child who becomes a star.

LANDAU, JACOB M., 1958, *Studies in the Arab Theatre and Cinema*, Philadelphia.
Heroic first attempt to sketch the impact of Western theatre and subsequently cinema on Arabs, and to review its subsequent indigenous development. Research seems to have been done in Israel and the USA. Film themes analyzed: farce; historical; melodramas, dramas; comedies; political films. Poignant: 'There is hardly an Arab film which is not largely musical', p. 199.

LAPIERRE, MARCEL, 1948, *Les Cents Visages du Cinema*, Paris.
Bulky history of the cinema. First half on France. Chapters on almost every other country of the world. A little attention is given to social background and to censorship, otherwise easy-going and undemanding when not at home in France.

LARABEE, ERIC, 1962, *The Self-Conscious Society*, New York.
Lightweight essays on American culture, including a level-headed contribution to the mass culture debate suggesting mass culture is inimical to class culture for it makes choices available.

— and MEYERSON, R., 1958, *Mass Leisure*, Glencoe.
A reader on leisure and its uses, with an extensive bibliography. Wolfenstein expatiates further on 'The Emergence of Fun Morality', pp. 86–96.

LARSEN, OTTO N., 1964, 'Social Effects of Mass Communication', in Faris, R. E. L., ed., *Handbook of Modern Sociology*, Chicago.
Excellent general survey. Distinguishes effective communications from successful communications by whether the point is got across, or whether there is conversion to it as well. Expounds and comments on Klapper (1961) and Berelson (1961).

— ed., 1968, *Violence and the Mass Media*, New York.
Out of thirty items in this reader only four deal with films, but the rest are of absorbing interest including a fascinating confrontation between Klapper, Berkowitz and Wertham.

LAURITZEN, E., 1962, *The Swedish Film*, New York.
Notes on selected Swedish films 1909–57.

LAWSON, J. H., 1946, 'Hollywood – Illusion and Reality', *Hollywood Quarterly*, 1: 233.
The Hollywood stereotype (e.g., Chandler, Rosten, Isherwood) has not been manufactured accidentally – as long as the average citizen thinks of Hollywood as a glamorous funnyhouse, he cannot think of it as a place where a public trust is fulfilled and where freedom of thought and communication must be preserved.

307

BIBLIOGRAPHY

LAZARSFELD, P. F., 1947, 'Audience Research in the Movie Field' *Annals* (1947), 160–8.

Control, content, audience and effect are the main categories of audience research. There are problems defining the filmgoer. The dominating factor in audience structure is age, with age rise there is a sharp fall off in film attendance, less so with more education. Reasons: 1) films are a social activity and young people have more social activities; 2) films involve leaving the house, i.e., trouble; 3) films are patterned to the tastes of youngsters. Rural people go less – because of the lack of cinemas. People go most frequently with friends. They like films about themselves, not complementary to their experience. Word-of-mouth advice is the key to the audience-penetration index. There exist people especially likely to be taste leaders: 1) young (under 25); 2) in the same class as those they advise; 3) frequent filmgoers themselves, read magazines and hear more radio, in general more aware, they get around more socially, 4) they are influenced in *their* choices by publicity, magazines, etc.

— and KENDALL, P., 1948, *Radio Listening in America*, New York.

In surveying the radio audience, reading and movie habits were also recorded. Radio and movies tended nicely to complement one another. Light listeners are light moviegoers. Heavy listeners are heavy moviegoers. Their interests and opportunities are similar. Book readers are more likely to be movie fans, but there is no relation with radio listeners. Exception: lots of movies are based on best-sellers. Moviegoing is related to age. Peak age is 19. More free evenings, less responsibilities, willingness to go out, lack of settled social activities. Single people more than married whatever age, men more than women if unmarried; no difference if married. Less in rural areas.

MOVIES SEEN DURING PREVIOUS MONTH ACCORDING TO AGE

Attendance	21–29	30–39	40–49	50–59	60+
None	19	31	36	51	73
One	15	18	16	15	9
Two or three	26	26	27	18	9
Four or five	23	16	14	11	6
Five +	17	9	7	5	3
Total %	100	100	100	100	100

— and MERTON, R. K., 1944, 'The Psychological Analysis of Propaganda' in *Writers Congress* (1944), 362–80.

Aim to analyze propaganda and predict unexpected response [*sic*]. Utilize content analysis and response analysis. The famous case of the radio talk warning the audience against X-raying by quacks is cited, because it boomeranged from puzzlement, to impatience, to mistrust of what was said about X-rays and about licensing practitioners. He spoke into a psychological void, ignoring the mental set of the audience, which was very different from his. While mistrust of 'mere propaganda' is rife, there is a readiness to accept the 'propaganda of facts'.

308

BIBLIOGRAPHY

LELOIR, MAURICE, 1929, *Cinq Mois a Hollywood avec Douglas Fairbanks*; Max de Cuvillon, *Films Muets Films Parlants*, Paris.
Charming memoir by a seventy-four-year old period expert invited to Hollywood to supervise design detail on *The Iron Mask*. He is lively and sympathetic and provides witty sketches of Hollywood studio life; his descriptions are mainly visual since he speaks no English. In a second part his son-in-law details the technical matters of film production.

LEPROHON, PIERRE, 1945, *L'Exotisme et le Cinéma*, Les 'Chasseurs d'Images' à la Conquête du Monde, Paris.
Long and detailed study of the cinema's treatment of exotic subjects and locales, including the many exploring expeditions which took film of their travels.

LERNER, D., 1958, *The Passing of Traditional Society*, Glencoe.

LEROY, M. and CANFIELD, A., 1953, *It Takes More than Talent*, New York.

LEVANT, OSCAR, 1965, *Memoirs of an Amnesiac*, New York.
Fascinating, gossipy tales about the making of some of the most famous Hollywood musicals. Interesting life, too.

LEWERANZ, A. S., 1929, 'An Analysis of the Academic Achievement and Mental Level of 257 Elementary School Pupils in Relation to Frequency of Attendance at Motion Picture Theatres', Los Angeles City School District, Psychological and Educational Research Division, typescript, unpublished, on file in USC library.
'It would seem that motion pictures are not a help to a child in his school work and, in fact, excessive going may be a detriment to academic achievement' (average going makes no difference?).

LEWIS, H. T., 1930, *Cases on the Motion Picture Industry*, Harvard Business Reports, 8: New York.
Business school analyses of case studies mostly concerning distribution and exhibition but with a few examples of how banks and finance companies scrutinize producers.

— 1933, *The Motion Picture Industry*, New York.
Sane descriptive survey of the industry, trying to show the relation of the industrial structure to what is made. 'It is probably safe to say that in many respects the central problem confronting the motion picture industry is the problem of what pictures to produce', p. 81.

— 1933, 'Motion Pictures – Industrial Development' *Encyclopaedia of the Social Sciences*, New York, 11: 58–65.
Unexciting industrial history, not nearly as clear as Hellmuth (1950).

LEYDA, JAY, 1960, 'A Chinese Adventure', *Films and Filming*, 6: September, 11f.

309

BIBLIOGRAPHY

— 1961, *Kino*, A History of the Russian and Soviet Film, London. Authoritative and scholarly, if rather long and poorly written. Explains clearly how, until cinema was brought into the first five-year plan in 1928, most effort was put into organizing the medium rather than regimenting its style. In twenty years of Stalin the industry was re-organized nine times, degenerating to the production of sycophantic historical travesties, and things came to such a pass that in 1953, only five fiction films were made. See review by Thorold Dickinson in *Sight and Sound*, 1960, 29: 202–3.

LIPPMANN, MAX, 1967, *Film:* Ein sozialpsychologisches Phänomen. Die Darstellung des judischen Menschen im Film. Wangen. Two essays by a German/Jewish film critic published in memoriam.

LIU, A., 1966, 'Movies and Modernization in Communist China', *Journalism Quarterly*, 43: 319–24. How films were mobilized to aid the Great Leap Forward and also its retrenchment. Film shows were integrated 'agitprop' sessions, with talk before, during and after. There was a decentralization of newsreel and documentary production.

LO DUCA, G. M., 1957, 1960, 1962, *L'Erotisme au Cinéma*, 3 vols., Paris. Duca is the cinema's rival to Ashbee, the Victorian bibliographer of pornography – except that Duca sticks to pornographic suggestions made in quite legal films. If his text, with graphs and equations, is intended as serious that's too bad. I prefer his explanation that he started out to write a thesis but found that stills said more than words and his publisher J. J. Pauvert agreed!

LOOS, ANITA, 1966, *A Girl Like I*, New York. Sparkling autobiography by a writer who knew everyone in Hollywood in the teens and twenties.

LOUNSBURY, MYRON O., 1966, The Origins of American Film Criticism 1909–1939, Ph.D. thesis, University of Pennsylvania, unpublished. (1) Has the prevailing tone of American film criticism always been liberal-thematic, or is this only a post-war phenomenon? (2) Has film literature ever before entered the form-content debate? Yes to both. Serious reviewing begins in 1909 and is mainly in trade and entertainment journals. In the twenties we see regular newspaper and magazine reviewing and the first specialist journals. The output levels off in the thirties, and the decade concludes with Lewis Jacobs (1939) which codifies a tradition of judgement and taste. Before 1909 the movies were treated as a scientific or economic phenomenon. In 1909 films about the Thaw scandal produced threats from New York's chief of police and a counter-attack was mounted by scenario writers who argued against censorship because the film was a genuinely artistic medium which would improve as time went on.

LOVAAS, O. I., 1961, 'Effect of Exposure to Symbolic Agression on Aggressive Behavior', *Child Development*, 32: 37–44.

When children could choose between toys (ball or 'aggressive' doll), those who had been exposed to agressive cartoon film engaged in more play behavior with the hitting dolls than did those who had been exposed to the nonaggressive film. Either the children gained 'increased sensitization to behavior with aggressive consequences' or 'the film constituted a discriminative stimulus marking the occasion when aggressive behavior would be reinforced positively or at least not punished' p. 43.

LOVELL, ALAN, ed., 1968, *Don Siegel – American Cinema*, London.
A study of Siegel, concluding with a questionnaire about Hollywood, which an array of British critics staunchly defend.

LOW, RACHEL and MANVELL, R., 1948, *The History of The British Film*, Vol. I, 1896–1906: London.

— 1949, *The History of The British Film*, Vol. II, 1907–1914.: London.

— 1951, *The History of The British Film*, Vol. III, 1914–1918: London.
Authoritative, officially sponsored (by the British Film Institute and the British Film Academy), highly detailed history.

LUCHAIRE, JULIEN, 1924, 'Relations of the Cinematograph to Intellectual Life', memorandum submitted to the League of Nations Committee on Intellectual Co-operation, reprinted in Seabury (1929), 235–64.
Against 'silly sentimentality or . . . fantastic adventures' in films and for films as art. It is too exclusively plebeian now. Seabury describes it as 'a brilliant memorandum'. [In the light of Gans (1966) I would say 'haven't we travelled a long way since then?']

LUDWIG, EMIL, 1946, 'The Seven Pillars of Hollywood', *Penguin Film Review*, 1: 90–5.
How Hollywood ruins and destroys talent; its incompetence will lead to its downfall.

LUNDERS, L., 1963, *L'Attitude Actuelle des Jeunes devant le Cinéma*, essai de synthèse, Bruxelles.
Elaborately documented and tabulated Catholic analysis, trying to show that more family films should be produced as they are more profitable than adult films.

LURASCHI, LUIGI, 1947, 'Censorship at Home and Abroad', *Annals* (1947), 147–52.
In addition to screening material that might be bought and produced, studio censorship departments have to be sensitive to the odd sensitivities of foreigners who especially dislike: 1) period films which clash with the local view of events; 2) almost any treatment of the Second World War and its aftermath by Hollywood; 3) light comedies set in the USA.

MACCANN, R. D., 1951, 'Documentary Film and Democratic Government', an Administrative History from Pare Lorentz to John Huston. PhD thesis, Harvard University (Government Dept.), typescript unpublished.

— 1962, *Hollywood in Transition*, New York.
Informative survey of Hollywood's major structural change, much of the book consisting of strung-together short pieces. No startling conclusions.

— 1964, *Film and Society*, New York.
Excellent anthology confined only by the paucity of material to draw from. Not much on the social organization of film making or evaluating.

MACCOBY, ELEANOR, 1964, 'Effects of the Mass Media', in M. Hoffman and L. Hoffman, eds., *Review of Child Development Research*, New York, 323–48.
Useful review of the literature with respect to effects on children, arguing, among other conclusions, that media-addiction is a psycho-social danger signal, but also that effects can be counteracted and even nullified by the teaching and example of the significant people in the child's life.

—, LEVIN, H. and SELYA, B. M., 1955, 'The Effect of Emotional Arousal on the Retention of Aggressive and Non-Aggressive Movie Content', *American Psychologist*, 10: 359*ff*.
The hypothesis that if the viewer is angry at the time of viewing he will tend to recall: 1) more of the aggressive material; 2) less of the non-aggressive material than viewers who are in a more neutral state, was tested and confirmed.

—, LEVIN, H. and SELYA, B. M., 1956. 'The Effects of Emotional Arousal on the Retention of Film Content: "A Failure to Replicate" ', *Journal of Abnormal and Social Psychology*, 50: 3–11.
The thesis of their (1955) that 'the nature of the movie content recalled by . . . children a week later was . . . a function of their emotional state at the time of viewing' is refuted. Children in an induced highly frustrated and aggressive state remembered slightly less well the aggressive content of a film. The hypothesis underlying was either selective perception (in an aggressive state one focuses on material congruent with the drive state) or the drive-reducing function of the aggressive fantasies may increase their 'recall probability'.

— and WILSON, W., 1957, 'Identification and Observational Learning from Films', *Journal of Abnormal and Social Psychology*, 55: 76–87.
Learning is by *doing*. Yet we learn from films. We identify. We identify with those like us for gratification, with those unlike us to escape guilt (by displacement). 'We suspect that anxiety over the expression of aggression is one of the sources of children's preference for animal heroes or space men', p. 77. While identification goes with class of aspiration, remembering is not significantly related to what the identificand is doing, except where aggression is involved, and this may be explained as selective perception based on need. Each sex identifies with itself, boys remember more aggression, girls remember Girl Alone and Girl Interaction situations. 'Memory for movie content appears to be influenced *both* by

identification with a character in the movie and by the "need relevance" of a particular kind of content for the viewer', p. 86.

—, — and BURTON, R., 1958, 'Differential Movie-Viewing Behaviour of Male and Female Viewers', *Journal of Personality*, **26**: 259–67.
Identification is related both to the 'need relevance' and the similarity in sex between viewer and character identified with. Eye movements were studied to decide if one watches who one is identifying with, or who the character one is identifying with is watching. Male viewers spend more time watching the males, than females do the females.

MCCORMACK, T., 1961, 'Social Theory and the Mass Media', *Canadian Journal of Economic and Political Sciences*, **27**: 479–89.
The mass media function to socialize and as a means of social control: they impose a coherence, a synthesis of experience, an awareness of the whole.

— 1966, 'Intellectuals and the Mass Media', *American Behavioral Scientist*, **9**: 31–6.
Mass society is biased towards interpretative rather than creative or critical communication. Intellectuals and journalists therefore need to co-operate, as academic freedom and freedom of speech may be inadequate safeguards.

MACDONALD, DWIGHT, 1954, 'A Theory of Mass Culture', *Diogenes*, Summer 3: 1–17, reprinted in White and Rosenberg (1957).
His famous elitist theory of the tripartite division of High Culture, Folk Art and Mass Culture, with the latter seen as posing a threat as it oozes over the others, blurring boundaries and lowering standards. Mass Culture = *kitsch*. '. . . the silent film had at least the theoretical possibility, even within the limits of Mass Culture, of being artistically significant. The sound film, within those limits, does not.', p. 8. See the counter-attack of Brogan in *Diogenes*, **5**: 1954, 1–13.

MCKECHNIE, SAMUEL, 1932, *Popular Entertainment Through the Ages*, London.
Popular history which is a useful corrective to all notions of the corruption of mass culture, etc. Chapter on film only goes up to 1907.

MACLIAMMOIR, M., 1952, *Put Money in Thy Purse*, London.
Hired to play Iago to Welles' *Othello*, Macliammoir narrates the vicissitudes of the making of that film, mainly in Morocco. A sort of tribute to Welles' extraordinary powers of survival in the film jungle, and his undiminished creative energy, for the result was a marvellous film.

MCLUHAN, H. M., 1951, *The Mechanical Bride*, New York.

— 1962, *The Gutenberg Galaxy*, Toronto.

— 1964, *Understanding Meda*, New York.

— 1967, *The Medium is the Massage*, New York.

BIBLIOGRAPHY

— and CARPENTER, E., 1960, *Explorations in Communication*, Boston.

— and FIORE, Q., 1968, *War and Peace in the Global Village*, New York.
The codified works of McLuhan are these, plus Stearn (1967), which has a complete bibliography, and Rosenthal (1968). They are not difficult, and are the only way to approach seriously the thought of the master. See the appendix to this volume for my use of them and some comments.

MCPHERSON, MERVYN, 1956, 'Memoirs of a Publicist', *Films and Filming*, 2: April, 6–7; May, 15; June, 16–17 and 34; July, 9.

MCVAY, D., 1967, *The Musical Film*, London.
Chronological annotated list of American musicals.

MCWILLIAMS, CAREY, 1946, *Southern California Country*, New York.
Chapter XVI, entitled 'The Island of Hollywood', is an incisive sociological and historical analysis of both the suburb and the state of mind.

MADDISON, J. and OLDFIELD, R. C., 1947, 'The Social Sciences and the Cinema', BBC Third Programme talk, unpublished.
A conversation à propos the Paris conference on 'filmology' organized by Cohen-Séat. Oldfield stressed the selective and reconstructive aspects of seeing films – even to the distant screen apparently looming large. Maddison mentions that in Nigeria, a panning shot of a building was seen as a building rushing by.

— and VESSELO, A., 1947, 'The Cinema and the Narrative Arts', BBC Third Programme talk, unpublished.
Civilized exchange comparing the cinema with the theatre and the novel, stressing literalness of cinema and cliché's of narrative devices. Vesselo defends, stating that film versions of classics should concentrate on their integrity as films.

MALRAUX, ANDRE, 1946, *Esquisse d'une Psychologie du Cinéma*, Paris.
Trite observations like 'Un acteur de théâtre, c'est une petite tête dans une grande salle; un acteur du cinéma, une grande tête dans une petite salle', p. 34. Lack of entr'actes, compares film with novels, sequences with chapters, etc. US cinema (circa 1939 when the essay was written) is good journalism not literature. 'Marlene Dietrich n'est pas une actrice comme Sarah Bernhardt, c'est un mythe comme Phryné', p. 51.

MANVELL, A. R., 1944, *Film*, Harmondsworth.
My generation was breast-fed on the milk of his tolerant liberalism and gentle social consciousness. Yet we had to grow up and demand solid foods – some of which, naturally, turned out to be ginger pop (*Cahiers, Movie*, etc.).]

— 1946a, 'The Philosopher at the Cinema', *Sight and Sound*, 15: 18–20.
Decent and balanced review of Cohen-Séat (1946) and Mayer (1945).

— 1946*b*, *A Survey of the Cinema and its Public*, London.
Part III, 'The Influence of the Film On Society', calculates that a couple
attending twice-a-week may spend £24 p.a. Although US studies suggest
delinquency (i.e., Payne Fund, q.v.), here the roots are thought to be
deeper. Stars and documentaries are touched on.

— 1953, 'Britain's Self-Portraiture in Feature Films', *Geographical
Magazine*, August, 222–34.
Regionalism gives richness; understatement is demanded, so music
becomes especially important (Bax, Vaughn Williams, Walton, Bliss,
Alwyn, Rawsthorne); and heavy reliance is placed on skilled actors. There
was hardly any indigenous film in the quota days of the thirties. The war
films were understated. The quintessential film which made foreigners at
last understand was *Brief Encounter*. Post-war there was the naturalistic
style and the theatrical style. Our best films are indigenous.

— 1955, *The Film and the Public*, Harmondsworth.
Excellent popular introduction to some of the sociological questions raised
in the text of this volume; chapter 3, on the Industry and chapter 4, on the
audience are especially clear-headed.

— 1967, *New Cinema in Europe*, London.
A hasty survey of European cinema since 1945. Too short to pay attention
to style, speaks instead of schools and plots. Good stills.

— 1968, *New Cinema in the USA*, London.
Companion to (1967). Prolific, solid and indefatigable, Manvell argues
that 'American film making, at its best, has never been higher in standard
than during the 1950s and 1960s; the better films have become more
varied, more individual and enterprising, and more striking in their
technical presentation than they have been in the past', p. 8. Argues at
p. 23*ff*. that the Hollywood system was undermined by 1) HUAC; 2) the
Anti-trust suit; 3) Television. Quotes Dilys Powell quoting Kubrick (p.
26): 'The source of supremacy of the majors was their power to make
money. When they stopped making money, they sent for the independent
producers'. His argument on p. 25, 'Hollywood had for the most part been
bad for the film maker' – because of competition, distance from mainstream of American life, enervating sunshine and smog – is surely mistaken.
[Competition is a forcing house, it enforced discipline and created standards of sheer professionalism which still mark off American television and
films from all competition. This volume seems rather hastily written,
resuming plots; in fact he is so abrupt at the end there is the impression he
is running out of space. Good stills.]

—1969, *New Cinema in Britain*, London.

MARGOLIS, HERBERT F., 1947, 'The American Scene and the Problems of
Film Education', *Penguin Film Review*, 2: 54–63.
Problem of audience tastes and standards.

— 1948, 'The Hollywood Scene: The American Minority Problem', *Penguin Film Review*, 5: 82–5.
Crossfire stimulates a few notes on Hollywood's record in dealing with the themes of anti-semitism and anti-negro prejudice; hopes are e. pressed for the future.

MARLOWE, FREDERIC, 1947, 'The Rise of the Independents in Hollywood', *Penguin Film Review*, 3: 72–5.
The mushrooming of independent production is due to the high profitability (and thus low risk) of film making; the desire to share these profits on the part of directors, writers and actors; and the tax advantage that allows such gains to be taxed at 25% as capital gains rather than at up to 90% as income. Studios also allow cells of independents: viz. DeMille and Wallis at Paramount; Bette Davis and Errol Flynn at Warners; Dudley Nichols and Leo McCarey at RKO; Mark Hellinger and Mervyn LeRoy at Universal International. Marlow itemizes the various advantages of this development and even hopes that more poetry and realism will be a by-product.

MARX, GROUCHO, 1959, *Groucho and Me*, London.
Chapter 18 *et seq.*, recounts their experiences in Hollywood after their arrival in 1931. Told with crackling and wit and intelligence, but no real explanation of why they broke apart and stopped making films, except perhaps Groucho's feeling he was getting on.

MARX, HARPO, 1961, *Harpo Speaks*, New York.
A disappointment to those wanting the inside story or insights into some of the most hilarious films ever made.

MAUERHOFER, HUGO, 1949, 'Psychology of Film Experience', *Penguin Film Review*, 8: 103–9.
The cinema situation would be one with no light or sound which did not come from the screen. Time seems to go more slowly, space is perceived differently. The spectator needs heightened action and he is passive as in sleep. Films are daydreams, private and anonymous, which have a psychotherapeutic function.

MAY, M. A. and SHUTTLEWORTH, F. K., 1933, *The Social Conduct and Attitude of Movie Fans*, New York.
'That the movies exert an influence there can be no doubt. But it is our opinion that this influence is specific for a given child and a given movie. The same picture may influence different children in distinctly opposite directions. Thus in a general survey such as we have made, the net effect appears small . . .'

MAYER, ARTHUR, 1953, *Merely Colossal*, New York.
Amusing, anecdotal account of the business by a man in it from way back.

BIBLIOGRAPHY

— 1956, 'Myths, Movies and Maturity', *Saturday Review*, **39**: 7–8.
Reviews the crisis of Hollywood's great contraction, the urge to gimmickry,
the concentration on blockbusters – *Marty* being an exception to prove the
rule. '. . . when, frequently before it is realised, the word leaks out that a
film has that indefinable something called B.O. [box office], the hardships
of babysitters, parking, and high admissions are as nothing . . . How this
advanced information is disseminated is a mystery that the industry has
not fathomed in all its fifty years', p. 8.

MAYER, GERALD M., 1947, 'American Motion Pictures in World Trade',
Annals (1947), 31–6.
One-third of the finished negative cost is recouped abroad. Despite their
popularity, American pictures are discriminated against. Not only an
economic, but a cultural export.

MAYER, J. P., 1945, *Sociology of Film Studies and Documents*, London.
Follows Blumer (1933) in thinking children must have difficulty in coping
with film experience because it is always so extreme.
Denny and Meyersohn: 'An excellent attempt to analyze films for once
through the audience and through film content. Interesting investigation
of film influence, particularly interviews conducted through *Picturegoer*
magazine in Britain which asked for the influence of movies on personal
decisions and on dreams'.
Fearing (1950): 'his discussion . . . is marred by commitment to the
doctrine that the reaction of the audience to the film is non-rational and
childlike. He makes use of the conceptions of Levy-Bruhl, the philosopher-
anthropologist, in regard to the alleged prelogical character of the
primitive mind'.
In *Penguin Film Review*, 3 Kay Mander criticizes it for being turgid, too
wide-ranging and somewhat oddly based on questionnaires answered by
the readers of *Picturegoer*.

— 1948, *British Cinemas and their Audiences*, London.
This is a thin follow-up to his (1945), using even more of the questionnaire
data. Reviewed in *Penguin Film Review*, 9: 121*ff*. He thinks the data shows
the audience is not getting what it wants: he cites Box (1943).

MAYERSBERG, PAUL, 1967, *Hollywood, the Haunted House*, London.
A book describing producing, acting, directing, writing in Hollywood in
the form of travel notes, commentary and selections from interviews with
a few co-operative Hollywood personalities. Basically rather slight, by a
young Englishman who spent a few months there writing a script.

MEAD, MARGARET, 1959, *The Study of Culture at a Distance*, New York.
Selection from some studies including attempts to read anthropological
information from Chinese films.

MEADOW, ARNOLD, 1944, *An Analysis of Japanese Character Structure*,
Based on Japanese Film Plots and Thematic Appreception Tests on

Japanese Americans, unpublished report of the Institute for Inter-
cultural Studies, New York.
Problem: to explain the aggressive character trait of the Japanese. Using
'modern' psychoanalytic ideas (Fromm, Horney, Kardiner), and basing
himself on seven films, plus the tests, he finds the Japanese are aggressive
because of institutional factors which systematically cause severe conflict
and then threatening frustration. [Uses only plots, not the style or treatment of the films: he is not really interested in what the films *qua* films
tell him at all.]

MELUCCI, M., (1942?), *Redemption in Hollywood*, A Translation of Movie-
fanship into Philosophical Pathos, Newark.
Referred to in Melucci (1943). I have not managed to trace a copy.

— 1943, *Political Cinematology*, How Motion Pictures and TV will shape
the political destiny of America, Newark.
Prescient work, addressed to Republicans, about how conventions and
presidential candidates acceptable to the people have to have been made
real on the screen. Analyses Wilkie's poor screen presentation and warns
about Dewey's. The screen could remedy indifference and it does reveal the
real man.

MENDELSOHN, HAROLD, 1966, *Mass Entertainment*, New York.
A systematic attempt by a social psychologist to argue the value of the
mass media as gratifications, as socializers, as communicators, and as
potentially the vehicles of culture. Outstanding bibliography.

MERCEY, A. A., 1947, Review of Kracauer (1947) in *Annals* (1947), 173–4.

METZGER, C. R., 1947, 'Pressure Groups and the Motion Picture Industry',
Annals (1947), 110–15.
Hollywood is pressured both inside and out: by law, religion, government,
unions, professions, races, internationally, by trade, political and other
groups.

MEYERSOHN, ROLF B., 1957, 'What do we Know About Audiences?',
Journal of Broadcasting, 1: 220–31.
Comparison of radio and television, arguing that the high costs of the
latter demand millions more viewers than the lesser costs of the former. It
follows that there can be many radio stations, each catering to different
tastes, and it is the proper medium for educational broadcasting.

— 1961, 'A Critical Examination of Commercial Entertainment', in R. W.
Kleemeier, ed., *Ageing and Leisure*, New York, 243–72.
Books require more mental exertion than films or television. They are less
predigested. It is 'better' to produce than to consume entertainment, better
to play baseball than to watch it. Do they encourage newcomers? Do they
discourage experts? Creativity = personal creativity regardless of the
audience. The mass audience is undifferentiated, the mass media product

is undifferentiated, there are only trivial differences in it, or purely commercial differences. Television doesn't programme for older people as they are not an attractive marker or prospect. It could be useful to bridge the generation gap, but it doesn't.

MICHAEL, DONALD M., 1951, *Some Factors Influencing the Effects of Audience Participation on Learning from a Factual Film*, Human Resources Research Laboratories. Headquarters Command, USAF, Technical Research Memorandum, Washington.
Practice at answering questions about film content is much more significant than motivation: *knowing* you are going to be questioned produces the best performance.

— and MACCOBY, N., 1953, 'Factors Influencing Verbal Learning from Films Under Varying Conditions of Audience 'Participation', *Journal of Experimental Psychology*, 46: 411–18.
Learning from films is improved by audience participation. Is this due to the practice they get at recalling the material, or because they have higher motivation to recall, knowing they will be involved in discussion? Experiment shows the former.

'Milestones of Musicals', 1956, *Films and Filming*, 2: January, 5.

MILLARD, W., 1955, 'A Study in the Sociology of Communication: Determinants and Consequences of Exposure to American Motion Picture Films in the Near and Middle East', PhD thesis, Columbia University, typescript unpublished.
Studied Greece, Turkey, Jordan and the Lebanon. Persons already oriented towards the West differ in their moviegoing behaviour from those who are not. Those groups which lack social standing (the young, the better educated, the women) may be more inclined to turn their attention to a medium which pictures life in another land than are groups which are respected and well-established in the social structure. Moviegoing weakens loyalty to traditional values and is an agent for cultural change. Frequent moviegoing increases the likelihood of holding an unfavourable image of Americans – who are seen as fun-loving, frivolous, little concerned with serious thoughts, rude and immature, not morally strict, more interested in money and a good time than in virtue. Americans appear to worship romantic love, 'leg shows', and violence.

MIRAMS, G., 1951, 'Drop That Gun', *Quarterly of Film, Radio and Television*, 6: 1–20.
A New Zealand censor says there is a cult of death and violence in movies!

MITNICK, L. and MCGINNIES, E., 1958, 'Influencing Ethnocentrism in Small Discussion Groups Through a Film Communication', *Journal of Abnormal and Social Psychology*, 56: 82–90.
A group shown an anti-enthnocentrist film – *The High Wall* – and a group shown this and discussing it, showed changes in attitudes against control group. 'Attitude change in response to a persuasive sound film was a joint

function of opportunity for discussion of the film and initial attitude. Predisposition alone was not related to attitude change', p. 87. Effects face in the film-alone group more quickly.

MITRY, JEAN, 1963, *Esthetique et Psychologie du Cinéma*, I, *Les Structures*, Paris.
Attempt to update Arnheim by going beyond the simple problem of the differences between life and screen life to ask how and why. Discusses how 'the author' is a variable from film to film, country to country. 'On pourrait dire d'un film que c'est un ensemble de variables géométriques dont la mobilitié est organisée selon une composition arithmétique de la durée', p. 28.

MOELLENHOFF, F., 1940, 'Remarks on the Popularity of Mickey Mouse', *American Imago*, 3: 19–32.
Mickey Mouse is a hermaphrodite, a desexualized phallus. His world is one of childhood wishes and fantasies in which adult-figures and machines are cheerfully vanquished. Action proceeds like in dreams. He is the pleasure principle incarnate.

MOLEY, RAYMOND, 1938, *Are We Movie-Made?*, New York.
Presentation in popular form of the argument of Adler (1937).

— 1945, *The Hays Office*, New York.
Sycophantic history of the self-regulation agency of the United States motion picture industry.

Monopolies Commission, The, 1967, *Films: A Report on The Supply of Films for Exhibition in Cinemas*, London.

MONTAGU, I., 1929, *The Political Censorship of Films*, London.
Film censorship has grown up under fire regulations and is used to prevent or discourage politically controversial films. 'Power without responsibility is the negation of the English Constitutional Principle. Realization of the position must lead to its revision', p. 21.

— 1964, *Film World*, Harmondsworth.
'Purist' look at the film – emphasizing the visuals and arguing that when speech and speaking control the rhythm, then 'the result will be dull, dreary and certainly less eloquent and moving then a well-constructed "silent" film'. See Rotha and Griffith (1963).

MONTANI, A. and PIETRANERA, G., 1946, 'First Contribution to the Psychoanalysis and Aesthetics of Motion Pictures', *Psychoanalytic Review*, 33: 177–96.
The unconscious stream of pre-logical and a-causal images has a natural affinity to the motion picture. A director who allows them to well up without the intervention of literary translation can create 'pure cinema' – a source in the human psyche long waiting to be tapped. 'Motion picture is

... an expressive natural disposition of man, which until our century sought a proper technical means for the practical recording of its products ... *There is a psychic film at the base of our unconscious thought'*, p. 179. 'Motion-picture, like the dream, must follow pre-logical ways', p. 183. As a dream can compress a great deal into a short time, so can a film. The attraction of motion and movement is phallic. In the vulgar pictures the audience identifies with stars; shares an equality as parts of a mass; regresses to infantile narcissism in the darkness. How could this pure cinema of unconscious images be understood? It would have no literary meaning at all, but a meaning of its own, like a symphony. [This illiterate, but extraordinary, paper deserves comment. The crucial error, it seems to me, is the notion that art is self-expression. A symphony has a meaning as an ordered and disciplined piece of music – usually variations on a set of themes. The welling-up of unconscious images is not an ordered or disciplined creation at all – indeed it is the reverse. I would contend their pure cinema would be private and unintelligible, no more art than the results of a free-association exercise. Films have extra-literary conventions, it is true, but not in the way this odd theory requires.]

Monthly Film Bulletin, 1933 to date, London.
Essential reference journal, reviews all feature films released in the UK, and a selection of the documentaries and shorts. Indexed by title and director. Of late has developed a series of 'check lists' of the work of important personnel.

MOORE, COLLEEN, 1968, *Silent Star*, New York.
Contains many good anecdotes and much information on what it was like to be a player in the silent era. The youth of the girls is explained by the harsh revealingness of primitive film stock. In the early days everyone seems to have been far from corrupt.

MORIN, EDGAR, 1954, 'Préliminaires à une Sociologie du Cinéma, *Cahiers Internationale de Sociologie*, 17: 101–11.
Plea for an anthropology of the cinema which incorporates all the social sciences, and does not founder on the dichotomy of art *versus* industry.

— 1956, *Le Cinéma ou l'homme Imaginaire*, Paris.
The cinema reveals the atavistic tendencies towards magic and primitive attitudes of modern man. Product of a technological era, this seventh art presents the archaic, partially imaginary reality found in dreams and myths.

— 1960, *The Stars*, New York.
'The star is a specific product of capitalist civilization; at the same time she satisfies profound anthropological needs which are expressed at the level of myth and religion. The admirable coincidence of myth and capital, of goddess und merchandise, is neither fortuitous nor contradictory. Star-goddess and star-merchandise are two faces of the same reality: the needs of man at the stage of twentieth century capitalist civilization'. p. 141.

Special chapters on Chaplin and Dean. Uneven, but useful. Excellent selection of stills.

MORRIS, LLOYD, 1949, *Not So Long Ago*, New York.
At pp. 16–217 there is an informal social history of films and of Hollywood, following Ramsaye to 1926 mostly, and then overlapping with Hampton, Jacobs and Rosten. Some original research and freshly written.

Motion Picture Producers and Distributors of America, Inc., 1932, 'The Motion Picture Industry', in J. G. Glover and W. B. Cornell, eds., *The Development of American Industries*, New York, pp. 745–61.
Panegyric to itself, a cursory history, 'the social importance of any art may be said to depend largely upon the number of people it serves', p. 748. The marked social progress of the screen is made evident by how the Boy Scouts and the YMCA, *et al*, recommended so many films for children and family. Its indirect contribution to the world of business staggers the imagination. 'The clothing of the farm boy cannot be distinguished from that worn by the city boy . . . they fashion their clothes . . . after those seen on the screen', 751. Invested capital $2 billion. This article compares ill with that of Hellmuth (1950).

MULLALLY, F., 1946, *Films: An Alternative to Rank*, An analysis of power and policy in the British film industry, London.
An attack on the Rank company's grip on the industry, its vertical integration, and a proposal for a government distributing agency to help independent producers and frustrate American power in British industry.

MULLER, HANS, 1957, *Der Film und sein Publikum in der Schweiz*, Zurich.
Elaborate questionnaire study of Swiss production, audience, and other media.

MUNSTERBERG, HUGO, 1916. *The Photoplay: A Psychological Study*, New York.
1) The limitations of the medium serve to free and isolate things and events – Arnheim develops this theory; 2) film bears special relations to the processes of human consciousness. Pudovkin, Eisenstein and Spottiswoode hold this view; 3) photography has a specially intimate relationship to 'reality'.

NATHORST-BOOS JR., ERNST, 1935, *Om Amerikas Filmindustri*, Stockholm.
Studio by studio description of Hollywood, interesting photos of the top executives of the time.

National Council of Public Morals, 1917, *The Cinema: Its Present Position and Future Possibilities*, Report of the Cinema Commission of Inquiry, London.
Priests, teachers, chief constables, social workers, censors, in an extraordinary convulsion of small print, call for tighter censorship, brighter

cinema lighting (cf. 'the moral danger of darkness', the vestibule as 'danger point' for 'young girls'), and for films exciting the finer emotions.

NEBLETTE, C. B., 1926, 'The Place of the Motion Picture in Modern Life', *Photo-Era*, 57: 175–80.

NELSON, DONALD M., 1947, 'The Independent Producer', *Annals* (1947), 49–57.
All producers were once independent. The desire for independence is not so much financial as a drive to be free. There were around 100 independents in Hollywood in 1946. Disproportionately, many of the most successful films were independent productions. The anti-trust suit will help independents.

NIELSEN, GERHARD, 1965, *Filmens Psykologiske Virkningen*, Copenhagen. General Study.

NOBLE, PETER, 1948, *The Negro in Films*, London.
Impassioned account of the negro in films and the improvement latterly. Relates backwardness to social factors. Argues that a better attitude could also be good business. Lots of material on negro actors and negro background.

— 1950, *Hollywood Scapegoat*, the biography of Erich von Stroheim, London.

— 1956, *The Fabulous Orson Welles*, London.

NOLAN, W. F., 1965, *King Rebel*, New York.
Lively biography of John Huston, with no serious intention of appraising his career or the effects on his work of the loss of Hollywood discipline.

NUSSBAUM, M., 1960, 'Sociological Symbolism of the "Adult Western" ', *Social Forces*, 39: 25–8.
'Every culture has at some precise time in its growth created a folk-type art form in response to its inner turmoils and strivings to satisfy its need for expression of its character', p. 25. Why now? Westerns involve: 1) the equivalent of foreign adventure; 2) an heroic hero; 3) individualism; 4) uncomplicated contact with nature; 5) a mixture of good and evil, with some characters on the right side of the law and some on the wrong; 6) gun as *deus ex machina*. They appear now as a revolt against reason, over our powerlessness in a world of machines, Heisenberg, and Godel. [N.B.: the author fails to answer his own questions.]

ODLUM, FLOYD B., 1947, 'Financial Organization of the Motion Picture Industry', *Annals* (1947), 18–25.
Of the box-office dollar, theatre expenses take up 0·83 (i.e., salaries 0·16, rent 0·15, operating costs 0·20, film rent 0·32). Of the 17 cents profit, six goes in tax, leaving a net of some 11 cents. Of the 32 cents paid for film

rent, 12 goes for cost of prints, transport, and advertisement, leaving 20 cents for Hollywood. This is broken up as follows:
Film production

Screenplay	0·01
Producer	0·01
Plant and materials	0·07
Cast	0·04
Overhead	0·04
	0·17
Tax	0·01
Net profit	0·02

Rate of recoupment (*domestic*)
43% of total in 13 weeks
73·5% of total in 26 weeks
nearly 100% in 60 weeks.

In the years 1942–5, the rate of return on capital was 14% compared with 9·8% in all manuracturing. Films have low elasticity of demand, i.e., they fluctuate less than 8% for a 10% change in disposable income (Department of Commerce definitions). While between 1929 and 1933, outgoings on two other items with low elasticity of demand – shoes and food – dropped 41% and 40% respectively, films fell only 33%.

O'FLAHERTY, LIAM, 1935, *Hollywood Cemetery*, London.
Savage satire on Hollywood. Jack Mortimer, producer, discovers a colleen *in flagrante* and takes her to Hollywood as a mystifying woman. Complications involving an Irish novelist, Mortimer's secretary, backers, and wife, climax in the colleen and writer happy in Mexico, and a transvestite subsitute for the mysterious goddess of love leading a triumphal religious procession.

O'HARA, ROBERT C., 1964, *Media for the Millions*, New York.
A textbook on communications, stressing selection, simplification, stereotyping and myths of media, paying due attention to films, not just television.

OLSEN, M., 1960, 'Motion Picture Attendance and Social Isolation', *Sociological Quarterly*, 1: 107–16.
'People go to the movies because they cannot find other more personal forms of recreation . . . movies act as a substitute form of recreation for people who lack close friends', p. 108. Social isolation – measured by population increase, rate of house moving, and an urbanism index – turns out to be fairly highly correlated with film attendance.

ORTON, W. A., 1933, 'Motion Picture – Social Implications', *Encyclopaedia of the Social Sciences*, New York, 11: 65–9.
A mass art run by Jews for hicks cannot be expected to aspire very high. There is no disinterested patronage – except in Russia [sic]. Uninfluenced

by the Film Societies 'the commercial film has . . . followed rather than led the herd mentality', p. 66. The industry is conservative and placatory to the moralists. In Germany, Italy and Japan the State takes a hand. The film does not affect children much, what is needed is constructive not restrictive policies. Film exports may spread culture (how high is dubious) but also exacerbate international tension.

OSTEN, GERD and LUNDKVIST, ARTUR, 1950, *Erotiken i Filmen*, Stockholm. Predecessor to Lo Duca (1957, etc.) q.v.

PALACHE, ALBERT, 1944, *Tendencies to Monopoly in the Cinematograph Film Industry: Report of a Committee Appointed by the Cinematograph Films Council*, London.

PALMER, EDWIN O., 1937, *History of Hollywood*, Hollywood.
Charming but dull parish history of Hollywood, from Pleistocene to the Oscar ceremonies, written by a leading citizen of pre-movie times, a doctor-cum-banker. Some useful details on early movie-making; more on how to finance hospital building.

PANOFSKY, E., 1947, 'Style and Medium in the Motion Pictures', *Critique* 1: 5–18 and 27–8, reprinted in Talbot (1959).
Useful, sane, unsnobbish account of the force and vitality of the cinema. Suggests that Hollywood adopts the axiom 'give the public what it wants', when they could get away with 'the public wants whatever we give it'.

PATALAS, ENNO, 1963, *Sozialgeschichte der Stars*, Hamburg.
Headings include: young girls, *femmes fatales*, comics, flappers, etc. Proceeds by category and then star by star, with sketches of careers – includes a geneaology tracing one star's 'relations' to others, which is the *reductio ad absurdum* of all such classifications.

— 1967, *Stars, Geschichte der Filmidole*, Frankfurt and Hamburg.
A second paper edition of (1963) by a different publisher, with an epilogue at the end of stars and with the geneaology and booklist missing.

Payne Fund Studies, The, 1933–5, New York.
See under Blumer (1933), Blumer and Hauser (1933), Charters (1933), Cressey and Thrasher (1933), Dale (1933), Dale (1935a, 1935b), Dysinger and Ruckmick (1933), Holaday and Stoddard (1933), May and Shuttle-worth (1933), Peters (1933), Renshaw, Miller and Marquis (1933), Thurstone and Peterson (1933). These studies in a way marked the high point of the campaign begun in the 'twenties in America to agitate about the immorality of Hollywood and its films. In a decade which saw prohibition, the producers tried various means of presenting a united front of responsibility to the world. The publication of these studies coincided with the black year when the Production Code was codified, beginning of nearly twenty-five years during which special ingenuity had to be devoted to developing a code of nuances to convey what the Code would not have

portrayed. As to these studies, Adler (1937) summed it up thus: 'In short, the scientific work that has been done is of little or no practical value to the prudent man. On the crucial point – the influence of motion pictures on moral character and conduct – science has not improved o: altered the state of existing opinion. In those few instances in which the scientific work has been well done and reported with proper scientific restraint . . . the findings do not warrant any moral judgments about the effects discovered. We must proceed, therefore, without the benefit of science'.

Penguin Film Review, 1946–49, Harmondsworth.
A bi-annual journal of research and criticism, succeeded by *Cinema*. Short-lived, alas; scholarly and useful. Too highbrow.

PERLMAN, W. J., ed., 1936, *The Movies on Trial*, The Views and Opinions of Outstanding Personalities Anent Screen Entertainment Past and Present, New York.
More fall-out from the controversy stemming from the Payne Fund studies and leading by way of Adler and Moley's contributions. Some contributors, e.g., judges, say films are great, others, e.g., priests and highbrows, froth at the mouth. This is the first reader on the social side.

PERRY, C. A., 1923, *'The Attitude of High School Students Towards Motion Pictures'*, New York.
37,500 high school students surveyed and found not to attend too much or to choose too foolishly, and to have their reading stimulated not stunted. Published by the National Board of Review.

PETERS, C. J., 1933, *Motion Pictures and Standards of Morality*, New York.
Is conduct in films above or below previously held standards of morality? Adler summarizes: '. . . suggests that there may be a way of condemning the movies no matter what one finds. If they deviate at all they are bad; if they deviate towards the disapproved end, they are also bad; perhaps, even if they deviate towards the approved end, they are bad; and maybe if they do not deviate at all, they are bad because they should deviate towards the approved end'.

PETERSON, T., JENSEN, J. W. and RIVERS, W. L., 1966, *The Mass Media and Modern Society*, New York.
Textbook on the sociology of the media, including the industry, audience, and effects. Sensible, but scanty as it insists on covering all the media under each heading. Movies rarely get more than a page in each chapter. Selective and not very useful bibliography.

PHILLIPPON, O., 1952, 'L'Influence du cinéma sur l'enfance et l'adolescenes, l'enquête nationale francaise', *Nouvelle Revue Pedagogique*, 7: 526–30.
'A child or an adolescent who frequents the movies more than once a week needs psychiatric attention and should be looked after', *Psychological Abstracts*, 27: 7088.

BIBLIOGRAPHY

PHILLIPS, GIFFORD, 1966, *The Arts in a Democratic Society*, Santa Barbara.

PICKFORD, MARY, 1956, *Sunshine and Shadow*, New York.
Autobiography of the first and the biggest star; unfortunately as sweet and anodyne as those 'life is beautiful' volumes she used to produce when active in films.

Political and Economic Planning, 1952, *The British Film Industry*, A report on its history and present organization, with special reference to the economic problems of British feature film production, London.
Authoritative economic and organizational history of the British film industry. Suggests that Rank's loss of nearly £3½ million in 1948 made the industry inescapably dependent on public funds; it came about because the industry was geared exclusively to high-cost production. Useful comparative chapter. Brief chapters on audience and effects drawing mainly on government statistics and Dale (1935a). Lucid account of finance (front money, end money, front part of the end money, completion guarantees, etc.).

Political and Economic Planning, 1958, *The British Film Industry 1958*, London.
Up-dates the 1952 report in the light of the shrinkage of cinema numbers, the attempts made to prevent the showing of films on television, and deplores the continuing mystery concerning how much British films make overseas.

POPPER, KARL, R., 1962, *The Open Society and Its Enemies*, London.

Positif, 1957 to date, Paris.
A critical journal peddling an inimitable French intellectual's mixture of Marxism and popcult.

POWDERMAKER, HORTENSE, 1947, 'An Anthropologist Looks at the Movies', *Annals* (1947), 80–7.
An anthropologist must analyze films, study the audience, and learn how pictures are made to do functional analysis. The film functions on an emotional level to produce day dreams. *Belief* in the dichotomy between business and art creates conflicts. In them love is emphasized at the expense of work, friendship, etc. Money-making is rarely a motive – despite the high salaries of Hollywood. Stars seen in intimate close-up on screen and in fan magazines, are a substitute for personal relations in the increasingly impersonal and lonely modern urban society. Films also are an escape, a means of self-understanding, killing time, taking a rest, a courtship pattern.

— 1950, Hollywood, *The Dream Factory*, New York.
Chapter I, hypothesis: 'The social system in which they are made significantly influences their content and meaning', p. 3; 'Like all institutions, they both reflect and influence society', p. 15.

Chapter II. Hollywood dominates Los Angeles and is an ingrown community. Salaries are high there and yet there is no other Hollywood to compete. Sex is talked of, but not excessively done. The conflict between art and commerce is based on a false either/or philosophy. An industry badly needing creative people should be aware that to them industrialization is anathema. Success and failure are contagious. There is an unplanned crisis atmosphere. Anti-intellectualism. Social controls include option contracts, high salaries, censorship, 'give the audience what it wants', and there being no security of employment. The personalism and friendliness conceal impersonal manipulations. Hollywood could have a different social organization – that it does not raises a problem. Chapter III. Hollywood strives to mass produce by formulas, i.e., 'message pictures lose money', 'a love story is the most important element in an A picture', 'no picture can be about prize fighting'. [Powdermaker contentiously maintains that only formula westerns make money, other formulas are no good and the exhibitors complain that returns are falling off. Cf. the contrary thesis maintained by Alloway (1964) and myself that cycles can lead to exploration and invention – is the explanation of bad films not the formulas, but creative poverty?] The pollster is the wrong person to advise on the production and editing of films. The audience cannot like a film until it has seen it, and shackles on a creative artist make him inefficient. [Yet does her solution, more knowledge of the audience, really solve the studios' very genuine problem?] By 1946, one-third of production was by independents, (p. 51). The basic conflict of mass production: uniformity is cheap; but originality is expensive. Summary of production code prohibitions pp. 58–65. Taboos. The code is puritannical, 'does not belong to this world' p. 78, conflicts with Christianity, creatively restrictive and yet does not work and is easily evaded. Pp. 71–72 a general attack on Hollywood's cardboard stereotypes. Code ignores some values like truth, understanding, and freedom to choose, tries to impose mechanically a single set of values on a pluralistic society.

Chapter IV. 'Front Office'. Front office men are rarely admired as skilled film men. Power relations are feudal because people are property, everyone has his price. High salaries, concealment of picture profit, 100% profit is normal. Insecurities revealed in the need for colossal box office successes, and the attribution of this to an 'instinct' for what the public wants. There is a frantic pace and a desire to cap each success.

Chapter V. 'Men Who Play God'. The businessmen worship profits not creativity and they bully the artists.

Chapter VI. 'Lesser Gods But Colossal'. Producers mediate between the creative and the business personnel. They grew out of 'supervisors'.

Chapters VII, VIII and IX. 'The Scribes', 'Assembling the Script'. 'The Answers'. There is a preponderance of hacks and compromisers among the writers because what they get out of it is a rain of dollar bills (p. 183). [She glosses the problem of whether the talent for screen writing differs from journalism, plays, novels.]

Chapter X. 'Directors'. They have a key role yet most are reduced to glorified traffic cops. They only have first cut rights.

328

Chapters XI, and XIII. 'Acting in Hollywood', 'Stars', 'Actors are People'. The breaks. Talent. Option contracts equal semi-slavery. Stars are sex-symbols, pp. 252–3. Stars do not sell films. Good script plus lightweight cast is more likely to do well at the box office. Starless films do well.
Chapter XIV. 'Emerging from magic'. 'The breaks' is a primitive, magical, anti-intellectual philosophy out of kilter with the technical sophiscation of Hollywood's culture.
Chapter XV. 'Hollywood and the USA'. Hollywood is totalitarian in its domineering attitudes and interest in power for power's sake. Can it democratise?
[All in all a very thoughtful and informative book, inclined not to discriminate between what people do and what they say they say they do; also rather keen (like practically everything published between 1935 and 1950) to warn us of the Terrible Dangers looming.]

— 1966, *Stranger and Friend*, New York.
In this professional autobiography, the anthropologist confesses that of all her field studies – in Melanesia, Mississippi, Africa – the most difficult was in Hollywood. She was never able to become accepted in the community and she always felt alien.

PRATT, G. C., 1966, *Spellbound in Darkness*, Rochester.
Extremely rich collection of contemporary comment on silent films.

PRATT, JOHN, 1954, 'In Defense of the Western', *Films and Filming*, 1: November, 8.
Western as the central tradition of American film making. Two themes: central or epic tradition of winning the West; and the thrilling suspenseful personal drama. They show the American attitude to culture and shifting experiences that give universal appeal.

PRICE, BYRON, 1947, 'Freedom of Press, Radio, and Screen', *Annals* (1947), 137–9.
Censorship and government control was resisted during the war and must be resisted now 'for no civil liberty once lost can easily be regained' p. 138.

PRICE, IRA, 1938, *A Hundred Million Movie-Goers Must be Right*, Cleveland.
While vigorously defending the judgments of the box-office against those of the critics he admits that films could be a little more serious from time to time.

PRIESTLEY, J. B., 1937, *Midnight on the Desert*, A Chapter of Autobiography, London.
Chapter X, pp. 166–202, is his reflections after a short spell of work in Hollywood. His problem is why Hollywood films are good but not better. He explains this by the geographical isolation of Hollywood where the

main concern is with making films – this makes them good, although Los Angeles is a tawdry, overgrown, small town, but their isolation from the rest of the world prevents their professionalism from drawing from anything except itself. If the economic restrictions under whic'ı films have to be made applied to books or plays the effect would be disastrous.

PRODOLLIET, ERNEST, 1963. *Kleines Lexikon des Wilden Westerns, Geschichte und Filme*, Zurich.
Alphabetically arranged.

QUIGLEY, M., 1937, 'Public Opinion and the Motion Picture', *Public Opinion Quarterly*, 1: 129*ff.*
In their early days of popularity, films told more about their audiences than they told their audiences. Pressure groups like the Legion of Decency were set up to correct that. Films influence fashion, promote American exports, and, if left to compete freely, American films are peerless throughout the world. Little educational use has been made of them as yet, but as costs fall there will be.

— 1947, 'The Importance of the Entertainment Film', *Annals* (1947) 65–9.
Legalistic-wordy defence of the entertainment film as vicarious escape, and of the Production Code as 'the best conceivable instrument' of control.

— 1948, *Magic Shadows*, Georgtown.
Subtitled *The Story of the Origin of Motion Pictures* This is 'the guide to the discovery of the principle and techniques behind movies'.

QUIGLY, ISABEL, 1968, *Charlie Chaplin the Early Comedies*, London.

RABIL JR., ALBERT, 1968, 'The Future as History and History as the End: An Interpretation of Marshall McLuhan', *Soundings*, 1: 80–100.
Competent and sympathetic analysis, showing McLuhan as a Fall of Man and Redemption through Apocalypse theorist. Suggests he evades the problem of the ends to which technology is put.

RAMSAYE, TERRY, 1926*a*, *A Million and One Nights*, New York.
This bulging history of the cinema up to 1926, is sometimes cited as an authoritative work, which it is not. Much of the information is all right, but there are also myths – especially challenged are those connected with Edison. Its industrial history needs to be closely compared with that of Hampton (1931) and Jobes (1966).

— 1926*b*, 'The Motion Picture' in *Annals of the American Academy of Political and Social Science*, 128: 1–19.
Very condensed summary of his (1926*a*).

— 1947, 'The Rise and Place of the Motion Picture', *Annals* (1947), 1–11.
The humble peoples' art costs millions and can only cater to the majority. Those who resist censorship expect the family theatre to meet the standards

of the art museum. The public has no stake in the current anti-trust suit. The theatre had retreated to the metropolitan centres and become so sophisticated that when sound cinema raided plays, a censorship outcry arose and the Production Code was upon us.

RATHBUN, J. B., 1914, *Motion Picture Making and Exhibiting*, Chicago.
Charming period handbook on everything from Muybridge's studies of movement to positioning carbon arcs.

RAYNOR, HENRY, 1950, 'Nothing to Laugh At', *Sight and Sound*, 19: 69*ff.*
Attack on what *Sequence* (q.v.) called 'Huggetry' (after the post-war British comedy series centred around the lower class Huggett family), i.e., the class snobberies of British film makers as revealed in their amused and patronizing attitude to working class types.

— 1950, 'Heaven Lies About Us', *Sight and Sound*, 19: 319*ff.*
The appeal of films about children to adults has a tinge of idealization.

REED, REX, 1968, *Do You Sleep in the Nude?*, New York.
The collected interviews with show business people by the highly talented, young, and very perceptive writer. His sessions with Ava Gardner and, especially, Warren Beatty, are in the realm of *tours de force*.

REID, J. H., 1961, 'Both Sides of the Camera', *Films and Filming*, 7: February, 15–16; March, 31–2 and 39.
An analysis of Otto Preminger's work in the cinema.

REID, L. R., 1938, 'Amusement: Radio and Movies', in H. E. Stearns, ed., *America Now*, New York, 3–35.
Hollywood is geared to the mentality of twelve-year olds, and its weird business organization, extravagance, equation of quality with expenditure, makes it fall far short of what its great technical capability gives it potential for.

REISZ, KAREL, 1951, 'The Showman Producer', *Cinema 1951*, 160–7.
Study of de Rochemont, Hal Wallis: contrasts the UK and the USA and points up the lack of showmanship in UK producers.

— 1952, 'Substance into Shadow', *Cinema 1952*, 188–205.
Discussion of the transforming of novels into films: *Maltese Falcon, To Have and Have Not, Intruder in the Dust, A Walk in the Sun*.

— 1953, 'Hollywood's Anti-Red Boomerang', *Sight and Sound*, 22: 132*ff.*
Argues that Hollywood's crop of anti-Communist films is ludicrously inept.

RENAN, S., 1967, *An Introduction to the American Underground Film*, New York.
A factual guide-book rather than a critical appraisal.

RENSHAW, S., MILLER, V. L. and MARQUIS, D., 1933, *Children's Sleep*, New York.
Moley: '. . . children do not sleep as quietly after seeing a motion picture as after not seeing a motion picture', p. 30. Now Adler: 'The most that can be said for this piece of research, in the light of our present knowledge of fatigue and sleep, is that the movies were found to produce changes in the motility of children's sleep in the direction of more quiet and more restless sleep than usual. What this means . . . can be determined "only after more intense research studies have been carried out", only after we have more knowledge of the physiology of sleep and fatigue in relation to each other and to health', quoted in Moley, p. 31.

Report of the National Recovery Review (Darrow) Board Relating to the Motion Picture Industry, 1934, Washington.
Referred to in a number of works. Huettig (1944) lists it under unpublished data.

RHODE, E. and PEARSON, G., 1961, 'Cinema of Appearance', *Sight and Sound*, 30: 160–8.
Jungian view of films.

— 1966, *Tower of Babel*, London.
Intelligent essays, perhaps too highbrow-literary.

RICE, JOHN R., 1938, *What is Wrong with the Movies?*, Grand Rapids.
Answer, chapter II is titled 'Movies are Made by Sinful, Wicked People, Unfit to be Examples'. Author explains why he quit the habit and why *Snow White and the Seven Dwarfs* is bad because 'Children will get accustomed to thinking the movie theatre is a proper place to be entertained', p. 13. Cf. Harding (1942).

RICHARDSON, TONY, 1961, 'The Two Worlds of the Cinema', *Films and Filming* 7: June, p. 7f, reprinted in Geduld (1967).
Reflections on the industry, comments: 'I'm thrilled I went there because I know that I never want to make a film in Hollywood again . . . When one enters the Hollywood set-up one is always promised the earth, and you think you can beat them at their own game and that you can handle these people. But you can't, because the underlining [tape mistranscribed? 'undermining,?] is not big and dramatic. It is not as though there are great issues in which one refuses in a black and white way not to compromise, it's in every tiny detail that the whole quality of the picture is eroded away leaving nothing. At no time can you win on a particular issue. Everything slides away, and everyone who works on the film is in that atmosphere. The product starts as a mirage which gradually slips away as reality takes over'. 'It is impossible to make anything interesting or good under the conditions imposed by the major studios in America'.

RICHIE, DONALD, 1961, *Japanese Movies*, Tokyo.
A readable and rapid historical survey of the Japanese cinema.

BIBLIOGRAPHY

— 1965, *The Films of Akira Kurosawa*, Berkeley and Los Angeles.
A film by film survey of the career of perhaps the most brilliant film maker in the world.

— 1966, *The Jcpanese Movie*, Tokyo.
A running commentary on films one needs to have seen, especially later in the volume. Mostly theme analysis, little of style. A companion to his and Anderson's (1959) and his (1961). This volume traces the film as the history of Japanese popular thought, on self, society, resignation or acceptance, social conscience, faults of governments, emancipation of women, end of feudalism, assertion of individuality.

RICKETSON, F. H., 1938, *The Management of Motion Picture Theatres*, New York.
Everything is covered from publicity stunts to how often to police the rest rooms. A Bonus 600-word glossary, many of them very esoteric, e.g., brail, standee, shuttle sheet, snipes, travel ghost, etc.

RIEGEL, O. W., 1938, 'Nationalism in Press, Radio and Cinema', *American Sociological Review*, 3: 510–15.
The media are channels for nationalism, and only modification of the economic and political bases of nationalism will cause it to wither.

RIESMAN, DAVID, 1956, 'The Oral Tradition, The Written Word, and the Screen Image', *Film Culture*, 2, no. 3: 1–5.
Oral societies are face-to-face small groups. Empires, larger in space and time, require transportable information and permanent record. Oral communication tends to freeze social structure, though occasionally a prophet can wreak change. Post-literate society structurally unstable. Orality binds people, print loosens bonds, creates space, even isolates. Those in touch with media, e.g., radio, have an utterly different horizon of expectations.

—, GLAZER, NATHAN and DENNY, REUEL, Abridged edition, 1955, *The Lonely Crowd*, New York.
Full of fascinating asides about films and media, fitting filmgoing and film-content into their theories of society and personality-formation. Their feel for the differences between the media and their effects is good, but their cursoriness comes out when they use mainly plot summaries – e.g,. discussing the little girl's family problems in *Curse of the Cat People* and ignoring the main focus of the film.

— and E. T., 1952, 'Movies and Audiences', *American Quarterly*, 4: 195–202.
'. . . films are too mature, move too fast for older people to catch on to and catch up with . . . The realization that the old have to learn the languages . . . would be a first step toward appreciating some of the ambiguities of communication in which the movies and other media are involved – ambig-uties related to the tensions between the generations, between social

classes, and between character types', p. 195. '. . . young people . . . resort to the movies . . . in order to understand complex networks of interpersonal relations . . . connected with a change . . . from . . . "innerdirection" to . . . "other-direction" ', p. 196. Radio and television research went ahead because of the need to show advertisers the effects.

RIEUPEYROUT, J. L., 1952, 'The Western: A Historical Genre', *Quarterly of Film, Radio and Television*, 7: 116–28.
'Far from being glamorized fiction, the Western is rather a faithful representation of a too-often unrecognized reality. It is the expression of a typically American mythology. Its heroes and its gods offer us a thousand epic pictures and unfold on the screens of the universe a new, gigantic, and vivid Bayeux tapestry' p. 128. Mainly discusses Fords' *My Darling Clementine* and *Fort Apache* and defends their historical liberties in the name of verisimilitude.

— 1953, *Le Western*, Paris.
History of the *genre*.

— 1963, *La Grande Adventure du Western*, (1895–1963), Paris.
Authoritative and important French historical analysis.

RILEY, J. W. and M. W., 1959, 'Mass Communications and the Social System', in Merton, Broom and Cottrell Jr, eds., *Sociology Today*, New York.
A sketch of communications research. Looking at the recipient we can discuss his motivation, his audience self-selection, and his (selective) perception. Looking at the recipient and his primary group we can consider reference group theory, i.e., the reference of behaviour to the values of the groups belonged to. Then we can go on to look at the recipient in the context of the wider society where sociological analysis in general applies. Then we can look at the communicator and the many factors influencing him (p. 564). There are instrumental versus expressive messages. [This article is mainly a literature survey aimed at articulating a programme for a sociological approach to mass communications.]

RIMBERG, J., 1959, 'Motion Picture in the Soviet Union 1918–1952: A Sociological Analysis', PhD thesis, Columbia University, unpublished.
'Film content and the volume of film production in the Soviet Union are determined by a process of compromise between Communist Party officials, film industry artists and the Soviet audiences who constitute the primary potential market for the exhibition of Soviet Films.' The party aims at political films, artists at works of art, audience at entertainment. Most writers consider only two groups, forgetting all three have power and can be shown to use it.

— 1960, 'Social Problems as Depicted in the Soviet Film – A Research Note', *Social Problems*, 7: 351–5.
During the NEP, 15% of films did not deal with social problems at all,

and less than 50% featured Communist solutions. Later, 100% showed social problems and 80% Communist solutions. 1934–40 saw again some frivolous films, but two-thirds of all films had Communist solutions to social problems. After the war no films featured unsolved problems, 80% featured problems and Communist solutions. Throughout it was frequently the non-Party non-Komsomol person who provided the Communist solution.

RIVKIN, A. and KERR, L., 1962, *Hello Hollywood*, New York.
Anthology of pieces on Hollywood, largely by writers, many extremely witty and unusual.

ROAD, SINCLAIR, 1946, 'The Influences of the Film', *Penguin Film Review*, 1: 57–65.

ROBERTS, J. M., ARTH, M. J. and BUSH, R. R., 1959, 'Games in Culture', *American Anthropologist*, 61: 597–605.

— and SUTTON-SMITH, B., 1962, 'Child Training and Game Involvement', *Ethnology*, 1: 166–85.

—, SUTTON-SMITH, B. and KENDON, ADAM, 1963, 'Strategy in Games and Folk Tales', *Journal of Social Psychology*, 61: 185–99.

ROBINSON, DAVID, 1968, *Hollywood in the Twenties*, London.
Elegant survey in the series with Baxter (1968) and Higham and Greenberg (1968).

ROBINSON, W. R., 1967, *Man and the Movies*, Baton Rouge.
An adventurous anthology of original pieces mainly by academic literati and none the worse for it. Range is from skin flicks (Chappell) through westerns (McMurty) to Antonioni and Bergman. Especially good also Dillard on horror films, Peck on films versus television, Robinson on the experience, Hardison on Hitchcock, Fiedler on novels of Hollywood, and Slavitt on critics. Excellent bibliography, partly annotated. Highly recommended.

ROCHE, CATHERINE DE LA, 1949a, 'That "Feminine Angle" ' *Penguin Film Review*, 8: 25–34.
Examination of the alleged woman's picture and woman appeal.

— 1949b, 'No Demand for Criticism', *Penguin Film Review*, 9: 88–94.
Outlines the social structure and value of professional criticism.

ROGERS, GARET, 1963, *Scandal in Eden*, New York.
Novel.

Rôle Intellectual du Cinéma, Le, 1937, Paris: Société des Nations, Institute International de Co-operation Intellectuelle, New York.
The first part is a country-by-country review of the history of the cinema

Second part has some papers on the intellectual role of the cinema by various hands. 'Langage, le cinéma a tous les vices et toutes les vertus d'un langage; il sert à l'excellent et au pire. Les pêcheurs puritains qui le condamnent ne voient pas sa face brillante; les thuriféraires qui l'encensent aveuglément se bouchent les yeux devant son hémisphère ténébreux.', Arnoux, p. 163. Of special interest are the essays by A. Consiglio and Walt Disney abstracted elsewhere.

ROSENBERG, B. and WHITE, D. M., 1957, *Mass Culture*, Glencoe.
Bulky reader containing six pieces on the cinema: Gans (1957), Elkin (1950), Kracauer (1950), Powdermaker (1950), Wolfenstein and Leites (1950), Larrabee and Riesman on *Executive Suite*. Bibliography of 75 items at 338–40.

ROSENTHAL, RAYMOND, 1968, *McLuhan: Pro and Con*, New York.
Another anthology of writings on McLuhan, some very good, none overlapping with Stern (1967), but also lacking an interview with the master. The McLuhan secondary material is rapidly getting out of hand.

ROSENTHAL, S. P., 1934, 'Changes of Socio-Economic Attitudes Under Radical Motion Picture Propaganda', *Archives of Psychology*, No. 166.
Rosenthal wanted to study the effect of propaganda on a wide range of attitudes. Education is to train us to handle data, draw conclusions and be critical; propaganda presents conclusions to be swallowed. Psychology students were shown a Russian silent propaganda 'newsreel'. This effectively changed attitudes on a wide range of socio-economic problems in the direction intended by the propaganda. It was more effective on attitudes related to the subject matter of the film than on those remotely related. There may be a boomerang effect. Dislike of stereotyped terms is easier to arouse than eradicate. Age and radicalism are not correlated. Intelligence and radicalism are.

ROSS, BETTY, 1955, 'Back to the Golden Era', *Films and Filming*, 3: August, 7.
On the Mexican industry. New book, *Mexican Cinema* is announced. I can find no trace of it.

ROSS, LILLIAN, 1950, *Picture*, New York.
Story of the making of John Huston's film *The Red Badge of Courage* in Hollywood in 1949, from scripting to final print. Written originally for the *New Yorker*, this hilarious piece of acid-throwing understandably got Miss Ross banned from MGM forever. Her thesis seems to be How Good Artistic Intentions Were Thwarted by Executive Idiocy; I say 'seems' because the author makes no first person comments of any significance at all.

— and ROSS, HELEN, 1962, *The Player*, New York.
A series of self-descriptive and ruminative interviews with some top players of stage and screen.

ROSS, MURRAY, 1941, *Stars and Strikes*, New York.
The Hollywood work force is a quarter of a million people, their payroll is 400 million dollars. Organized labour used Hollywood as a trojan horse to invade 'open shop' Los Angeles. They first tried to unionize the craft in 1916. As a result the MPA was formed. By 1921, there had been three strikes. In 1925, inter-union disputes stopped. 1926, the Motion Picture Alliance signed the Studio Basic Agreement. There were lots of jurisdictional problems, and problems of contract labour. The Academy of Motion Picture Art and Sciences was originally an industry-wide employee's organization and very successful. Later it was stripped of its union functions. Central Casting was a triumph. Executives ignored craftsmen because of the 'cynical belief which pervades Hollywood that unless one is very highly paid he is not to be favoured with the attention and time of film magnates', p. 216. Dealing with such people is delegated to minor officials. NRA helped unionization. Unions resist change. Musicians fought canned music in the name of theatre orchestras (p. 218).

— 1947, 'Labor Relations in Hollywood', *Annals* (1947), 58–64.
From Los Angeles being an open, to its being by the time war came, a closed, shop, films have had a stormy labour history.

ROSTEN, LEO, 1941, *Hollywood, The Movie Colony, the Movie Makers*, New York. Denny and Meyerson: 'Three years' first hand research in the movie city has produced a major presentation of the life, practices, and values of the community'. Not only that; it is witty, and throws cold water on several myths, including that of the highly paid actors, and the gripes of the well-paid writers.

— 1947, 'Movies and Propaganda', *Annals* (1947), 116–24.
As HUAC sets out to investigate Hollywood propaganda, the question arises what is propaganda? Books and magazine serials are not accused of it, any more than are newspaper reports. But films involve groups. Film producers have posed as purveyors of uncontroversial entertainment, distinguishing entertainment from propaganda sharply. Intentions and controversy are essential in propaganda, therefore the audience is involved: in Russia a film on free elections is propaganda, in the USA not. The Senate investigated war propaganda in films and producers demanded their constitutional freedom. There are some significant differences between films and newspapers and radio: 1) they gain no advertising revenue; 2) they are dependent on a mass referendum (b.o.); 3) they are more costly; 4) they depend upon overseas revenues; 5) they have no 'local' audience; 6) they have no 'local' identity; 7) they have no interlocking directorates; 8) there is no one-film town, i.e., no absence of competition. But the film makers should resist the temptations of the anodyne and use the freedom the constitution gives them wisely.

— 1956, 'Hollywood Revisited', *Look*, 20: 17–28, reprinted in Rivkin and Kerr (1962).
He notes four great changes since his (1941): television; wide-screen; middle age; and smog. Producers are no longer gods, are more business-

like; there is less nepotism, fewer professional sycophants, less high spending. There is still a lot of egocentricity, boasting about psychiatrists, a few night clubs. Most popular television programmes originate in Hollywood, this involves, e.g., Disney producing the equivalent of four features per week for television. In 1945, there were 790 actors and actresses on contract, in 1956 only 209. In 1940, 240 writers were on contract, in 1956 only 67. After the Second World War, Hollywood no longer had to work hard to convince everyone films were significant. The HUAC row tore Hollywood apart in feuds not yet forgotten.

— 1961, 'The Intellectual and the Mass Media: Some Rigorously Random Remarks', in Jacobs (1961), 71–84.
A commonsensical defence of the media, pointing out that the criticisms come from a guilty elite (cf. Shils (1957)), that the *New York Times* versus the *Daily News*, the BBC versus the ITA, cases, show what the public really prefers. He shows that the maligned profit motive can be replaced by a BBC that suppresses Churchill, and would have crumpled if it had had to suffer the furore CBS survived when it interviewed Kruschev. 'It seems to me that most of the horrors of human history have been the work not of skeptical or cynical or realistic men, but of those persuaded of their superior virtue', p. 79.

ROTHA, P. and GRIFFITH, R., 1963, *The Film Till Now*, London.
Latest edition of the massive history of the film by Rotha up to 1930, on to 1948 by Griffith (very wrong-headed) and in later editions again, but more cursorily, by Rotha. This book, and those of Arnheim (1933), Balazs (1952) and Montagu (1964) are the work of intellectual critics who swallowed the aesthetics of Eisenstein and Pudovkin whole, and who never reconciled themselves to the coming of sound or the triumph of Hollywood. They die hard with their Russian heroes – Arnheim and Balazs have barely altered their views in thirty years, Montagu's book must surely have been written then and rapidly up-dated. Together they form something like the orthodox canon of criticism if we include also Manvell (1944) and Jacobs (1939).

ROWSON, S., 1935, *A Statistical Survey of the Cinema Industry in Great Britain in 1934*, London.
Just that.

RULE, J. T., 1953, 'Movies and TV: Murder or Merger', *Atlantic*, 192: 55–9.
Discusses 3-D, wide-screen, predicting that they will rescue films when properly used, and that films on television will become the fashion and they will be assets to theatre-showing, like music-on-record or theatre. Pay television will come too.

SAFILIOS-ROTHSCHILD, C., 1968, ' "Good" and "Bad" Girls in Modern Greek Movies', *Journal of Marriage and the Family*, 30, 527–31.
Twenty five movies were analysed and all make the traditional Greek distinction between 'good' girls – chaste until marriage – and 'bad' girls

who engage in premarital sex and who are thus dishonoured and un-acceptable marriage partners. Good girls are always faithful, never initiate the relationship, motherly, and do not demand reciprocation of their goodness; bad girls are sexually and otherwise aggressive and adopt a take it or leave it attitude towards others. Good girls are poor or working class, bad girls are rich or venal. The rich are shown as eccentric, unscrupulous, cruel. This maybe because up to the 1950s the only way to get rich was to compromise standards. Author suggests the stereotypes are *a*) true, *b*) self-serving in that many poor girls are rivalled by rich ones (marriage to a rich woman is an avenue to upward mobility), so a happy ending for the poor and virtuous is reassuring.

SALUMBIDES, V., 1952, *Motion Pictures in the Philippines*, Manila (?).
Not even any straightforward statistics.

SANDER, A. U., 1944, *Jugend und Film* ' "Das Junge Deutschland" Amtliches Organ des Jugenführers des Deutschen Reichs', Berlin.
Theoretical essay in Nazi ideas on the role of film for German youth.

SANDERS, TERRY B., 1955, 'The Financing of Independent Feature Films', *Quarterly of Film, Radio and Television*, 9: 381-9.
Valuable description of the setting up of finance.

SANT'AGATA, C. R., 1966, 'Motion Picture Advertizing in the United States: A Study to Determine Its Changes', MA thesis, UCLA, un-published.
History of advertising techniques up to *West Side Story*.

SARRIS, ANDREW, ed., 1967, *Interviews With Film Directors*, New York.
'Unfortunately, most scholarly works on the cinema are still written from a predominantly sociological viewpoint, and most directors are still sub-ordinated to both the studio and star system that allegedly enslave them', p. iii. Introduction is a good survey of the history of film history and criticism and a plea for the director and for Hollywood. The interviews vary, most are pretentious.

SCHARY, DORE, 1950, *Case History of a Movie*, New York.
'As Told to Charles Palmer': step by step account of the making of *The Next Voice You Hear*. Quite revealing (as, e.g., the non-inclusion of director William Wellman in editing discussions between Schary, Chief Editor Margaret Booth and editor Dunning).

SCHICKEL, R., 1964, *The Movies*, New York.
A good general introduction. See my favourable review (1966).

— 1968, *The Disney Version*, New York.
Excellent study of Disney and his relations to the dream of small-town America the Beautiful. This highly sensitive study was written without help from Disney or his organization.

SCHMIDT, G., SCHMALENBACH, W. and BACHLIN, P., 1948, *The Film*, Its Economic, Social and Artistic Problems, London.
Fruits of a Basle exhibition in 1943, this book uses pictures, tables and diagrams to do the job of books like Manvell (1944). Its view is the usual one, although it also stresses the passivity of the filmgoer who submits to the tyranny of monopoly.

SCHRAMM, W., ed., 1948, *Communications in Modern Society*, Urbana.
Set of conference papers giving useful elementary introduction to communications, with an annotated bibliography.

— ed., 1949, *Mass Communications*, Urbana.

— ed., 1955, *The Process and Effects of Mass Communications*, Urbana.
Readings on the theory and effects of mass communications. No piece more than mentions the film in passing.

— 1964a, *Mass Media and National Development*, The Role of Information in the Developing Countries, Stanford.
The importance of information flow in promoting social change is very great and the mass media are effective means of channelling information. Developing countries should make more use of them and who knows what wonders will result.

— ed., 1964b, *The Effects of Television on Children and Adolescents*, Paris, UNESCO, reports and papers on mass communications, No. 43.
Annotated bibliography plus introductory essay summarizing all studies to date.

— LYLE, J. and PARKER, E. B., 1961, *Television in the Lives of Our Children*, Stanford.
Excellent study which shifts the emphasis from, what does television do to children, to, what do children do with television. Overall results coincide with Himmelweit, Oppenheim and Vince (1958). Really good annotated bibliography.

SCHULBERG, BUDD, 1949, 'Hollywood', *Holiday*, 5: 34–49, 126–9.
Clever, but naive, portrait of Hollywood and its crisis. No awareness of the coming of gimmickry. Denny and Meyerson: 'Useful as a touchstone to both public and professional views of Hollywood, 1946–9, when the film industry was under its greatest postwar pressure to reform'.

— 1941, *What Makes Sammy Run?* New York.
From rags to riches as a film executive.

SCHULMAN, GARY, 1965, 'The Two-Step Flow Hypothesis of Mass Communication: A Reformulation Using Cognitive Dissonance Theory', PhD thesis, Stanford University, unpublished.
The two-step flow hypothesis is a poor predictor as it is existential and can only be confirmed, not falsified. People engage in interpersonal com-

munication to reduce cognitive dissonance and to avoid dissonance increase. This yields predictions which were confirmed.

SCHUMACH, MURRAY, 1964, *The Face on the Cutting Room Floor*, New York.
Scholarly and lively history of censorship in the USA.

SCHWARTZ, D., 1955, 'Mary Pickford: The Little Girl in Curls', *New Republic*, 132: 17–20.
Review of Pickford (1955) – Mary as the child-girl with sexual undercurrents. She was succeeded by Clara Bow: 'this exhibits Hollywood's sensitivity to national moods and the quickness with which it responds', p. 18.

SCHWARTZ, J., 1960, 'The Portrayal of Educators in Motion Pictures 1950–1958', *Journal of Educational Sociology*, 34: 82–90.
On the basis of plot summarizes in *Variety* and *The Green Sheet*, concludes that teachers are portrayed as frustrated, unattractive, unmarried. They pursue romance only outside the profession, either with outsiders, or after quitting it. Female educators are usually helpful, males often violent. Their non-academic pursuits are usually show-biz and crime.

SCOTT, E. M., 1957, 'Personality and Movie Preference', *Psychological Report*, 3: 17–19.
'Results seem to support the hypothesis that movie attendance is related, in some instances, to the central aspects of personality: (a) movie preferences serve as substitute outlets and (b) social values appear to determine the serious or less serious movie choice', *Psychological Abstracts*, 32: 1958, #4129.

SEABURY, W. M., 1926, *The Public and the Motion Picture Industry*, New York.
Idealistic attempt, inspired by the League of Nations, to advocate the conversion of the industrial and commercial regime of 'the greatest force and instrumentality in the world for the cultivation and preservation of the world's peace and for the moral, intellectual and cultural development of all people' (p. ix) into a public utility.

— 1929, *Motion Picture Problems*: the Cinema and the League of Nations, New York.
Because 'pictures produced in America, many of which are undesirable, unwholesome and unworthy of America, monopolize as much as 90 per cent of the screen time of the cinema theatres in many countries . . .' (p. 13), Seabury escalates his public utility idea to League of Nations Control. All well-meaning, but dreary and beside the point.

— 1930, *The Futile Exhibitor*: how the industry shackles your local movie manager, New York.

SEEMAN, MELVIN, 1966, 'Alienation, Membership and Political Knowledge A comparative Study', *Public Opinion Quarterly*, 30: 353–67.

341

We learn in accord with expected outcome and value of outcome. But also in accord with powerlessness/alienation. Alienation means poor learning of power-giving information; membership means good learning of power-giving information.

SELDES, GILBERT, 1924, *The Seven Lively Arts*, New York.

— 1937, *Movies for the Millions* (*The Movies Come From America* in the US), London.
History-cum-introduction to the art of. . . .

— 1951, *The Great Audience*, New York.
Seldes' first return to the mass media since his (1937) to argue, in his own words (1956) 'a rather ominous warning that these . . . popular arts which are also mass media might be used to keep us complacent and perpetually immature'. Very interesting material on the industry: argues that mediocre run-of-the-mill pictures help audiences decline. Audience habit does not carry over into middle and later years. Claims much of the satisfaction from the cinema is suited only to the immature and so becomes less acceptable with age. Films are myths by-passing the mind; by familiarity and by their capacity for endless repetition. On pp. 74 *ff* maps some of the imaginary rules of the world produced by the Production Code. The Code and the distribution system have purged the audience of the mature and thoughtful.

— 1956, *The Public Arts*, New York.
A disorganized report on the films, radio and television, arguing that their public character and their effects for good and ill require that some sort of control of their use be exercised by the public. It is odd that an author who so loves the media as they are, should feel the need to change them so radically.

Sequence, 1947–52, Oxford and London.
Short-lived, alas, brilliant, personal, enthusiastic journal of criticism edited originally out of Oxford to *épater* the BFI. Subsequently one of its founders, Gavin Lambert, took over *Sight and Sound* (and he in turn was succeeded by a veteran of *Sequence*, Penelope Houston); the other, Lindsay Anderson, went on to an active film, theatre, and television career.

SHAH, PANNA, 1950, *The Indian Film*, Bombay.
Charmingly breathless history of the Indian film, written as a PhD thesis in sociology and therefore containing some sociological emphasis but not much structural analysis. Stars pictured in Indian costume unintentionally revived dress and make-up modes of the past.

SHAW, ARNOLD, 1968, *Sinatra*, Retreat of the Romantic, New York.
Bulky biography of Sinatra's life and loves: unadulteratedly worshipful.

SHAW, IRWIN, 1949, 'Hollywood People', *Holiday*, 5: 53–61.
Everyone in Hollywood is connected with or yearning for the cinema.

Many are in other jobs only because they failed to get into films. The relaxed life and beautiful people produce remarkable children.

SHELLEY, FRANK, 1946, *Stage and Screen*, London.
Contrasts the two – theatre is less superficial, more humanizing. Cinema acting almost as interesting as stage acting.

SHILS, E., 1957, 'Daydreams and Nightmares! Reflections on the Criticism of Mass Culture', *Sewanee Review*, 65: 587–608.
Article-review of Rosenberg and White (1957) and Hoggart (1957) – pointing to the preponderance in the communications field of Disappointed Marxists. 'The critical interpretation of mass culture rests on a distinct image of modern man, of modern society and of man in past ages. This image has little factual basis. It is a product of disappointed political prejudices, vague aspirations for an unrealizable ideal, resentment against American society, and at bottom, romanticism dressed up in the language of sociology, psychoanalysis and existentialism', p. 596. Its roots are in a historical fantasy of community – 'they were all ideologists, hostile to human beings as they are, and this they share with Marxism'. The *Institut für Sozialforschung* in Frankfurt, tried to explain why the masses submitted to Fascism. Because modern industrial man was alienated and uprooted he accepted the spurious ethnic community offered by Nazism, *mutatis mutandis*, mass culture. 'the present pleasures of the working and lower middle classes are not worthy of profound aesthetic, moral or intellectual esteem but they are surely not inferior to the villainous things which gave pleasure to their European ancestors from the middle ages to the nineteenth century', p. 605. 'The culture of these strata, which were dulled by labor, illness and fear, and which comprised a far larger proportion of the population than they do in advanced societies in the twentieth century, was a culture of bear-baiting cock-fighting, drunkenness, tales of witches, gossip about the sexual malpractices of priests, monks and nuns, stories of murders and mutilations', p. 604–5.

— 1961, 'Mass Society and Its Culture' in Jacobs (1961), 1–27.
Mass society involves mass participation in society, there are no longer outsiders within the society (in contrast to the 'mass society is atomization' theories). The status of authority is lowered, the power of tradition weakened; there is more civility and enhanced individuality. Three levels of culture, refined, mediocre and brutal. Refined is rich in stock of items accumulated, so is brutal – the items are preserved in traditions; mediocre is short-lived. All levels are expanding, and especially the bottom two. The persistence of strength of tradition and orally transmitted culture as against centrally produced culture, shows the futility of making social diagnoses from centrally produced films, broadcasts, etc. (cf. Kracauer). The cultures overlap and feed on each other, the less, the greater their distance apart. Refined culture has not been specially threatened by mass society, creators not specially tempted or seduced, they still have an

343

audience. The audience for refined culture is a bit scattered in US, but prospects are good.

SHULMAN, IRVING, 1964, *Harlow*, London.
Scandalous and scandalized biography of the star Jean Harlow, who died mysteriously at the age of 26. Based on the memoirs of a publicist close to her.

SHURLOCK, G., 1947, 'The Motion Picture Production Code', *Annals* (1947), 140–6.
Description of the origin and working of Hollywood's self-censorship, the Production Code Administration, stressing how reasonable, helpful and universalist it is, not mentioning the $25,000 fine for non-compliance (see Brady (1947*b*)). 'The basic moral aspects of the code seem fundamental for all time', p. 145. [The code was drastically reformed nineteen years later after being violated repeatedly. Surlock seems unaware of the ludicrousness of the code's moralism to the outside world.]

SIEDZINSKI, E., 1958, 'A Study of Television Viewing Habits and a Comparison of these with the Interests and Habits of Radio, Motion Pictures and Reading, as Shown by Students in Selected High Schools in Metropolitan New York', PhD thesis, Fordham University.

SIEGEL, A. E., 1956, 'Film Mediated Fantasy, Aggression and Strength Of Aggressive Drive', *Child Development*, 27: 365–78.
Children shown a mild and then a violent (Woody Woodpecker) cartoon then left to play with a friend after each show, displayed no significant differences in aggressive drive. Conclusion: scores are not indices of drive strength. 'Fantasy aggression' was 'mediated' by the violent cartoon, i.e., violence = aggression, etc.

Sight and Sound, 1933 to date, London.
Official organ of the British Film Institute, this journal blossomed – under the editorship of Gavin Lambert (1949–1956) – into a sophisticated and literate, if a trifle staid and orthodox, journal of English criticism.

SINCLAIR, UPTON, 1933, *Upton Sinclair Presents William Fox*, 'A Feature Picture of Wall St. and High Finance' in 29 reels with a Prologue and Epilogue, Los Angeles.
Peeved by being ousted from his own company, William Fox sought out Sinclair and 'told all'. The book is a study in the economics of tycoonery in the film business. At p. 97, the main investment banking house line-ups are described:

Warners	..	Goldman, Sachs
Paramount	..	Kuhn, Loeb
Universal	..	S. W. Straus
Fox ..	..	Halsey, Stuart & Co, Hayden, Stone and Co.

These are the superbankers Fox turned to when needing fifty million dollars (p. 75). Mentions that the film *The Automobile Thieves* was shown before auto thefts had begun (circa 1905?), and the *New York World* began a campaign about films corrupting public morals (p. 36). The Motion Picture Patents Company (a trust) fixed the price of a scenario at $62.50, and no writers or actors names were to appear on the screen by their edict (pp. 39–40). This trust was bust by actions brought under the Sherman Act of 1912. On p. 51 he mentions the origins of the other executives: Laemmle was a clothing merchant; Lasky a band musician; Warner a shoemaker; Zukor a fur dealer.

Singapore, 1951, *Committee on Film Censorship, Report,* Singapore. A rather restrictive attitude is displayed in this report and directive to censor, written by C. H. Parkinson; e.g., the censor 'will bear in mind that the lowest standard of sophistication will be the one to be considered when assessing a film's suitability', p. 17.

SINHA, D., 1954, 'Sociological Aspects of Film', *Science and Culture,* 20: 281–3.
Films appeal to a bigger audience than radio and the press because they are cheaper than the former, and do not demand literacy as does the latter. In the anonymity of the cinema, in a dreamlike state of escape, the cinema-goer is highly receptive to influence. There has been much debate about the effectiveness of this influence, which has tended to cast doubt on its long-term persistence. Films should produce desirable sociological effects as well as entertain.

SISK, J. P., 1955, 'Life in the Movie Magazines', *Commonweal,* 61: 634–5.
Film magazines offer a vision of paradise, and a caricature of materialist values. The glamourization of the body is a form of disgusted reaction, a manifestation of the Manicheism which taints modern civilization.

SJÖMAN, VILGOT, 1963, *L. 136 Dagbok med Ingmar Bergman,* Stockholm. Diary of the making of *Winter Light* by a friend of Bergman's, who is also a film maker in his own right. French translation appeared in *Cahiers du Cinema.*

— 1967, *Jag var Nyfiken, Dagbok med mig själv,* Stockholm. Diary of the making of *I am Curious – Yellow.* Smug, and rather pleased with itself.

— 1968, *I am Curious Yellow,* New York. Scenario of the film, translated into English and lavishly illustrated.

SKINNER, JOHN, 1955, 'Censorship in Films and Dreams', *American Imago,* 12: 223–40.
'Motion pictures are modern substitutes for the myths and fairy tales of earlier times'. Story themes may be consciously borrowed from mythology

and may 'reassert timeless unconscious themes'. Some plots and some emotional conflicts are reproduced with monotonous regularity. The roles of men and women are often distorted in the Hollywood picture, e.g., *Adams Rib, Red River, The Outlaw.* The enjoyment of the motion picture is essentially a passive activity; while there may be a momentary release of tension, the original emotion returns, perhaps with additional force. *Psychological Abstracts,* 30: 1956, #4498.

SKOURAS, CHARLES P., 1947, 'The Exhibitor', *Annals* (1947) 26–30.
Standard industry equation of popularity and quality (Shakespeare was a box-office hit, etc.), attacks on intelligentsia and pedants. Defines 'grind house' (cheap downtown theatre for transients); 'road-show' (pricey showings, months in advance of general release); 'day and date first runs' (premiering a film in several theatres simultaneously); 'moveovers' (to smaller first-run house); and 'flexible booking' (extended runs).

SLESINGER, DONALD, 1941, 'The Film and Public Opinion', in Waples, D., ed., *Print, Radio and Film in a Democracy,* Chicago.
'How can we make the public pay for what it doesn't want?', p. 82. Film can carry a trend (like fashions in clothing), but not go against it. Ideas must be relatively acceptable and repeated in film after film. Newsreels, documentaries, government films, film societies. Research is going on.

SMITH, HENRY NASH, 1950, *Virgin Land,* Cambridge (Mass.).
Chapter IX: 'The Western Hero in the Dime Novel', Chapter X: 'Dime Novel Heroine', trace the origin of popular western myths. Such rapidly written, mass produced, formula fiction 'tends to become an objectified mass dream, like the moving pictures, the soap operas, or the comic books . . . The individual writer abandons his own personality and identifies himself with the reveries of his readers', p. 101.

SMYTHE, DALLAS W., *et al.,* 1955, 'Portrait of a First-Run Audience', *Quarterly of Film, Radio, and Television,* 9: 390–409.
Regulars 53%. Less than 10% over 45. Three-quarters under 30. One-third younger than 21.

Twice a week	34·2
Once a week	37·8
Two or three a month	13·8
Once a month	7·8
Less	6·4

Regulars are other-directed, casuals inner-directed. The former selecting largely on the basis of newspapers, stars, and their friends. The latter select by type, academy awards, etc. Musicals are the most popular type. The comedy syndrome (musicals, comedy, slapstick) *genre* is preferred; followed by serious films; then by action films. Of the most-liked pictures, most are serious.

BIBLIOGRAPHY

SNYDER, R. L., 1968, *Pare Lorentz and the Documentary Film*, Norman (Okla.).
A sober and scholarly biography of a documentary film hero, whose career was short and output small (three films).

SOMLO, J., 1948, 'The First Generation of the Cinema', *Penguin Film Review*, 7: 55–60.
Useful material on how different countries dominated the international film market before Hollywood became paramount. In 1908, France (Pathe) was on top. In 1912, the Italians came out on top with the first feature-length films (Ambrosio, Itala, and Cines, companies). Then in 1914, Denmark (through the business sense of one Ole Olsen) took over. Both the German and American industries were created by the 1914–18 war. The Germans were blockaded. The USA was neutral until 1917 and had the run of the international market. After the war all the European industries had to have protection from US competition. The first was Germany. Hollywood's response was to buy European talent. Since then she has been on top. However, World War II saw UK production out-doing Hollywood [*sic*].

SONTAG, SUSAN, 1966, *Against Interpretation*, New York.
Collected criticism. The title essay argues against content, meaning, for the immediate sensuous experience. Also pieces on Bresson, Godard, science fiction films, Jack Smith, Resnais and the Novel versus the Film.

Spain. Diplomatic Office of Information. 1949, *The Spanish Cinema* Madrid.
Of principal interest are the production statistics:

1939	15	1944	36
1940	20	1945	37
1941	45	1946	36
1942	35	1947	49
1943	55	1948	45

SPIEGELMAN, J. M., 1952, 'Ambiguity and Personality in the Perception of a Motion Picture', PhD thesis, University of California at Los Angeles, unpublished.
What are the characteristics of ambiguity? Is there a relation between what is perceived in a communications situation and the personality patterns of the perceiver? Can clinicians assess a communicator by his communication? Ambiguity is a univocal dimension of content, but ordered. A film was analysed. Questions were shot at a group seeing it and another not. The groups were Rorshached. The film maker had his Rorshach read, and then his film read by others. The questions received affirmative answers. The film used was *Uirapuru*, an MA film made in Brazil by a UCLA student, in colour, in which natives of Brazil's Amazon jungle act out a legend of the bird of love—music by Villa Lobos.

— 1955, 'Effect of Personality on the Perception of a Motion Picture', *Journal of Projective Techniques*, 19: 461–4.
'Individual differences in the perception of a motion picture are a function of global aspects of personality as defined by Rorshach'.

SPOTTISWOODE, RAYMOND, 1935, *A Grammar of The Film*: An Analysis of Film Technique, London.

SPRAGER, H. K., 1952, 'Hollywood Foreign Correspondents', *Quarterly of Film, Radio, and Television*, 6: 274–82.
'Critics . . . often criticize the industry for making pictures which give foreign countries a distorted impression of Hollywood and American life. As a group, the foreign correspondents are in no position to join in the criticism, for their writings do very little to place the American motion picture industry in proper perspective', p. 282.

SPRAOS, J., 1962, *The Decline of the Cinema*, An Economist's Report, London.
Pessimistic economic analysis of the prospects of the cinema.

STANBROOK, ALLAN, 1960, 'Break with the Past', *Films and Filming*, 6: March, 9–11 and 30; April, 13–14 and 30.
An outline of what the Japanese cinema is all about.

STANTON, F. and LAZARSFELD, P., 1949, *Communications Research 1948–9*, New York.
Newspapers, comics and radio are studied in various papers – not films. Merton anticipates Katz and Lazarsfeld (1955).

STEARN, GERALD, 1967, *McLuhan Hot and Cool*, New York.
See McLuhan, H. M.

STEINBERG, C. S., 1966, *Mass Media and Communications*, New York.
Contains excerpts from Inglis (1947), Powdermaker (1950), and Hovland (1954).

STEINER, GARY A., 1963, *The People Look at Television*, New York.
The people are remarkably satisfied with television; they are not out for uplift. They would like less violence, less westerns, less intrusive commercials, all programmes a little better rather than a few oases in the trash. They say more about themselves than about television when they respond.

STEPHENS, H. B., 1926, 'The Relation of the Motion Picture to Changing Moral Standards', *Annals*, 128: 151–7.
Very exercised over the exposure of the young to risque pictures – even meritorious ones like *Woman of Paris*. Suggests a circulating library of approved films to be shown in schools or community theatres.

STEPHENSON, W., 1967, *The Play Theory of Mass Communication*, Chicago.

BIBLIOGRAPHY

Mass communications can be looked at as forms of play as well as forms of social control.

STEVENSON, E. F., 1929, *Motion Picture in Advertising and Selling*, New York. Cf. Box (1937).

STOCKWIN, HARVEY, 1965, 'India's Escapist [Film] Industry,' *Far Eastern Economic Review*, 48, No. 9: 27 May, 433–5.
Second only to Japan in size, the Indian film industry is devoted exclusively to stylized and escapist films. Yet Indians need to be brought face to face with reality. How to do this without falling into the absurdities of socialist realism (another form of escape)?

STORCK, HENRI, 1950, *The Entertainment of Film for Juvenile Audiences*, Paris, UNESCO.
Survey of films made for children in several countries and of the juvenile audience. Plea for moderation in the portrayal of violence. Research is needed. Abstracted in UNESCO (1961).

STRAND, PAUL, 1950, 'Realism', *Sight and Sound*, 19: 23*ff.*
Confused discussion equating realism with involvement, lack of prettification, on the side of 'progressive' values. [The blatant way the Left appropriates to its exclusive use perfectly ordinary words is a scandal.]

STUCKRATH, F. and SCHOTTMAYER, G., 1955, *Psychologie Des Filmerlebens in Kindheit und Jugend*, Hamburg.
Elaborate study of the impact of films on children.

SUCKOW, RUTH, 1936, 'Hollywood Gods and Goddesses', *Harper's*, July, 173: 189–200.
Stars represent national ideals reduced to lowest common denominator. Early stars were western heroes. But the real gods are perfect-lover ideals. Valentino was the eternal gigolo. Clark Gable is as American as popcorn or BVDs. Only Mary Pickford has remained a goddess. Clara Bow was sex appeal. Garbo is adolescent mysteriousness. Marlene is a demi-goddess, disillusioned European femininity. Joan Crawford is a success who became a mask. Katherine Hepburn is a junior leaguer. The fan-magazines are intimate-personal. But actors love their image too. These broad typifications are an unconscious social [sic] document rather than art.

SYLVESTER, DAVID, 1954, 'Them!', *Encounter*, 3: November, 48–50.

— 1955*a*, 'Orwell on the Screen', *Encounter*, 4: March, 35–7.

— 1955*b*, 'The Innocence of Marilyn Monroe', *Encounter*, 4: May, 50–2.

— 1956, 'The Anglicisation of Outer Space', *Encounter*, 6: January, 69–72.
For an all-too-brief period, the art critic Sylvester turned his hand to writing about films.

349

TABORI, PAUL, 1959, *Alexander Korda*, London.
Affectionate biography of a genuine British-Hungarian film tycoon of the thirties, forties and fifties, who seemed never quite to consolidate his successes into a financially sound structure. A bit superficial on the workings of the industry compared to Wood (1952, 1954).

TALBOT, DANIEL, 1959, *Film: An Anthology*, Berkeley and Los Angeles.
Useful collection covering social aspects as well as aesthetics.

— ed., 1960, *Concerning a Woman of Sin and Other Stories of Hollywood*, New York.
Anthology of stories by Ben Hecht (title story), John O'Hara, William Faulkener, Christopher Isherwood, Scott Fitzgerald, William Saroyan, Irwin Shaw, Budd Schulberg and Ring Lardner.

TALBOT, F. A., 1912 and 1923, *Moving Pictures: How They are Made and Worked*, London
First edition is a quite sophisticated account of how films are made, if uncritical. It contains a precious photograph of the Selig Company in Los Angeles. Much space is devoted to trick effects, now called special effects. The second edition is considerably revised, but equally lively and thorough.

Tavistock Clinic, 1952, *A Psychological Study of Films Produced for Child Audience*, by Petroleum Films Bureau, London.
Three road safety films were shown and one was written by children. Children disliked being taught, talked down to, and jumped on technical errors. Films need to take account of the child's point of view, desire to be in the know, and need of adult approval.

TAYLOR, J. R., 1962, *Anger and After*, London.
Detailed description of the playwrights of the 'new English drama'. Especially good on Pinter. See my review (1964b).

— 1964, *Cinema Eye, Cinema Ear*, London.
What the title means is a matter of conjecture. Consists of eight thorough and well argued essays on Fellini, Hitchcock, Bergman etc. This is how to do a book on the cinema, cf. Houston (1963) and Rhode (1966).

— 1965, Review of Huaco (1965) in *New Society* 6, 9 September: 31.

TEIXEIRA DE SALLES, F., 1962, 'Aspectos Politicos-Sociais do "Western" ', *Revista Brasiliera de Estudos Politicos*, 14: 129–54.
Rather Leftish analysis of the social and political significance of the development of the western in America.

TERLIN, ROSE R., 1936, *You and I and the Movies*, New York.
'The problem . . . is . . . to secure some measure of control over incidental social education . . .', p. 56.

BIBLIOGRAPHY

TERRAINE, JOHN, 1957, 'End of the Trail', *Films and Filming*, July, 3: 9 and 30.
The West's appeal is: scenery; violence; movement; and the ready-made heroes, 1) the individual hero, 2) the cavalry, 3) the Indians, 4) no heroes, just guns and bravery.

THOMAS, BOB, 1967, *King Cohn*, New York.
Biography of the 'czar' of Columbia studios, showing him to be ruthless, indeed, but also a producer with real flair and a tolerance of intellectuals.

— 1969, *Thalberg: Life and Legend*, New York.
First biography of the short life of the 'genius' of MGM, Irving Thalberg. A public, rather than a private, life.

THOMAS, DONALD and MEHRA, H. K., 1953, 'The Indian Film', *Atlantic*, 192: October, 131-3.
Quick sketch of the Indian industry and its shortcomings.

THOMSON, DAVID, 1967, *Movie Man*, London.
Intriguing attempt to argue that film fills and permeates our world, has modified our sensibility, plays crucial roles in history, and has heavily influenced all the hitherto established arts. Today's man is film man: who makes, acts in, is portrayed in, or sees films.

THOMPSON, D., ed., 1964, *Discrimination in Popular Culture*, Harmondsworth.
The title promises a disquisition on race prejudice but it is in fact a series of papers on standards in popular culture, or rather, standards by which to condemn popular culture. The authors more or less follow the position Thompson and Leavis pushed in *Culture and Society* 1933. Standards are, as usual, vague, socially conscious and serious, and have never a kind word for the professional and entertaining standard product. There is the usual Reith-ian stuff about progressing from Muzak to Mozart, and you can't love the Beatles and Bach, or in a comparable way. In fact, the Leavisite basic equipment is no more than a scary and abusive rhetoric. See Hunt (1964).

THORP, M. F., 1947, *America at the Movies*, London.
Postwar British reprint of her *The Movies Come From America*, 1939. Reviewed jointly with Mayer (1945) by Kay Mander in *Penguin Film Review*, 3: 92-3.

THURSTONE, L. L. and PETERSON, R. C., 1933, *Motion Pictures and the Social Attitudes of Children*, New York.
Motion pictures affect attitudes and the effect is lasting. Fearing (1950) comments that this, the best of the Payne studies, 'established an experimental design fundamental for such investigations'.

351

TONNESSEN, H. O., 1952, *Ungdom Og Kino*, Oslo.
Every country seems to have its survey of childrens' cinema habits in the fifties. This one takes 12–18 as the boundary ages and has few surprises. See UNESCO (1961).

TREACY, D., 1966, 'The Effects of Mass Communication: A Survey and Critique', Ph.D., thesis, University of Illinois, unpublished.
Various approaches are classified together and criticized: the psychological behaviourist approach, the cognitive approach, the sociological approach and the functional approach. They are not integrated, and all neglect man as actively involved.

TRUFFAUT, F., 1967, *Hitchcock*, New York.
Exhaustive study of the films in an interview with the director which extended over *days*. Some of the most famous sequences are analyzed in great detail, and Hitchcock resists all attempts to impose profundity and messages on his work.

TUCKER, N., 1968, 'Who's Afraid of Walt Disney', *New Society*, 11: 502–3.
Constant theme is parent/child relations. *Lady and the Tramp* is about jealousy of a new baby. Exaggeration and child-identification. *Dumbo* is separated from mother and humiliated. in *Bambi*, the unspeakable loss of the mother may be realized for the first time alone in the darkness. Most disturbing of all: *Snow-White*, the (bad) mother who wants the death of her child. Many other terror moments. The good characters are sickly. Film is more disturbing than a book: book is read on mother's lap, can be edited, closed; film engulfs. 'For young children, confused between reality and unreality, what they see in the cinema in conditions of heightened susceptibility can be as real as anything else that they see happening in front of their eyes . . . some scenes in Disney quite literally have a nightmare quality', p. 503.

TYLER, PARKER, 1944, *The Hollywood Hallucination*, New York.
Movies are the day dreams, the struggle to penetrate the darkness. Elaborate psychological analysis of content and the play between the content and the medium itself. Too involved to summarise.

— 1947, *Magic and Myth of the Movies*, New York.
'Analysis of motion picture content based wholly on Freudian concepts' (Fearing (1950)). His analyses are described as 'fascinating' by Catherine de la Roche in *Penguin Film Review*, 1948, 7: p. 35.

— 1967, *The Three Faces of the Film*, New York.

— 1969, *Sex, Psyche Etcetera in the Film*, New York.

TYNAN, K., 1951, 'Cagney and the Mob', *Sight and Sound*, 20: 12*ff*.

UNDERHILL, FREDERIC, 1964, *Post-Literate Man and Film Editing*: an application of the theories of Marshall McLuhan, Boston.

A paper set out like a poem and with stills, trying to expound and exemplify McLuhan.

UNESCO, 1950, *The Film Industry in Six European Countries*, Paris. Comparative study of the industries of Denmark, Norway, Sweden, Italy, France and the United Kingdom, with most space given to the first named.

— 1954, *Film and Cinema Statistics*, Paris.
A volume of very useful, even essential statistics.

United Kingdom, 1944, Board of Trade. *Tendencies to Monopoly in the Cinematograph Film Industry*, Report of a Committee Appointed by the Cinematograph Films Council, London.

— 1950*a*, *Report of the Departmental Committee on Children and the Cinema*, London.
Sane report on the habit and children, advocating revision of the U, A and H categories of film classification into C, U, A and X.

— 1950*b*, Social Survey. No. 164, *Audience Reaction to the Film 'The Undefeated'*.

United States, various dates, Trade Information Bulletins, as below:
467, 1927, *Chinese Motion Picture Market*
499, 1927, *Market for Motion Pictures in Central Europe, Italy and Spain*
520, 1927, *Markets for Industrial and Educational Motion Pictures Abroad*
522, 1927, *Short-subject Film Market of Europe*
542, 1928, *European Motion Picture Industry in 1927*
544, 1928, *Short-subject Film Market in Latin America, Canada, Far East, Africa and Near East*
533, 1928, *Market for Motion Pictures in Scandinavia and Baltic States*
608, 1929, *Motion Pictures in Australia and New Zealand*
614, 1929, *Motion Pictures in India*
617, 1929, *European Motion-Picture Industry in 1928*
619, 1929, *Motion Pictures in Argentina and Brazil*
634, 1929, *Motion Pictures in Japan, Philippine Islands, Netherlands. East Indies, Siam, British Malaya, and French Indo-China*
641, 1929, *Latin American and Canadian Markets for American Motion Picture Equipment*
694, 1930, *European Motion-Picture Industry in 1929*
701, 1930, *Markets for American Motion-Picture Equipment in Asia Africa and Oceania*
722, 1930, *Motion Pictures in China*
752, 1931, *European Motion Picture Industry in 1930*
754, 1931, *Motion Pictures in Mexico, Central America and Greater Antilles*
756, 1931, *Small Island Markets for American Motion Pictures*
797, 1932, *Motion-Picture Industry in Continental Europe in 1931*
801, 1932, *Motion Picture Industry in the United Kingdom in 1931*
815, 1933, *European Motion-Picture Industry in 1932*

— 1928. Federal Trade Commission. *Trade Practice Conference of the Motion Picture Industry, New York, October 10–15, 1927*, Washington.

— 1936, Office of National Recovery Administration, Divisic n of Review, Industry Study Section, *The Motion Picture Industry*, Washington. See also Bertrand (1936). This item is listed in Huettig (1944) as unpublished data.

— 1938, Foreign and Domestic Commerce Bureau, *Review of Foreign Film Markets During 1937*, Washington.
Those who think Germany has a monopoly on efficient data-compiling bureaucracies should glance at this exhaustive survey of the markets for US films in eighty-five countries and territories. Hong Kong, e.g., made fifty-three films in 1938, seventy in 1937, for twenty-eight theatres.

— 1941, Congress Temporary National Economic Committee, Investigation of Concentration of Economic Power, monographs No. 43, *The Motion Picture Industry – a Pattern of Control*, Washington.
See Bertrand, Evans and Blanchard (1941).

— 1953a, Senate, Select Committee on Small Business Report *Problems of Independent Motion Picture Exhibitors*, Washington.

— 1953b, Office of the High Commissioner for Germany. Office of the Executive Secretary, Historical Division, *Press, Radio and Film in West Germany, 1945–1953*, Bad Godesberg-Mehlem.

— 1956, *Motion Pictures and Juvenile Delinquency*, 84th Congress, Senate Reports on Public Bills, 1008-A, Report of the Committee on the Judiciary, Interim Report of the Subcommittee to Investigate Juvenile Delinquency, Washington.
A throwback – films thought definitely to shape attitudes, but only suggests Code and its operation should be revised.

VAN LOAN, CHARLES, 1914, *Buck Parvin and the Movies*, New York.
Buck is an extra who rises to western stardom. There are nine loosely connected stories set in the Titan Studios where David Seligman is the boss and Jimmy Montague is the actor-director. Amusing. 'Buck was a moving-picture cowpuncher, acting during every waking moment. His street costume consisted of a widebrimmed hat of grey felt, a blue flannel shirt, a red bandanna for a cravat, a leather vest thickly studded with shining disks of brass, lavender trousers tucked into highheeled boots; and on special occasions he wore angora chaps and enormous spurs, which tinkled musically as he walked. His hatband was made of rattlesnake skin, and distributed about his person he wore several pounds of Indian beadwork and Mexican silver jewellery. Buck Parvin was one character actor who never left his make-up in the dressing room at the end of the day's work . . .' p. 19.

VAN VECHTEN, CARL, 1928, *Spider Boy*, New York.
Classical Hollywood novel which tells how Ambrose Deacon, timid

author of stories of small-town life published in the *Saturday Evening Post* and of a hit play, is waylaid on the train west by star Imperia Starling, and director Herbert Ringrose, who somehow inveigle him to Hollywood. Terrified, he announces his inability to work for the movies, and escapes to Santa Fe. He is pursued, and persuaded to sign up. A willing hack does the work and turns out egregious trash that is hailed as a smash. He marries Wilhelmina and decides to return to New York to write another play and prove he really is something.

VARDAC, NICHOLAS, 1949, *Stage to Screen*, theatrical method from Garrick to Griffith, Cambridge (Mass.).
Scholarly examination of the outgrowth of cinema from theatre. Argues that the realistic-romantic-melodrama grew up in the nineteenth century in parallel with animated pictures, then animated photographs, thence motion pictures. The theatrical striving for realism is the necessity that is the mother of the invention of the cinema. Then, instead of the reaction setting in after the extravagances of Irving, Belasco, and Mackaye, the cinema carried that theatre tradition to new heights, especially Porter, Griffith, and the spectacles. Belasco continued to compete for a time. *Birth of a Nation, Orphans of the Storm, Ben Hur* were in this tradition.

VARGAS, A. L., 1949, 'British Films and Their Audiences', *Penguin Film Review*, 8: 71–6.
British films preserve their technical efficiency and gloss and lose content. Whatever happened to the spirit of *Brief Encounter*?

VESSELO, A., 1947, 'The Cinema and the Unconscious Mind', a BBC Third Programme talk, unpublished.
A critique of Kracauer (1947) suggesting that the cinema's dream-like quality, mid-way between the conscious and unconscious worlds, between literature and music, explains their capturing of phenomena Kracauer stresses.

VIDAL, GORE, 1968, *Myra Breckinridge*, New York.
Outrageously queer novel about a sex-changed film maniac who formerly held that Hollywood vintage 1935–45 was the high point of western culture, and who is writing a book called *Parker Tyler and the Films of the Forties or, the Transcendental Pantheon*, celebrating Tyler's insight – the only important one of the century – that films are the unconscious expression of age old myths. She (he) now confesses that the television commercial engages the attention of the world's best artists and technicians. Pandro S. Berman, 'with the exception of Orson Welles and Samuel Fuller, Berman is the most important film-maker of the forties', p. 67.

VIDOR, KING, 1954, *A Tree is a Tree*, London.
Autobiography of the famous director who went from silents to *Solomon and Sheba* (with the incomparable *War and Peace* along the way). Many

amusing anecdotes, as, e.g., a script conference on the way to a funeral dressed in open shirts, slacks and sneakers.

VIOTTI, SERGIO, 1954, 'Britain's Hepburn', *Films and Filming*, 1: November, 7.
Defence of Hepburn after *Roman Holiday* and *Sabrina Fair*, and her expressed wish to break out of Cinderella roles.

— a 1955, 'Vogues in Vamps', *Films and Filming*, 1: February, 5.
Vamps were killed off by the Second World War.

VON STERNBERG, J. V., 1966, *Fun in a Chinese Laundry*, New York.
The acid, literate and ungracious (one might almost say slightly misanthropic) memoirs of a superior director who, as his egomania grew, found increasing difficulty in getting work.

WADES, SERENA E., 1966, 'An Exploration into the Media Behavior of the Creative Adolescent', Ph.D. thesis, Stanford University, unpublished.
Hypothesis: the creative adolescent will make only limited use of media because of other activities. More catholic in selections, integrate media more fully into daily life. Confirmed.

WAGENKNECHT, E., 1962, *The Movies in the Age of Innocence*, Norman (Okla).
Memoirs of silent film viewing by an intellectual fan who remembers it all. Very appealing, personal and unpretentious.

WALEY, D. H. and SPENCER, D. A., 1939, 1956, *The Cinema Today*, Oxford.
Chapter XII on 'The Social Uses of the Cinema' – frightfully superficial: cinema an escape, needs to be censored, specialized films are made for children and the film is used in education.

WALKER, ALEXANDER, 1966, *The Celluloid Sacrifice*, London.
A series of essays, some on censorship, which are all very well, and a series on female stars which culminate in a brilliant study of Elizabeth Taylor showing how her life and her art intertwine both for her and for her public.

WALL, W. D., *et al.*, 1948–9, 'The Adolescent and the Cinema I and II', *Educational Review*, 1: 34–46 (October 1948), 119–30 (February 1949).
These results come from studies of upwards of 5,000 boys and girls in the Midlands.
'The cinema is a force to be reckoned with in the wider education of the young. It is so much a part of the pattern of adolescent and adult life that an effort must be made to understand and control its impact', p. 127.
'Specific scenes, even specific shots, remain longer in the mind than do generalizations which have been drawn by the viewer . . . the viewpoint of many films is distorted if not entirely unreal, the values offered shallow or worse, and the way of life such as to suggest false standards of success',

| | | Frequency | | | |
| | Less than | | | | |
Never	1 pw	1 pw	2 pw	2 pw+	Average
Secondary modern					
13–16					
Boys	1·4	16	23	40	20	1·6
Girls	0·2	23	36	30	11	1·7
Grammar					
Boys	0	46	27	23	4	1·0
Girls	0	57	27	13	4	0·9

p. 128. There is a need to help develop critical standards. Brief annotated bibliography.

— and SIMSON, W. A., 1949, 'The Effects of Cinema Attendance on the Behaviour of Adolescents as seen by their Contemporaries', *British Journal of Educational Psychology*, 19: 53–61.
Adolescent cinema-going is up sharply and a questionnaire shows that 'the prestige of a cultural medium like the cinema is such that it induces in a considerable proportion of adolescents the desire to imitate a number of apparently superficial modes of behaviour [dressing, dancing, hair style, make-up, manners, amusement, talking, walking], it is at least arguable that its influence extends to less readily observable and probably psychologically and educationally more important fields', p. 62.

— and SMITH, E. M., 1949, 'The Film Choices of Adolescents', *British Journal of Educational Psychology*, 19: 121–36.
Children are very critical of films' verisimilitude where they can be, otherwise they are notably thirsty for information on human relationships. Aesthetic approach no good; a matrix of knowledge of human relationships and social conditions must be developed in school that they can use as a background.

— 1951, 'The Emotional Responses of Adolescent Groups to Certain Films', *British Journal of Educational Psychology*, 20: 153; and 21: 81–8.
'Only a few of the many films shown and seen make a lasting impression or are likely radically to modify the attitudes of an adolescent audience', p. 161. But there may be a cumulative effect, and a temporary effect. In dreaming and fantasizing it seems likely children 'selected what they dwelt upon afterwards, in accordance with their own developmental needs', p. 87.

WANGER, WALTER, 1963, *My Life With Cleopatra*, New York.
Wanger's memoirs of the making of the 1963 version of *Cleopatra*.

WARNER, JACK L., 1965, *My First 100 Years in Hollywood*, New York.
Very lively and anecdotal autobiography by one of the old-guard executives who survived to be bought out.

357

BIBLIOGRAPHY

WARSHOW, ROBERT, 1948, 'The Gangster as Tragic Hero', in (1962), 127–33 and Deer (1967).
In a happiness culture the gangster is tragic. '... the gangster film is simply one example of the movies' constant tendency to create fixed dramatic patterns that can be repeated indefinitely with a reasonable expectation of profit' (p. 157 in Deer). 'For such a type to be successful means that its conventions have imposed themselves upon the general consciousness and become the accepted vehicles of a particular set of attitudes and a particular aesthetic effect.' Appeals to the experience of reality only in the ultimate sense; immediate appeal to previous experience of type itself, creates own field of reference. The western is folklore and the gangster film is a universally experienced rejection of Americanism. There is a conflict between the need to succeed, and success as aggression to be punished. The gangster dies for us.

— 1962, *The Immediate Experience*, New York.
Posthumously collected pieces of a much admired critic, several on films.

WATKINS, G. S., 1947, ed., *The Motion Picture Industry, Annals of the American Academy of Political and Social Science*, **254**: Philadelphia.

WEAKLAND, J. H., 1966, 'Themes in Chinese Communist Films', *American Anthropologist*, **68**, 477–84.
Dominant themes: old *versus* new China, emancipation of women, anti-individualism – are analysed. Films are better sources than literary works because 1) they are more representative as a group product, for a mass audience, 2) yet relate general themes and particular situations, 3) they preserve something of the difference between saying and doing.

— n.d., 'Conflicts Between Love and Family Relationships in Chinese Films', Office of Naval Research, Group Psychology Branch, Technical Report #2.
Both communist and non-communist films deal with family conflicts, the former siding with the young, the latter showing more sympathy with the old. Both resolve by traditional Chinese values – *not* love should conquer all, but accept authority, subordinate self to wider social ends.

— 1968, 'Chinese Communist Images of Invasion and Resistance', Office of Naval Research, Group Psychology Branch, Technical Report #4.
Chinese films portray invasion as equivalent to sexual invasion and rape, the young wife situation parallels that of the invaded motherland. Hence great sensitivity to encroachment.

— 1971, 'Real and Reel Life in Hong Kong – Film Studies of Cultural Adaptation', *Journal of Asian and African Studies*, forthcoming.
Films like myths are a cultural distillate. They provide easy to study, concrete images of behaviour. Perception of them and the responses evoked are culturally structured. Films provide commonly shared interpretations of society and culture and are consonant with the basic orientation of their audience. They are a group product. They reflect conscious as

well as unconscious premises and preoccupations. The verbal and visual dimensions act as checks on each other, discrepancies will be particularly interesting to the researcher. Hong Kong films can be sampled because they are repetitive. Themes should be sought out, then specific treatments analysed, then comparisons made with mainland and Taiwan films. The depiction of technology, business and western elements, as well as traditional Chinese themes, e.g. family relationships, should prove interesting. Contrast the Mandarin and Cantonese films. Mandarin films might be expected to show more western influence.

WEIGAL, A., 1921, 'The Influence of the Kinematograph Upon National Life', *The Nineteenth Century*, 139: 661–72.
Fair play, orderliness, honesty and modesty are sterling British virtues. 'But what is happening in regard to the kinema? The photoplays which are being presented to British audiences are, for the most part, written and produced in Western America by a comparatively small group of persons . . . In regard to fair play several of the smaller producers hold the views of the less reputable elements in the sporting circles of the States: . . . that the player . . . may attempt to win by any form of trickery . . . As to law and order, some of them have the standards made notorious in the past by the American police force . . . As to honesty, they hold that no man is above suspicion . . . And in regard to modesty or the suppression of the more blatant forms of heroics, they very frequently offend against the laws of good taste', pp. 667–8. The answer is a stricter and more subtle censorship – if we regard our racial virtues as worth preserving.

WERTHAM, F. C., 1954, *Seduction of the Innocent*, New York.

WEST, MAE, 1959, *Goodness Had Nothing to do with It*, New York.
Scintillating autobiography of the all-time champion of good-time girls.

'The Western', 1962, *Cinema 62*, 68: July–August.
The usual thorough French treatment, with Rieupeyrout (q.v.) doing his thing on the real versus the film characters. Bibliography.

WHITE, D. M. and AVERSON, R., 1968, *Sight, Sound and Society*, Boston.
Useful anthology; several pieces on films.

WHITE, D. M. and ABEL, R. M., 1963, *The Funnies: An American Idiom*, Glencoe.

WHITE, PETER, 1931, *Investigation Into an Alleged Combine in the Motion Picture Industry in Canada*, Ottawa.
Finds Famous Players Canadian Corp. Ltd, a combine in restraint of trade against the public interest.

WHITEHALL, RICHARD, 1964a, 'Crime Inc.', *Films and Filming*, 10: January, 7–12; February 17–22; March 39–44.
Elaborate survey of the gangster film.

— 1964, 'One . . . two . . . three', *Films and Filming*, **10**: August, 7*ff.*
Discussion of war films.

'Why You Go to the Pictures', 1965, *Films and Filming*, **11**: June, 4*f.*
Report of a BBC survey.

WILDER, BILLY and DIAMOND, I. A. L., 1963, *Irma La Douce*, New York.
Illustrated script of Wilder's much-underrated film.

WIESE, M. and COLE, S., 1946, 'A Study of Children's Attitudes and the
Influence of a Commercial Motion Picture', *Journal of Psychology*, **21**:
151–71.
Free association technique was used after viewing of *Tomorrow the World*
(about Nazi boy brought to the USA). Pioneering acknowledgment that
the cultural framework plays a primary role in determining how an
individual will be affected by a motion picture.

WILENSKY, H., 1964, 'Mass Society and Mass Culture', *American Sociological Review*, **29**: 173–97, reprinted in Berelson and Janowitz (1966)
293–327.
Social differentiation persists, even increases. Nevertheless, cultural
uniformity grows. Structure and culture change at varying rates but their
individual variation is greatest at the highest levels of modernization.
There is considerable independence among separate institutional spheres.
There is a long-run strain towards consistency: 1) among values and
beliefs in diverse emotional spheres (incompatibility of high rate of mass
behaviour in consumption, low in politics (UK) or low rate of mass consumption and high rate in politics (France)); 2) among behaviour patterns
in diverse spheres; 3) between culture and social structure (incompatibility
of elite educational system and continued growth of mass culture (France),
or high rate of mobility and stable, insulated leisure styles (class subcultures in the UK, ethnic subcultures in the USA)).
Until college, educational level is unimportant: what is important is
completing college and a good college at that. More education will protect
individuals against ennervating amounts of the media's shoddiest, but
will not cause a mass breakthrough in the mediocrity barrier.
1) Differentiate age, religion, occupation and quality and content of
college education, 'white collar', 'working class' too crude: 'obscure most
of what is central to the experience of the person and the structure of
society', p. 317. We must return to the study of group life.
2) Television has become central to the leisure routine of majorities at
every level.
3) Structural differentiation and cultural uniformity are transitional. In
undeveloped societies they go together. At our level they part. They will
come together again. 'Men who have confidence in the major institutions
of American society distrust television and radio networks; men who trust
the media distrust other institutions . . . To be socially integrated in
America is to accept propaganda, advertising, and speedy obsolescence in

consumption . . . those who fit the image of pluralist man in the pluralist society also fit the image of mass man in the mass society', p. 319. The Happy Good-Citizen consumers tend to be unusually prone to personality voting, dependent on the media for opinions on issues, susceptible to advertizing and mass behaviour generally.

WILLIAMS, RAYMOND and ORROM, MICHAEL, 1954, *Preface to Film*, London. Films should use fully the expressive resources of all the arts that can go into it: drama, poetry, dance, music, design, as well as its intrinsic art.

WILNER, DANIEL M., 1951, 'Attitude as a Determinant of Perception in the Mass Media of Communication: Reactions to the Motion Picture *Home of the Brave*', PhD thesis, typescript, UCLA. Groups ranked by prejudice were shown the film and asked to describe facial expressions, feeling states of characters, their motives, then whether they liked or disliked the characters, and what they would have done in the circumstances. Is missing the point of an anti-prejudice film a direct perceptual experience, or a function of further cognitive activity?

WILSON, JOHN, 1961, 'Film Illiteracy in Africa, *Canadian Communications*, summer, 1: 7–14. A still picture, to those untutored in reading in three dimensions, remains obstinately flat. A health film was shown and the audience, asked what they saw, spoke of the chicken. They hadn't seen a story and they hadn't seen whole frames – they had scanned it for details and had spotted a chicken scurrying across the screen which the educators had barely noticed. Westerners habitually focus a little in front of the screen to take in the whole frame. A picture is a convention. The audiences wanted to know where a man was going when he went off screen. Panning and moving into close-up were seen as the landscape moving, the person growing bigger, or us walking closer, etc. Simpler conventions had to be adopted until the film language had been mastered. Audience participation, i.e., a question-and-answer commentary, helped. To learn film literacy took three to four years.

WILSON, J. A., 1952, 'Film and Society', in *Cinema 1952*, Harmondsworth, 152–7. The function of the cinema is to give knowledge of the world we live in and to create values by which we live. It is presently doing this very poorly – both in Russia and the West, the one being didactic, the other escapist.

WIND, EDGAR, 1963, *Art and Anarchy*, London.

WINNINGTON, RICHARD, 1950, 'Negro Films', *Sight and Sound*, 19: 27*ff*.

WISEMAN, T.. 1957, *The Seven Deadly Sins of Hollywood*, London. After six weeks in Hollywood, Wiseman lists the sins as Snobbery, Gossip, Sycophancy, Shoptalk, Egomania, Salesmanship and Parochialism.

— 1964, *The Cinema*, London.
A brief and relaxed illustrated history of the cinema, without undue emphasis on the earlier period, and due weight given to Hollywood.

— 1965, *The Czar*, London.
Novel: Compare Thomas (1967) and Schulberg (1941), not to mention Fitzgerald (1949) and a character in Lambert (1963).

WOELFEL, NORMAN, 1947, 'The American Mind and the Motion Picture', *Annals* (1947), 88–94.
America is in a bad way and needs unity and purpose. The media are vital and can only stay 'private' if they perform their necessary task. At the moment they are just escapist, they should become serious and educative.

WOLF, C. and BAGGULEY, J., 1967, *Authors Take Sides on Vietnam*, New York.

WOLFENSTEIN, M. and LEITES, NATHAN, 1947, 'An Anlaysis of Themes and Plots', *Annals* (1947), 41–8.
The most frequent pattern is that the hero and heroine meet casually, a pickup. They are more alone when they meet than in the final clinch. Sexy = bad, good = dull, therefore there has evolved the good/bad girl. Americans want a girl to be all things, more so than Europeans, hence high divorce rate – the search for perfection. The increasing sexual availability of good girls, the glamourization of the housewife, and the easing of taboos are undermining the equation sexy = bad.

— 1950a, 'The Unconscious versus the "message" in an Anti-Bias Film – Two Social Scientists view *No Way Out*', *Commentary*, 10: 388–91.
The apparently liberal surface of the film conceals: ambiguity about black murdering white; negroes initiating violence against white, including women; theme of violating a white body to save a negro; dependence of the negro on whites to fight his battle; self-abasement; negroes as a burden, a moral obligation, a guilt – but this may increase hostility; a downfallen girl learns to overcome prejudice and to be upwardly mobile; negroes are shown eating heartily, eating is rare in films and this emphasizes the stereotype of negroes preoccupied with bodily pleasures; even the title is ambiguous.

— 1950b, *Movies, A Psychological Study*, Glencoe.
Denny and Meyersohn: 'A pioneer, content-analysis study of the public daydreams of American movie-goers, e.g., "The Good-Bad Girl". Analysis of all American "A" films with an urban setting from 1945 to 1950. Recurrent problems; comparison with European movies. Statement of themes; statement on the psychological processes of movie-makers and audiences; some assumptions about life-patterns in American culture. The analyses are acute and go together with the work of Mead, Bateson and Gorer on American character. But little attention is paid to the quality of the films and their styles. Here are some samples to give the flavour: 'Where these productions gain the sympathetic response of a wide

BIBLIOGRAPHY

audience, it is likely that their producers have tapped within themselves the reservoir of common daydreams', p. 13. 'Thus French films dramatize the breaking down of the ideal image of the woman, American films, the justification of this image. British films in contrast to both American and French tend to see women more as possible victims of men's violence or betrayal', p. 23. 'Another film reflection of the popular girl with her many escorts is a frequent dance pattern in musicals where a girl dancer appears with a chorus of men. Her relation to them is stylized and superficial as she dances with each in rapid succession, not favouring one more than another. The male chorus alternate their attentions to the girl with routines in which they dance together in amicable accord', pp. 32–3. 'The belief in the unchangingness of love is probably related to the tradition of monogamy combined with the demand for continuous pleasure. It is also related to the characteristically American denial of the evanescent aspect of life . . . Instead, one plans to move to California, to take a course in the Charm School. The only kind of change which is readily admitted is improvement and this tends to apply to technology rather than to human relations. There seems to be a high capacity for retaining early preferences with undiminished intensity. The child-hood taste for ice-cream is little superseded by acquired tastes for more subtle delicacies; and comic strips continue to be read alongside Pocket books. The grown man retains his boyhood enthusiasm for baseball, and shares with his son the admiration for its heroes', p. 48. 'Since goodness morality and fun morality both operate in contemporary American culture, we frequently find a movie heroine using a masculine approach and appearing as a good-bad girl', p. 82. 'American films are preoccupied with showing events from a variety of viewpoints. We have seen what importance is attached to discrepancies between appearance and reality; the hero and heroine in melodramas frequently appear different from what they really are. We are shown how the hero appears to the police, as a criminal, how the heroine appears to the hero, as a wicked woman. The plot is less one of action than of proof or rather disproof. The incriminating false appearances must be dispelled. It must be proved that what was supposed to have happened did not happen. The potentialities of the hero and heroine for serious action are realized only in a false appearance, which indicates what they might have done if they had been carried away by dangerous impulses. This is what we have called the eat-your-cake-and-have-it aspect of American films. We can see the hero and heroine carrying out forbidden wishes and in the end see them escape penalties since these acts are shown to be merely a false appearance. Hence the character who sees things mistakenly has a special importance in American films. It is from his point of view that we can see the fulfilment of forbidden wishes, while at the same time we get the assurance that nothing happened', pp. 243–4. 'The false appearances in either case represent the fulfilment of wishes that remain unacknowledged or are not acted out', p. 244. 'In comedies, in contrast to melodramas, false appearances are more gratifying and less anxiety-provoking; they correspond to wishes phrased in less disturbing terms, and at the same time taken less seriously', p. 252. The elderly, bald, fussy and ineffectual father figure blunders about getting things wrong as do the police in melodrama. 'The comic onlooker embodies the suspicions of the child about things which he does not see. We in the audience are encouraged to laugh at him and enjoy the fantasy that if we could see everything we could see that nothing happens. The peculiar elation in American film comedies in demonstrating that nothing happens would seem to derive in part from this source', p. 257. The comic onlooker is an adult-child, crawls under tables and listens in, he is bald, sexless, likely to misunderstand and is a nuisance. 'The position of the American father as surpassable makes him an eligible object for the projection of supposedly foolish childish mistakes no less than for repressed dangerous impulses', pp. 257–8. 'Films with a happy romantic ending frequently close with a shot of the onlooker rather than of the happy couple. This may have the function of shifting the audience back to a recognition of their own position as onlookers, easing them out of their identification with the hero and heroine', pp. 266–7.

— 1955, 'Trend in French Films', *Journal of Social Issues*, 11: 42–51.
Fifty films since 1950 analysed and eight themes distinguished, the common denominator of which is 'a presumably increasing feeling of incapacity to cope with crushing circumstances'.

WOLLENBERG, H. H., 1946, 'Exploring the Psychology of the Cinema', *Sight and Sound*, 15: Autumn, 99–101.
Reviews books and articles by Gregor, Stoetzel, Ayer, Altenloh, Cohen-Seat.

— 1949, 'The Jewish Theme in Contemporary Cinema', *Penguin Film Review*, 8: 46–50.

WOOD, ALAN, 1952, *Mr Rank*: A Study of J. Arthur Rank and British Films, London.
Lucid account of the British film industry: 'The only industry where increasing the geographical extent of the market does not increase the demands for the product. The requirements of a small town . . . can be met by about 400 films a year. The requirements of the whole world can be met by 400 films a year . . . And Hollywood was quite prepared to make every one of the 400 films itself', p. 48. In 1923, only 10% of films shown in the UK were British, by 1926 5%. The quota act of 1928, resulted in evasions and 'quickies'. '. . . you are always better off owing a lot of money than if you only owe a little money . . . the man with an overdraft running into millions . . . knows that, whatever happens, his bank cannot possibly afford to let him go bankrupt', p. 100.

— and MARY, eds., 1954, *Silver Spoon*, being extracts from the random reminiscences of Lord Grantley, London.
Richard Norton, aristocrat and financier, contributes his anecdotes about film making in the thirties among Lady Yule, Korda, Pascal, Ludovico Toeplitz de Grand Ry, Filippo Del Giudice and other fabulous characters, not to mention the rising Mr Rank.

BIBLIOGRAPHY

WOODS, FREDERICK, 1959, 'Hot Guns and Cold Women', *Films and Filming*, 5: March, 11 and 30.
Ritual of the westerns. The chivalry in gunfighting is quite unhistorical. 'Hostesses' were really vicious and unscrupulous prostitutes. Johnny Concho was mainly about a spring-hinged holster. 'Chivalric codes, and stories based upon them, can flourish only in one set of historical circumstances. Firstly, the world in which they are set must be new and continuously expanding. Secondly, society must be loosely organized, so that not only is sporadic and systematic lawlessness possible, but it is also necessary for the law to be taken into the hands of good men who must administer it according to the dictates of their own consciences', p. 30.

WOOLF, VIRGINIA, 1926, 'The Movies and Reality', *New Republic*, 47: 308–10, reprinted as 'The Cinema' in *The Captain's Death Bed and Other Essays*, London, 1950, 166–71.
Says that the cinema is a case of the savages beginning not with two bars of iron and working up to Mozart, but with grand pianos and nothing to play. Seems to be against narrative and for movements and abstractions.

WRIGHT, C. R., 1959, *Mass Communications*, New York.

WRIGHT, VIRGINIA and HANNA, DAVID, 1944, 'Motion Picture Survey', in *Writers Congress* (1944), 402–11.
Review of the truthfulness or otherwise of Hollywood films dealing with Nazis and Japanese, concludes that after a bad and cowardly start. things improved radically.

Writers Congress, 1944, The Proceedings of the Conference held in October 1943 under the Sponsorship of the Hollywood Writers' Mobilization and the University of California, Berkeley and Los Angeles.
Fascinating set of papers and discussions as writers try to maximize their war effort by ruminating on the nature of their craft. Contributors include Robert Rossen, Thomas Mann, Dudley Nichols, James Wong Howe. Items by Wright and Hanna (1944), Lazarsfeld and Merton (1944) and Fearing (1944).

YOUNG, DONALD RAMSEY, 1922, *Motion Pictures*, A Study in Social Legislation, Philadelphia.
Early discussion of 'the problem of social standards, of ideals, of morals', p. 6. 'Social standards are influenced by motion pictures . . . and . . . by the fact that the audience, often young boys and girls, are packed in narrow seats, close together, in a darkened room[1] . . . the phrases, "movie masher" and "knee flirtation" are coming into use', p. 6. 'It is unessential that any evidence be advanced to show that the type of picture seen by mo.ion picture audiences . . . influences their thoughts and subsequent activities', p. 82. Suggests Federal censorship impracticable; goes instead for State boards. (Footnote 1 reads: '1 ". . . Under cover of darkness, evil communications readily pass and bad habits are taught.

Moving picture theatres are favourite places for the teaching of homosexual practices" Healy, Wm., *The Individual Delinquent*, p. 308'.)

— 1926, 'Social Standards and the Motion Picture', *Annals*, 128: 146–50.
Films tend to mould vastly different peoples and ways of life into a universal social pattern. But somehow enlightened public opinion needs to educate and raise standards to sweep away false values, like farm folks trying to emulate city slickers.

YOUNG, VERNON, 1953, 'The Witness Point', in *New World Writing*, 4th Mentor Selection, New York.
Analysis of forms available to control content. The witness point is the controlling viewpoint of the film: monovisual, subjective, following one person, etc., *Crossfire, Rashomon*, play on conflicts of witness point.

ZABBA, SAM, 1956, 'Casting and Directing in Primitive Societies', *Quarterly of Film, Radio, and Television*, 11: 154–66.
Must treat people as human beings and participate in their culture, otherwise they will not co-operate. How to convey what they are doing to people who have no idea what a film is? But once you pay an actor, the price goes up.

ZIERER, C. M., 1947, 'Hollywood – World Center of Motion Picture Production', *Annals* (1947), 12–17.
History of the relocation of the industry from the east coast to Hollywood.

ZIMMERSCHEID, KARL, 1922, *Die Deutsche Filmindustrie*, ihre Entwicklung.
Organization und Stellung in Deutschen Wirtschaftsleven, Stuttgart.

ZUKOR, ADOLPH, 1953, *The Public is Never Wrong*, New York.
Autobiography of the movie mogul who imported Bernhardt in *Queen Elizabeth* and thereby introduced feature-length films to the USA. He founded Famous Players on the slogan of Famous Players in Famous Plays, and exported the star system of the theatre to the cinema. Features brought in the carriage trade. Terry Ramsaye said he was Napoleonic; he denies it, but some pages later justifies his easing out of Sam Goldwyn thus: 'My aim was the building of a large and wide-flung organization, while he operated in the moment', p. 179. 'Stardom is a matter over which only audiences have any real control . . . Suppose the producer consciously tries to build . . . he tries with a hundred where he succeeds with one', pp. 182–3.

ZWETSLOOT, JAN., 1913, *De Bioscoop – Een middel tot volsontwikkeling envolksbederf*, Leiden.
Possibly the earliest book on the uses and misuses of the cinema, does it educate or corrupt?

INDEX

INDEX OF SUBJECTS

('*t*' indicates that a term is discussed; '*n*' that the reference is to be found in a footnote.)

INDEX OF NAMES

('*n*' indicates the reference is in a footnote. Names mentioned in the abstracts of the bibliography have been indexed, but not those which are alphabetically listed. Authors' names have, then, to be checked both in this index and in the bibliography.)

INDEX OF FILMS

(Where possible, films mentioned are listed by title, director, country and year. The principal authorities used are the lists provided in Andrew Sarris, *The American Cinema*, New York, 1968, and the *Monthly Film Bulletin*.)

Titles in This Series

1.
Roy Armes. Patterns of Realism. 1971

2.
Iris Barry. D. W. Griffith: American Film Master: with an annotated list of films by Eileen Bowser. 1965
bound with
Richard Griffith. Samuel Goldwyn: The Producer and His Films. 1956

3.
Ingmar Bergman. Four Screenplays: Smiles of a Summer Night, The Seventh Seal, Wild Strawberries, The Magician. 1960

4.
Luis Bunuel. Three Screenplays: Viridiana, The Exterminating Angel, Simon of the Desert. 1969

5.
Jean Cocteau. Cocteau on the Film. 1954

6.
Bosley Crowther. The Lion's Share. 1957

7.
Cecil B. DeMille. The Autobiography of Cecil B. DeMille. 1959

8.
Denis Gifford. The British Film Catalogue, 1895–1970. 1973

9.
Abel Green and Joe Laurie, Jr. Show Biz from Vaude to Video. 1951

10.
Robert M. Henderson. D. W. Griffith: His Life and Work. 1972

11.
Charles Higham. Hollywood Cameramen. 1970

12.
Ian C. Jarvie. Movies and Society. 1970

13.
John Howard Lawson. Film in the Battle of Ideas. 1953

14.
John Howard Lawson. Theory and Technique of Playwriting and Screenwriting. Revised edition. 1949

15.
Michael F. Mayer. Foreign Films on American Screens. 1965

16.
Vladimir Nilsen. The Cinema as a Graphic Art. 1959

17.
Robert Richardson. Literature and Film. 1969

18.
Donald Richie. George Stevens: An American Romantic. 1970

19.
Lillian Ross. Picture. 1952

20.
Roberto Rossellini. The War Trilogy: Open City, Paisan, Germany—Year Zero. 1973

21.
Robert Rossen. Three Screenplays: All the King's Men, The Hustler, Lilith. 1972

22.
Mack Sennett. King of Comedy. 1954

23.
Albert E. Smith, with Phil A. Koury. Two Reels and a Crank. 1952

24.
Bob Thomas. Selznick. 1970

25.
Bob Thomas. Thalberg: Life and Legend. 1969

26.
Parker Tyler. Chaplin: Last of the Clowns. 1948

27.
Parker Tyler. The Hollywood Hallucination. 1944

28.
Parker Tyler. Magic and Myth of the Movies. 1947

29.
Luchino Visconti. Two Screenplays: La Terra Trema, Senso. 1970

30.
Luchino Visconti. Three Screenplays: White Nights, Rocco and His Brothers, The Job. 1970